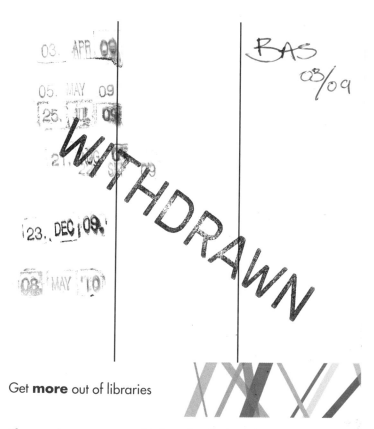

ACTS *of* WAR

ACTS of WAR

RICHARD HOLMES

WEIDENFELD & NICOLSON

Cassell
Wellington House
125 Strand
London WC2R 0BB

Originally published as *Firing Line*
Copyright © Richard Holmes, 1985
First published in Great Britain by Random House, 1985
This edition 2003

British Library Cataloguing-in-Publication Data
A catalogue record for this book is available from the
British Library

ISBN 0-297-84668-X

Printed and bound in Great Britain by Clays Ltd, St Ives plc

Contents

Contents

Introduction to the 2003 Edition

This is a book that occupies a particular place in my development as a military historian. When I wrote it I was becoming convinced that the human being was the central weapon of war, and the events of the past twenty years have done nothing to change my mind. The more I see of battlefields – and I spend about a third of my year trudging haunted acres from Anzio to Bunker Hill and Cassino, and from Wissembourg to Yorktown and Zorndorf – the more I am struck by the fact that individuals really do make a difference. At the higher levels, of course, it is senior commanders that grab our attention. Can we imagine Issus without Alexander, Austerlitz without Napoleon or Chancellorsville without Jackson and Lee? At a lower level, brave and clear-sighted regimental and brigade commanders have often had more effect than their modest rank would suggest. It is impossible to study Gettysburg, for instance, without being struck by the extraordinary impact of William Barksdale for the Confederacy or Joshua Chamberlain for the Union. And it was a major who led three companies of the Worcestershire Regiment in a counter-attack at Gheluvelt on 31 October 1914 and restored the tattered British front line, with little behind it but the Channel Ports.

Yet this book was always intended to be about the led, not their leaders, about what British military doctrine (something not yet officially articulated when the book was written) would now term 'the moral component of fighting power.' If we descend to war's most fundamental level, that of the individual combatant, it seems to me that preparedness to take risks, determination to succeed, and, ultimately, ability to endure are qualities which are as fundamental to military success at the beginning of the 21st Century as they were at Hastings or Bannockburn. And, though I emphasise that my estimation of the deed's impact in no sense implies approval of its motives or execution, the attack of 11 September 2001 again put the human being at the very centre of conflict.

If America and its allies are to win 'The War against Terrorism' then they will need to recognise that human qualities are crucial in the struggle, and that winning tactical victories with superior technology or technique will not necessarily win the war. Indeed, recognition of the centrality of moral qualities ought to suggest that persuading potential opponents not to fight in the first place will be every bit as important as engaging them when they do take the field. And although regard for technology and an understandable desire to minimise both friendly casualties and (dreadful phrase) collateral damage, will encourage some combatants to favour the use of smart long-range weapons, there will remain times when the ultimate symbol of a nation's commitment is to put its young men (and, these days, its young women too) in harm's way. An infantry section can say some things far more eloquently than the most agile of cruise missiles. I thought this twenty years ago, and having seen British soldiers on operations since then I am more impressed than I would once have thought possible by the worldly wisdom of young men and by their ability to enthuse about the tasks endemic in the hugely complex work of rebuilding collapsed states.

Were I writing the book today I would certainly do some things differently. In particular, I would pay more attention to Omer Bartov's views on political indoctrination on the Second World War Eastern Front. In *The Barbarisation of Warfare* he argued that conventional arguments about the primacy of small-group cohesion made little sense in an army where the sheer volume of casualties wreaked comprehensive and repeated havoc on these groups: the German Army, he argues, needed a deeper level of belief. Although I am not wholly persuaded by the argument (for instance, how might we relate it to British infantry on the Western Front in 1916–18, where comparable disruption did not displace small-group cohesion?) I would certainly pay more attention to the impact of big ideas on individual combatants. And, while I would try to avoid easy clichés about the importance of religion in sustaining morale, I would write more about the bedrock of often ill-defined belief which gave more comfort to British soldiers of the First World War than once I thought. Islam too merits more attention than I have given it. Indeed, one of the defining characteristics of our age in which strategists are fond of talking about 'asymmetric warfare' is likely to be cultural asymmetry, and the importance of belief in the complex and heady chemistry of culture cannot be underestimated.

There are areas where I was more right that I would have hoped. In the 1980s several distinguished historians predicted the imminent end of war, an activity which, they suggested, had outstripped man's ability to wage it. I would rather have had them right and me wrong, but, writing as I do with another Gulf War apparently imminent, it seems to me that, if we have got better at hedging war about with legal constraints (and even this is debatable) we retain an extraordinary capacity for inhumanity to our fellow man. While I was probably wrong to place battle quite as much in the centre of war's stage, I have been struck, even over the past few years, by the similarity between the battles described in these pages and small-unit action in the Gulf, Sierra Leone or Afghanistan. Things like Global Positioning Systems, body armour and personal radios have naturally made a difference, but they have not yet transformed low-level combat, if, indeed, they ever will.

It seems to me, therefore, that successful armed forces must continue to value the qualities which enable their people to fight, even though the actual incidence of combat might remain relatively infrequent. These qualities may easily be eroded by a variety of factors, many of them wholly proper consequences of social and political development. Discipline must, in its way, reflect the mores of the times, but discipline there must be. Low-level leaders will need to take battlefield decisions in circumstances when a legally-imposed duty of care may urge reflection: but the successful commander on the 21st Century battlefield will be the one who grasps the 80% solution and does not await the absolute certainty which rarely comes.

Armed forces need to be more open with both their political masters and their national constituencies. While minimising casualties may be desirable it may not always be possible, and it is part of the paradoxical logic of war that he who strives to preserve his life may indeed loose it. Wounds and death remain the currency of war, and the fact that this cruellest of coinage must occasionally be paid does not mean that the transaction was necessarily an error. Good men die, in war as in medicine, even though nobody has blundered. Single men in barracks are no more inclined to grow into plaster saints than they were in Kipling's day. Neither are many of their civilian contemporaries, and yet local newspapers still find 'Soldier resists arrest' an appealing headline where 'Baker resists arrest' might not be. Good armed forces recognise that they differ from civilian corporations for sound functional reasons: they do a different job in trying circumstances, and the way they behave must ultimately reflect this. This duty to be different – for such it is – might be better understood if it was more clearly articulated, and not regarded, as it sometimes is, as a matter of belief that eludes rationalisation.

Armed forces are value-based or they are nothing. This is not to suggest that servicemen are interest-free: erode their pay and allowances, house them badly, neglect them in painful retirement, or shift them about as if they were warrior monks without family ties and they will show the strains. But ultimately what nerves them in the sorts of circumstances described in these pages are values. These will vary from time to time and place to place, with a variety of factors influencing the precise mix. These values, so many of them the old-fashioned virtues like courage, loyalty and duty, work within the interlocking network of personal bonds that link soldier to soldier; the wider circles that join units within the services; and a broader national – or even supra-national – sense of purpose. For if battle, as this book suggests, is ultimately about people, so too are the organisations that fight it, and they forget this at their peril.

Richard Holmes
Ropley, 2003

Acknowledgments

I acknowledge with thanks permission to include in this volume quotations from: Charles Anderson, *The Grunts* (Presidio Press, Novato, California); Patsy Adam-Smith, *The Anzacs* (Hamish Hamilton Ltd); Mark Baker, *Nam* (William Morrow & Co Inc.), Copyright © Mark Baker; Charles Carrington, *Soldiers From The Wars Returning* (Hutchinson Books Ltd); W.S. Churchill, *The Malakand Field Force* (Longman Group Ltd.); Robert Graves, *Goodbye to All That* (Penguin Books Ltd); Max Hastings and Simon Jenkins, *The Battle for the Falklands* (Michael Joseph Ltd); Fred Majdalany *Cassino* (The Bodley Head); William Manchester, *Goodbye, Darkness* (Michael Joseph Ltd) ; Martin Middlebrook, *The Kaiser's Battle* (Allen Lane), Copyright © Martin Middlebrook, 1978, and *The First Day on The Somme* (Allen Lane), Copyright © Martin Middlebrook, 1971, both reprinted by permission of Penguin Books Ltd; Tim O'Brien, *If I Die in a Combat Zone* (Marion Boyars Publishers Ltd); Guy Sajer, *The Forgotten Soldier* (Weidenfeld & Nicolson Ltd); Al Santoli, *Everything We Had* (Random House Inc.), Copyright © Al Santoli and Vietnam Veterans of America; Stephen Westman, *Surgeon with the Kaiser's Army* (William Kimber & Co Ltd).

Mr Paul P.H. Jones allowed me to quote from the papers of his uncle, P.H. Jones; Mrs Cate Marshall authorised me to print sections of S.L.A. Marshall's *Men Against Fire;* Mrs Glen Gray granted me permission to quote from J. Glenn Gray's *The Warriors: Reflections on Men in Battle*; and Mr Andrew S. Railton permitted me to use quotations form the diaries of the Reverend David Railton. Most of my Australian material came from Bill Gammage's admirable book, *The Broken Years* (Australian National University Press), and I acknowledge not only Dr. Gammage's work but also the repositories of his sources, notably the Australian War Memorial Library, Canberra, the Mitchell Library, State Library of New South Wales, and the La Trobe Library, State Library of Victoria. The American Medical Association granted me permission to reproduce a graph from R.L. Swank and W.E. Marchand, 'Combat Neuroses: Development of Combat Exhaustion' in *The Archives of Neurology and Psychiatry*, vol 55 (1946), pp. 236–47, Copyright © 1945 American Medical Association.

I would also like to thank the following for permission to reproduce illustrations: E.C.P.A., Paris, Pierre Ferrari, nos 14 and 28; Raymond Cauchetier, no. 18; Harenberg Kommunikation, Dortmund, fig. 2; Imperial War Museum, nos 4, 6–8, 10, 12, 15, 24 and 27; Kameradschaftliche Vereinigung ehemaliger 67er, Köln, no. 5; Catherine Leroy, nos 11 and 20; Library of Congress, nos 21 and 23; Burk Uzzle, Magnum Photos, New York, no. 3; Andrew Mollo, Historical Research Unit, nos 25 and 26; Musée de l'Armée, no. 9; Royal Military Academy, Sandhurst, no. 1; Suddeutscher Verlag GmBh, Munich, no. 16; Sergeant Ronald Haeberle, *Life* © Time Inc. 1968, no. 30; Goya's *This is Worse*, Victoria and Albert Museum, no. 29; United Press International, New York, no. 2; U.S. Army, no. 19; U.S. Marine Corps, no. 22; Weltwoche Bildarchiv, no. 13.

I

Start Line

The start line is the forward edge of the forming up place ... It must be secure and should be at right angles to the objective. It is used to help align the attacking troops with the objective.

Land Operations 1971, vol. II

Jubilee Covert

The battle started well enough. My company crossed the start line a little late, but moved across the bare field in front of the covert well spread out in assaulting formation, with two platoons up and one in reserve. There was no sound except for the swish of boots through wet grass, and the occasional low-pitched order as an officer or NCO adjusted the line.

I had little enough to feel romantic about. I was bone-weary, having snatched perhaps three hours sleep in the last forty-eight. My chin was sore where my respirator had rubbed it during a period spent in NBC protective suits the preceding night, and an ominous griping in my stomach suggested that the colour-sergeant's cuisine was about to wreak its dire revenge. But when I looked at my hundred or so soldiers as they tramped forward towards the neatly-ranked pine trees of the covert, I was gripped by a feeling of corporate unity so profound that I could easily have wept. This was only an exercise: our enemy were genial regulars from the Royal Hampshires rather than the Soviet motor riflemen of some often-imagined future conflict, and the only real danger was to reputations rather than to lives. Yet as we played our part in the charade I was overwhelmed with images of battle, and thought of our ancestors going steadily forward across the open ground at Minden, our great-great-grandfathers climbing the slopes above the Alma, and our grandfathers shaking out into their own assaulting formation on the chalk uplands on the Somme.

We started losing men long before we reached the covert. The ground shuddered from the charges of plastic explosive representing the mortar and artillery fire that would have protected the forward edge of the enemy position, and umpires dashed about, dealing death with outstretched arm and pointed finger. We were about a hundred yards from the wood, when a steady popping from our left announced that one of the other companies had not secured its objective, and we were being raked by flanking fire. An umpire ran past my headquarters group and, almost as an afterthought, swung round and shouted: 'Dead. Lie down. Don't move. Switch your radios off.'

I flopped down and undid the belt of my webbing equipment. My radio operators, relieved to be spared the hiss and crackle of their sets, lay back and were soon asleep, and my company sergeant-major produced some polish and began to repair the damage done to his toe-caps by three hundred yards of damp grass. All along our line of advance small groups of soldiers lay where umpire-delivered death had caught them. A few sat up and chatted, but most capitalised on the opportunity for sleep, and soon assumed the untidy sprawl of real corpses, as if in some strange way they sought to complete the masquerade of battle by counterfeiting death.

As the sounds of fighting died away into the wood, I soon stopped worrying about how the company would perform: the platoon commanders had had their surviving soldiers well in hand when I had last seen them and there would in any case have been little I could have done to help them in a close-quarter battle amongst the pines. Concern for the fate of my company was replaced by a growing sensation of irony. As a professional military historian and amateur soldier, I had just acted out a scene that I had so often described. Just as my imagination had painted my advancing company with the scarlet of Minden and the Alma and the khaki of the Somme, so now it coloured the tranquil scene along the wood edge with the crimson of slaughter. Alongside the silent dead would have been the wounded, some struggling, some appallingly injured and crying out in pain. Men I had known for a decade, dead and dying: the massive and apparently indestructible Sergeant-Major Fairfax, the rubicund Corporal Wickham, and the quiet and wiry Corporal Mitchell, our irreplaceable Scots medical orderly. We were all very mortal and, had we been taking on a real enemy on a real battlefield, most of us would have been very dead.

But how would I have described the scene in print? It might merit a line or two in a formal 'battle piece' of official history-style prose:

> Unfortunately, C Company failed to secure its objective, enabling the enemy to engage A Company from a flank. Although the company commander and about one-third of his men became casualties before reaching Jubilee Covert, Lieutenant McGhie took command of the remainder and eventually succeeded in clearing the wood.

The flanking company's failure would have been 'unfortunate', we would have 'become casualties', a savage close-range fight with bullet and grenade would have merited the domestic euphemism 'clearing', and the narrative would then have moved on dispassionately to consider the events elsewhere before summing up the day's fighting with a well-chosen overview; it might have been 'disappointing', 'encouraging' or even 'disastrous'.

There was always the possibility of making more of it. I could, perhaps, start by feeling for the right phrase to

3

describe the misty dawn, and by dredging *Roget* for the correct description of that flanking fire.

> As they pressed on through the half-light of dawn, the exhausted soldiers of A Company were deluged by shellfire, while machine-guns ripped into them from a flank. Heedless of the mangled corpses of their comrades, the survivors fought their way into the wood, and in a long hour of bitter hand-to-hand fighting secured three hundred square yards of shell-torn woodland.

This might be getting dangerously close to the purple prose of the 'rattle of machine-gun fire' and the 'acrid tang of cordite', but, as nearly fifteen years of fencing with publishers had shown me, there was a seemingly insatiable public appetite for this blood-and-guts style of narrative. It would also be dressed up with plenty of human interest. There was a hero – my surviving platoon commander – and a villain – the company commander who had not secured my flank. And even a tragedy of conscience: a battalion commander who, under pressure from a thrusting brigadier, had embarked upon a plan of attack which was simply too ambitious. In any event, however, something could be made of the episode, and, book or article, it would all be grist to my mill.

The popularity of military history is such that it has, in the words of Paddy Griffith, 'assumed the proportions of a minor industry'. There are a number of possible reasons for this. The psychologist Professor Norman Dixon, in his thought-provoking *On the Psychology of Military Incompetence*, suggests that:

> The popularity of books and films dealing with war and violence (particularly evident after a prolonged period of peace), like that for pornography following an age of sexual repression, attests to the pleasure provided by the vicarious satisfaction of hitherto frustrated drives.

There is undoubtedly a measure of truth in Professor Dixon's assertion, although as the surge of literary activity of the

1920s, and, more recently, the flood of books dealing with the Falklands conflict demonstrate, there is a very considerable interest in military history even in the aftermath of a war. John Connell believed that there was a deep-seated human interest in war which found its expression in military history:

> War has had us in its thrall. It has horrified us and fascinated us ... The stench of war has seeped into our souls. We have talked endlessly about peace; but in the recesses of our imagination we have brooded, often feverishly, on war, and we have written about it more copiously, I suppose, than any previous generation: memoirs, novels, poetry, histories official and unofficial, and (increasingly) theoretical studies of greater prolixity than profundity.[1]

It is, of course, possible to argue that the prime function of military history is to provide vicarious experience of war, and to illustrate that, however superficially attractive it might seem to those who have never been caught up in it, war is, in General Sherman's much-quoted opinion, hell. The Elizabethan poet George Gascoigne summed it up well:

> My promise was, and I record it so,
> To write in verse (God wot though little worth)
> That war seems sweet to such as little know
> What comes thereby, what fruits it bringeth forth:
> Who knows none evil his mind no bad abhors,
> But such as once have felt the scorching fire,
> Will seldom efte to play with flame desire.

There are, though, difficulties inherent in this approach to military history. As Professor Dixon points out, the very horror of the events being described can afford the reader a curious sense of satisfaction or even *schadenfreude*: it is no accident that some of the best-selling military history is that which adopts an almost ghoulishly forthright approach to battle, or which catalogues the excesses which war drags in its wake.

My reflections on military history as I lay outside Jubilee

Covert waiting for the 'war' to end reminded me of Clemenceau's accusation that military historians beat their drums with the bones of the dead. Had I suffered physical or mental injury in a real battle, I would probably not have taken kindly to someone who either dismissed my experience with a word or two or, worse still, wrote of it without care or feeling. But my experience of Jubilee Covert did a good deal more than this. It crystallised a long-standing dissatisfaction with my own practice of military history, a dissatisfaction based, not simply on moral grounds, but on more practical foundations.

In *A History of Militarism*, Alfred Vagts complained that military history has played no small part in the process of militarising minds, and that it is generally written

> with polemical purpose for the justification of individuals or armies and with small regard for socially relevant facts ... A very large part of military history is written, if not for the express purpose of supporting an army's authority, at least with the intention of not hurting it, not revealing its secrets, avoiding the betrayal of weakness, vacillation, or distemper.

Vagts's criticism contains elements of truth. Yet neither his strictures on the defensive nature of establishment military history, nor the wider disdain in which military history is held by adherents of the 'Whig tradition', who argue that battles are at once unpleasant and unimportant, seem altogether valid. More serious is the fact that, for all that it is concerned with one of the most passionate dramas in which the human spirit can be engaged, military history all too often reduces it, at the one extreme, to a knockabout affair dripping with clichés, and at the other, to a desensitised operational narrative in which the individual is lost in a welter of arrows on maps. As John Connell noted, too many observers have concentrated on the enormousness – and the enormity – of war: 'The soul of man, in all its majesty and mystery, has been dwarfed by the war game.'[2] There is certainly room enough for both racily popular and studiously academic military history – indeed, without the framework of detail provided by operational history any form of analysis would be difficult. But it remains true to say that too little serious work is done on the individual soldier's experience of battle, on the sum of complex instincts and emotions that have led generations of soldiers to their own Jubilee Covert. My experience on that July morning persuaded me to make my own attempt to redress the balance: this book is the result.

Actualities of War

'If I had time and anything like your ability to study war,' wrote Field-Marshal Lord Wavell to Basil Liddell Hart,

> I think I should concentrate almost entirely on the 'actualities of war' – the effects of tiredness, hunger, fear, lack of sleep, weather ... The principles of strategy and tactics, and the logistics of war are really absurdly simple: it is the actualities that make war so complicated and so difficult, and are usually so neglected by historians.[3]

Wavell was certainly not the first man to stress the importance of the actualities of war. Tolstoy, writing almost a century earlier, acknowledged that he was fascinated by war, not in the sense of great manœuvres, but in: 'the reality of war, the actual killing. I was more interested to know in what way and under the influence of what feeling one soldier kills another than to know how the armies were arranged at Austerlitz and Borodino.'[4]

Tolstoy's inquiry into the human spirit in war was conducted for primarily philosophical motives, and his own experience of war in the Caucasus and Crimea formed the basis for that interest in 'the physiognomy of war' which is so evident in *War and Peace*. However, the very actualities of war which Wavell and Tolstoy describe are themselves one of the reasons why the history of war has, as Professor Geoffrey Elton complains, been addressed by 'astonishingly few' professional historians.[5] The fact that war is so catastrophic in human terms has engendered a moral revulsion against it on the part of many historians, while others have felt that their own lack of direct acquaintance prevents them from studying it adequately.

It is easier to sympathise with the 'moral revulsion' argument than to discover a logical basis for it. Studying war need neither imply a commitment to the values of militarism nor betray an unhealthy interest in carnage. The fact that some military historians have indeed championed traditional military values of the most Prussian sort, while others have dwelt longer on the uglier side of war than a balanced view might warrant, does not prove the point, any more than the practice of necrophilia by a few morticians would condemn the entire profession. Even Clausewitz, often accused of being the apostle of total war, was well aware of the frightful nature of battle, 'the bloodiest solution ... the character of battle, like its name, is slaughter [*schlacht*] and its price is blood'. But at the same time he warned: 'It is to no purpose, it is even against one's better interest, to turn away from the consideration of the affair because the horror of its elements excites repugnance'.

Lack of personal knowledge of war need not disqualify the historian from studying it. He may, of course, experience the sort of moral reservation at profiting from the misfortunes of others that I have already discussed, or, as John Keegan mentions early in *The Face of Battle*, recognise a fundamental difficulty in describing something outside the bounds of his own experience. Liddell Hart put the question in perspective:

> Direct experience is inherently too limited to form an adequate foundation either for theory or for application. At best it produces an atmosphere that is of value in drying and hardening the structure of thought. The great value of indirect experience lies in its greater variety and extent.[6]

Nevertheless, the historian without personal experience of war has to overcome a stop in the mind if he is to write valuably about it. Even if he does this, he will have to contend with those who argue that lack of personal experience is a disqual-ification *per se*. In his first-hand account of the life of an infan-tryman on the Western Front during the First World War, W.H.A. Groom attacks the historian John Terraine, arguing that: 'Terraine was not in the war and has no knowledge of the mental strain of the front line.'[7] Historians would have a thin time of it if they could only discuss events of which they had personal knowledge: nevertheless, it is hard not to sym-pathise with the veteran who feels that what he may regard as 'his' war in an almost proprietary sense is being misrepre-sented by those who have no first-hand experience of it.

But Liddell Hart's point remains valid. Direct experience is, of necessity, limited, and the writer who extrapolates only from personal knowledge risks discovering a universality where none might exist. Indirect experience, culled from as wide a variety of sources as possible, is more likely to illumi-nate the real truth. Yet how is this experience to be collected and distilled? Wellington averred that soldiers could remem-ber only sporadic and random fragments of the events in which they participated. 'Write the history of a battle?' he asked. 'As well write the history of a ball.' The issue of the soldier's ability accurately to recall the events of the battlefield is more fully explored later: nevertheless, it is worth recognis-ing, at this early stage, that recall is likely to be patchy and selective. Furthermore – and this is an argument dovetailing with the veteran's assertion that he alone knows what happens on the battlefield – there are frequent complaints that those who really understand war never write about it. Rudolf Bind-ing believed that the history of the First World War would never be adequately written, because: 'Those who could write it will remain silent. Those who write it have not experienced it.' Precisely the same point was made by one of the American soldiers quoted in Robert Jay Lifton's *Home from the War*. Despite all that had been written on Vietnam, he suggested that 'very little was understood about what either GIs or Vietnamese really experienced there'.

Simply finding the language to describe the sensations of battle, either in words or on paper, is no easy task. Guy Sajer thought that language was altogether inadequate to describe his own experiences on the Eastern Front. Nat Frankel had encountered veterans:

> with an actual lust to tell their tales of Armageddon. But once they start, even the most articulate of them fall tongue-tied. What was Iwo Jima like? It was ... it was ... it was fucking rough man! I know that, but what was it like? Really ... really ... really tough! So the very experience of war, what would seem to be the prerequisite for describing it, precluded any actual, palpable narrative.

If written accounts of war risk being flawed on the one hand by the difficulty that the participant experiences in both rising above the subjective level and meticulously recalling events, and on the other by the inability of those who were not present to comprehend fully what took place, how then is the historian to proceed? Firstly, by accepting that there is a good deal of merit in first-hand accounts, subjectivity, inaccuracy and all. Binding's own book is a valuable contribution to that very history which he feared could never be written. Secondly, by recognising that there is a wealth of insight on war to be obtained from talking to soldiers: Lifton's work goes a considerable way towards explaining the anguish that the Vietnam War imposed on a generation of young Americans.

A.J.P. Taylor is sceptical about oral history, which, he warns, can degenerate into 'old men drooling over their youth'. His cutting observations on the professional recollectors who forget the truth and manufacture myth are not, however, sufficient cause for condemning oral history *in toto*. One needs to apply the same care in the evaluation of oral evidence that one must to its written counterpart. Nevertheless, both recent improvements in recording techniques, and the parallel but unrelated decline in the practice of keeping diaries argue strongly in favour of the maintenance of oral archives. Oral history is of particular value to the military historian. Many of those who know most about battle will be unlikely to write about their experiences. It is an inescapable fact of military life that the infantry tends to be, as S.L.A. Marshall put it, 'relatively the most slighted of all branches' in terms of its recruitment and, in Brigadier Shelford Bidwell's words, to experience 'the severest stresses in combat'. Thus the very soldiers who have the closest personal relationship with battle are those least likely to commit their feelings to paper. There are many honourable exceptions to this rule – one needs only to think of Frank Richards and Frederick Manning for the First World War alone – but the broad truth remains valid. Moreover, oral evidence can be collected relatively soon after the event. It is vulnerable to the vagaries of subjectivity and recall, but it is still far fresher, and no less accurate, than much written evidence.

It is deceptively easy, having assembled a wealth of evidence, oral and written, to present it as an anthology, with quotations from participants, either standing alone, or interspersed with judicious comment. At its best this can be both valuable and stimulating. Martin Middlebrook and Lyn Macdonald both deserve great credit for preserving the experiences of soldiers of the First World War. Indeed, without Middlebrook's *The First Day on the Somme* and *The Kaiser's Battle*, and Macdonald's *Somme* and *They Called It Passchendaele*, my own task would have been infinitely harder. This approach can, alas, easily degenerate into what John Keegan calls 'the historian as copy-typist', when there is little attempt to do more than collate personal accounts and string them together with bluff assertions that the evidence speaks for itself.

The study of battle experience by analysts who use the tools of sociology can also come close to the truth. A great deal of valuable work has been carried out by military sociologists – if one can use that term not unfairly. Specifically, examination of the role of the group in influencing the individual's behaviour on the battlefield, an aspect of analysis upon which a number of sociologists have concentrated, has proved particularly illuminating. Some broader-based studies are of lasting importance: *The American Soldier*, by Samuel Stouffer and his colleagues, is an invaluable source of information on the Second World War GI's attitude to military service and to combat. Yet here also the pitfalls are legion. Sometimes the human element is removed from combat altogether, and we are simply presented with statistics which indicate that 19·8 per cent of soldiers have red hair while only 7·2 per cent are left-handed. It is uncomfortably evident that at least some sociologists lack what C. Wright Mills called 'the sociological imagination'. Their studies are flawed by precisely that tendency which limits the impact of some of the anthologies of battle experience: there is no real attempt to rise above the discipline of the card-index.

There are similar difficulties with a good deal of operational research. As Colonel Trevor Dupuy (whose own work on the evaluation of historical data has brought him into conflict with the operational research establishment) has observed, most operational research is 'rigorously scientific', and is 're-lated to weapons systems and the operation of the physical laws of nature in the context of sophisticated modern technology'. Operational research will, for example, establish the hit probability of a certain weapon at given ranges. It is of much less value in suggesting just how that weapon will perform on a battlefield: the combat variables – weather, season, terrain and, above all, the firer's state of mind – are factors which it is impossible to quantify scientifically.

Colonel Dupuy's own approach to the analysis of battle, set out in *Numbers, Predictions and War*, employs the Quantified Judgment Method of Historical Combat Analysis, QJMA for short. Its inventor claims that it is 'the only known model that reliably represents real life combat over the course of history ...' He is very probably right. But this method of analysis tells us as much about the nature of battle as a gynaecological textbook does about the nature of human eroticism. Colonel Dupuy is, of course, quite entitled to claim that he is examining not the face of battle but the anatomy of war. Nevertheless, despite the undoubted merit of QJMA as a model of historical combat, its inventor acknowledges that 'behavioral considerations' – none other than the actualities of war – explain the discrepancies between the projected outcome of a battle and the actual result.

Anthony Kellett's recent *Combat Motivation* is a formidable piece of work by an experienced operational analyst. It demonstrates at once the strengths and weaknesses of what might best be termed the enlightened operational research approach. It is a scholarly and deeply-researched exploration of the behaviour of men in battle which deserves, as Richard Gabriel has suggested, to be required reading for all officers and scholars interested in this field. But despite its very considerable value, it falls short on two counts. In the first place, it is rather heavy going, and thereby risks rendering itself inaccessible to the very regimental officers who are so intimately concerned with the major issues which the author explores. Secondly, like many other works of the same *genre*, it is sometimes no more than a canter through the literature, which ultimately fails to grasp the essence of the human spirit on the battlefield: capable though its author is, he is more concerned with synthesis than with hypothesis.

There are, however, other analysts of battle, often men with personal military experience, who go far beyond cataloguing the evidence, but use the results of their research to produce general theories on the soldier's behaviour. In the 1860s the French Colonel Charles Ardant du Picq circularised his brother officers and used the information from their (remarkably rare) replies to postulate, in *Études sur le Combat*, his concept of the primacy of morale. The American, S.L.A. Marshall, who combined service as an infantry officer in the First World War with a journalistic background, studied the performance of American soldiers during the Second World War, using the after-action interview as his source. Marshall's *Men Against Fire* remains a classic account of the infantryman's behaviour on the battlefield. Like du Picq, Marshall was not content with merely accumulating facts: he too sought to illuminate general truths by the analysis of a large number of particular examples. Although most modern analysts would disagree with at least some of Marshall's conclusions, or might suggest that his research methods are not always reliable, there can be no doubting the importance of *Men Against Fire*. Marshall carried out similar studies during the Korean and Vietnam

Wars, although his later works lack the wide relevance of *Men Against Fire*.

More recently, a growing interest in what may broadly be called battlefield stress has led to an increasingly important psychological input into the analysis of combat. Indeed, the stress bandwagon seems to roll on irresistibly, impelled both by 'stress studies', like that conducted at the Staff College, Camberley, and a profusion of articles in professional military journals. Concern with the psychology of battle is, of course, nothing new. Lord Moran's *The Anatomy of Courage* was a brilliant fusion of Moran's experiences as a regimental medical officer on the Western Front with a wider conceptualisation of the nature of courage. Major-General Frank Richardson's *Fighting Spirit* also addressed the question of morale from the point of view of an experienced medical officer, while Brigadier Shelford Bidwell's too little-known *Modern Warfare* successfully linked sociological, psychological and historical evidence to produce a gripping and penetrating study.

Finally, there are some historians pure and simple who have studied battle from the standpoint of their own discipline. John Keegan's *The Face of Battle* is without doubt the most important of these historical examinations of the battlefield, and it is true to say that it has had a profound impact upon military historiography. Paddy Griffith's *Forward into Battle* also deserves honourable mention, and goes further towards explaining what actually happens in battle than many more widely-known studies. But there is, alas, still something to quarrel with even in these, the most admirable of their school. The understandable tendency for historians to shun excursions to the wilder shores of psychology sometimes leaves the reader with the feeling of having been deprived of a prize that was almost within reach. Furthermore, *The Face of Battle*, either because of the conditions prevailing in the world in the early 1970s when it was written, or because of its author's moral *Weltanschauung*, concludes optimistically that battle may have abolished itself, a judgment which, sadly, seems unduly sanguine a decade later.

If this brief review of the literature does nothing else, it should at least suggest that the subject is far from being virgin territory. Why, then, does it merit further study? What new light can be thrown upon it? It is my contention that the actualities of war can best be illuminated by the use of the evidence, both oral and written, of those who have participated in battle. While some historians have approached the subject by using chronologically arranged case-studies, I have chosen a more thematic approach, looking at different areas of individual behaviour on the battlefield over a wide timescale, considering such things as the soldier's preconceptions of battle, his sensations on first making contact with the enemy, his changing attitudes towards combat as his experience of it grows, and his feelings towards his adversary. My oral sources consist of information from some 150 soldiers, serving and retired, European and American, Middle Eastern and African, who have participated, as members of combat sub-units in close contact with the enemy, in one or more of the World Wars, the Korean conflict, the Arab-Israeli wars, the Vietnam War, an assortment of minor conflicts in the post-1945 period and, finally, the Falklands War of 1982. Some of these men completed a written questionnaire, dealing far more kindly with impertinent questions from a complete stranger than I either expected or deserved. Others were reluctant to commit their views to paper, and requested an anonymity which I am bound to accord them.

It will already have become evident that I have limited sympathy for the anthological approach to military history. Having said that, I do include quotations which I believe to be apposite, although I hope that I have not fallen into the trap of producing the not unfamiliar *olla podrida* of other people's experiences in a thin sauce of my own opinion. There are two other serious issues which merit discussion at this juncture. The first concerns the relationship between history and psychology. Despite the self-evident risks of venturing into a discipline in which I have no formal training, I have come to the conclusion that, in an attempt to explain some aspects of battlefield behaviour, I must at times leave the *terra firma* of military history for the quicksands of psychology. This is bound to affront some historians, who will maintain that such fudging of the boundaries of academic disciplines is dangerously unprofessional, as well as some psychologists, who will resent the appearance of yet another interloper in a field which attracts so many trespassers. Norman Dixon sought to achieve 'a cheerful marriage of history and psychology', and was doubtless not surprised by the fact that some objected to what they regarded as a shotgun wedding. Yet whatever the flaws in Dixon's book – and I would be the first to acknowledge that its author is a better psychologist than he is a historian – it seems to me that the book attains its very considerable stature largely by virtue of the fact that its author was prepared to make the perilous leap between disciplines. If I land even half as smoothly as Professor Dixon, I shall be well pleased.

Finally, it should be clear that I believe that there is a moral dimension to the practice of military history. This is not to say that I advocate polemic, either depicting war as unrelieved horror on the one hand or as a rather vigorous form of outdoor sport on the other. War contains elements of both farce and tragedy. But it is vital to remember that we are dealing with the most passionate drama of all, which has a profound impact, not only upon those personally involved in it, but also, through what T.E. Lawrence called 'the rings of sorrow', upon their families and friends. In this context I acknowledge a powerful personal feeling of ambivalence which it is hard to rationalise and harder still to describe.

I had never wanted to be much other than a military historian. Like many schoolboys, I was fascinated by 'drum and trumpet' military history, by richly-embroidered narratives of battle. I could – and, given half a chance, did – recite by heart the stories of the repulse of the Imperial Guard at Waterloo, of Colonel Lacy Yeo and his fusiliers at the Alma, or of Major Raynal's *biffins* defending Fort Vaux. Somehow, although I recognised that it must have been decidedly unpleasant to have got in the way of a roundshot or to have found oneself in the cone of fire of a machine-gun, I was not unduly alarmed by the butcher's bill.

By the time I was studying military history more seriously, I was conscious of charting the geography of a realm where death was king. My research on the French army of the Second Empire was more concerned with the routine grind of training and administration than with the high drama of battle. Nevertheless, while struggling through the records of the ill-fated *Armée du Rhin* in the delightful surroundings of the Vincennes archives, I was constantly reminded of the mosaic of human tragedies which underlay the faded copperplate of staff officers and *Intendance* officials. The letter-books of the Imperial Guard, a useful source of information in internal administration, recorded that, on 24 July 1870, with mobilisation under way, Colonel Cousin of the 3rd Grenadiers requested permission to marry. An interesting reflection, I thought, upon military bureaucracy. A month later to the day, the same book gave instructions for the disposal of the colonel's horse. Another piece of routine paperwork, and scarcely worth recording. But what had happened between the formal marriage application and the routine sale of a bay gelding? On 16 August, as Bazaine tried, ineffectually, to break out from Metz down the Verdun road, the Guard, bringing up the army's rear at Gravelotte, went forward into the teeth of heavy shellfire to support the sorely tried 2 Corps. The tired infantry shouted 'Vive la Garde' as the grenadiers came up, and the episode merited several square yards of canvas in Detaille's panorama of the battle. But Cousin never had the opportunity to compliment the painter on the accuracy of his uniforms or his feel for the action. As he waved the regimental colour to rally his men, shouting 'Au drapeau, mes enfants,' a Prussian shell killed him.

Before long I grew wary of taking an interest in an individual figure, almost sure that some misfortune would befall him. Reading *Glory Road*, one of Bruce Catton's American Civil War trilogy, I was impressed by the bald-headed, red-bearded Colonel Cross of the 5th New Hampshire, who quelled a rowdy party in the officers' lines by stalking in, drawn sword in one hand and pair of handcuffs in the other. Cross was wounded at Fredericksburg and survived the desperate fighting at Chancellorsville. Commanding a brigade at Gettysburg, he shouted cheerily as he rode past the ambulances: 'We shan't want any of your dead carts today.' It was an unwise prophesy: he was mortally wounded in the bitter combat in the wheatfield on the second day of the battle, and died before midnight, gasping, 'I think the boys will miss me.'

These are two isolated examples of the way in which the practice of military history is, for me at least, filled with constant reminders of what lies behind the casualty statistics. And so, while twenty years ago I might have thought of the battle of Solferino in terms of trim little French *chasseurs* pressing nimbly up the vine-terraced hills, I now think almost as much of Colonel Dieu, a handsome and well-connected staff officer whose spine was smashed by a bullet and who lived, in what Germain Bapst termed indescribable agony, for a year after the battle. I am sure that this preoccupation with the human tragedies of war would have made me an appalling regular soldier, and it may well make me a worse military historian, reluctant to see the wood because of an excessive concern for the trees.

So much for our point of departure. Before setting off in search of the complex and elusive factors which influence the individual soldier on the battlefield, it is worth bearing in mind the words of Ardant du Picq, whose own fascination with 'the dark beauty of violence' was, like Colonel Cousin's, to end fatally on the Verdun road in August 1870:

The smallest detail taken from an actual incident in war is more instructive to me, a soldier, than all the Thiers and Jominis in the world. They speak for the heads of state and armies, but they never show me what I wish to know – a battalion, company or platoon in action. The man is the first weapon of battle. Let us study the soldier, for it is he who brings reality to it.

War on the Mind

It was Shelford Bidwell who astutely observed that the problem of discovering what actually happens in combat lay on
'dangerous ground because the union between soldier and
scientist has not yet passed beyond flirtation'. Nevertheless, if
psychology is, as F.C. Bartlett called it, 'a systematic attempt
to understand the conditions of human activity', no study of
the individual in battle can be complete without it. It would
be pleasant to begin what is, of necessity, a somewhat bumpy
journey through the psychological and sociological theory
which bears upon the soldier in battle with an easily-under-
stood statement of a widely-recognised fact which might serve
as a basis for further inquiry. Such, alas, is not to be the case,
for the most basic of questions concerning man's approach to
battle, that of whether or not he is innately aggressive, admits
of no easy answers. Indeed, as so many of those who have
addressed it have noted, the question straddles numerous fields
of study, including psychology, neurophysiology, animal
psychology and anthropology, and demands inter-disciplinary
investigation of the most rigorous sort.

This question is at the root of a long-running debate
amongst ethnologists and anthropologists. In *On Aggression*
Konrad Lorenz maintained that aggression is 'really an essential part of the life-preserving organization of instincts.
Though by accident it may function in the wrong way and
cause destruction, the same is true of practically any functional part of any system.' The aggressive drive is, suggested
Lorenz, inherited from man's anthropoid ancestors, and it
causes him to fight members of his own species. Other species
generally possess some mechanism for avoiding serious aggression within the species. Perhaps a 'pecking order' is established, or perhaps combat is ritualised: piranha fish employ
their lethal teeth on other species, but fight members of their
own species by administering sharp but harmless raps with
their tails, and rattlesnakes bite man but wrestle with one
another.

Lorenz attacked the concept of a 'Golden Age' when man

was a harmless herbivore. 'Peking Man,' he wrote, 'the Prometheus who learned to preserve fire, used it to roast his brothers ...' Because man lacks the natural weapons of keen teeth and sharp claws, he does not possess the safety devices instinctively built in to 'professional' carnivores, all of whom have reliable inhibitions which prevent the destruction of their own species. Man has developed and employed weapons without having the benefit of this instinctive safeguard. Moreover, the improvement of weapons has actually helped to reduce such inhibitions as do exist:

> The distance at which all shooting weapons take effect screens the killer against the stimulus sensation which would otherwise activate his killing inhibitions. The deep, emotional layers of our personality simply do not register the fact that the crooking of the finger to release a shot tears the entrails of another man.

Variations on this theme were expressed by Robert Ardrey in *The Territorial Imperative*, Desmond Morris in *The Naked Ape*, and Irenäus Eibl-Eibesfeldt in *The Biology of Peace and War*. The latter vigorously defended Lorenz, and went on to provide strong circumstantial evidence in favour of an aggressive drive in man. He noted the important role played by cultural pseudospeciation – something which we shall encounter in later pages – in the organisation of violence. 'The fact that the other party is often denied a share in our common humanity', he wrote, 'shifts the conflict to the interspecific level, and interspecific aggression is generally destructive in the animal kingdom too.'

In *The Anatomy of Human Destructiveness*, Erich Fromm attacked the view that violence is instinctive. It was, he declared, attractive for men to believe that violence stemmed from their animal nature, and he complained that this tenet inhibited serious study of the real causes of human destructiveness. Fromm went on to draw a distinction between benign aggression, which was instinctive by nature, and reactive in effect, and malignant aggression, which was not phylogenetically programmed, and was a behaviour peculiar to humans. Fromm's study includes some concepts – notably that of group narcissism – which will be useful in furthering our understanding of human behaviour in war. Nevertheless, on balance, his judgment on the nature of violence seems less satisfactory than that of his adversaries. As Robert Fox wrote, 'there is really no point and no future in trying to prove that man is *not* an aggressive or violent animal'.[8] Galloping technology has created a new context in which man's naturally violent activities must operate, and this, suggested Fox, endows human aggression with particular menace. There is a wide measure of agreement that violence, like the drives towards sex or food, is deep-seated within the human organism, although, while the drive for food cannot be sublimated, the drives towards sex and violence are more malleable, and can be suppressed, sublimated or ritualised. This debate on the nature of human violence is of more than merely academic interest: it abuts on several areas of crucial importance, in particular the soldier's attitude towards his adversary.

This conflict between anthropologists as to the nature of man is, in a sense, a microcosm of a broader dispute over the nature of human society. Some societies, though mercifully few of them, have been motivated by Social Darwinism, believing that it was only through war that a nation gained its right to exist and earned its continued survival. But even at a less extreme level, there remains a radical difference between those who regard war, in Clausewitzian terms, as the continuation of politics by other means and an indispensable device in the whole apparatus of intercourse between states, and those who argue that war is an aberration, in a sense the opposite of politics rather than its continuation.

While this particular debate may have little bearing upon events on the battlefield, it does have a profound effect upon the way people write about war, and is, no doubt, part of the reason why, as Professor Elton regretted, military history attracts relatively few professional historians. In *War and the Liberal Conscience*, Michael Howard – by any reckoning one of the notable exceptions to Professor Elton's rule – wrote that,

'Erasmus despised the profession of arms with a scorn which generations of intellectuals were to inherit: "Military idiots, thick-headed lords ... not even human except in appearance".' Erasmus's strictures on the warriors of his own age found an answering echo in Einstein, who announced that man's great brain was wasted on the soldier: a spine would have been quite adequate. It is, perhaps, no accident that Erasmus and Einstein, both men of outstanding intellect, attacked soldiers by using phraseology designed to deprive them of their human characteristics. Both were, no doubt unconsciously, employing that cultural pseudospeciation which is such a common feature not only of war itself but even of conflicts of an overtly less violent sort. It should be pointed out, in fairness, that soldiers often do very much the same thing, although they tend to use phraseology designed to deprive their opponents of the attributes of manhood rather than those of humanity.

The theories of the great psychologists similarly leave us with no single smooth and easy path to follow. Much as one might sympathise with Frank Richardson in deploring 'the tendency of some psychologists to explain in complex jargon things which are perfectly obvious to all of us from our own experience of life', too much of what happens on the battlefield relates to psychological theory for us to shun the subject. The concepts of Sigmund Freud, C.G. Jung and Alfred Adler are all relevant in one way or another.

Freud divided the mind into the three key elements. The *id* is its most primitive part, containing all functions of an instinctual nature. The contents of the *id* do not reach consciousness directly, but manifest themselves in dreams and neurotic symptoms. The *ego* is a development of the *id*, and links it to the outside world. Most of the *ego's* activities are conscious: it assimilates and retains external stimuli and controls our voluntary activities. Finally, the *super-ego* is concerned with moral codes and standards of behaviour: it is formed in early life by the unconscious influence of parents and teachers. The *id* is dominated by the pleasure principle and the *ego* by the reality principle, and conflict can occur between them as mechanisms for the defence of the *ego* distort reality. Central to Freudian theory is the conviction that events during an individual's early life have a profound effect on the personality of the adult. Although much of Freud's early work centred upon sexual drives, latterly he focused on the conflict between the life instinct (*Eros*) and the death instinct (*Thanatos*). As Dr Bruno Bettelheim has demonstrated in *Freud and Man's Soul*, translators, interpreting Freud's work as science, have tended to devalue its humanist, philosophical elements. In particular, he objects to the Latinising of Freud's three 'provinces of the soul', suggesting I, It and Above-I as more suitable translations.

If the theories of Freud, particularly as developed in his later period, are of obvious relevance to battlefield behaviour, the concepts of Adler are no less significant. Adler argues that all human beings have a deep-seated desire for superiority, and crave to be respected, admired and loved. Advance towards this Goal of Superiority is impeded by feelings of inadequacy or inferiority. In most cases these feelings prove transient, but sometimes they assume an importance which renders the Goal of Superiority utterly unattainable. Some of the psychiatric disorders afflicting soldiers may be seen as having their origin in this conflict between feelings of inferiority and the Goal of Superiority. Richardson asserts that the soldier's Goal of Superiority is bravery. This is something of a generalisation which may not apply in all cases, for example to conscript armies engaged in unpopular wars. None the less, despite this it is clear that Adler's theories relate intimately to matters of individual heroism and group cohesion.

Finally, the Jungian system of analytical psychology emphasised the influence of the racial or collective unconscious, and divided mankind up into a number of personality types. The belief that combat performance was determined as much by an individual's race as by such things as training and tactics was widely held in the nineteenth century. For example, the French took up Clausewitz's teaching about battle and morale with a fierce intensity, encouraged by national mystique about *furia francese* and popular philosophy which stressed *l'élan vital*. The concept of a racially-determined personality is anathema to most Western liberals. Nevertheless, there is considerable evidence that battlefield performance is influenced, if not by race in the biological sense, at least by a society's culture and norms.

The fact that soldiers are organised in groups – sections, platoons, companies, battalions, and so on – means that the theories of psychologists and sociologists whose prime concern is with group behaviour are also of great importance. In 1895 Gustave Le Bon, in *Psychologie des foules*, made the crucial statement that, even if we understand the individual, we are forced to acknowledge that he acts differently in a group. Le Bon argued that, whatever the occupations, character and intelligence of the individuals who make up a group, the fact that they have been transformed into a group gives them 'a sort of collective mind' which causes them to think and act in a manner quite different from that which might be expected of the isolated individual. He went on to suggest that a 'racial consciousness' emerged within the group. The group displays a number of special characteristics: it has a sensation of power, springing from its numbers; its members lose their sense of individual responsibility; feelings can be communicated within the group by an almost hypnotic 'contagion', and the group has a wide suggestibility of which this contagion is only a small element. The individual's conscious personality disappears, and an unconscious personality emerges: 'He is no longer himself, but has become an automaton who has ceased to be guided by his own will.' Le Bon propounded a number of patterns of group behaviour, some of which will strike chords in the pages that follow. Groups go to extremes: suspicions become certainties, and antipathy becomes hatred. They respect force, and demand strength from their leaders; they have a marked distrust for innovations and a profound regard for tradition.

It would be surprising if Le Bon's work, written as it was nearly a century ago, had not undergone considerable modification by his successors. Nevertheless, his findings have provided a useful springboard for others. Wilfred Trotter's

Instincts of the Herd in Peace and War made much of man's gregarious characteristics. Man, argued Trotter,

> is intolerant and fearful of solitude, physical or mental ... He is more sensitive to the voice of the herd than to any other influence ... He is subject to the passions of the pack in his mob violence and the passions of the herd in his panics ... His relations with his fellows are dependent upon the recognition of him as a member of the herd.

Writing with particular reference to the First World War, Trotter suggested that one of the sensations produced by war was isolation, an 'urgently unpleasant' loneliness. Furthermore, as the physical proximity of his fellows dispelled this loneliness, so the soldier's morale improved. Thus, whatever the tactical wisdom of adopting dense formations on the battlefield, it was clear to Trotter that powerful psychological pressures encouraged men to bunch together under fire. Morale could be seen as a reflection of the herd instinct: 'The peace of mind, happiness, and energy of the soldier come from his feeling himself to be a member in a body solidly united for a single purpose.'

It will come as no shock to the reader who is, by now, doubtless becoming accustomed to the academic in-fighting that surrounds most theories, be they anthropological, psychological, or even historical, to discover that Trotter's findings have been disputed. Freud, in particular, complained that Trotter's concept devalued the leader, who was thrown in with the herd, almost by chance. In place of the herd, Freud created the horde: man was not a herd animal but a horde animal, 'an individual creature in a horde led by a chief'. None the less, it is interesting to note the similarity between Trotter's view of the herd and Tolstoy's concept of the nature of war. In *War and Peace*, Tolstoy wrote: 'Millions of men, repudiating their common sense and their human feelings, were bound to move from west to east, and to slaughter their fellows, just as centuries before hordes of men had moved from east to west to slaughter their fellows.' The instincts of the swarm were supreme, and the king was the slave of history.

Sociologists have approached the study of the group from a different standpoint, but many of their findings mesh well with those of the psychologists. In *The Human Group*, G.C. Homans studied the face-to-face – or primary – group. Group experience was, he maintained, an immediate and pervasive human characteristic: 'From infancy onwards we are all members of families, childhood gangs, school and college cliques, clubs and teams – all small groups.' He distinguished between the external systems of group behaviour, designed to enable a group to survive in its environment, and internal systems, the expression of sentiments towards one another developed by members of the group in the course of their life together. Homans's opinions on the feelings of the members of a group for one another is of great importance as far as battlefield morale is concerned. Interaction within the group, he wrote,

is accompanied by friendliness among the members of a group only if the group as a whole is maintaining itself in its environment. If the group fails in its purposes and starts to break up, its disintegration will be hastened by the increasing antagonisms and mutual incriminations of its members.

Conversely, warmth of feeling between companions could be greatly enhanced by the group's successful completion of a difficult task. This friendliness within the group tends, however, to be accompanied by some degree of hostility towards outsiders.

An essential part of a group's culture is its norms – its ideas of what behaviour should be. Homans's case studies examine the employees of an electrical wiring workshop, the members of a street corner gang and a south-sea islands community. Although a military organisation may have little resemblance to these groups, in their norms we can see sets of behaviour values which are not dissimilar to those within armies. In the wiring workshop the men had a self-imposed upper and lower output limit, and applied sanctions to the 'rate-busters' and 'speed-kings' who did too much, as well as to the 'chiselers' who did too little. These look remarkably similar to the norms of the American infantrymen studied in Korea by Lieutenant-Colonel Roger Little, where 'chiselers' and 'rate-busters' were paralleled by 'duds' and 'heroes'.[9]

Homans's views on leadership are also of interest. 'The leader is the man', he maintained 'who, on the whole, best lives up to the standard of behaviour that the group values.' The real source of his authority is his ability to carry his followers with him. 'He controls the group,' wrote Homans, 'yet he is in a sense more controlled by it than others are since it is a condition of his leadership that his actions and decisions shall conform more closely than those of others to an abstract norm.' Members of a group comply with the group norms because of the group's social control. This need not necessarily have the force of law, but it will be supported by some sort of sanction within the group: in the case of the wiring workshop the usual sanction was 'binging', a sharp blow on the arm. The control of reciprocity is based upon the theory that 'if a man does a favour for you, you must do a roughly equivalent favour for him in return'. In *Trench Warfare*, his examination of fighting on the Western Front during the First World War, Tony Ashworth postulated that it was this norm, applied to front-line soldiers as a group rather than to any nationality in particular, which accounted for the unofficial truces which were such a frequent occurrence.

A.H. Maslow linked an individual's behaviour to that of the group by suggesting that the individual has a 'hierarchy of needs'. This starts with basic physiological needs for food, drink and sleep, and moves on to safety needs for security and protection. Next come social needs, for a feeling of belonging, social activity and leisure; his self-esteem needs, for status and recognition; and finally his self-realisation needs for growth, personal development and accomplishment. These needs affect not only the individual's relationship with a given group, but also his attitude to its leaders.

The group is likely to respond to some change or crisis in its existence by ritual, which often has the effect of restoring the group to equilibrium or easing its transition to some new state. Arnold van Gennep, in *The Rites of Passage*, wrote that:

> The life of an individual in any society is a series of passages from one age to another and from one occupation to another ... there are ceremonies whose essential purpose is to enable the individual to pass from one defined position to another which is equally well defined.

Inherently armies are deeply ritualistic organisations, and some of their ritual is devoted to the marking of important events in the individual's service – his oath of enlistment, passing-out from recruit training, and so on. Other rituals set out the parameters of the military day, mark a unit's arrival in or departure from a garrison, and celebrate its return from a victorious campaign. But much ritual is far less obvious. It goes on beneath the surface, and the reasons for it may be unclear even to those who carry it out. Sometimes, like 'official' ritual, it may have the effect of marking a new transition, but often it serves a talismanic function, and is adopted because it gives the individual the sensation of being preserved from harm. There is a close connection between anxiety and ritual, a connection which, as we shall see, intimately concerns many soldiers.

The prime purpose of military training is to produce effectiveness on the battlefield. Much of it is devoted, either directly or indirectly, to enabling the soldier to cope with the stress-filled environment of combat. General theories on coping with stress can be applied to the particular circumstances of the battlefield, although, as Peter Watson observed in *War on the Mind*, some psychologists would argue that the stresses of the battlefield are so severe as to be totally different from the stresses which an individual might encounter in the course of his everyday life. In *Psychological Stress and the Coping Process*, R.S. Lazarus acknowledged that stress was in itself a broad term, which included the overlapping sensations of conflict, frustration, anxiety, defence, and emotions such as fear and anger. Some stresses may be obvious, with easily recognisable external stressors: others may be well concealed, and result from conflict within the psyche, in one of the ways suggested by Freud or Adler. Although it is dangerous, by concentrating upon Lazarus, to accord primacy to what is after all only one of a number of scholarly works on stress and its effects, the Lazarus model is so appropriate to military circumstances that it is worth examining in some detail.

Lazarus suggested that there are, in general, two methods of coping with stress. They are by no means mutually exclusive, and an individual may employ either or both. The first is direct action. The individual under stress alters the relationship between himself and the source of the stress. He may do this by some practical form of preparation against harm, by aggression or by escape. The individual may be unwilling or unable to take direct action. On the battlefield, for instance, direct action is often impossible. The soldier under bombardment can neither attack the source of his discomfort nor flee from it without adding to the danger. Indeed, this very inactivity produced by bombardment is one of the characteristics that renders heavy shelling so damaging to morale. In the second method of coping with stress, palliation, the individual adopts mechanisms which do not alter his relationship with the stressor, but which make him feel better. Palliation is as common on the battlefield as ants in an ant-hill. It includes a wide variety of 'inter-psychic modes' affecting the individual's subconscious, such as denial, in which he simply denies that a threat exists, displacement, when he 'escapes' from the battlefield in spirit although not in body; ritualisation; humour, and so on. The process of palliation may be assisted by the use of drugs or alcohol, which, similarly, make the situation no safer – they may actually make it more dangerous – but help the soldier to deal with stress by making his plight seem less threatening.

Various factors determine an individual's ability to cope with stress, and help establish the means he uses to do so. Some of these stem from his cultural background. Lazarus cited the different ways in which Spanish-Americans and Anglo-Americans react to death. Spanish-Americans tend to regard it fatalistically: they dramatise death as high tragedy, with lavish ritual and openly emotional mourning. Although Anglo-Americans are unable to deny death, they attempt to de-emphasise it by reducing ritual and mourning to a minimum and trying to make corpses as lifelike as possible. The Adlerian overtones of this are evident, and it has clear implications not only for the soldier's treatment of the dead on the battlefield, but also for the way in which his morale may be blunted by casualties. The strength of an individual's *ego*, in itself notoriously difficult to assess, also affects his ability to withstand stress. Here we shall later observe an ebb and flow of opinion amongst military psychologists and psychiatrists, as views on the importance of the pre-stress personality have evolved over the past fifty years or so.

So much for the theoretical background. What follows is a study of the soldier's feelings and behaviour from his training for war, through his experience of battle, and on into its aftermath. It seeks neither to glamorise war on the one hand nor, on the other, to deny that it contains moments of satisfaction or even pleasure. I have already emphasised the need to remember that war is a gripping crisis for all involved in it, and that the cost of even a relatively petty skirmish is absolute enough for those who comprise the statistics. My concern is unashamedly with what some might regard as microscopic detail, but it is the sum of such detailed brushwork that makes up the broad canvas of war. Wellington observed that 'one must understand the mechanism and power of the individual soldier' before it is possible to grasp the nature of war. This is my own attempt to comprehend that mechanism and to fathom that power.

2

Mysterious Fraternity

a mysterious fraternity born out of smoke and
danger of death

Stephen Crane

New Baptism

However much sociologists might argue that we live in an age
of 'narrowing skill differentials', when many of the soldier's
tasks are growing ever closer to those of his civilian contemporaries, it is an inescapable fact that the soldier's primary
function, the use – or threatened use – of force, sets him apart
from civilians. This separation is more marked in the case of
the combat arms than it is in the case of the supporting arms
and services, for whom a perfectly natural preoccupation with
logistics or communications can easily obscure the blunter realities of war. It is equally understandable that those armies
which recruit by means of voluntary enlistment should emphasise the fact that they teach skills and instil values which
will be of use to the individual when he leaves the service.
Nevertheless, the fact remains that someone who joins an
army, even the benign army of a democracy in time of peace,
is both crossing a well-defined border within the fabric of
society, and becoming a member of an organisation which, in

the last analysis, may require him to kill or be killed. Thus, while entry into military service may vary greatly from place to place and from age to age, it is always distinguished by its own rite of passage, and is followed by a process designed to inculcate professional skills, produce conformity to certain norms, and create a framework of ritual and relationships which will enable the soldier to withstand the impact of battle.

All armies impose some sort of oath on their recruits. St Cyprian equated the Roman military oath, the *sacramentum*, with the Christian initiation rite of baptism, and the comparison is an apt one. The Roman legionary swore an oath to the state and, until 216BC, to his comrades as well. The form of the Roman military oath, with its emphasis upon public affirmation of allegiance and pledge of brave conduct, has proved remarkably durable. At times, as the Swiss poet Ulrich Braker, who was impressed into the Prussian army during the reign of Frederick the Great, observed, the finer points of the ceremonial tended to be lost.

> They conducted us into a hall, which seemed as big as a church, and brought up several badly-holed colours and ordered each of us to take a corner. An adjutant, or whoever he was, read us a whole screed of articles of war and pronounced a few formulae, which the others murmured after him. I kept my mouth shut and fixed my attention elsewhere – I believe I thought about Annie [his girl friend]. Lastly he swung a colour over our heads and dismissed us.[1]

This type of oath has survived in some armies to the present day. In the Soviet army, the recruit swears a military oath on his regimental colour in the presence of his comrades: like his Roman predecessor, he not only swears allegiance to the state, but undertakes to fight 'as a brave soldier' and to incur penalties should he fail to do so.

It is easy to regard the military oath as a meaningless charade which has little practical value. To do so is, however, to underestimate the importance of the first ritual in a ritualistic profession. The impact of the oath upon German officers and soldiers was recognised by Hitler, who, after the death of Hindenburg in 1934, had the impersonal oath of the Weimar Republic replaced by one in which the soldier swore personal allegiance to the *Führer* himself. Telford Taylor wrote that the oath 'constantly emerged as a seemingly insurmountable obstacle to any decisive opposition to Hitler within the officers' corps'. And it was not only officers who felt the oath to be a powerful bond linking the individual to the *Wehrmacht*. Guy Sajer took the oath after retraining for service in the *Grossdeutschland* division. 'For me, only half German,' he mused, 'this ceremony may have had even more significance than for the others. Despite all the hardship we had been through, my vanity was flattered by my acceptance as a German amongst Germans, and as a warrior worthy of bearing arms.' In their study of cohesion and disintegration in the *Wehrmacht*, Edward Shils and Morris Janowitz observed that deserters often sought to appease their consciences by claiming that they had signed their oaths in pencil, or that the sergeant who administered the oath had his back turned. Such elaborate excuses would not have been needed had the oath not possessed considerable moral authority.

The fact that the American oath was rather less elaborate did not prevent it from having a profound effect. Glenn Gray, whose book *The Warriors* is a remarkable personal reflection on men in battle, was surprised how many American civilian soldiers appeared to place great weight upon taking their soldier's oath. He frequently heard the remark: 'When I raised my right hand and took that oath, I freed myself of the consequences for what I do. I'll do what they tell me and nobody can blame me.' In this instance the oath was seen as freeing the individual of personal responsibility for his actions, and, at least in this context, has an obvious similarity to the otherwise markedly different German oath. In the Vietnam era, when young Americans seemed to set less store by ritualistic formalities than previous generations had, the oath still had an important symbolic effect even on some of those who were unenthusiastic at the prospect of military service. A black GI, David Parks, recalled: 'the officer told us to step right foot forward, raise our right hand and take the oath. It was all over in about a minute. I felt trapped.'

A physical metamorphosis accompanies the mental rite of passage marked by the oath. At the same time as the recruit is made to feel that he has become a soldier, he is made to look like one. His appearance is transformed by the addition of uniform and the removal of long hair. The almost obligatory military haircut is often justified on grounds of practicality: it facilitates the control of head-lice, is more comfortable in the field, and, in conscript armies where military service is unpopular, it helps to identify the deserter. In fact, the short hair now associated with military service is a relatively recent phenomenon. The armies of the seventeenth and eighteenth centuries wore their hair long, or concealed it with wigs. Ironically, the recruit of that period would be likely to discover that enlistment was followed, not by the short back and sides of the twentieth century, but by the addition of false hair, in the form of a military pigtail, or even, particularly for hussars and grenadiers, false moustaches.

Whether the assault on the soldier's hair involves lengthening or shortening, the aims – in addition to the practical justifications mentioned above – are always the same. Firstly, hairdressing produces a uniformity of appearance which submerges the recruit's individual identity. David Parks noticed how the stringent US army haircut of the 1960s cut across racial and cultural divides. 'I never saw so much hair in all my life,' he wrote. 'It was all mixed up on the floor together, white hair, Spanish hair and soul hair – all going the same route.' Secondly, a radical transformation of appearance helps to impress on the recruit his change of status: it is an outward symbol of the inner transformation produced by the oath. The third major function of military hairdressing applies less in the twentieth century than it did in preceding ages. Long hair and moustaches were once considered particularly frightening. A private soldier in the British 71st Regiment described the attack of French grenadiers in the Peninsula: 'Their hats, set round with feathers, their beards long and black, gave them a fierce look. Their stature was superior to ours; most of us were young. We looked like boys; they like savages.' The grenadiers may actually have been no older than their opponents, but their appearance was calculated to give every impression of maturity, size and ferocity. The shaving of the upper lip was forbidden in the British army until 1916, and one may be forgiven for suspecting that the impressive function of facial hair is not entirely a thing of the past: the broad-shouldered, narrow-hipped image of the parachutist is completed by an almost obligatory moustache.

If the rigours of the military haircut are one of the best-known landmarks of induction, the issue of uniform, with all its puzzlement and peril, is scarcely less notable. As he exchanges his comfortable and familiar civilian clothes for what is all too often a strange and resistant uniform, the recruit feels acutely conscious of his change of status. He may compare his own ungainly air with the snappy dress of his instructors or the manly figures on recruiting posters. Sometimes recruits suffer because the best equipment is sent to units on active service, or is simply diverted by the 'barrack rats' who seem to be such a regular feature of depot life. When Philippe de Pirey joined the French Colonial Parachutists in 1950 he emerged from the quartermaster's stores 'dressed like a Guy Fawkes in flapping trousers and a denim jacket split at the back from top to bottom'. More often, however, the recruit suffers from simply not understanding how to put on his uniform or assemble his equipment, and has to contend with boots that need breaking in and a beret that obstinately refuses to assume the shape of his head. Simply learning the myriad of dodges which have always been associated with uniform since it came into general use in the seventeenth century is an important part of the process of socialisation into the ways of the army. Duly sworn in, his hair transformed in accordance with the prevailing military fashion, and his unfamiliar uniform sitting uneasily upon him, the recruit is ready to embark upon basic training.

On the Square

Basic training has two clearly identifiable functions. Its most obvious task is to instil exactly what its name suggests, an adequate level of training in such things as weapon handling and minor tactics. Its second, though by no means less important, function is to inculcate the military ethos in recruits, and to ensure that the individual values which prevail in most civilian societies are replaced by the group spirit and group loyalties which underlie all military organisations. These two functions are by no means as distinct in practice as they may appear in principle, and the overlap between them helps to explain some aspects of basic training which might otherwise seem stupid, illogical, or simply brutal.

Military historians often give short shrift to training, preferring to concentrate on the dramatic and moving events of battle rather than the mundane and often repetitive process of training for it. But by doing so they risk missing a crucial point, for a great part of a man's behaviour on the battlefield, and hence of the fighting effectiveness of the army to which he belongs, depends upon training. In his admirable book *Fighting Power*, Martin van Creveld takes as his starting point the 'consistently high performance' in victory and in defeat of the *Wehrmacht:* his book is, in essence, an examination of the secret of the German army's prodigious fighting power. Trevor Dupuy had already noted that 'the Germans consistently outfought the far more numerous Allied armies that eventually defeated them', and numerous eye-witnesses had paid their own tribute to the effectiveness of the *Wehrmacht*.

One aspect of the German army's performance which repeatedly surprised observers was its ability to cobble together *ad hoc* units, often battle groups known by the name of their commander, and to use them successfully to plug gaps amongst the *bocage* of Normandy or on the open steppe of the Eastern Front. British and American attempts to extemporise similar units usually failed, albeit for different reasons in each case. Much of the reason for the German army's fighting performance in general and for the impressive achievements of many of its *ad hoc* formations was that, despite the growing demands of war, the *Wehrmacht* persisted in giving its recruits a solid basic training: sixteen weeks for an infantryman for much of the war, falling to twelve to fourteen weeks in 1944. Armoured troops received longer training, though there was a tendency, from 1944 onwards, to make do with 'a mere sixteen weeks'.

The British and Americans, by contrast, spent less time in basic training, with the result that even in 1944-5 the German army, contending with insatiable demands on its manpower and imminent threats to the territory of the *Reich*, was generally committing a better-trained soldier to battle than were its opponents. Basic training is, of course, only part of the story: most soldiers, Allied or Axis, received further training once they reached their units, and in any case other factors – organisation, administration and leadership – played their part in generating the German army's awesome fighting power. But the role of basic training is noteworthy, and there can be no doubt that the *Wehrmacht*'s formidable achievements had their foundations in sound training.

Marshal Gouvion Saint-Cyr doubtless echoed the less delicately phrased question of countless recruits when he asked rhetorically: 'What do your exercises and parades matter to me, and what have they in common with war?' It is evident that while training aimed at the learning of purely practical skills clearly has an easily-recognised application to war, much other training has a far less obvious purpose. Norman Dixon noted that soldiering falls into the category of human activities that are broadly instinctual. While attempts to professionalise instincts are comparatively easy in some cases – and here Dixon cites prostitution and pie-eating as examples – they are far more difficult in the case of soldiering. The sheer size of human warring groups has brought with it problems of motivation and control; and military training, therefore, needs to include devices which, in Dixon's words, ensure cohesion, incite hostility, enforce obedience and suppress mutiny. It is this aspect of training, rather than that which is concerned with the attainment of what General Sir Richard

Gale called 'mechanical perfection', which is the most elusive, and which is my prime concern in the pages that follow.

In the era of close-order battle, which lasted until the nineteenth century – though exactly when in that century is a matter of considerable debate – the main emphasis of basic training was upon the constant repetition of drill movements until they became so firmly engraved upon the mind that they were, in effect, conditioned reflexes, producing predictable actions which had nothing to do with conscious thought. It was widely recognised that conscious thought was likely to prove a disadvantage on the smoky and confusing battlefields of the eighteenth century: Frederick the Great noted cynically that if his soldiers began to think, not one of them would remain in the ranks. As Shelford Bidwell has pointed out, the disadvantage of this sort of training is that it can easily result in the extinction of initiative, leaving the soldier puzzled or inert in the absence of orders.

Repetitive training designed to produce a conditioned reflex is often used to teach weapon-handling. There must be thousands of middle-aged men today who, with their military service years behind them, can still field-strip a Bren gun or a Browning automatic rifle, so deeply were the drills for doing so impressed upon them in their youth. Drills learnt in this way are often remembered even at times of supreme crisis, as John Masters recounted in *The Road Past Mandalay*, describing a Gurkha Bren detachment in action against the Japanese.

The No 1 was seventeen years old – I knew him. His No 2 lay on the left side, beside him, head towards the enemy, a loaded magazine in his hand ready to whip onto the gun the moment the No 1 said 'Change!' The No 1 started firing, and a Japanese machine gun engaged them at close range. The No 1 got the first burst through his face and neck, which killed him instantly. But he did not die where he lay, behind the gun. He rolled over to the right, away from the gun, his left hand coming up in death to tap his No 2 on the shoulder in the signal that means *Take over*. The No

2 did not have to push the corpse away from the gun. It was already clear.

Glenn Gray believed that soldiers under the stress of battle reached the point where they lost 'all sharpness and consciousness'. At this stage:

> they can function like cells in a military organism, doing what is expected of them because it has become automatic. It is astonishing how much of the business of warfare can be carried on by men who act as automatons, behaving almost as mechanically as the machines they operate.

The Soviet armed forces pay great attention to the problems created by stress in battle. Russian pilot training seeks to produce a 'dynamic stereotype in the cerebral cortex' – a conditioned reflex – for some set manœuvres. 'The training is geared', wrote Christopher Donnelly, 'to producing complex reflex actions which do not depend upon intellectual effort but will be performed semi-automatically in the high-stress situation of the cockpit of a plane under attack.'

Values, as well as drills, can be instilled by repeated emphasis on them during training. In the French Foreign Legion, for instance, it was a point of honour not to allow weapons to fall into the hands of hostile tribesmen. *Légionnaires* were constantly told of the importance of preventing the capture of their weapons, regardless of circumstances. In May 1911 part of Captain Labordette's company of the 1st *Régiment Étranger* was ambushed at Alouana in Morocco. When the remainder of the company came up, two of the dead were found to have removed and hidden their rifle-bolts so that the tribesmen would not capture usable rifles. The badly-wounded *Légionnaire* Siegel of the 4th Regiment was surrounded in a fierce hand-to-hand battle in Morocco in 1925. Before he died he hurled his rifle over the heads of the enemy into French lines.

Even the close-order drill which originated in the horse and musket age is more than an elegant ceremonial survival. True, it is unlikely to be regarded with affection by some soldiers,

39

who feel that it has little to do with the business of war. When Robert Graves was an instructor at the 'Bull Ring' at Harfleur early in 1916, he received a complaint from Canadians who 'asked what sense there was in sloping and ordering arms, and fixing and unfixing bayonets. They had come across to fight, and not to guard Buckingham Palace.' A similar protest was made by an unidentified Second World War American soldier, who wrote of his basic training that: 'Too much time is spent on close-order drill, which is pretty to see but doesn't make fighters. You won't stop a tank by doing present arms in front of it.'

There is no doubt that emphasis on close-order drill during basic training can become excessive, merging with other sorts of 'bull' to produce a sterile and oppressive climate where drill and bull become substitutes for thought and are constant and grating reminders of the hierarchical nature of armies. But both drill and bull are not without their uses. The psychologist J.T. MacCurdy argued, in *The Structure of Morale*, that, whatever the defects of drill, 'no one has as yet devised any other system which will so quickly inculcate the habit of automatic obedience'. Provided that this obedience is not produced by totally extinguishing initiative, then MacCurdy's point is valid. Numerous soldiers with practical experience of war also argue in favour of drill. Herbert Sulzbach, a German gunner officer in the First World War – and a British officer in the Second – made an eloquent case in its favour.

> Drill as the means to an end is indispensable to every army. It cannot be replaced by individual training nor by sporting instinct. A man, unless his inherent worth is beyond all doubt, must have obedience drilled into him, so that his natural instincts can be curbed by the spiritual compulsion of his commander even in the most awful moments.

An American drill-sergeant put it rather more succinctly: 'Give me control of their *instinct* and you can have their *reason*.' Robert Graves answered the objections of his Canadians by telling them that, 'for some reason or other', the troops that fought best were 'those that had guts and were good at drill'. Some of Graves's colleagues in the mess suggested that drill did more than produce mutual confidence and natural obedience. It was the foundation of tactics and musketry, and, when 'open war' eventually came, it would be won by 'the simple drill tactics of small units fighting in limited spaces, and in noise and confusion so great that leadership is quite impossible'.

What Graves's fellow instructors were describing was 'battle drill'. Just as parade-ground musketry had been the basis of tactics in the eighteenth and early nineteenth centuries, so new drills of conditioned reflex and automatic response could be developed for use on the battlefields of the twentieth century. Denis Sheil-Small, commanding a company of 4/8th Gurkha Rifles in Burma in 1944–5, spent some time during a pause in the advance down Burma in training which included learning 'The Rifleman's Creed', a series of slogans like 'One bullet – one Japanese'. 'It is not, perhaps, a strange thing', he wrote, 'that when I became involved in my first battle and the numbness of surprise at a sudden onslaught threatened to paralyse my reactions, the slogans of the creed sprang to my tongue as I shouted to my men to encourage them.'

All twentieth-century armies have evolved set drills for minor tactics: fire and manœuvre at section or squad level is the bread-and-butter of basic tactical training. Even if the circumstances of battle are totally unlike those of the training area, the principles of fire and manœuvre are second nature to the well-trained soldier. A group of Falklands veterans from a parachute battalion recalled that: 'skirmishing [the set drills for fire and manœuvre] went to pot ... You did what you thought was best, but you knew that you had to win the fire fight, and get automatic fire down to cover you when you moved.'

If the responses created by battle drill are not battle-winners in themselves, at least they ensure that well-understood tactical ploys are readily available to meet a wide variety of situations. Dixon rightly points out that bull is, *inter alia*, a substitute for thought. So, to some extent, is battle drill. As such it may, at times, restrict initiative and produce inflexibility: but it is also likely to increase confidence as a small unit falls unconsciously into the appropriate well-rehearsed battle drill, secure in the knowledge that 'the eight o'clock Bren' will be in the right place. Part of the stress of battle stems from its puzzling and capricious nature: battle drills help to minimise the randomness of battle, and give the soldier familiar points of contact in an uncertain environment, like lighthouses in a stormy sea.

Even in an age when the value of battle drill is widely recognised, its ancestor, close-order drill, still survives. In part this is because it is believed to impart attention to detail: as Rudolf Binding, a First World War German cavalry officer, put it, 'If the fellow forgets his button here he will forget his ammunition up there.' Precisely the same point was made in a Soviet military journal in 1973, in answer to a correspondent who questioned the wisdom of polishing buttons and carrying out repeated parades in an age of Inter-Continental Ballistic Missiles and electronic warfare.

> One must be concerned with drilling, and not just parading. And the badges must be polished bright even more energetically than before ... An operator [of electronic equipment] who had been lazy in cleaning his boots ... will scarcely show industry and patience in servicing the equipment.

There is, of course, the danger that the balance of priorities will become distorted: as a clear-sighted article in the *British Army Review* in 1971 warned, it is all too easy to penalise faults such as dirty boots or a dusty beret on the drill square, but to ignore the potentially more serious forgotten spare radio battery on exercise.

Finally, close-order drill has an important ritualistic and morale-building role. Just as the dance plays an important part in the African warrior tradition, as both a physical preparation for war – (witness the Zulu war-dances which mirrored the tactics of the *impi*) – and as a status marker, so drill binds a unit together in a way which even unwilling soldiers may find to be curiously pleasurable. The poet Edmund Blunden disliked drill, but nevertheless acknowledged its strangely attractive quality:

> Harrison, with his gift of being friend and commander alike to all his legion, was at our head: everyone was outwardly censorious and inwardly happy when he paraded the battalion by the bleak hop-garden at Vlamertinghe for arms drill. It was cold, but he put life into us, and there is a religious or poetic element in perfecting even one's dressing by the right.

Charles Carrington, on the march with his battalion of the Royal Warwickshire Regiment in 1916, experienced a similar sensation:

> We are passing through a village where another regiment has its headquarters, and its quarter-guard 'pays the proper compliment' by turning out and presenting arms, to which we reply, giving 'eyes right' by platoons. This is a bore, but it is only for a moment and is in a curious way enjoyable. This is our display of pride, our publicity, and we are ready to show them what good soldiers look like.

Close-order drill, despite its distant origins and lack of practical application on the modern battlefield, nevertheless remains an essential ingredient of basic training. Not only does it make men look like soldiers but, far more important, it makes them feel like soldiers.

Instruction during basic training is carried out mainly by non-commissioned officers. Under most circumstances they will have been specially selected for their instructional ability, although, on occasion, particularly when the pressures of war impose serious strains on trained manpower, there is a temptation to keep the 'first team' at the front and use second-rate officers and NCOs – or even those who have proved inadequate in action – for training. The consequences of yielding to this temptation are usually serious and may even prove disastrous. One of Robert Graves's colleagues at Harfleur, a captain in a line battalion of a Surrey regiment, told him:

> Our battalion has never recovered from the first battle of Ypres. What's wrong is that we have a rotten depot. The drafts are bad, so we get a constant re-infection ... In both the last two shows I had to shoot a man of my company to get the rest out of the trench.

During the First World War the most serious lapses of discipline in the British army took place at training depots, and were caused partly by the fact that the ties linking officers, NCOs and men were weakest at depots, and partly by the fact that many instructors were not up to their jobs, but were, in Norman Gladden's words, 'buying with their souls a brief respite from that other hell'. Charles Carrington considered the great mutiny at the Étaples 'Bull Ring' to be the consequence of 'acts of petty tyranny by tactless officers' in an environment where 'men of all units exchanged complaints and did not know the officer in charge'. It is significant that the collapse of the Russian Imperial Army in 1917 spread from the depots and rear areas to the front, and that front-line units were always more prepared, after the February Revolution, to accept discipline and replacement officers. Part of the problem lay in the fact that nearly half Russia's trained manpower had been destroyed in 1914, with the result that there were too few officers and NCOs to meet the demands of field formations and the scarcely less crucial needs of the training depots.

The importance of the instructor is underlined by the disproportionate impact of basic training upon soldiers. It is, after all, their first experience of army life, and its events and personalities are likely to be remembered for the remainder of a man's military service, and often for long after it. An American study of basic training, published in 1976, concluded that 91 per cent of trainees had a positive view of their drill-sergeant, and no less than a quarter of them took him as their role model and strove to be like him. Indeed, so powerful was the impact of the drill-sergeant that the officers and NCOs encountered by the soldier when he reached his unit were often something of a let-down in comparison.[2] David Parks described what was almost a love–hate relationship with his drill-sergeant in terms that will be familiar to many who have undergone basic training. 'He'd be shocked to hear it, but I respect him as an instructor,' admitted Parks. 'He's got all the answers. But he does keep his foot up my backside.' Asa Baber, who served in the Marine Corps during the Vietnam War, wrote of his instructor, Sergeant Danny Gross, with evident affection, and made the telling observation that: 'men like Sergeant Gross serve as examples for the rest of us and that we men look for role models as we grow and try to mature. We don't always find the right models but that doesn't mean we aren't looking.'[3] The psychiatrist Dr Peter Bourne, author of a number of studies of the behaviour of American soldiers during the Vietnam War, was more clinical – or, as some might say, more cynical. 'The whole of Basic Training', he maintained, 'has evolved in the guise of a masculine initiation rite that often has particular appeal to the late adolescent struggling to establish a masculine identity for himself in society.'[4]

The figure of the firm-but-fair instructor recurs constantly in memoirs and interviews. Writing of his service as a guardsman during the Second World War, Gerald Kersch described the Guards warrant officers who, then as now, left their indelible brand upon recruits passing through Pirbright.

> I have a great affection for old Charlie Yardley who, by sheer solid kindness and patience has made thousands of men love, honour and obey him. I don't believe that he has ever had to punish a man ... Another Sergeant-Major who inspired a strange kind of affection was the great, the fabulous Freddy Archer of the Scots Guards. They cursed him from hell to breakfast but would not have parted with him for his weight in gold.

45

The influence of such men extends far beyond the confines of depots and training camps. Many a soldier has gone into battle riven by fear but feeling that, in the words of a very young private soldier in a parachute battalion in 1982, 'if I bottled out I'd be letting down Sergeant X, who got me through the depot'.

The instructor's separateness tends to be emphasised not only by distinctive items of dress, such as the broad-brimmed hat worn by drill-sergeants in the American army, but also by the careful cultivation of an immaculate appearance: John Parrish, conscripted into the US navy as a medical officer during the Vietnam War, noticed that, somehow or other, his instructor was the only man in the room not perspiring.

Language is also important. The instructor is likely to have an inimitable line in profanity: Asa Baber recalled being called 'a pinheaded, no-brained, foreskin-chewing, pogey-bait maggot, lower than worm life', and he was, no doubt, luckier than many. The cult of virility is underlined by the employment of terms of abuse which cast doubt upon the recruit's masculinity. There can be few soldiers in the English-speaking world who have not, at some time or other, been called the bluntest of all Anglo-Saxon synonyms for what my dictionary terms 'the female pudenda'. Peter Bourne observed that language was yet another of the factors which helped to create the military identity. 'Even his [the recruit's] accustomed language pattern must be renounced, and college graduates are reduced under the taunts of sarcastic drill sergeants to a vocabulary of monosyllabic conformity interspersed with obscenities adopted from their mentors.'

Yet alongside this sort of abuse goes the language of the family. Recruits are, collectively, likely to be called boys or lads rather than men, while the same sergeant who vilifies a recruit on the parade-ground will call him son in a gentler moment. This paternalistic language goes far beyond basic training, and has done for centuries. Sir Jacob Astley launched the Royalist foot at Edgehill in 1642 with the shout, 'March on boys', and Colonel Cross died at Gettysburg murmuring that he thought the boys would miss him. Frederick the Great, for all his insistence on rigid discipline, got on well with his soldiers at the purely personal level: he often rode about his regiments on the line of march, greeting them with a genial 'Good day to you, lads!' When the Prussian infantry reeled before searing Austrian fire at Prague in May 1757, old Field-Marshal von Schwerin grabbed one of his regiment's colours and led his men back into battle, calling 'Heran mein Kinder!' One hundred and thirteen years later Marshal Bazaine trotted ahead of a battalion as it moved forward under a blazing August sky at Rezonville, with a cheery shout of 'Allons, mes enfants, suivez votre maréchal.'

But there is another side to the picture. In all armies – even in the 'enlightened' Israeli army with its lack of emphasis on formal discipline – there is a toughness about basic training that can sometimes become brutality. At least part of the harshness is justified by the need to accomplish what Parrish called the 'rearranging of young men's thinking' which is essential for the triumph of group identity. Spartan accommodation, a long working day and collective punishments for individual transgressions help build a group identity in an atmosphere of shared privation. Indeed, many training systems are deliberately designed to break recruits down to a lowest common denominator before building them up again.

There is a direct link between the harshness of basic training and the cohesiveness of the group which emerges from it. Two American psychologists who conducted experiments into the relationship between the severity of initiation and members' affection for their group concluded that subjects who underwent a severe initiation perceived the group as being considerably more attractive than those who had undergone a mild initiation. This may be attributed to Festinger's theory of cognitive dissonance. Festinger stated that an individual always finds some unattractive characteristics even in a group he otherwise likes. If entry to that group has followed a difficult initiation, his cognition that he has gone through this unpleasant process for the sake of membership of the group is dissonant with his cognition that he dislikes some of the group's characteristics. He strives to reduce this dissonance

47

either by convincing himself that the initiation process was not particularly unpleasant, or by exaggerating the positive characteristics of the group at the expense of its unattractive aspects. In a military context he is likely to do the latter, subconsciously persuading himself that the organisation which he has gone through such pains to join is close to perfection.

This process is at its most marked in the basic training carried out by specialists like parachutists and marines. The rigorous nature of training for such units, with its high failure rate and its emphasis upon physical fitness and mental toughness, welds young men from diverse backgrounds into highly-motivated and cohesive fighting units, which think of themselves as being not only markedly different from, but also considerably better than, the remainder of the armed forces. Whether this is in fact true is almost irrelevant: what matters is that the men who undergo such training come to think of themselves as being élite. They regard themselves as a different species: their basic training initiates and their service together completes what is in effect a process of cultural pseudospeciation. Their sense of tribalism is marked by both appearance and language: American airborne soldiers scorn 'straight leg' infantry, while British parachutists look upon anyone not fortunate enough to wear the red beret as a 'craphat'.

Furthermore, just as Irenäus Eibl-Eibesfeldt had noted, 'the bond within the group is reinforced if aggression is directed against third parties and unity is thus demonstrated against a common, often imaginary, enemy'. The training of specialist units encourages feelings of aggression which are directed not only towards a potential battlefield adversary but also towards almost anyone outside the tribe. When the soldiers of Theodore Eicke's *Totenkopfdivision* were stationed near Stuttgart in the winter of 1939-40, the district commander of the *Wehrmacht* field police formally complained that bands of SS soldiers were roaming the town at night and becoming involved in fights with regular soldiers.

Churlish though it may seem to discuss British parachutists and marines in the same breath as the *Waffen SS*, it is an uncomfortable fact of life that the disciplinary record of these units is similarly chequered. Soldiers of 3 Para were involved in a large-scale brawl within a year of their return from the South Atlantic, and there was fighting between Royal Marines and Danish youths when the former were in Denmark on Exercise Ample Express in September 1983. Indeed, several paras commented on the importance of inculcating aggression during training and maintaining it subsequently. A company commander in 2 Para believed that the fact that his men were 'good gutter fighters' had proved invaluable, while a lance-corporal in 3 Para attributed part of his unit's success to the fact that 'the lads are all scrappers anyway'.

The rigours of basic training, and the pressures which force soldiers together into groups, go some way towards explaining the curious fact that regimes are often defended most stoutly by those who, in logical terms, have little reason to support them. The Prussian Regiment of Anhalt-Bernburg was filled up with impressed Saxons during the Seven Years War. These unfortunates had little sympathy for the Prussians, against whom many of them had already fought, and they can scarcely have found the savage discipline of the Prussian army enticing. In July 1760 the regiment was routed by an Austrian sortie from Dresden, and subjected to an unprecedented collective punishment, under whose terms the common soldiers lost their swords while the officers and NCOs had to give up the braid round their hats. A month later the regiment, still in the deepest disgrace, and still full of Saxons, distinguished itself at Liegnitz, spearheading a breakthrough which decided the battle.

Military history is strewn with similar examples. In July 1758, only thirteen years after the bloody suppression of the Jacobite rebellion of 1745, James Abercromby's infantry assaulted Montcalm's strongly-held position at Ticonderoga. The 42nd Regiment (the Black Watch) contained many Scots with strong personal motives for disliking a government which had harried the Highlands, banned Highland dress and executed, imprisoned or exiled their friends and relatives. Nevertheless, the regiment made gallant and repeated attempts to storm the position, and lost half its rank and file and no less than twenty-five of its officers in the process. In *The Winter War*, their account of the Falklands conflict of 1982, Patrick Bishop and John Witherow pointed out that many of the men in British marine commandos and parachute battalions came 'from Britain's economic wastelands: the Clyde, Ulster, the north-east, and they had better experience than anyone else in the country of its imperfections and injustices. They joined up in many cases because there was nothing else to do.' But these men demonstrated remarkable toughness and determination in the battle for East Falkland.

Another convincing explanation for the apparent paradox inherent in such behaviour is furnished by Erich Fromm, who suggests that a group's narcissism – its tendency to self-worship – is commensurate with its members' lack of real satisfaction in life outside the group. Those who 'lead a life of unmitigated boredom' are more inclined to fanaticism, and fit more happily into a narcissistic group, than those who enjoy more material and cultural benefits. An individual's doubts about himself may be submerged beneath affection for the group, and the tendency for group identity to be formed by aggression leads to a situation in which:

> The narcissistic image of one's own group is raised to its highest point, while the devaluation of the opposing group sinks to its lowest. One's own group becomes a defender of human dignity, decency, morality and right. Devilish qualities are ascribed to the other group; it is treacherous, ruthless and basically inhuman.

There is, as we shall see, a good deal more to the business of moulding unit identity and *esprit de corps* than rigorous basic training and the fostering of aggression against those outside the group. However it is evident that *esprit de corps* can be a decidedly double-edged weapon, producing on the one hand high morale and formidable battlefield performance, but on the other risking extravagantly heavy casualties and a disregard for the humanity of the enemy which can easily lead to atrocities.

Sometimes the pressure which forms a legitimate part of basic training is allowed to become excessive. Most armies have their own horror stories of 'beasting' or 'bastardisation' that has got out of hand. In 1956, for example, a DI in the United States Marine Corps camp at Parris Island, South Carolina, marched seventy-four recruits into a tidal swamp in the dark: six of them drowned. In 1980 a British court martial revealed that recruits at an infantry depot had been subjected to a variety of unofficial punishments, including a mock execution, and a year later the suicide of a young soldier was partially attributed to bullying at a depot. These are, admittedly, particularly notorious examples. More usual is the sort of casual brutality described by William Manchester, who wrote of Parris Island that 'in my day it was quite common to see a DI bloody a man's nose'. One of the Vietnam veterans interviewed by Mark Baker for his book *Nam* remembered how a joke on the DI turned sour. 'It was really funny,' he said, 'a take-off from Gomer Pyle. The guy within arm's reach of the Marine was laughing just like everybody else. Smokey Bear [the DI] whipped around and smacked him right in the face, knocking him half way through the window.' Similar excesses, perpetrated either by the instructors or by the recruits themselves – often in an effort to 'improve' a slovenly comrade whose behaviour or turnout has brought the group into disrepute – have been regular features of basic training in almost all armies.

Officer-training academies have, traditionally, been every bit as harsh as the depots attended by ordinary recruits, although in these institutions it has usually been the cadets themselves, rather than their instructors, who have been responsible for the worst barbarity. St Cyr was notorious for its *brimades*, crude and often dangerous practical jokes, of which one of the least aggressive was boring holes in the victim's chamber-pot. German cadet academies also witnessed considerable brutality, while the Royal Military College, Sandhurst, was well up to the standards of its continental counterparts in this respect: the future Field-Marshal Montgomery was reduced to the rank of gentleman cadet from that of lance-corporal for setting fire to a junior cadet's shirt. Montgomery had clearly gone too far, but less harmful sorts of mischief were, if not officially approved, at least not discouraged. Just as basic training socialised the recruit into the military life, so the military academy, and the officer cadet school in wartime, provided what Stouffer called: 'a kind of purgatory, a definite demarcation from the candidate's enlisted incarnation ... It has some of the characteristics of a conversion experience, or the ordeal of the medieval knight.'

Much of the harshness in recruit training results, then, from the need to cement the group together under adversity. There is also more than a little of the psychological phenomenon which Julian Huxley associated with exams, but which applies equally well to military training, many of whose pressures stem from 'the subconscious desire of the adult to revenge himself for past ordeals by subjecting the young to the same unpleasant trials to which he himself was subjected'.

There are, though, other reasons for the application of what is often very severe stress to the recruit. A drill-sergeant at Fort Polk justified his harshness as an essential preparation for the pressures of combat. 'You have got to have harassment', he claimed, or the recruit would be unable to withstand battle for, 'if you can't take the training, you damn sure can't take that.' US Marine Lieutenant-General Chesty Puller, speaking for the defence at the court martial which followed the Parris Island tragedy of 1956, used very much the same argument. 'The definition of military training is success in battle,' he contended. 'Without discipline, an army becomes a mob. In my opinion the reason American troops made out so poorly in Korea was mostly due to lack of night training.' Twenty years later, General Louis H. Wilson, commandant of the Marine Corps, acknowledged that the creation of stress in training was important, because the ultimate aim of a training organisation was 'to train a man to be able to take care of himself and to live in the stressful situation of battle'. His Soviet counterpart would probably not disagree, for Suvorov's maxim 'hard and heavy on the training ground, light on the battlefield' has long been an axiom of Soviet military training.

The fact that training is designed as preparation for war has encouraged various attempts to recreate, in a training environment, many of the stresses of the battlefield. Clausewitz believed that manœuvres should prepare the soldier as realistically as possible for the disjointing and depressing consequences of war, and S.L.A. Marshall complained that this was exactly the sort of training which a soldier did not receive. While he might be told about his country's war aims, his allies, and so on, 'he does not get what he most requires – the simple details of common human experience on the field of battle'. While Marshall was undoubtedly right to suggest that there was too little emphasis on telling the soldier what to expect of battle, there were certainly considerable efforts made by all major combatants during the Second World War to ensure that the soldier was familiar with at least some of the sights and sounds of the battlefield.

Battle inoculation is an attempt to accustom the soldier to the din of battle. By 1943 almost all men under training in the United States army had been put through a course which required an eighty-yard crawl over rough ground, with live machine-gun fire passing overhead. Similar training was used in the British army, and there were a number of variations, in which mortar and artillery fire fell the minimum safety distance away from the troops under training, and explosive charges were set off near by to represent shellfire.

Although John Ellis suggested that 'the only really effective combat training was that received on the battlefield itself', there was a wide measure of agreement that battle inoculation was useful. One-third of the combat veterans who provided the information used by Stouffer and his colleagues believed that more exposure to battle simulation would have helped them, and 81 per cent felt that this sort of training was 'very important'. 'Make it as real as possible, using real ammunition,' advised one soldier. 'A few will get killed, but the others will learn. They will know the score, that this is war and no picnic.'

Unfortunately attempts to create realism could go too far. In 1941–2 some British battle schools, despite opposition from psychiatrists, introduced battle inoculation which included the use of animal carcasses and was designed to inculcate hatred and aggression. It proved markedly unsuccessful, and many of the best students lost interest in their training as a result. It was finally prohibited in May 1942. Nevertheless, the battle inoculation which was continued, and which centred upon overhead machine-gun fire and close explosions, was generally regarded as being helpful in that it did give the soldier some idea of the sound of battle.

This sort of training inevitably entails the risk of casualties. German SS units took part in particularly realistic training with live ammunition, in which 5 per cent casualties were tolerated. The armies of Western democracies have tended to be more cautious, particularly in peacetime, when death or injury in training is likely to become the subject of official inquiry, and combat training is hedged about with so many restrictions that it often becomes either impracticable or ineffective. Not so in the Soviet army, where combat simulation and battle inoculation are as realistic as possible, and include the use of chemical agents which other armies might regard as impossibly risky.

Let us turn from the harder edge of military training to what might superficially seem to have little to do with training: sport. Konrad Lorenz suggested, however, that sport originated from highly ritualised fighting, describing it as 'a specifically human form of non-hostile combat, governed by the strictest of continually developing rules'. Sport is more akin to serious fighting than animal play is, and contains aggressive motivation. It is therefore not surprising that sport and military training are often closely linked. Sport has several useful military functions. Geoffrey Best identified two of them in *The Victorian Public School:*

Sport concerned the military in two ways: firstly, as the straight road to physical health and strength, indispensable to the good soldier; secondly, because of the special value attributed to team games in training the essential qualities of the officer and leader.[5]

Robert Graves supports the latter point. Commanding a platoon in an officer-cadet battalion in Oxford in 1917, he recalled that 'Our final selection was made by watching the candidates play games, principally rugger and soccer. Those who played rough but not dirty, and had quick reactions, were the sort we needed ...'

It is tempting to regard this sort of emphasis on sport, which smacks of Waterloo being won on the playing fields of Eton, as antiquated and excessive. But fast-moving team games do indeed call for quick decisions under pressure, and often involve physical contact calling for physical courage and determination. Moreover, as Lorenz indicates, such games educate man in the control of his own fighting behaviour. Irenäus Eibl-Eibesfeldt asserted that 'warlike cultures actually practise more combative sports than unwarlike cultures'. Stouffer and his colleagues detected a strong connection between sport and military behaviour: they discovered that there was a marked correlation between interest in body-contact sports and adjustment to army life. Keen team sportsmen, in other words, made the keenest soldiers.

Norman Dixon took the argument on sport a stage further, noting the frequency with which military men hunt and shoot. Few other professions, he observed, carry their professional responses thus far into their leisure activities. Here Professor Dixon's evidence is unreliable. The examples he cites are from Britain in the Victorian era, when not only army and naval officers, but also that segment of civilian society from which most of them sprang, hunted and shot. It is therefore not remarkable that Victorian and Edwardian officers spent a great deal of their leisure time astride horses or wielding shotguns: it would have been surprising had they not done so. There is, though, more than a little truth in the general point made by Erich Fromm that there are well-established similarities between war and blood sports. Hunters, for example, rarely enjoy the suffering of their quarry, and often feel affection towards it, mingled with guilt. These sensations are, as we shall see, not dissimilar to those experienced by many a soldier towards his enemy, who may, in a sense, simply be 'the most dangerous game'.

The conclusion of basic training is marked by a passing-out ceremony, designed to emphasise the change of tribal status from youth to warrior. Just as ritual welcomed the recruit into the army, so ritual marks this, a crucial transformation. At the very least the transition will be celebrated by a parade, which may be carefully designed to impress the importance of the occasion upon the soldier's mind: recruits to the Israeli army's armoured corps, for example, pass out at a torchlight ceremony at Masada. There will also be a demonstrative change in plumage, as the fledgeling takes on the distinctive markings of maturity. Red or green berets, arm patches, lanyards: the marks of the fighting caste vary from army to army. But whatever they are, they form part of a ritual designed to demonstrate that the recruit is no longer an object of scorn, the butt of drill-sergeants and the despair of officers: he is a man, a comrade and a soldier.

Virgin Soldiers

There can have been few periods of peace so assured that soldiers have not considered, however peripherally, the prospect of their own participation in war. Moreover, for men who join armies while hostilities are actually in progress this speculation can assume the proportions of obsession. Colonel Elmar Dinter, a serving West German officer and author of a brilliant study of morale in battle, suggests that 'hero or coward?' is every soldier's unspoken question to himself.[6] My aim, at this juncture, is to examine the soldier's preconceptions of battle early on in his service, before the stage when battle is imminent and expectation is sharpened into anticipation.

There is more than a superficial similarity between the sense of anticipation which precedes a soldier's first battle and that which precedes his first experience of sex. In both cases he will have stretched his mind forward in an effort to grasp the sensation, and will probably have talked to those who have already undergone it. He may well regard both experiences as essential milestones along his own route to full masculinity. 'I wanted to go to war,' said a Vietnam veteran. 'It was a test that I wanted to pass. It was a manhood test, no question about it.' True, the comparison cannot be taken too far, for battle clearly contains risks which sex does not. Nevertheless, it is no accident that there is considerable overlap between the language of sex and that of battle. A soldier who served with 2 Para in the Falklands described his battalion's attack on Wireless Ridge, delivered with lavish artillery support, as 'the most exciting thing since getting my leg across', while one of Mark Baker's subjects proclaimed that 'a gun is power. To some people carrying a gun was like having a permanent hard-on. It was a pure sexual trip every time you got to pull the trigger.' In more general terms, Ali Mazrui is right to draw attention to 'the interplay between martial and sexual prowess in man's ancestral heritage'.

I make no apologies for the fact that sex rears what some will regard as its ugly head in various places in this book. I am, at least, in good company. Glenn Gray devoted a chapter to 'Love: War's Ally and Foe', and emphasised soldiers' preoccupation with sex. The interplay between war and sex is obvious enough in the context of Freudian psychology, and love – whether in the sense of erotic love between the sexes, what Gray calls 'preservative love', independent of distinctions of sex, or that easily-misunderstood friendship between men which is quite literally 'passing the love of women' – plays far too great a part in the soldier's life to be ignored.

Although the process of basic training will have attempted to crystallise the soldier's preconceptions of battle, and give him confidence in himself and his weapons, it will have been, at best, only partially successful in doing this. Lord Moran believed that, though courage was an expendable commodity and every man had his breaking point, certain men – notably the 'weak creatures from the towns' – were predisposed to breakdown and would crack first. During the Second World War there was also a tendency to explain breakdown in battle as the result of a deep-seated neurotic disorder or personality defect: battle cracked a man along an existing fissure. Later, particularly as psychologists moved more into the combat zone, so 'realistic explanations for psychiatric breakdown were found in the environmental and situational circumstances of combat itself'.[7] In Vietnam, however, a war subjected to a greater degree of psychiatric scrutiny than almost any other, there was something of a reversal of this trend of opinion, and Peter Bourne observed that psychiatric casualties were composed mainly of psychoneurotic and personality disorders. Moreover, Lazarus argued that the strength of the *ego* – something extremely difficult to measure – was an important factor in the individual's resistance to stress, and that 'the development of pathological behaviour patterns in combat situations must be understood in terms of the prestress personality'.

Some instances of breakdown resulting from a deep-seated neurosis are clear enough. In *Childhood and Society*, Erik Erikson describes the case of a soldier who remembered nothing after having a sub-machine-gun put into his hands shortly after landing on a Pacific island during the Second World War. This was not a result of the pressures of battle, but was rooted in the man's childhood, when he had promised never to touch a gun. Most cases of breakdowns related to the pre-stress personality are less simple. Nevertheless, there is a wide measure of agreement among psychiatrists that a significant proportion of the soldier's behaviour in battle is accounted for by events which occurred long before he joined the army.

The practical consequences of this are potentially serious. S.L.A. Marshall established that, on average, only some 15 per cent of American infantrymen fired during actions in the Second World War. Marshall blamed failure to fire upon the values inculcated into the soldier during his upbringing. The soldier, argued Marshall, bore all the marks of the society which produced him. 'The Army cannot unmake him,' he wrote. 'It must reckon with the fact that he comes from a civilisation in which aggression, connected with the taking of life, is prohibited and unacceptable.' Military training may find itself in conflict not only with an individual's *super-ego*, but also with more conscious cultural norms. There is thus a fruitful source of psychiatric illness and of a less dramatic but

militarily equally damaging failure to participate in a firefight.
And, while basic training may succeed in obliterating these
conscious norms, and, as J.A.Blake put it, in socialising men
into violence, it cannot deal with the *super-ego*, and the potential for conflict between it and the conscious personality
remains.

The soldier's preconception of battle is shaped, not only by
his upbringing, education and training, but also by the influence of the art, literature and film to which he has been
exposed. The arts, in their broadest sense, play a more important role in creating images of war than is generally recognised. Even exposure to the journalistic coverage of war can
both sketch the outlines of battle and foster that curious fascination which violence often has. Christopher Isherwood
grew up during the First World War, and acknowledged that:

> Like most of my generation, I was obsessed by a complex
> of terror and longings connected with the idea 'War'. War
> in this purely neurotic sense meant The Test. The test of
> your courage, of your maturity, of your sexual prowess: 'are
> you really a man?' Subconsciously, I believe, I longed to be
> subjected to this test; but I also dreaded failure. I dreaded
> failure so much – indeed, I was so certain that I *should* fail
> – that, consciously, I denied my longing to be tested alto-
> gether.

Ironically, portraying war in all its harsh realism often has
the effect of making it more rather than less attractive. In
Violence in the Arts, John Fraser warned that it can be peculiarly
pleasurable to give way to a desire for the uglier and seamier
side of life, and quoted the philosopher William James who,
as long ago as 1910, wrote that 'showing war's irrationality
and horror is of no effect upon [modern man]. The horror is
the fascination. War is the *strong* life; it is life *in extremis*.'

Myron Smith's *War Story Guide* suggests that literature is
one of the most important ways in which Americans have
'attempted to gauge the thrust and reality of combat', and
goes on to outline the role of war fiction as an educational

tool in spreading vicarious experience of war. Certain sorts of literature create their own preconceptions. William Manchester acknowledged that his own ideas of what war was actually like had been partially shaped by what he had read. 'I read Kipling, not Hemingway.' he wrote, 'Rupert Brooke, not Wilfred Owen; *Gone with the Wind*, not Ambrose Bierce and Stephen Crane.' John Baynes believed that popular literature played an important part in determining attitudes in Britain before the First World War. Books like *Jackanapes* and *The Story of a Short Life* were 'full of noble sentiments, glorious deaths and fervid patriotism', while the historical novels of G.A. Henty, with their emphasis upon manly virtues and clear-cut values, played an important part in conditioning British middle-class youth for the First World War. 'I became a keen reader of G.A. Henty's books on war,' said a machine-gunner of the First World War, 'and later read Rudyard Kipling's books. I loved to be in the company of soldiers.'

No single author played a greater part in this conditioning than did Rudyard Kipling. In 'Only a Subaltern', he described Bobby Wicks, the classic public-school Englishman, honest, loyal, bursting with both moral and physical courage. Charles Carrington wrote in his biography of Kipling that 'he moulded a whole generation of young Englishmen into that type. They rose up in their thousands, in 1914, and sacrificed themselves, in the image Kipling had created.' It is ironic that Kipling himself knew war only at second hand, and his early stories of fighting on the North-west Frontier were themselves derived from 'books, or from soldiers' yarns about their experiences'. Those who modelled themselves on Kipling's heroes were, in fact, imitating a type which owed almost as much to Kipling's imagination as it did to the realities of life – and death – on the frontier.

During the Second World War, V.M. Yeates's *Winged Victory*, a gripping novel about the air war over the Western Front in the last year of the First World War, became so popular with bomber pilots that it changed hands at up to £5 a copy, a substantial sum in those days. Those who read it told Henry Williamson that it was the only book about war

flying which 'wasn't flannel', but there may have been more
to it than this. Yeates's characters, flying mission after mission
with dwindling odds against survival, had much in common
with the crews of bomber command: if the latter were to have
any fictitious role models, then, surely, Yeates's tired warriors
were they.

It is interesting to speculate upon what books – novels,
'faction' or memoirs – most influence the present generation
of young soldiers and junior officers. There is certainly a taste
for strong meat. Guy Sajer's *The Forgotten Soldier* and Robert
Elford's *The Devil's Guard* are both popular, and the almost
surrealistic novels of Sven Hassel, which describe the fighting
on the Eastern Front in the most explicit terms, are read
avidly by the young men who, two generations ago, would
have lived out the very horrors the books depict. The Vietnam
War has produced at least two books of lasting importance,
Michael Herr's *Dispatches* and Philip Caputo's *A Rumour of War*.
Although both are likely to appeal to a rather more cultiva-
ted taste than that which relishes *Legion of the Damned* and *Wheels
of Terror*, they none the less pull no punches, and leave the
reader in no doubt that war is a brutal and bloody business.

Many young men wish to be assured of the horror of war,
either as part of that craving after the ugly side of life which
John Fraser describes, or because of a desire to gain a foretaste
of what might come if humanity does slip over the rim of the
crater into hell. What one might term 'military pornography'
vies with pornography of a more predictable type in the backs
of the armoured personnel carriers that grind their way across
the sandy training areas of northern Germany. Three years
ago, on a NATO exercise on the Danish island of Zeeland, as
my battalion braced itself to meet a simulated invasion, I
noticed that my radio operator had his nose deep in a book:
it was a novel about the experiences of a tank commander in
the Third World War.

The impact of photography has been particularly striking,
if only because of the limitations of pictorial art. The busy
canvases of battles all too often reflected what the artist wished
to believe had taken place rather than what had actually

happened. The late nineteenth-century French artists Édouard Detaille and Alphonse de Neuville were notable for their attention to detail but, even so, Detaille believed that there were some things which the artist should avoid. 'Disfigured corpses, wounded with neither arms nor legs' could not be represented, and a similar restraint prevented many other artists, albeit with significant exceptions such as Callot and Goya, from showing war in its true lights.

There are few better examples of the triumph of illusion over reality than Horace Vernet's painting of Arcola. It depicts a French attempt to cross the Alpone on 15 November 1796, and Vernet has chosen the moment when Bonaparte – then a young general with his career before him – seized a tricolour and led an attack on the bridge at Arcola. Vernet, painting in 1826, when the follies of the First Empire had been forgotten and many Frenchmen yearned for charismatic leadership, was concerned to show Napoleon in a heroic light. But his picture is more than mere Bonapartist propaganda. Vernet is showing war the way people wished to imagine it. He permits a blast of cannister to bowl over a few unfortunates and to splinter some woodwork, but the French infantry seem barely inconvenienced by the gusts of death blowing at them from across the narrow river. The dead are killed cleanly, and the wounded hit 'in some mentionable place'. Most of the French have managed not only to retain their cumbersome headgear but also to preserve the crispness of their linen: they stand, soldierly endeavour glinting in every eye, almost like costume figures in the *Musée de l'Armée*.

The image is a travesty of reality. The *Armée d'Italie* was tired and battleworn: its 'weakness and exhaustion' alarmed even its commander. The crossing was so firmly held by Austrian infantry and guns that French troops were reluctant to advance: close-range artillery fire slashed through their ranks, tearing off limbs and blowing men to ribbons. Bonaparte did briefly grab a colour, but was almost immediately knocked into the river in the confusion, to be hauled out bedraggled just before the Austrians counter-attacked. The battle raged on for another two days, and was not decided at the bridge at

Arcola, still less by Bonaparte's gesture there. Vernet's picture is a heroic fraud: it resembles an attempted river-crossing under heavy fire less accurately than 'Star Trek' represents the problems of manned space flight.

The approach of popular artists to the First World War was scarcely better. Caton Woodville, with his neatly-bandaged head-wounds, manly and heroic expressions, and curiously splay-legged runners, gives the distinctive flavour of a generation of popular war artists who painted battle in anything but 'the woeful crimson of men slain'.

Even if the painter was determined to portray battle as honestly as he could, the technical limitations of his art were such that he was usually unable to capture the fleeting moment. The crammed canvases of most nineteenth-century military painters fail to reflect a battlefield which was, in the participants' view, more often empty than crowded. They also do not do justice to the clouds of thick powder-smoke which blackened hands and faces, 'broke down' uniforms far more effectively than the efforts of any theatrical costumier, and often reduced observation to a few yards. Captain Cavalié Mercer, commanding a battery at Waterloo, was in the very forefront of the battle. But he saw little of it. 'What was passing to the right and left of us I know no more than the man in the moon,' he wrote. 'The smoke confined our vision to a very small compass, so that my battle was restricted to the two squares [of infantry] and my own battery.'

The shortcomings of these artistic representations of battle, obvious though they may seem to us, were far less remarkable at the time. One of the things which surprised participants in nineteenth-century battles was how little like battle pictures the real thing actually was. Young Georges de Moussac, who charged with the 3rd *Cuirassiers* at Froeschwiller on 6 August 1870, compared the reality of this action with the paintings of it. His colonel was killed, not neatly and gallantly during the charge, but before it, by a shell which ripped his head off, tore the hand of another officer and killed three men and their horses. There was no hand-to-hand contact with the Germans at all, and de Moussac recalled, not the splendour and gravity of what was to become a classic episode of French military history, but the fact that he was too thin for his cuirass, which flopped about in the most irritating fashion.

In their desire to portray either the whole of a battle, or at least the totality of an episode within it, artists did soldiers – and, indeed, historians – a disservice. They implied that battlefields were full, whereas, from the evidence of combatants, it is abundantly clear that they often felt and looked empty. The gulf between pictorial conjecture and harsh reality was often utterly dislocating, especially to men brought up in the tradition of crowded paintings. Colonel Lyman fought for the Union in two pitched battles in the American Civil War. 'I have scarcely seen a Rebel save killed, wounded or prisoners,' he admitted. 'I remember even line officers, who were at the battle of Chancellorsville, saying: "Why, we never saw any rebels where we were; only smoke and bushes, and lots of our men tumbling about."'

Photography did not revolutionise the image of war overnight. The first few war photographs were taken in Mexico in 1846 or 1847, and a British surgeon, John MacCosh, took some photographs in the Second Sikh and Second Burma Wars. Roger Fenton recorded the hirsute heroes of the Crimean War, and Felice Beato captured the dusty squalor of India during the Mutiny. It was not until Matthew Brady exhibited his pictures of the dead of Antietam in the autumn of 1862 that war photography came of age. The *New York Times* commented that Brady's photographs made the battlefield a reality. It was 'like a funeral next door', although, just as a funeral might excite morbid curiosity, so too the photographs aroused 'a terrible fascination'. In *America's Bloodiest Day*, William Frassanito indicates the essential difference between these photographs and the paintings, lithographs and woodcuts that had preceded them. 'The dead and wounded were invariably present,' he observed, 'but somehow they always appeared intact – never mutilated, bloated or rotting in the sun – and the aura of martyrdom usually triumphed, blending well into the excitement of living forms struggling for victory.'

Brady and his colleagues were not above rearranging the dead to make a better picture, and the substantial limitations imposed by their cumbersome equipment prevented them from photographing battle itself rather than its aftermath. Nevertheless, as the apparatus at their disposal improved, so photographers began to freeze the very face of battle. Many of the photographs during the First World War were either posed or deliberately sanitised so as to be non-controversial. Despite this, the camera recorded the purgatory of the Western Front, from the wilderness of desolation in the Ypres salient to a Frenchman crumpling to a German rifle in Nivelle's vain offensive above the Aisne. But it was still difficult to photograph battles in the same sense that artists had painted them. For, while the artistic imagination had been able to pierce the fog of war, the camera's lens could not. 'Battles of the First War', pointed out Charles Carrington, 'were rarely spectacular since the shrapnel obscured visibility. A great noise and a smoke-cloud filled the valley in which now and then one saw distant figures moving aimlessly it seemed, like ants in a disturbed anthill.'

During the last fifty years the camera has recorded a striking portrait of the battlefield, and has caught vignettes of combat, if not of the broad spread of battle itself. Robert Capa, whose approach to combat photography is summed up by his comment 'If your pictures aren't any good, you're not standing close enough', covered two decades of war with remarkable distinction before he was killed in Indo-China. During the Vietnam War, Tim Page – described in Michael Herr's *Dispatches* as one of the 'young, apolitically radical, wigged-out crazies' – took a series of photographs that somehow seemed to seize the essence of the war, from tattered corpses in a paddy-field to a soldier with *Hippie* written on his helmet-cover sitting in an APC turret with a mauve umbrella. Wilfred Owen had written of that 'Incomprehensible look, which men will never see in England ... it was not despair or terror, it was more terrible than terror, for it was a blindfold look, without expression, like a dead rabbit. It will never be painted, and no actor will ever seize it.' That look, those 'sad

65

infinite eyes, like those of a newborn beast of burden', as Federico García Lorca put it, that face transfixed by the 'thousand yard stare', may have eluded the artist, but they have not escaped the camera, and live on to haunt us in the work of combat photographers.

These photographers have increased the impact of war in a way in which artists, however inspired, could never have done. But they have done more than bring the Vietnam War on to the news-stands of London, or immortalise the death of a frigate in San Carlos Water. They have provided successive generations of young men with their own images of battle, images which pre-date their military service and are often more compelling than those imparted during basic training. There is, however, room for inquiring whether the photographers of the twentieth century are not creating an image of battle which may, at least in some of its aspects, be as misleading as the work of the artists of the nineteenth. Photographers are naturally inclined to photograph what is there rather than what is not. Photographs of bleak moorland, virgin jungle or bald desert do not sell newspapers or make reputations. The essential emptiness of the battlefield is rarely captured, and it still numbs soldiers.

The battlefield 'is the lonesomest place which men share together,' wrote S.L.A. Marshall. 'The harshest thing about the field is that it is empty. No people stir about. There are little or no signs of action.' Memoirs, anthologies and interviews, whether they deal with the World Wars, Vietnam or the Falklands, lend emphasis to the words of an American soldier: 'By God, there was never a situation like it. We saw no one. We were fighting phantoms.' Second-Lieutenant W.H. Crowder, a British Field Artillery observer quoted in Middlebrook's *The Kaiser's Battle*, recalled:

I had always imagined that I should see some sort of fight in front of us with our men fighting the Germans but it was so misty and I had to wear one of those horrible gas-masks that I saw nothing – just an occasional figure. I kept bobbing up and down and observing and then bobbing down and reporting. I could see just a few figures in the mist but couldn't tell which side they were on.

A soldier's glimpses of the enemy – and often of his friends – are summed up by this British parachutist:

> There was a lot of smoke about: some of it was ours and some came from the burning gorse. A lot of shit got thrown up by the shells and that didn't help. You could see their trenches all right, but I didn't really see any Argies properly until they'd started surrendering ... I could see the other blokes in the section, and when one of them got hit he was thrown back so hard by the bullet that I was sure he'd had it but he was OK ... It was unbelievably confusing, far, far worse than even the most confusing exercise.

If photographs have been influential, films have been even more so. Although the precise role of film and television with regard to violence is hotly disputed, it seems certain that they have had the effect, in Fraser's words, of 'raising the shock threshold'. The striking fact about many war films is that, whatever line they might take over war as a moral issue, they often portray it in what appears to be a realistic way. It may well be that this realism is more apparent than real. General Sir John Hackett wrote:

> Battle scenes in films often make people who have been in battles restless. On the screen there are particular conventions to be observed. Men blown up by high explosives in real war, for example, are often torn apart quite hideously; in films, there is a big bang and bodies, intact, fly through the air with the greatest of ease. If they are shot ... they fall down like children in a game, to lie motionless. The most harrowing thing in real battles is that they usually *don't* lie still; only the lucky ones are killed outright.[8]

It is also rare for films to grasp the emptiness, puzzlement and disorganisation of the battlefield, although John Ford's *Lost*

Patrol is an honourable exception. Nevertheless, because films seem to be realistic, they have furnished the soldiers of the last forty or so years with a credible image of battle.

And they have done more than this. Just as many recruits tend to take their instructor as their role model, so soldiers often unconsciously take the character from a film as their role model before they even enter the army. While in the process of shooting *The Outsider* at Camp Pendleton in 1960, Delbert Mann asked a group of Marine recruits why they had chosen the Marine Corps. Half of them answered that it was because of the John Wayne films that they had seen. In *Sands of Iwo Jima* John Wayne played the classic firm-but-fair Sergeant Stryker, the archetypal role-model for young Marines for the next twenty years. Ron Kovic, a Vietnam veteran, recalled that: 'Like Mickey Mantle and the fabulous New York Yankees, John Wayne in *Sands of Iwo Jima* became one of my heroes.' Josiah Bunting, author of *The Lionheads*, served as an officer in Vietnam, and believed that infantry officers, particularly lieutenant-colonels, were influenced by 'this whole area of machismo ... The influence of John Waynism, if you want to call it that, on these people was terribly profound.' Middle-ranking infantry officers in Vietnam in the late 1960s would have been in their early teens when *Sands of Iwo Jima* first appeared: it is, perhaps, not surprising that its impact was so tremendous.[9] John Parrish endorsed these comments. He noticed that a soldier wore his dog tags outside his T-shirt 'just like in a World War II movie'. 'I was John Wayne,' he wrote, describing how he had helped wounded on to a helicopter under fire. 'I was covering the retreat from the beaches of World War II. I was the star of the war comics.'

This almost conscious role-playing is a notable feature of the wars of this century. Soldiers often conform to their preconceived image of what a soldier should be, and this image is usually a photograph or a frame from a film. Robert Graves depicted: 'Myself in faultless khaki with highly polished buttons and belt, revolver at hip, whistle on cord, delicate moustache on upper lip, and stern endeavour a-glint in either eye, pretending to be a Regular Army captain.' It was an image which could easily be misunderstood. An Australian officer complained that the British New Armies 'have not the pluck of a louse and all their officers think of doing is to ape the regular officer when on parade'.

John Parrish's self-portrait, although from a different war and another continent, was similar to Graves's. 'A .45 on the hip and two bars on the collar gave rise to a sense of personal prestige and power analysed by a few, accepted by most, and needed by some,' he wrote. 'Boys who watched World War II movies, read war comics, and played war games on vacant lots were men now.' Lieutenant William Calley, court-martialled for his role in the My Lai massacre, was quite specific, firstly, about the influence of films on his behaviour. 'We thought', he recalled, 'we will go to Vietnam and be Audie Murphys. *Kick in the door, run in the hooch, give it a good burst –* kill.' Secondly, he remembered how, on his arrival in Vietnam, he conformed to the image of the rough-tough infantryman. 'I stood in the trailer truck like the meanest, the most tremendous, the most dangerous weapon there is,' said Calley. 'My rifle slung low. My helmet pulled down. I even scowled!' He must have looked curiously like Second-Lieutenant John Kincaid, marching off to embark for the Walcheren expedition in the spring of 1809.

> With the usual quixotic feeling of a youngster, I remember how very desirous I was, on the march to Deal, to impress the minds of the natives of my importance, by carrying a donkey-load of pistols in my belt, and screwing my naturally placid countenance up to a pitch of ferocity beyond what it was calculated to bear.

Finally, the soldier is given a foretaste of what is to come – often no more accurate than that provided by artists, photographers or film-makers – by the war stories of his relatives, instructors and, as battle draws closer, his comrades. All are likely to slant their recollections in one direction or another. Older relatives may simply not talk about what was for them a harrowing experience or, unconsciously using selective recall, may dwell upon only those espisodes which they think will bear repetition. Nevertheless, the influence of these men is often greater than they realise. Alfred de Vigny traced his own fascination with armies to his childhood. 'I have always enjoyed listening,' he wrote,

> having early acquired this taste as a child at the wounded knees of my old father. He began by telling me the stories of his campaigns and, sitting on his knee I found war at my side. He made war live for me in his wounds, in the patents of nobility and the heraldic blazons of his ancestors, in the great armoured portraits which hung in an old manor house in the Beauce.

'I was very keen on becoming a soldier,' a First World War NCO told me. 'I had two uncles, both regulars who served throughout the South African War of 1899–1902. As a youngster I was thrilled by their stories.' Tim O'Brien mused on how he and his friends were influenced by their fathers' war:

> We bought dented relics of our fathers' history, rusted canteens and olive-scented, scarred helmet liners. Then we were our fathers, taking on the Japs and Krauts ... I rubbed my fingers across my father's war decorations, stole a tiny battle star off one of them and carried it in my pocket.

William Manchester's father had served in the Marine Corps during the First World War, and, feeling that he owed his father a debt, the young Manchester joined the Marine Corps in an effort to be amongst the first to fight the Germans.

Mothers, though they have no war stories to tell, have a deeper influence than many a young soldier is prepared to acknowledge. 'The psychological influence of the mother should not be under-rated,' wrote Major-General Frank Richardson. 'It is a touching fact that men, dying in battle, often call upon their mothers. I have heard them do so in five languages.'

The values instilled during upbringing play their own important part in determining the soldier's attitude to military service in general and to battle in particular. 'You could never expect another generation to do what we did,' stressed a First World War infantry officer. 'We had been bred to it in a funny sort of way: certainly the soldiers of the next war could never have put up with it.' *Musketier* Wilhelm Boscheinen of the 230th Reserve Regiment, recalling his own sensations while waiting to attack on 21 March 1918, added: 'But at that time we were brought up through school and parental discipline in the spirit of the military Empire of the Kaiser.' The influence of the patriotic schoolmaster was pronounced in pre-1914 Europe: the figure of Kantorek in Remarque's *All Quiet on the Western Front* is drawn from life. William Manchester argued that the marines of his generation were shaped by the values of a world in which: 'Debt was ignoble. Courage was a virtue. Mothers were beloved, fathers obeyed. Marriage was a sacrament. Divorce was a disgrace.'

The war stories swapped by off-duty soldiers help to socialise the recruit into the military family. General François du Barail, a nineteenth-century French cavalryman, believed that old soldiers played an important role in training recruits. It was their duty to 'tell the jolly military stories in the barrack rooms, sing old songs on the march, and perpetuate the types of Brin d'Amour, Fanfan la Tulipe and Ramée'. As battle draws closer, so the tales are likely to be decidedly less jolly. A newly-arrived soldier may find himself the unspoken target of stories which either emphasise the bitterness of the fighting he has just missed or elaborate on atrocities. Raleigh Trevelyan, a twenty-year-old subaltern attached to the Green Howards at Anzio in 1944, was surprised that his brother officers were unable to resist talking about previous battles when out of the line for a few days: '"God, the Fortress was a picnic compared to the cemetery at Minturno," etc. etc. Then they started off on How We Crossed the Catania Plain. As if I were interested.' A US Marine officer had a similar experience on his first night in Vietnam. 'I spent the night in some officers' hooch,' he said. 'They came in and were talking about this and that, the worst things they could come up with. Half their conversation is aimed at me, although I'm not included.'

By the time that the soldier reaches the point where speculation becomes apprehension, he is likely to have at least a dim version of the experience he expects to undergo. Effective and realistic training and, for soldiers in the latter part of the twentieth century, exposure to fiction and documentary on film and television, may have created an image which accords with reality. The soldiers of the two parachute battalions in the Falklands constantly emphasised how the war had resembled an exercise for which live ammunition had somehow been issued. Similarly, an American infantry officer described his first action in Vietnam in 1970 as 'a textbook situation' which conformed to his expectations, while a British platoon commander at Arnhem told me that 'combat seemed to be simply an extension of training – only with a real enemy and a higher degree of danger'.

On the other hand, veterans of the Malaya campaign of 1941–2 are almost unanimous in describing how the reality of war conflicted with their preconception of it. H.L. Payne, an artillery officer, wrote of the 'formidable worry' of embarking upon jungle warfare without any training. Lieutenant-Colonel Peter Halford-Thompson complained, not unreasonably, of being 'pitchforked' into an unfamiliar environment. Another artillery officer, A.D.B. Arroll, used almost the same form of words, and told of being 'pitchforked in at the deep end ... things were very hectic and also discouraging ... there was no time for either acclimatisation or training, or to get to know the Indian Army to which we were attached'. Sergeant Kenneth Harrison of the Australian 4th Anti-Tank Regiment contrasted his inexperienced comrades with their Japanese enemy. 'Compared with these battle-tested veterans,' he wrote,

we were babies. Apart from firing six shots out to sea from a few old French 75s, none of us had ever handled an artillery gun since we enlisted. We were going into action with a two-pounder gun we had never fired, except in theory.

It was strictly amateurs versus professionals. Fortunately we were not aware of it.

The risks of such gulfs between preconception and reality are colossal. Battle is a traumatic experience at the best of times. But if it produces not only all the stresses of noise and danger but also the dislocation of expectation, then the risks of failure and breakdown loom large. Marshall believed that the average soldier goes to battle, the 'supremely testing experience of his lifetime almost as a total stranger'. Grinker and Spiegel, too, argued that most men had an essentially unreal concept of battle. Certainly, most soldiers set off on the road to battle conscious of the fact that they are about to embark upon an experience which, for good or ill, is unique. As Lieutenant Alan Hanbury-Sparrow wrote as he went to war in August 1914, 'What's all the knowledge of the world compared with what we are about to discover?'

3

The Painful Field

We are but warriors for the working-day;
Our gayness and our gilt are all besmirch'd
With rainy marching in the painful field
                                        Shakespeare, *Henry V*

The Components of War

'Combat', declared Stouffer, 'is the end toward which all the manifold activities of the army are oriented, however indirectly.' This undoubtedly remains true even in an age when the strategic posture of deterrence can sometimes mislead armies into forgetting that, even if war-prevention is their most usual function, war-fighting is their ultimate task. Yet the essential truth of Stouffer's statement must not be allowed to obscure the fact that battle is rarer than it seems, even during wars of apparently high intensity. Moreover, it may involve a relatively small proportion of the soldiers of the contending armies. War and battle are anything but synonymous: indeed, a bone of contention amongst the classical strategists was the degree to which battle was even a desirable component of war. Much of a soldier's experience will, even in wartime, be of the everyday minutiae of military life rather than the climax of battle, and many of the stresses which affect him will come as much from army life in general as from battle in particular.

It is deceptively easy to form the impression that battle is a frequent occurrence in war. Like so many first impressions, this will not stand close scrutiny. Even the period of European history which labours under the blanket description of 'Napoleonic Wars' contained perhaps two hundred days of pitched battle in twenty years. During the Peninsular War – a conflict of high intensity for its period – there were, between the French occupation of Madrid in March 1808 and Wellington's crossing of the Pyrenees over five years later, twenty-two major battles and about as many formal sieges. The very rapid Austerlitz campaign began in September 1805 and ended with Napoleon's overthrow of the combined Austro-Russian armies three months later: even if one blurs the line between large-scale skirmishes and pitched battles, there were not more than ten days' fighting during the whole of the operation. Nor were the World Wars much different. Tony Ashworth maintains, not without reason, that for much of the First World War large sections of the Western Front lapsed into unofficial truce, while on all fronts during the Second World War there were lengthy periods in which sporadic shelling, mortaring and low-level patrol activity were the rule while battle was the exception.

Similarly, battle – or, at least, the specifically combative element of it – has always involved fewer men than might be thought. Even before the advance of technology increased the size of an army's tail at the expense of its teeth, large numbers of soldiers avoided battle either because their duties lay in administration and supply or simply because their unit was elsewhere when the battle actually happened. Napoleon's *Grande Armée* began the Austerlitz campaign with a total effective strength of 210,500 men. About 73,000 were present at Austerlitz, and by no means all of them came within musket-range of their enemy. Wellington's field army for the Waterloo campaign comprised nearly 94,000 men. Some 4,500 of them became casualties at Quatre Bras on 16 June, but there were still only 68,000 men in or near the Waterloo position on the 18th, and over 15,000 of them did not fire a shot in anger.

By 1865, as Peter Parish observed in *The American Civil War*, what happened on the field of battle was 'more than ever the tip of the military iceberg'. In the century that followed the tip became smaller still while the base steadily grew. For the Second World War, even taking the most generous definition of combat – a definition which, in practical terms, included all units within field artillery range of the enemy – Stouffer concluded that 'less than half the men in Europe could reasonably have been called in combat at any one time'. 'There are millions who have done a great and hard job,' wrote the American soldier-cartoonist Bill Mauldin. 'But there are only a few hundred thousand who have lived through misery, suffering and death for endless 168-hour weeks ...' By the 1960s, the balance was even more heavily weighted, and Charles Moskos wrote that 'approximately 70 per cent of the men in Vietnam cannot be considered combat soldiers except by the loosest of definitions'.

This academic objectivity, with all its niceties of terminology, seems out of place to the soldier himself. Many of those soldiers not involved in combat in either the Second World War or Vietnam actually thought that they were. Peter Bourne suggested that, although only 14 per cent of Americans in Vietnam were fully involved in combat, most of the remainder believed themselves to be. Similarly, Stouffer discovered that, while only 11 per cent of soldiers in rifle companies gave full combat status to their comrades in forward headquarter and service units, nearly one-quarter of the latter saw themselves as combat soldiers. William Manchester made the telling point that a soldier's perception of front and rear was purely relative.

> Your definition of it depended on your own role in the war. To the intelligence man out on patrol near the jap wire the platoon CP was rear echelon; to the platoon it was the company CP ... until you reached the PX men who landed at D-plus-60 and scorned the 'rear echelon' back in the States.

The front-line soldier's definition was likely to be harsh indeed. Henri Barbusse, whose harrowing First World War novel *Le Feu* was based upon personal experience, reckoned that there were no less than 250 *embusqués* in a two-battalion infantry regiment – orderlies, cooks, clerks and so on.

Friction between front and rear is a well-documented aspect of military history. It is encouraged by the belief that food and equipment tend to get stuck along the lines of communication. John Ellis records that, when the British Second Army in north-west Europe made a special effort to give all fighting soldiers two suits of battle-dress and three blankets, many of these items failed to reach the front, and most of the men at base had three suits of battle-dress and at least five blankets. Mauldin acknowledged that the same thing happened in the American army, where new clothing was often 'shortstopped by some of the rear echelon soldiers who wanted to look like the combat men they saw in the magazines'. The same complaints were made about food: W.H.A. Groom argued that food in forward units on the Western Front during the First World War was bad because soldiers in the rear echelons always purloined some. Every war produces its abusive description of rear echelon personnel, from the First World War German army's *Etappenschweine* to the REMF (Rear Echelon Mother-Fuckers) of Vietnam.

The gap between teeth and tail is often widened by the tactless behaviour of those engaged in duties, however essential, in the rear. Contempt for rear-area personnel crosses the front line. Rudolf Binding bitterly resented the tendency of parvenu officers on lines-of-communication duty to wear spurs, complaining: 'The caste is being dishonoured.' The same point was made in a First World War British cartoon which showed a horsy railway transport officer, dressed for the hunting field rather than the loco shed, being greeted by a muddy battalion commander with an inquiry as to whether the engines were a bit frisky that morning. The future Lord Slim, while still a junior officer, fell foul of a lieutenant-colonel in the Indian army's Supply and Transport (unkindly nicknamed Sausage and Tum-tum) Corps. 'He looked very fierce and military,' wrote Slim: 'officers who dealt with bully-beef and biscuit in the back areas so often did ...' In Slim's case the experience proved useful, for few Second World War commanders were more successful in bridging the gulf between front and rear than 'Uncle Bill'. 'When one of the forward formations had to go on half rations, as throughout the campaign they often did,' he wrote,

> I used to put my headquarters on half rations too. It had little practical effect, but as a gesture it was rather valuable, and did remind the young staff officers with healthy appetites that it was urgent to get the forward formations back to full rations as soon as possible.

It goes without saying that much of the conflict between teeth and tail is illogical. After all, those personnel in an army's rear areas are, in the main, carrying out tasks upon which the forward units depend, and their own tendency to grant themselves 'combat soldier' status may reflect doubt of their own standing in comparison with that of the undoubted warriors in the front line. The fact that the command structures of armies are usually dominated by teeth-arm officers who may mistrust or misunderstand logisticians only complicates the problem. Many of the shortcomings of the supply services in campaigns from Napoleon's invasion of Russia in 1812, through the Crimean War to Burma in 1942–3 stemmed more from military systems which emphasised the honing of the cutting edge at the expense of welding the hilt than from the failings of the logisticians themselves. But, where matters of the human spirit are concerned, we are dealing with belief rather than with logic. A rifleman in the front line does not stop to consider that he may be on short rations because his line of communications runs for hundreds of miles over inhospitable terrain, and that the supply service is doing its overstretched best to cope. As far as he is concerned, some blanket-stacker with clean finger-nails and a dry sleeping bag is not doing his job. As Bill Mauldin put it: 'Soldiers who are in danger, feel natural and human resentment to those that aren't.' The fact that this resentment may be both unfair and illogical in no way reduces its intensity.

Battle, then, is relatively rare, and involves a small proportion of an army's soldiers. Its prevalence has been exaggerated in a number of ways. Firstly, the process of memory tends to emphasise the peaks and troughs of experience at the expense of the great grey level plain between. Thus, it is the searing events of battle – though not, perhaps, its most utterly horrifying moments – rather than the tedium of the barrack-room or transit-camp which stick in the mind or emerge in memoirs. Secondly, historians, whether writing original work of their own or editing first-hand accounts, tend to focus upon battle as the event which has all the elements of excitement, drama and, in a broader historical perspective, decisiveness. Finally, because battle is the end to which an army's activities are ultimately directed, it is only natural that it should be the crescendo of battle rather than the andante of day-to-day military life which attracts the lion's share of interest. The net result of this is that we tend to concentrate upon events on, rather than off, the battlefield. While my major aim is indeed to examine the individual in battle, much of what happens to him can be fully understood only in the context of the war of which battle forms such a small, if crucial, part. It is with the non-battle elements of war that this chapter is primarily concerned.

It Breaks My Heart to Go

While some of the pressures which bear upon the soldier off the battlefield are physical, others are mental and usually attract less interest than they deserve. Foremost among them are the strains arising from the soldier's separation from his home and family and his induction into the army. The process of basic training, and the subsequent welding of the individual into a unit, will have gone some way towards giving the soldier a military identity in which home and family are of diminished importance. Indeed, the veteran Marshal Bugeaud argued that a man could not properly be termed a soldier until his civilian identity had been completely submerged.

> A man is not a soldier until he is no longer homesick, until he considers his regiment's colours as he would his village steeple; until he loves his colours, and is ready to put hand to sword every time the honour of the regiment is attacked; until he has confidence in his leaders, in his comrades to right and left, until he loves them, until they have eaten soup together for a long time.[1]

This total extinction of the civilian identity is rarely possible. Furthermore, there are many who would argue that, in a greater sense, it is not even desirable. Bugeaud was writing of France in an age of long service and bad communications: a French soldier in the early part of the nineteenth century was quite likely to lose touch with his home altogether, a fact which was marked, in some areas, by the celebration of a requiem mass for the departing conscript. The soldier, be he conscript or regular, will usually carry with him into military service not only the unconscious values of the *super-ego*, but also conscious emotional ties which may conflict with his newly-acquired military loyalties.

For most soldiers induction into the army represents their first separation from home. Some never recover from a crushing feeling of homesickness, and to this is added a profound sense of their own loss of importance. A soldier of the British 71st Regiment during the Napoleonic period lamented that he was merely 'an atom of an army, unheeded by all, his comforts sacrificed to ambition, his untimely death talked of with indifference, and only counted by the gross with hundreds, without a sign'. This sensation of having left a familiar society of which one was a valued member is a common source of unhappiness. When W.H.A. Groom arrived at Étaples on his way to battle on the Western Front, what was hardest to bear was not anxiety at what was to come – that was something of a challenge – but the loneliness and isolation of a sensitive man in unfamiliar surroundings. The psychological damage inflicted by loneliness is widely recognised in other contexts: Lazarus cites the fact that hospital patients with serious illnesses profit from the mere physical proximity of other patients, which gives rise to a sense of shared difficulties. So it is with military service: a man who is unable, for whatever reason, to benefit from the 'we're all in this together' syndrome will find it hard and painful to adjust to his role as a soldier.

The soldier of the 71st and Private Groom had both volunteered for military service, and were buoyed up by a desire to perform well in a war they had gone to willingly. The conscript, however, may feel not only homesick and isolated, but bitterly resentful of a system which, in the words of a subversive pamphlet distributed amongst the French army before the 1870 Plebiscite, 'takes you away, during the best years of your life, from your loved ones, your civic duties ... [and] makes you almost a stranger in your own land'. Although not every reluctant conscript may examine his predicament as eloquently as John Parrish, the latter's comments will find a response in many who have faced the prospect of conscription for service in a war for which they had little sympathy. 'My free country', wrote Parrish, 'was forcing me to leave home for an undeclared war in a distant country. To what lengths was I in honour bound to serve my country? ... Where was my freedom of choice? Where were my rights as an enlightened citizen in an enlightened society?'

Moreover, however essential basic training may be, and however successful it may prove in inculcating military values into the majority of recruits, there will be some for whom it is little short of purgatory. The primitive and physical nature of recruit training is often difficult to cope with. 'Somebody six-foot-two, 275 pounds,' remarked one of Mark Baker's interviewees, 'is your new squad leader and no matter how dumb he is, he's in charge. The sergeant is the authority figure in the background, and this big kid is the bully on the block.' In this world turned upside-down, intelligence and civilian status count for less than physical strength and manual dexterity. David Parks saw 'studs from Brooklyn' work out their resentment against the inequalities of American society by beating up smaller white conscripts. Fear of losing status in this way may be one of the reasons why, as researchers in the mid-1970s found, the more educated a young man was, the less he was likely to favour military service.[2]

This particular phenomenon had already been well documented during the Second World War. The effect of conscription had been, as Stouffer observed, 'to place the top enlisted leadership in the hands of men who, on the average, had less education than the men they were trying to teach and lead'. This happens because regulars tend to dominate a wartime army's senior NCO structure, and these regulars are very often less well-educated than wartime conscripts. Now this need be no bad thing in principle, for education itself is no guarantee of military effectiveness. However, it is likely to embitter the well-educated private soldier. 'There is no more reason for making a fifteen-year Pfc [Private first class] a staff sergeant than there is for making a ditch digger a construction engineer,' complained a Second World War American soldier. It is scarcely surprising that Stouffer discovered that a man's satisfaction with the army would be likely to vary in inverse proportion to his educational level. A striking fact about his findings is the very high level of dissatisfaction with military service that they revealed among private soldiers.

Sometimes the social cocktail shaken by conscription is appreciated by the men who constitute it. A British infantry officer recalled his own service as a private soldier in the 1950s with evident affection:

> The fellow in the bed on my left came from Glasgow and would thump you as soon as look at you, and the chap on the other side came from the East End [of London] and wasn't much better. But we all got on remarkably well: I helped them write their letters home, and they helped me sort out my kit ... But for National Service I'd never have met them, and I'd have been poorer for it.

The Reverend David Railton, a First World War padre, hoped that the war would break down social barriers and open men's eyes to the plight of the less fortunate. 'Why are people so less sacrificing in peacetime?' he asked. 'If a Colonel – a gentleman – can give up his tent in a storm for the soldiers, why can't a gentleman of like position give up many luxuries for some injured workman? I hope such great things from this war.'

Nevertheless, for many military service is a burden to which they never become accustomed. In peacetime, rigorous selection processes and in-service screening will be likely to identify them and to ensure their discharge. But in wartime, when manpower is at a premium, they will be condemned to soldier on, as much to their own misery as to the resentment of their comrades. Lieutenant-Colonel Alan Hanbury-Sparrow, author of *The Land-Locked Lake*, a remarkable account of his service in the Royal Berkshire Regiment during the First World War, described a character who will be familiar to many readers who have themselves served in an army.

> When eventually you found the rest of the battalion it was heading in the wrong direction. Its leader and broken link was Private Ailey. This Ailey had been the curse of the battalion for more than a year. Feeble in body, he was feebler still in mind ... Too sub-normal to be able to keep up with the man in front, he had quietly lost touch, and such was the blackness of the night that not even his section commander, let alone the rear companies, realised what had happened.

That the luckless Ailey was no intellectual giant is not in question. But many cleverer men lost their way in the nightmare that was the Third Battle of Ypres. While sympathising with Hanbury-Sparrow's anguish at discovering that his battalion had become split up on the way to its start line, should we not also spare a thought for the broken link himself, for whom military service, let alone Third Ypres, was an insupportable burden?

Some of those for whom army life is a constant misery soldier on. Others decide to opt out, and desertion is their most frequent means of doing so. It is tempting to regard desertion as either a means of escape from a dangerous situation, or as a politically motivated gesture of protest against a particular war. In fact, it has been as marked in peacetime as it has in war, and it tends to appeal to those who, for a variety of reasons, have adjusted poorly to military service.

There is no doubting the impact of desertion upon the armies of history. Christopher Duffy described it as 'the bane of the Prussian army' during Frederick the Great's era, noting that, between 1740 and 1800, the *Regiment Garde* in Potsdam lost no less than 2 officers, 93 NCOs, 32 musicians and 1,525 men by desertion. These desertions were as much a symptom of discontent with army life as they were of a desire to escape injury in war. Indeed, war often worked to the advantage of the potential deserter, for it interfered with elaborate anti-desertion mechanisms built into the Prussian army and civil administration.

Things were scarcely better in the French army of the Napoleonic period. Half the conscripts from the Haute-Loire could be relied upon to desert, and in 1809 – while the war was still going well for France, and before the massive butcher's bills of later years – there were more than 20,000 deserters abroad in the south-west. The Lyons military division alone contained 8,000, and Prince Eugène de Beauharnais reckoned that there were 60,000 in the whole of Italy. When the *Grande Armée* took the field, literally thousands of soldiers left their regiments: some eventually returned, but others did not. The Duc de Fezensac suggested that 60,000 men disappeared after the battle of Eylau, while Marshal Bugeaud estimated that, for every army of 100,000 men, there were 20–25,000 skulkers trailing in the rear. Ardant du Picq was equally harsh in his judgment on the French army of the Second Empire, believing that there were 25,000 deserters in the *Armée d'Italie* in 1859.

The Union army during the American Civil War also experienced serious problems with desertion, and by the end of January 1863 there had been no less than 85,123 desertions from the Army of the Potomac. As Bruce Catton pointed out, most of these had not so much run away as drifted away.

They had been sloughed off by the army's own inefficiency. With many of them there probably had never been a conscious decision to desert, a moment when the soldier in his own mind ceased to be a soldier temporarily absent and became instead a civilian who was never going to go back unless somebody came and got him.

Much of this desertion sprang simply from discontent with army life and from a desire to get back home. There were, however, some spectacular, if untypical, examples of politically-motivated desertion: the 128th Illinois, recruited from the anti-Negro population of the southern part of that state, lost nearly all its members by desertion.

Desertion in the Allied armies during the Second World War remained within manageable proportions. Nevertheless, the American army acknowledged some 40,000 deserters, a number artificially decreased by a generous definition of absence without leave; and the British army had over 100,000 deserters, its desertion rate never running below 4·48 per 1,000 per year and peaking at 10·05 in 1940–1. That desertion should reach its height not only when Britain's fortunes seemed at their lowest ebb, but also when the *Luftwaffe*'s bombs filled many soldiers with fear for their families, is doubly significant, although it is impossible to be specific about the relative importance of these two motives for desertion.

There is no comparable figure available for the German army, but the combined total of desertions and AWOL probably reached nearly 300,000 for the period 1941–4, with the 1944 figure representing 21·5 per 1,000 strength. As we shall see shortly, this latter figure was brought about largely by conflicts of loyalty between the military and civilian identities of German soldiers, which often produced desertion whilst on leave.

Detailed study of the Allied statistics produces some interesting conclusions. In general, as John Ellis observed, they 'tended to show that a large proportion of deserters had been maladjusted in civilian life'. In the American army, it was discovered that the wartime deserter had very often been a schoolboy truant, while in the British army a survey of 2,000 deserters established that 73 per cent were under the age of twenty-six, whereas only 46 per cent of the British liberation army as a whole was in this age-group. Deserters of both armies often showed signs of mental deficiency or psychiatric illness.

The Vietnam era witnessed desertion from the American army which assumed almost epidemic proportions. But, as had been the case in the past, the politically-motivated deserter was less common than the soldier who simply found army life intolerable. 'The vast majority of deserters and those going AWOL during the Vietman era, as in previous wars,' noted Guenter Lewy, 'absented themselves not for political reasons but because of personal or financial problems or inability to adjust to military life.' Lowered induction standards combined with a growth in the number of inexperienced leaders to pro- duce higher rates of desertion towards the end of the war. The argument that desertion reflected opposition to the war is substantially undermined by the fact that, in the US Marine Corps, the desertion and AWOL rate was at its highest in 1975, after American withdrawal from Vietnam. In a profes- sional army soldiers may actually be *more* inclined to desert in peacetime, when they can easily feel bored by a repetitive routine of training. One parachute battalion under orders to depart for the Falklands in the spring of 1982 discovered that a number of illegally absent soldiers reappeared in an effort not to miss the campaign.

Desertion from the US army during the Vietnam War reached its peak in 1971, when 73·4 per 1,000 of the average enlisted strength deserted, and 176·9 went absent without leave.[3] Most desertions took place at the transition points in the soldier's military career, after basic training or during transit, when the pull of home was strongest and the bonds of military group loyalty were weakest. The same phenomenon had been noted in nineteenth-century France, where deser- tions peaked when a regiment marched near its own recruiting areas when changing garrisons.

Another means of escape from the army is a more final one.

The French sociologist Émile Durkheim was the first, a century ago, to note the close connection between suicide and military service. At this stage I am concerned with suicide in camp or barracks rather than with suicide as a release from intolerable stress or pain on the battlefield, or as the last act of a defeated commander. Durkheim pointed to what he termed the contagion of suicide in barracks in peacetime, remarking that 'perhaps no other phenomenon is so readily contagious'. The suicidal aptitude of the soldiers of Durkheim's day was markedly greater than that of comparable civilian groups, sometimes by as much as 900 per cent.

Perhaps surprisingly, Durkheim found that military suicide was most common among volunteers and re-enlisted men, often NCOs, and occurred most frequently amongst élite troops, and less often amongst troops with the least pronounced military character, such as the bridging-train and medical corps. Durkheim suggested that military morality was, in a sense, a survival of a primitive system of values, in which men were prepared to kill themselves for trivial reasons, such as the refusal of leave, unjust punishment, or a delay in promotion. In other words, it was the very men whose sense of military honour was most acute who were most prepared to react to a threat to it by killing themselves. It would be unwise to read too much into Durkheim's work, whose statistical evidence is, after all, drawn from the 1860s. Recent British statistics show that soldiers, as an occupational group, are well down the table, more likely to commit suicide than managers but less likely to do so than clerical workers. But it is worth noting that retired officers are amongst those professional groups with the highest rate of suicide, in part because the military values which they have acquired during their service often conflict with the values of civilian society.

Suicides are not infrequent in training depots, barracks and transit camps. In the eighteenth-century Prussian army, with desertion so difficult – though still achieved by many – suicide was an easier alternative. Frederick the Great's *Regiment Garde* had 130 suicides in the period 1740–1800. Reluctant soldiers have continued to kill themselves ever since. A typical case occurred in camp at Châlons in 1870, before the outbreak of the Franco-Prussian War, when a soldier of the 32nd of the Line shot himself. He had just been released from a military prison, and had immediately been awarded another eight days' *salle de police* for 'extreme dirtiness of person and equipment'. It is not difficult to envisage the despair of a perpetually scruffy soldier for whom life seemed to offer nothing but kit inspections and the guardroom. Charlton Ogburn described the suicide of a classic misfit as his unit, part of what was to become famous as Merrill's Marauders, moved through India on its way to Burma. He was a rather sad figure, who 'might have been one of the Huns who invaded Europe fifteen hundred years ago inexplicably come to life again as an American soldier'.

Most modern armies recognise that both efficient postal services and the provision of leave make useful contributions to morale. Not only does an effective postal system cheer soldiers who get mail but, in a deeper sense, it helps raise morale by illustrating the efficiency of the organisation to which they belong. During the First World War it rarely took longer than four days for a letter to reach the Western Front from England, although the addressee's name and regiment were all that was permitted on the envelope. The future Sir Richard Gale, then a subaltern in the Machine Gun Corps, wrote of the wonderful morale-raising effect of mail delivery in the front line. During the Second World War Bill Mauldin suggested that 'a soldier's life revolves around his mail', and in Vietnam David Parks wrote: 'If only the people back there knew how a few lines cheer you up, change your whole outlook.' Michael Morris, describing anti-guerrilla operations in Southern Africa in his book *Terrorism*, admitted: 'Strong men often cry on post-day.'

Impressive though this evidence is, the whole question of a soldier's contact with his family is decidedly ambivalent. In the First World War the proximity of the Western Front to the Channel ports encouraged some British soldiers to try to slip back home. Although this sometimes demonstrated nothing more complex than despair at the prospect of going back up the line, it was often instigated by trouble at home, which might break even a man for whom battle held few terrors. As Robert Graves wrote:

> Bad news from home might affect a soldier in one of two ways. It might either drive him to suicide ... or else seem trivial by contrast with present experiences ... an officer of the North Staffordshire Regiment heard from home that his wife was living with another man. He went out on a raid that night and got either killed or captured; so the men with him said. There had been a fight, and they came back without him. After two days he was arrested at Béthune, trying to board a leave-train; he had intended to go home and shoot up the wife and her lover.

Occasionally this sort of personal crisis can be resolved without the need for desertion: temporary absence will suffice. 'I know of one man', wrote Gerald Kersh,

> who absented himself for forty-eight hours to 'chastise', as he put it, his cousin who was 'annoying' his wife. Having given his cousin what he called a Lesson, he returned to Camp and gave himself up. His Commanding Officer gave him fourteen days' detention in the name of discipline, and a nod and a smile of moral approval as man to man.

Even the sternest resolve might wilt before a letter like this, written to a soldier in the London Trained Bands at the siege of Basing House in 1644.

> Most deare and loving husband, my king love, I remember unto you hoping you are in good health as I ame at the writing thereof. My little Willie have bene sick this fortnight. I pray you to come whome if youe cane cum saffly. I doo marfull that I cannot heere from you ass well other nay-bores do. I do desiere to heer from you as soon as you cane. I pray you to send me word when youe thenke youe shoude returne. Youe de not consider I ame a lone woemane, I

thought youe woald never leave me thuse long togeder, so
I rest evere praying for savese returne.

your loving wife

Susan Rodway

Ever praying for you till deth I depart. To my very loving
husbane Robert Rodway a train soudare in the Red Regiment under the commande of Captain Warrene. Deliver
this with all Spide.

It may be that Private Rodway never read this letter, to worry
about his lonely wife and his sick son. Captain Warren had
led an attack on Basing House, and it had been beaten off
with loss: perhaps Robert's silence had all too sinister a cause.

The concern aroused by bad news from home can eclipse
physical dangers. Raymond Cooper was about to move off
with his company on the approach march for an attack when
a man rushed up to him and 'blurted out in a hurried whisper
that by that morning's mail his wife had asked for a divorce.
"I'll talk to you in the morning," seemed an inept reply to a
man in his frame of mind with five hundred Japs between him
and the sunrise.' As Santiago and his comrades awaited the
British assault on the Falklands, some of them received 'Dear
John' letters. 'Those boys got very upset,' he told Daniel Kon,
'they cried in the trench.'

Some soldiers find that the arrival of news from home –
even if the news is good – can lower their morale by reminding
them that, as Francis Bacon put it, 'He that hath wife and
children hath given hostages to fortune'. A parachute officer
who served in the Falklands said that he dreaded the arrival
of mail because it reminded him that there he had another
persona: in addition to being merely a cog in a military machine and of little individual value, he was also a husband and
a father whose death would have devastating consequences.
Remembering his role as a family man made him feel uneasy
when the situation demanded that his military role should be
dominant.

This potential conflict of roles becomes even more evident
when a soldier goes home on leave from a theatre of opera-

90

tions. Many soldiers would, no doubt, agree with Major Martin Lindsay, second-in-command of a battalion of Gordon Highlanders in north-west Europe in 1944–5, that leave was entirely beneficial. 'I am feeling immensely better', he wrote, 'as a result of my leave. For the last month I had been getting very tired and irritable and, worst of all, increasingly jumpy.' But on the other side of the coin, Sergeant M. Warner, a mortar NCO in 7th Somerset Light Infantry, who went on leave at about the same time, recorded in his diary: 'Felt very low and depressed during this week, because of the delightful time we had last week at home.' Far from giving the soldier a well-earned respite from the pressure of war, home leave – or even rest and recreation (R&R) overseas – may only emphasise the physical discomforts of the front and remind him of what he stands to lose for ever. An American soldier regretted that he ever took R&R from Vietnam.

> Before I left for Hong Kong, I'd forgotten about napkins. I forgot about beds and sheets. I'd forgotten that when you wanted light on a dark night, you could just turn it on. You could put 15¢ in a machine and get a candy bar whenever you wanted. I'd almost forgotten about broads.

During the Second World War the German authorities recognised the damage that could be done if soldiers became preoccupied with worries about their families. The families of German soldiers were instructed to avoid references to deprivations and bombing when they wrote to their menfolk at the front, and party officials censored telegrams. But to ensure that this policy did not result in soldiers feeling isolated, families were encouraged to write to their menfolk, and efforts were made to ensure that soldiers without families received mail from friendly civilians.

This policy worked well enough with mail, but it could not prevent leave from increasing the psychological pressures on a soldier. As Edward Shils and Morris Janowitz discovered:

> When soldiers returned to visit their families, then the conflict between contradictory group loyalties became acute.

The hold of the military primary group became debilitated in the absence of face-to-face contacts. The prospect of facing, on return to the front, physical destruction or a prolonged loss of affection from the civilian primary group, especially from the family, prompted an increasing number of desertions while on furlough.

Sometimes a German soldier's will to fight collapsed completely once his home had been occupied by the Allies. The destruction of his home and family by Allied bombing, while undoubtedly a traumatic shock when it occurred, often had entirely the reverse effect, making the soldier fight harder because his military primary group no longer had any rivals for his affection.

Even if leave does not have the effect of unravelling the ties of military solidarity, there is every possibility that the soldier who goes home on leave will find it difficult to relate to the civilians he meets, and will return to his unit empty and unsatisfied. This was clearly the case during the First World War, when leave often did more harm than good. 'There was a complete lack of communication,' complained W.H.A. Groom. 'I simply could not get on the same wavelength with civilians.' 'Leave was thus an experience which began and ended with an overwhelming suddennesss and emotion,' elaborates Denis Winter in *Death's Men*, 'and was so different from what came before and after that men were left as baffled and unsatisfied as if they had been in battle.' Second World War German soldiers often felt much the same. The Germany they went back to was, in James Lucas's words, 'an empty shell, a glittering gem that turned out on closer inspection to be a tawdry bauble, a country whose people would not comprehend reality and were only playing at war.'

It would be rash to suggest that mail and leave do the soldier a disservice. But it must be recognised that they are not without risk, and may highlight the potential conflict within the soldier's personality. R.S. Lazarus discussed the case of a terminally-ill scientist who moved into his laboratory to work night and day in order to finish a series of experiments before he died: this single-minded devotion to duty cured him. Lazarus concluded: '*The possibility exists that periods of rest or holiday may add psychological burdens to the individual who is committed to certain efforts.*'[4] As far as the soldier is concerned, contact with home, however desirable it may be in many respects, can sometimes be counter-productive, re-opening the old wounds which the soldier's acceptance into the military family had previously cauterised.

Venus and Mars

The close affinity between love and war is an enduring feature of both history and mythology. At its most obvious and superficial level, this relationship is reflected by soldiers' almost universal preoccupation with sex. The very fact of becoming a soldier seems to have the effect of enhancing a man's sexuality. 'When we were in uniform,' admitted Glenn Gray, 'almost any girl had a strong erotic appeal for us.' He went on: 'the very atmosphere of large cities in wartime breathes the enticements of physical love. Not only are the inhibitions on sexual expression lowered, but there exists a much more passionate interest of the sexes in each other than is the case in peacetime.' Alan Hanbury-Sparrow had observed the same phenomenon during the First World War. 'It wasn't that you were in love with anyone in particular,' he said, 'it was simply that you took a quite especial delight in female society, and without really planning to, you yet did all in your power to attract them.' Lieutenant-Colonel John Baynes assessed the First World War British soldier rather more bluntly. 'Most soldiers', he maintained, 'were ready to have sexual intercourse with almost any woman whenever they could.'

There is some statistical support for the great mass of anecdotal evidence linking war and enhanced sexuality. In his study of Green Berets and war resisters during the Vietnam War, D.M. Mantell discovered that his sample of Green Berets – the archetype of the professional soldier – experienced sexual intercourse at the average age of fifteen, far younger than a comparable group of war resisters. Moreover, the Green Berets averaged a remarkable 28·5 contacts with prostitutes per man. In short, at least part of the complex chemistry which distinguished enthusiastic soldiers from vigorous opponents of war was sexuality.

Some soldiers, albeit a minority, succeed in sublimating their sexual desires, diverting the energy which might otherwise have been expended into an intense concern for their profession. Baynes suggests that many upper-middle-class Englishmen of the early years of this century blotted sex out of their lives altogether. 'It is fair to claim', he adds, 'that in many ways the repression of sexual instincts was a valuable asset to the army officer in his military life.' Baynes's single-minded regulars were in good company. That doughty sixteenth-century French warrior Blaise de Montluc had warned that the love of women was 'utterly an enemy to an heroic spirit', and a long series of martial groups have created and preserved all-male environments in which sex has – at least in theory – been sublimated or repressed.

But sublimation, or more straightforward repression, is not, alas, risk-free. Intolerable ideas or desires, even if they are banished from the conscious mind to the unconscious, still influence behaviour. However valuable the repression or sublimation of sexual instincts may be in the short term, there are long-term psychological dangers. It is no accident that many of these claustrophobic all-male groups, in which the cult of masculinity has been taken to extremes, have displayed behaviour patterns which have often made them a liability in military terms. Anti-effeminacy is a common military trait – witness the use of effeminate terms of abuse during training – and these groups tend to take it to absurd lengths, often regarding defence or withdrawal as effeminate and unmanly.

The Military Orders of the Latin Kingdom of Jerusalem, strong in arm and weak in tactical common sense, are striking examples of this. It is hard to discover a more notable instance of insistence on masculine virtues at any price than the disaster at the Springs of Cresson in April 1187. There was a brief discussion as to whether an inferior force of Frankish knights should attack a Muslim army which was watering its horses at the springs. Gerard of Ridefort, Grand Master of the Temple, taunted his Marshal, James of Mailly, with loving his blond head too well to want to lose it. 'I shall die in battle like a brave man,' replied James. 'It is you that will flee as a traitor.' With this, one hundred and thirty knights charged seven thousand Mamelukes and were cut to pieces. Gerard was one of the three Templars to escape. It would be simplistic to attribute the disaster at Cresson – or, indeed, the greater calamity at the Horns of Hattin just over a month later, for which Gerard must bear a large share of the responsibility – entirely to repressed sexuality and an exaggerated emphasis upon masculine virtues. But the very terms of the dispute between Gerard and James, with the use of expressions like blond head and brave man, suggest that it was primarily the knights' prickly virility which drove them to destruction.

The overwhelming majority of soldiers, who retain unabated sexual desires, provide their armies with problems which have both practical and moral dimensions. The practical problem stems from the fact that venereal disease has long been a major casualty producer. Between 1915 and 1918 there were 52,528 hospital admissions for VD in the Australian army alone, while the much larger British army reported 416,891 during the whole of the war. The VD rate in the Australian and Canadian armies ran at 150 cases per 1,000 embarkations, and in the British at 30 per 1,000. Comparable rates per 1,000 in the French and German armies were 83·19 and 110·2. Just over one-quarter of the diseases for which British soldiers were hospitalised were venereal. These figures must be seen in the context of relatively long periods of hospitalisation: stays in hospital averaged 52·2 days for Australian soldiers with syphilis. Venereal disease was, then, a serious drain on manpower as well as an added burden on already hard-pressed medical services.

In both wars the British army experimented with brothels staffed with medically-inspected prostitutes. A *maison de tolérance* set up at Rouen during the First World War was visited by 171,000 men in its first year, with only 243 reported cases of infection, but public opinion at home led to its closure. Robert Graves described how the army brothel in Béthune, containing three women, sometimes had a queue of 150 men waiting outside the door. He went on to observe that some young officers, trying to conform to the wartime image of the subaltern as a roistering blade, saved their lives by unwittingly incapacitating themselves for trench service through contracting VD. The American army had little choice in the matter. In February 1918 Clemenceau offered to help it to set up licensed brothels and thereby cut down on casualties from VD. General Pershing passed his letter on to Raymond Fosdick, head of the American commission on training camp activities, who showed it to Secretary of War Baker. 'For God's sake, Raymond,' said Baker, 'don't show this to the President or he'll stop the war.'[5]

During the Second World War, the brothels of Tripoli were allowed to remain open until Montgomery and his chaplain-general cracked down on them. Red-light areas in Italy were declared off-limits, and a prominent brothel in Delhi was closed down by public protests. These measures were often self-defeating. Shutting officially-controlled brothels led to a rise in the VD rate, and declaring an area off-limits rarely prevented the determined soldier from sampling its forbidden, if lingering, delights. Indeed, whatever official policy might have been, it is clear that, in both World Wars, many Allied commanders were prepared to turn a blind eye to the existence of well-patronised brothels within their areas of responsibility. Treating soldiers who contracted VD as 'sick through negligence', and confining them to special hospitals was, similarly, no answer to the problem.

The British and American armies during the Second World War adopted the uneasy compromise of warning soldiers of the dangers of VD, and issuing them with prophylactics, while not actually sanctioning brothels. Fred Majdalany, in Italy in 1944 with 2nd Lancashire Fusiliers, was struck by the VD warning posters which speckled the walls of Italian villages. Even the French and German armies, with their more robust approach to brothels, pointed out the dangers of illicit sex:

'Three minutes with Venus, three years with Mercury' was a warning repeated almost as often as it was disregarded. The 'short arm' inspection for the detection of VD was a regular feature of Second World War military life. 'One exhibitionist, anticipating an inspection of his short arm sooner or later,' recalled William Manchester, 'had submitted to excruciating pain for the sake of a practical joke. He had caused the words "Hi, Doc!" to be tattooed on the inside of his foreskin.'

The French army had, by long tradition, an enlightened and practical policy on brothels. During the 1840s General de Lamoricière inaugurated an official brothel to cheer up the garrison of Tlemcen in Algeria, and the brothel at Mourmelon, in the heart of the French training-camp at Châlons – the French equivalent of Sennelager, Salisbury Plain or Fort Benning – did a roaring trade during the huge summer training sessions of the 1860s. In June 1870, with the Franco-Prussian War looming, the headquarters of 2 Corps found time to record the particulars of a prostitute who was infecting soldiers, and to order the *Intendant* to arrange for a medical inspection.

Brothels catered for the needs of French soldiers in two World Wars, and far-flung garrisons were sustained by BMCs (*Bordels Militaires de Campagne*), with the specific aim of cutting down on rape, desertion and disease. They were staffed with volunteers, often women of the Ouled Nail tribe from the Constantine area of Algeria, who worked in them long enough to assemble their dowries. Two prostitutes were recommended for the *Croix de Guerre* in Indo-China for making a thirty mile march in forty-eight hours to relieve a distant outpost, and getting ambushed on the way back. Two BMCs, one Indo-Chinese and one Algerian, formed part of the garrison of Dien Bien Phu, and suffered all the horrors of the siege, capitulation and the aftermath.

There is, though, a great deal more to enhanced sexuality in wartime than the brusque physical appetite which brothels satisfy. Nat Frankel suggested that the average soldier who served from D-Day to the end of the war slept with twenty-five women, by no means all of them prostitutes. 'There was a great desperation in it and considerable satisfaction,' he wrote, 'but, just as it often began with a terrible yearning, it often finished that way too; with yearning of a deep and multi-faceted character.' Much of this yearning is for affection, not merely for physical gratification: it is for positive evidence that, despite the upheavals of military life, one still remains a valuable and valued person.

Memoirs confirm this need for love as well as sex. The Napoleonic *chasseur-à-cheval* Charles Parquin displayed light cavalry panache in the boudoir as well as on the battlefield. But although he was not averse to 'partaking of the forbidden fruit', his affairs always had the trappings of genuine emotion. 'Leaving a town where one has been stationed is always the same,' he recalled, 'the mutual sadness, the endless promises to think always of each other, never to forget each other, to write and so on'. To Raleigh Trevelyan, convalescing in Italy in 1944, the questionable delights of Teresa and Mici in the Colorado in Tamara paled into insignificance before an un-ruffled nursing sister called Celia, with whom he fell passion-ately in love. 'You are a necessary drug,' he lamented. 'What can I do to make you love me? Can I give you presents? I don't even know your tastes, what sort of things you like. To you I am only another patient in this hospital, temporary, a bird of passage.'

The whirlwind wartime romance may be a cliché, but it is a cliché founded on fact. The massive uprooting caused by war, and the maldistribution of the sexes which results from it, produces an environment in which there is as much desperate longing on the part of women whose husbands and lovers have themselves gone to war as amongst the soldiers of allied, or even enemy, armies with whom the fortune of war may bring them in contact. Protestant English officers eloped with Roman Catholic ladies during the Peninsular War: the amo-rous inclinations of Lieutenant Kelly of the 40th Regiment caused Wellington considerable chagrin, although Kelly made amends by marrying the lady in the end. Harry Smith of the 95th married the thirteen-year-old Juana after the sack of Badajoz, writing of her 'eye of light and an expression which then inspired me with a maddening love which from that period to this (now thirty-three years) has never abated under the most trying circumstances'. A town in Natal was later named after Lady Smith, as she became, and played its own brave part in another war.

American soldiers found that R&R from Vietnam offered them more than relief from physical frustration, a need to be satisfied as one might slake a thirst. It was common for them to hire a prostitute for the night, or even for the duration of their R&R, and to create a counterfeit domesticity in their brief time out of the war. Lieutenant Calley, describing a prostitute called Yvonne, admitted: 'I had something inside me that badly wanted to love her.' Stanley Goff, co-author of *Brothers: Black Soldiers in the Nam*, had a 'special relationship' with another prostitute, Suzanne. 'It was a great experience,' he said. 'I'd heard all kinds of stories about prostitutes myself – that they had no feeling and stuff like that, and that was all bullshit.'

During the First World War a British artillery officer wrote a series of letters to an American nurse he had met on leave. He never posted them, but their deeply introspective nature reveals quite clearly this aching need for affection.

> I should like to think that there are women in the world who will be very compassionate to us when the war is ended. The Frenchwomen are like that already. In their hospitals they call a wounded man *mon petit*, and take him in their arms and hold him against their breasts. That is what we need most when our strength is spent – women who are so shameless in their pity that they will mother us. We daren't ask for it ourselves. If you don't guess, we shall never tell you.

This need for female affection, as opposed to mere sexual gratification, is part of the reason why soldiers respond so well to female nurses. 'No male nursing orderly can nurse like a woman,' wrote Field-Marshal Montgomery, 'though many think they can.' Colonel C.A. McDowall, a staff officer in Burma, recorded his admiration for the nursing sisters: 'Theirs was the steady, unfailing courage peculiar to women, which will be remembered by the many thousands who owe their lives and health to these girls' devotion to duty.' It is not merely technical skill or female sensitivity that makes women so effective as nurses. Major Paul Grauwin, senior medical officer at Dien Bien Phu, believed, on the basis of his own extensive experience, that wounded men complained less with female nurses than they did with their male counterparts. Geneviève de Galard-Terraube, a French Air Force nurse, was marooned at Dien Bien Phu after her plane was destroyed. For the rest of the siege she nursed in Grauwin's underground hospital, whose conditions were enough to daunt the most stout-hearted.

> Blood, vomit and faeces mixed with the mud made up a frightful compound which stuck to the boots in layers. A pair of shorts was the only possible uniform. Sweat poured constantly over the forehead and the back, dripping from the armpits to the hands ... At the end of twenty-four hours the wounded all had their dressings damp and dirty; they had to be changed more often than that. With those in plaster, sweat caused terrible skin irritations which developed into sores, discharging matter and making sleep out of the question.

Geneviève worked tirelessly alongside her male colleagues, changing filthy dressings, cleaning maggots from wounds and soothing the dying. Grauwin was sure that men remembered their self-respect and accepted their pain more stoically when she was present. She, on the other hand, never lost her femininity despite the dreadful surroundings. 'Nothing can replace a woman at the bedside of a wounded man,' wrote Grauwin, 'not only at base hospitals but more especially at the front.'

It is ironic that Geneviève should have been at Dien Bien Phu at all, for the French army had decreed, a few months previously, that women should be removed from front-line medical units. This reluctance to expose female nurses to the perils of battle is only a small part of a wider argument concerning the usefulness of women on the battlefield. The debate is of deeper significance than might appear at first sight. Major R.L. Nabors goes to the heart of the matter by suggesting that much male opposition to the increase of women's military role stems from the fact that such an increase threatens the single-gender uniqueness from which men derive their self-identification and feelings of masculinity. While admitting that men do possess greater physical strength and stamina than women, Nabors argues that opposition to women in the army is culturally conditioned, and relies on sex stereotyping, paternalism and gender identification. After all, women are able to prove their femininity by bearing children, but for the man, 'the most observable, unique and honoured role . . . has traditionally been that of warrior'.[6]

There is a good deal of evidence in support of Nabors's argument. Irenäus Eibl-Eibesfeldt describes an experiment in which participants reacted to each other's behaviour by administering a reward (a blue light) or a punishment (an electric shock). The blood pressure of both males and females rose sharply after they were given an electric shock: in the case of males it dropped rapidly after counter-aggression, but not when they rewarded or reacted neutrally. Females, however, reacted in the opposite way, with a quick drop in blood pressure when they rewarded, but not when they reacted aggressively or neutrally. Eibl-Eibesfeldt suggested that this very different primary reaction might depend on a number of factors, but was none the less 'modifiable through individual experience'. Furthermore, Anne Campbell, writing on female aggression in *Aggression and Violence*, points out that much of our attitude to violence on the part of women is heavily influenced by our class perspective. In other words, there is anthropological as well as sociological support for the claim that it is primarily cultural considerations which deny women the role of warrior. There is certainly no conclusive physiological reason why women should be excluded from combat. Although they are, in general, less strong physically than men, most modern weapons do not demand great strength. Finally, the fact that women tend to be able to bear pain better than men is a positive advantage as far as their battlefield role is concerned.

History buttresses the Nabors thesis. During the seventeenth, eighteenth and nineteenth centuries women frequently passed themselves off as men and fought in the ranks of infantry and cavalry regiments. Other women followed their menfolk on campaign, helped carry their kit on the march and looked after them when they were wounded. Sometimes women were officially recognised as having a combatant role. The French expeditionary force sent to the West African kingdom of Dahomey in 1892 ran into fierce opposition from King Benhanzin's corps of Amazons. 'These female warriors fought with extraordinary courage,' wrote a French soldier, 'always in the lead, setting an example to the others by their fearlessness.' The Russians used women in combat units during the Second World War. Ludmilla Pavlichenko, history student turned sniper, was officially credited with killing 309 Germans. Three aircraft regiments – 586th Fighter, 587th Bomber and 588th Night Bomber (46th Guards) – were recruited entirely from women. More recently, women fought on both sides during the Vietnam War. Ho Thi Que, 'the Tiger Lady of the Delta', wife of the commanding officer of the 44th Vietnamese Rangers, was thrice decorated for bravery before being killed in 1965. On the other side of the hill, women served extensively with the Viet Cong and North Vietnamese Army. Finally, women – like Rose Dugdale and the Price sisters in Ireland, Ulrike Meinhof and Ingrid Siepmann in Germany – have played a prominent role in post-war guerrilla movements.

But merely establishing that it is primarily cultural conditioning that restricts the role of women in battle, and pointing to the many examples of women fighting on the battlefields of the past, does not necessarily prove that it is either easy or wise to extend women's military role. The fact remains that most societies, rightly or wrongly, are structured upon a sex stereotyping which has immense force. Indeed, those armies which have used women in the combat role have, like the Republican militias in Spain, the Soviet army or the North

Vietnamese army, usually been the products of far-reaching social revolutions which affected the role of women generally. It is unusual to find women in combat except as part of such an army or a revolutionary guerrilla organisation. Moreover, even in the case of these armies, it is easy to overemphasise the combat role of the female soldier. In the Soviet army in the Second World War, for example, far more women served as doctors, medical orderlies, traffic police, typists, telephonists or cooks than drove tanks or flew aeroplanes. The Israeli army is often cited as the apogee of integration but, as Samuel Rolbant stresses in *The Israeli Soldier*: 'It must be emphasised that, contrary to the widely held opinion abroad, women in the Israeli army are not employed in combat duties.'

For societies which have not undergone radical change, the use of women in combat roles is fraught with problems: not simply peril for the women themselves, but for its effect upon the morale of male soldiers. Military training, as we have seen, tends to emphasise masculinity, and young men have for centuries looked upon battle as the ultimate challenge to their manhood. It may well be, of course, that this should not be the case, and that it merely reflects an archaic and oppressive set of cultural values. But this powerful stereotyping of the man as the warrior undoubtedly does exist, is firmly entrenched and is likely to prove extremely resistant to change.

When women have appeared on the battlefield, their effect upon male soldiers has often been decidedly ambivalent. Sometimes, as in the case of nurses, they improve morale by enhancing a man's identification of himself as a warrior. Many of the women who appeared, in one guise or another, on the battlefields of the eighteenth and nineteenth centuries did just this. Annie Etheridge went to war in 1861 as laundress with the 3rd Michigan. She was later appointed officers' mess cook to Phil Kearney's division of III Corps, wore sergeant's chevrons on her black riding habit and drew a sergeant's pay. In May 1863, as the Army of the Potomac recoiled before the Confederate onslaught at Chancellorsville, she appeared beside a Union battery that had been badly mauled. The gunners were about to run, but Annie kept them at their task.

She smiled at them and cried, 'That's right, boys, now you've got good range, keep it up and you'll soon silence those guns.' The men raised a little cheer, made her go to the rear, and returned to the service of their guns. One sweaty cannoneer remarked that all the officers in the army could not have had as much influence with them just then as 'that brave little sergeant in petticoats'.[7]

Conversely, the death or wounding of a woman in battle has a disproportionately large effect upon male soldiers. Sir Francis Windebank, commander of the little Royalist garrison at Bletchingdon House, was simply not prepared to risk women being hurt as a result of his actions. Although he was an officer of proven valour, when Cromwell summoned him to surrender on 24 April 1645 he did so at once. His wife had invited some of her friends to visit the house: Windebank capitulated to spare them the horrors of an assault on the place. His chivalry cost him his life, for, when he got back to Oxford the next day, he was tried by court martial and shot. Although Israeli women soldiers are not now assigned to combat units, in 1948, when they found themselves in the front line, they suffered casualties. Men who might have found the wounding of a male comrade comparatively tolerable were shocked by the injury of a woman, and the mission tended to get forgotten in a general scramble to ensure that she received medical aid. Such is the strength of cultural conditioning that killing a woman, even when she is identifiably hostile, non-plusses many soldiers. Some tough *légionnaires* on the Dahomey expedition experienced a few seconds' hesitation about shooting or bayoneting a half-naked Amazon: their delay had fatal results. In *If I Die in a Combat Zone*, his moving account of the Vietnam War, Tim O'Brien describes the widespread feeling of grief and regret in his company when a Viet Cong nurse was shot and mortally wounded. O'Brien's comrades had no particular reverence for women as such: he recalls an occasion when two frightened Vietnamese women were beaten up by men who had just lost two friends to a booby-trapped artillery round. Nevertheless, the death of the nurse was profoundly disturbing, because the soldiers felt that a pretty black-haired girl should not be gasping her life away with a bullet wound.

This state of affairs is regarded as an affront by many feminists. In *Does Khaki Become You*, Cynthia Enloe complains about the way in which armies deprive women of their individuality and assign them to what are often humble duties. But, as John Keegan observed in a review of the book, they do exactly the same thing to men. Cynthia Enloe seems to favour a combat role for women. This is logical enough in view of the clear connections between social organisations and men's military role. Nevertheless, it is clear that, at least as far as most Western societies are concerned, soldiers regard battlefields as predominantly male preserves. The occasional women that appear on or near them are welcome only in so far as they contribute to a man's warrior ethos. John Laffin's conclusions in *Women in Battle* may be unacceptably sexist, but they seem to reflect Western man's perception of the woman's role.

A woman's place should be in the bed and not the battlefield, in crinoline or Terylene rather than in battledress, wheeling a pram rather than driving a tank. Furthermore, it should be the natural function of women to stop men from fighting rather than aiding and abetting them in pursuing it.

Doctrinaire attempts to change this view, however well-intentioned they may be, are unlikely to have much success, at least in the short term. The cultural identity of man the warrior is more firmly stamped upon us than we recognise.

There is, though, more to man the warrior than brute strength and physical courage. These archetypal male virtues are often shot through with streaks of gentleness and sentimentality. The Anglo-Saxon hero Beowulf and Chaucer's knight both included gentleness in their make-up, and 'brave and courteous' was a favourite Kiowa description of a warrior. Morris Janowitz saw military honour and the pursuit of glory as 'a mixture of toughness and sentimentality', and General Matthew B. Ridgway wrote that:

Professional soldiers are sentimental men, for all the harsh realities of their calling. In their wallets and in their memories they carry bits of philosophy, fragments of poetry, quotations from the scriptures, which, in times of stress and danger, speak to them with quiet meaning.

Even at the height of war, animals can provoke an affection denied to fellow-humans. Glenn Gray thought that this was because 'soldiers are moved by the impersonal compassion that the fragility and helplessness of mortal creatures call up in most of us'. Perhaps it is also a reflection of the need to bestow affection on something, linked to a sense of guilt at having had a hand in the catastrophe which has engulfed the animal. Individual soldiers have had their pets, and units their mascots, for centuries. Prince Rupert's dog 'Boye' was killed at Marston Moor, the Earl of Feversham's deerhound lies with his master on the Somme, and Major-General 'Uncle' Harper's 'Rip' – 'of breed uncertain, but about the size and build of a Newfoundland' – was well known throughout his master's division. Sir Henry Rawlinson kept a pet boar, known, like the general, as 'Rawly'.

Horses were long an essential ingredient of war, and their suffering caused grief to men who were inured to human tribulations. Alan Hanbury-Sparrow witnessed the 'martyrdom' of draught horses on the retreat from Mons, describing the decree that animals which could go no further were to be shot as 'perhaps the most senselessly savage order ever issued by the staff'. Norman Gladden saw German bombs injure men and horses. One of the latter 'dashed across the field with its entrails hanging down. Its awful bellow of pain, in protest against man's inhumanity, was more shocking than all the rest of that afternoon's nightmare.' As Robert Graves moved up into the Somme battle, he was 'shocked by the dead horses and mules; human corpses were all very well, but it seemed wrong for animals to be dragged into the war like this'. Dead horses amongst the wreckage of German transport in the Falaise pocket in 1944 disturbed British soldiers more than the German dead who surrounded them. During the Dhofar war the Sultan of Oman's aircraft strafed camels. As the enemy's main means of transport they were important targets. None the less, as John Akehurst records, the attacks 'caused great distress to many of the pilots ...'

Stray or deserted animals are befriended. Edmund Blunden chanced on a mongrel in the trenches and looked after him until he ran away. 'I gave him W.H. Davies' Corned Beef by mistake, an unpopular brand,' lamented Blunden, 'so he may have thought me a danger.' Graham Greenwell saw kittens kept safe in a trench, and, on the first day of the Somme, British soldiers carried small partridges to safety. During the Second World War, one of John Horsfall's fusiliers found a small tortoise in North Africa. He 'thought it too young to be running about by itself,' and it became a pet. The men of Raleigh Trevelyan's platoon found two of the creatures at Anzio. 'We are going to take them back to B Echelon,' he wrote: 'Baxter was to bore a hole in their shells so that they can be tethered, and he is also intending to polish them up with rifle oil.' In Normandy, Martin Lindsay's CO discovered a black kitten asleep on his bed. 'She has been named Jean after the legendary Duchess of Gordon,' noted Lindsay, 'and taken on the strength.' Later he saw 'a little ginger kitten asleep at the foot of a stretcher on which lay a corpse shrouded in the usual army blanket'.

The affection lavished on animals by fighting men who would kill an enemy soldier with little compunction testifies not only to a deeply-rooted need to give love, but also to a compelling desire to receive it. Some cultures have encouraged homosexual relationships between soldiers: the Theban Sacred Band owed much of its cohesion to the fact that lovers fought together in its ranks. Homosexuality is not uncommon even in armies which do not approve of it. Frank Richardson believed that homosexuality 'occasionally becomes a disciplinary problem, but far more often remains a personal one and may be a source of deep unhappiness to more of our men than we suspect'.

Charles Carrington went further, asking himself if there was 'a homosexual element in *esprit de corps*'. There is certainly nothing overtly sexual in the ties of comradeship that link man to man in a well-integrated unit. Nevertheless, in moments of stress or excitement, the physical signs of affection and encouragement – clasped hands, an arm around the shoulder, or even a comforting embrace – are neither unusual nor out of place. Indeed, we are accustomed to see similar things on the sports field. We can easily misjudge such gestures and the emotion which inspires them. At times it is undoubtedly love: not necessarily love in any sexual sense, but love nevertheless. Herbert Read earned the DSO and MC as an infantry officer on the Western Front, and was in every sense a warrior. Yet he recognised the powerful feelings which bound him to his company, and dreaded the moment when the relationship must end:

> I know that I'll wander with a cry:
> 'O beautiful men, O men I loved,
> O whither are you gone, my company?'

There is much more to love in wartime than the scramble for sex.

Living Rough

Military service in wartime takes the soldier from a familiar environment, deprives him of many of his accustomed social and sexual pleasures, projects him into a world where his civilian status counts for little, and, finally, may force him to risk his life. But even before it does this last, it will have subjected him to the pressures which arise from group life in what is often an uncomfortable environment, the rigours of terrain and climate, and the sheer physical exhaustion which stems from living in what Shakespeare's Henry V called 'the painful field'. A great part of what Clausewitz termed friction is created, not by the spectacular events of battle, but by the stresses and strains endemic in war itself. Writing of the First World War, Denis Winter maintained that, even in the dangerous environment of the Western Front, 'the real enemy was the weather and the side-effects of living rough'.

The process of military training and the routine of daily life within the unit play an invaluable role in the creation of sound morale and *esprit de corps*. But they can also have less desirable effects, as we have already seen in the case of training. It is the assault on privacy, inevitable in the cramped conditions of armoured vehicles or defensive positions, and likely even in the less restrictive circumstances of the barracks or transit camp, which many soldiers find hardest to bear. In a 1969 Boyer lecture Sir Zelman Cowen stated that 'a man without privacy is a man without dignity', and there can be no doubt that it is hard to reconcile the demands of dignity with the requirements of military life in wartime.

Some of these requirements are difficult for most Westerners to tolerate. Dr John Parrish found 'sleeping on sandy cots, existing on cold C rations and smelling like three weeks of accumulated body grime' an inconvenience, but 'somehow group defecation was damaging to one's dignity'. Lord Moran, serving as a regimental medical officer on the Western Front during the First World War, noticed that 'most of the boys were a bit ashamed of dirty feet', while Norman Gladden recalled being embarrassed at waiting in his underwear while his clothes were being deloused. 'The unavoidable intimacies of army life', he wrote, 'had apparently not killed the natural modesty in which most of us had been brought up.' Marc Bloch made a similar observation. 'Peasants and workers, whom one expects to be uncouth,' he wrote, 'are often remarkably sensitive.' Even the redoubtable Ernst Jünger, the very epitome of the battle-hardened infantry officer, coveted privacy. 'The vain search for a water-closet', he wrote, 'is the outstanding memory one has of the villages of Lorraine.'

These difficulties are not altogether insuperable. Even group defecation loses some of its horrors. In *Winged Victory*, V.M. Yeates writes: 'The morning latrine was quite a social affair. The squadron had an excellent five-compartment house with canvas walls, very convenient for conversation.' Remarque's hero sat with his friends in a circle of latrine boxes.

'We feel ourselves for the time being better off than in any palatial white-tiled convenience,' he wrote. '*There* it can only be hygienic; *here* it is beautiful.' But there were few such pleasures at the front. Fred Majdalany recounts how soldiers at Cassino would wait until dark before relieving themselves, and then 'you would see small groups of bare hindquarters showing white in the semi-darkness, like grotesque friezes: their owners fervently praying that they might complete the proceeding before a shell struck the area.' And well they might for, as Denis Winter put it, 'men in war seem to have an irrational fear of being under fire with their trousers down'.

The onset of dysentery or diarrhoea – both disagreeably frequent in a wartime environment – complicates matters. Often there is nothing for it but to soldier on regardless. Majdalany tells of Lieutenant B, who, afflicted with dysentery,

> was compelled to fulfil the exacting demands of his illness as best he could with empty bully-beef tins. They couldn't be thrown out of the shelter in the daytime as this would have given away the position. Despite these circumstances, Lieutenant B., who is twenty-one, commanded his platoon without a break.

Numerous English soldiers suffered from disturbed stomachs on the march to Agincourt: they removed their breeches to give the diarrhoea free run. Charles Ogburn saw Merrill's Marauders do much the same thing in Burma in 1944: 'one platoon had cut open the seats of its trousers so as to be handicapped as little as possible by dysentery in any combat emergency'.

While many soldiers do indeed adjust to this particular aspect of life in the field, it is a facet of daily routine that causes far greater discomfort and tension than its relatively infrequent mention might suggest. Constipation – less spectacular but scarcely less prevalent than its antithesis – is often caused as much by natural modesty as it is by an unbalanced diet: American troops in Korea suffered especially from problems caused by lack of privacy. Morale is also threatened. Richard Simpkin argued that 'no relationship, even marriage, can be sustained without reticences', and was sure that the question of privacy should be considered seriously by the designers of armoured vehicles. 'So modesty is a prime requirement,' he wrote, 'comprehending minimization of physical exposure, privacy in urination and defecation, suppression or localization of the odors of these processes and swift, private disposal of the products.'

Not all cultures place the same emphasis upon modesty. One of the aspects of the everyday life of the Vietnamese which seemed so alien to Americans was the propensity for people of all ages to relieve themselves in public places. Arab males, on the other hand, kneel to urinate and require privacy for the act: this fact meant that, during the Dhofar war of the 1970s, several Arab soldiers stepped aside from the beaten track to urinate and either trod or knelt on a mine left by the *adoo*. Like 'The Refined Man' of Kipling's poem, they paid their price to live with themselves on the terms that they willed.

War is, quite literally, a dirty business. Living in the field, in a trench, under a poncho or in the shelter of a ruined building, makes men dirty in a way that almost beggars description. George Orwell, an officer in the International Brigades during the Spanish Civil War, was surprised how easily people became accustomed to dirt.

> Dirt is a thing people make too much fuss about. It is astonishing how quickly you get used to doing without a handkerchief and eating out of the tin pannikin in which you also wash ... In eighty nights I only took my clothes off three times, although I did occasionally manage to get them off in the daytime.

A.W. Hancox, who served with the Royal Garrison Artillery on the Western Front during the First World War, describes a camp which was not untypical of many in France in the early years of the war.

The whole area where the troops lived was a sea of mud. Not the mud you would get on your Sunday boots after a hike in the hills at home, but ankle deep liquid. In this muddy lake, like the minarets in some eastern city, almost floating were hundreds of bell tents.

Each tent was the home for twelve men, with all their kit, thankfully only occupied at night when, feet to the pole, completely dressed and wearing sodden shoes, they eased themselves on to their groundsheet, covered themselves with greatcoat and blanket, and sought repose.

It goes without saying that conditions in the line were far worse.

With the dirt comes the added discomfort of lice. Norman Gladden affirmed that: 'We were beset by an itch that was barely tolerable except when fear overshadowed all bodily discomforts.' Marshal Chuikov, the defender of Stalingrad, ruefully observed that the louse 'is no respecter of rank, titles or honours', and one of his opponents said bluntly: 'The worst things in Russia are lice and snipers.' Orwell was moved by his own experience of lice to suggest a more general truth. 'In war', he wrote, '*all* soldiers are lousy, at least when it is warm enough. The men who fought at Verdun, at Waterloo, at Flodden, at Senlac, at Thermopylae – every one of them had lice crawling over his testicles.'

Under such circumstances, a bath and the issue of clean clothes do wonders for morale. As Charles Carrington wrote, 'De-lousing yourself was one of the pleasantest prospects of going out into rest.' Off-duty soldiers gathered in small groups in trenches or dug-outs to hunt out and destroy lice. A.W. Hancox found that immersing a lousy shirt in a bucket of petrol, and then running one's finger along the seams to remove the eggs did the trick, although 'it was a bit smelly for a time.'

Survivors pay tribute to the satisfaction to be obtained from the simple bath. Rudolf Binding's unit discovered a bath in the ruins of Passchendaele. 'This rich article is the envy of higher staffs,' he remarked. 'The bath is in the yard; rank is ignored in the queue; the General bathes after my clerk.' 'It had never occurred to me', wrote Charles MacDonald, 'that I could derive so much pleasure from a bath.'

Paul Fussell pointed out in *The Great War and Modern Memory* that the description of soldiers bathing is a common set-piece scene in First World War literature. 'There's hardly a better way of projecting poignantly the awful vulnerability of mere naked flesh,' he suggested, 'the stark contrast between beautiful frail flesh and the alien metal that waits to violate it.' Such accounts do indeed tend to stress the jovial innocence of soldiers bathing. Young Richard Gale of the Machine Gun Corps noted that 'it was a great sight to see the men all naked, clean and happy', and Lord Moran wrote of a similar occasion that 'they were like great children, these fellows'. Perhaps there was the unconscious influence of Tolstoy's description of Prince Andrei watching the men of his regiment bathing in a river in *War and Peace*: 'All that bare, white human flesh was splashing about with shrieks and laughter, in the muddy pool like carp floundering in a net ... "Flesh, meat, *chair à canon*," he thought ...'

Even if the contrast between naked flesh and spinning metal lends poignancy to the spectacle of soldiers bathing, there is more to the communal bath than merely washing away grime. The removal of uniform, and the reversion to a natural – and rankless – state reminds men of happier times when they splashed together with their boyhood friends or showered after a game. The bath provides time out of war in more than one sense: it not only cleans a grubby body, but it also affords a temporary relief to the hard-pressed mind.

Lice are not the only vermin with which the soldier has had to contend. The rats of the Western Front were notable for their size and persistence. One officer wrote that they were as 'big as rabbits, and so bloated that they hardly take the trouble to run – beasts'. Ernst Jünger found them particularly appalling, and could 'never help thinking of their secret doings among the dead in the cellars of the village'. Rats were not peculiar to the First World War. They have plagued armies for centuries, and were a dreadful ingredient of sieges, where the conditions were usually particularly favourable for them.

Sometimes their presence was not altogether unwelcome: during the siege of Paris in 1870–1 a rat cost fifty centimes, one-tenth of a labourer's daily wage, and the *Paris Journal* advised on how to 'fish for sewer rats with a hook and line baited with tallow'.

George Orwell found that the rats in Spain during the Civil War really were as big as cats: 'great bloated brutes that walked over the beds of muck, too impudent even to run away unless you shot at them'. Technology has provided no definitive answer to the problem of rats. The US Marine defensive position at Khe Sanh, just south of the De-Militarised Zone in Vietnam, was rife with them. The stinking bunkers and debris-strewn area outside the wire provided them with a fruitful breeding-ground. Sleeping marines were often bitten, and the only way of keeping the rats off was to sleep completely covered up.

Insects have caused equal discomfort. The mosquito not only inflicts irritating bites but also spreads disease. The development of the anti-malaria drug Mepacrine made it less dangerous, but Mepacrine pills were themselves bitterly unpopular, as they turned soldiers a yellowish hue and made them feel hot and uncomfortable. During the Vietnam War American soldiers were required to take yellow anti-malaria pills and pink salt tablets. Ensuring that these were taken was a command responsibility, and Charles Anderson suggests that this was a contributory cause of friction between the leaders and the led which sometimes resulted in 'fragging'. And, even if mosquitoes were no longer deadly, they remained distinctly unpleasant. 'Going out to an ambush one night, it rained so hard, I started to choke,' recalled one American soldier. 'I couldn't breathe. I bent over to create an airpocket under my chest. In that moment, it was filled with mosquitos.'

Flies may lack the mosquito's taste for human blood, but they play their own loathsome role in spreading disease. They were a particularly unpleasant feature of the Gallipoli campaign during the First World War. Trooper I.L. Idriess of the 5th Australian Light Horse was overwhelmed by flies immediately he opened a tin of jam.

I wrapped my overcoat over the tin and gouged out the flies, then spread the biscuit, held my hand over it, and drew the biscuit out of the coat. But a lot of flies flew into my mouth and beat about inside ... I nearly howled with rage ... Of all the bastards of places this is the greatest bastard in the world.

The assaults of vermin are often all the harder to bear because they fall upon a body which is already tired. C. E. Montague's account of the First World War soldier has wider application for twentieth-century war generally.

For most of his time the average private was tired. Fairly often he was so tired as no man at home ever is in the common run of his work.

If a company's trench strength was low and sentry-posts abounded more than usual in its sector, a man might, for eight days running, get no more than one hour off duty at any one time, day or night. If enemy guns were active many of these hours off guard duty might have to be spent on trench repair ... So most of the privates were tired the whole of the time; sometimes to the point of torment, sometimes much less, but always more or less tired.

The psychologist F. C. Bartlett emphasised the connection between physical fatigue and psychiatric breakdown in battle. 'In war', he wrote, 'there is perhaps no general condition which is more likely to produce a large crop of nervous and mental disorders than a state of prolonged and great fatigue.' There are two closely related aspects to the question of tiredness: the physical exhaustion produced by marching or manual labour, and the deprivation of sleep. Over the last hundred years the relationship between these two elements has changed as technology has affected not only transport but also the duration of battles. For all but the last century or so, the soldier's prime means of mobility, both strategic and tactical, was his feet. Clausewitz believed that a march of fifteen miles was a good day's work, while a single forced march might stretch to thirty miles and successive forced marches could average twenty miles a day. In practice, soldiers marched vast distances. In the Austerlitz campaign the French army covered almost 700 miles as the crow flies, from its camp at Boulogne to Austerlitz in Moravia. The average soldier marched perhaps 1,000 miles in four months, with his unit covering as much as eighteen to twenty miles a day. There can be few more spectacular examples of a forced march than the feat of Crawfurd's Light Division, which marched sixty-two miles in twenty-six hours to reach Talavera in July 1809.

The development of the railway during the mid-nineteenth century reduced the distances that soldiers needed to march by providing strategic transport at least as far as a country's border. Nevertheless, in August 1914 the soldiers of the German First and Second Armies covered 300 miles between their railheads on the Belgian border and the limit of their advance on the River Marne. The men of General von Kluck's First Army, on the outer flank of the wheeling German armies, marched up to thirty miles a day, and units of the British Expeditionary Force, falling back before them, covered similar distances. These marches took on an almost dream-like quality, as Captain C.A.L. Brownlow described:

> Of the rest of the night I have no clear recollection; it remains in my mind as a blurred nightmare, in which shadowy figures slept as they rode or slept as they walked, in which phantom teams halted in sleep, checking for miles a ghostly stream of men and in which the will more than ever wrestled with the desire to sleep.

Stephen Westman, then a young conscript serving with the German 113th Infantry Regiment, had a similar memory. 'We slogged on,' he wrote, 'living, as it were, in a coma, often sleeping whilst we marched, and when the column came to a sudden halt we ran with our noses against the billycans of the men in front of us.'

By the time of the Second World War motor transport was often available to reduce the distances marched by soldiers behind the battlefield. But it is wrong to assume that the development of the lorry or, more recently, the armoured personnel carrier or helicopter, has rendered long marches obsolete. The Second World War German army achieved a high degree of mechanised excellence in its *panzer* and *panzer-grenadier* formations at the expense of infantry divisions. In consequence, thousands of German soldiers marched over 700 miles in 1941 alone, in conditions well described in the war diary of the 112th Infantry Division.

> Even though the division had a good deal of experience in poor road conditions, what was now demanded of it vastly exceeded anything known in the past. The completely sodden forest paths, the areas of swampy marsh, and the sticky clay on open ground simply defy description ... The infantry regiments had spread out into unendingly long columns: the heavy vehicles were unable to keep up and had to be manhandled along.

Allied soldiers were usually more fortunate but, even so, long marches with a backbreaking load remained the infantryman's stock-in-trade. Fred Majdalany paints a realistic picture of British infantry coming out of the line at Cassino.

> They marched back from the battle in the way of the Infantry, their feet scarcely leaving the ground, their bodies rocking mechanically from side to side as if that was the only way they could lift their legs. You could see that it required the last ounce of their mental and physical energy to move their legs at all. Yet they looked as if they could keep on moving like that for ever ...
> They never once looked back. They just stared straight ahead with eyes that seemed to see nothing, and kept on following the man in front – some in pain, some asleep on their feet, some choked with sickness, many limping – but all managing to force one foot past the other in that steady, subconscious, mechanical rhythm which is the secret of the Infantry.

United States forces engaged in the Vietnam War enjoyed tactical mobility unprecedented in the history of war. The 1st Cavalry Division (Airmobile) was heliborne in its entirety, and a wide range of helicopters were available to assist units in everything from casualty evacuation to the delivery of mail or the transport of artillery. But there came a time when the soldier on the ground had to walk. Charles Anderson's account of the experiences of B Company, 1st Battalion, 3rd Marine Regiment on Operation Virginia Ridge in 1969 is an anabasis of shattering 'humps', from one 'of moderate length, 6,000 metres' on the first day, through days of trudging in the heat under a brazen sky, to the day when 'Captain Sam's travelling road show walked into the south gate of Con Thien late in the afternoon of June first'. Captain Sam's grunts might have been members of the most sophisticated army in the world, but they gained scant benefit from it. They were stripped as bare before the exhausting reality of the day's march as Napoleon's *grognards* or Kluck's *landser*.

> They rounded corners in the terrain and vegetation, grunted up rises and hills, stumbled, fell and rolled down rises and hills, tearing trousers, slashing arms and legs. They stumbled into occasional clearings after hacking and swearing at the stubborn growth, but still it was there. That sun rode the sky as if it had always been there, on top of everything, as if it had never been night; it resented anyone daring to move when it ruled above.

British forces carried out a prodigious feat of marching during the Falklands campaign. 'Yomping', as the marines called it, or 'tabbing', in army parlance, 45 Commando and 3 Para trudged squarely across the inhospitable terrain of East Falkland. It took 3 Para only five days to cover the forty miles of desolate country between the British beach-head at San Carlos and Estancia House, just short of the ring of Argentine positions round Port Stanley. Max Hastings describes the scene.

> The men marched in long files, 10 yards apart so that a moving commando stretched across 5 miles of East Falk-

land. Even if they managed to dry their feet during the night, each morning within a few minutes they had squelched through a marsh in the darkness, waded a stream or merely endured a torrential rain shower. Their canvas webbing stiffened and shrank on their shoulders, their hair hung matted on their skulls, the strain of stumbling across the hillside with grenades, weapons and linked-belt ammunition across their chests was etched into each face long before evening.

It is not merely the distances involved that make such marches so utterly tiring: the crushing burden of the soldier's pack adds its own numbing contribution. Armies have generally had two scales of personal equipment, one carried when contact with the enemy is imminent, and the other carried on the line of march. Now that motor transport or helicopters are often available, the soldier may legitimately expect that the more cumbersome part of his burden, such as pack and sleeping bag, will be carried for him for at least part of the time. Nevertheless, there will be times when, laden with weapon, ammunition, food and equipment, the twentieth-century soldier bears a load no lighter than that carried by the warriors of antiquity. True, his equipment is likely to be more durable and more scientifically designed than the hide packs and pipeclayed crossbelts of yesteryear, but the weights involved are still colossal.

The Roman legionary was appositely nicknamed 'Marius's Mule'. On the march he carried, in addition to his arms and armour, three days' rations, a mess-tin, hand-mill, chain, saw and hook, stakes for a palisade and, usually hung on a forked stick over his shoulder, a tool-bag and a basket for moving earth. This weighed around sixty pounds, and under exceptional conditions rations and so on took the legionary's burden to over 100 pounds. During the eighteenth and nineteenth centuries packs continued to weigh about sixty pounds. The Prussian infantryman was girt about with cartridge pouch, water flask, bread bag, and knapsack with such essentials as spare dickey, shirts, gaiter buttons, breeches, hose, foot bands, flints, gloves, hair powder, knife, fork, spoon and cleaning kit. Small wonder that when Ulrich Braker, serving in the notorious Itzenplitz Regiment, opened his shirt on the march to let in a little air, 'steam rose up as if from a boiling kettle'.

John Harris served in the infinitely more benevolent British 95th Rifles, but he too carried a leaden pack. 'I am convinced that many of our infantry sank and died under the weight of their knapsacks alone,' he wrote:

> so awkwardly was the load our men bore ... placed upon their backs, that the free motion of the body was impeded, the head held down from the pile at the back of the neck, and the soldier half beaten before he came to the scratch ... Many a man died, I am convinced, who would have borne up well to the end of the retreat, but for the infernal load we carried on our backs.

Infantrymen shouldered heavy burdens during the First World War. The French *poilu*'s load weighed eighty-five pounds. Henri Barbusse described the pack as 'monumental and crushing': it contained not only all the regulation items, but also a man's little treasures and comforts – tins of fruit, chocolate, candles, and so on. On campaign in North Africa the Foreign Legion marched twenty-five miles a day with 100-pound packs and, in the equally inhospitable terrain of Burma during the Second World War, British infantrymen in Wingate's Chindits carried at least seventy pounds, often increased to almost ninety. American soldiers landing in North Africa for Operation Torch shouldered nearly 132 pounds per man, and William Manchester, writing of his own war in the Pacific, observed that 'a marine in an amphibious assault was a beast of burden', laden with a pack weighing 84·3 pounds, while some unfortunates lugged 20-pound Browning Automatic Rifles, 45-pound mortar baseplates or 47-pound mortar bipods. American soldiers in Vietnam carried packs whose weight made them disinclined to crawl when under fire. They walked, wrote F.J. West in *Small Unit Action in Vietnam*, 'because they were tired and it was easier to move by standing.

The weight and bulk of their equipment contributed greatly to this fatigue.' Finally, British parachutists and marines in the Falklands carried loads weighing as much as 120 pounds.

For much of history these weights were the soldier's everyday burden on the march. It was, however, widely recognised that for battle he should divest himself of as much of it as possible. In 1744 Frederick the Great decreed that 'if time allows, the men must take off their knapsacks and all other impedimenta before every action'. By the time of the Second Empire French infantry invariably dumped their packs before going into battle, and in 1870 some of their German opponents experimented with a light battle order based on the rolled greatcoat, with mess tins and spare ammunition.

Sending a man into battle carrying more equipment than he needs makes his task infinitely harder. Sir James Edmonds, British Official Historian of the First World War, wrote that the infantry load of sixty-six pounds, carried by advancing troops on the Somme, 'made it difficult to get out of a trench, impossible to move more quickly than a slow walk or to rise and lie down quickly'. The distinguished military historian John Terraine has attacked this as a 'myth of remarkable tenacity', a statement which provoked a trenchant response from Lieutenant-Colonel Hew Pike, who commanded 3 Para in the Falklands.

> It is true that certain battalions of 3 Commando Brigade advanced across East Falkland carrying very heavy loads in record time. But it was ... 'impossible to move much quicker than a slow walk', just as in 1916. The difference was that we did not attack the enemy carrying such loads. If we had done so, the results might indeed have echoed 1916.[8]

Nevertheless, there are times when unanswerable tactical logic forces soldiers to carry very heavy weights indeed, even in battle. A Vietnam veteran believed that his clutch belt, supposedly light order, 'must have weighed forty-five pounds with a K-bar knife and a ·45 pistol and you name it'. American soldiers in the Hoa Hoi battle of 1966 went into action with 350 M16 rounds, six fragmentation grenades, one phosphorus and two smoke grenades, 2,000 rounds of link for their squad's machine-gun, three days' rations and two full canteens. British parachutists and marines in the Falklands went into battle bulging with ammunition. After Goose Green, soldiers in 2 Para carried 100 rounds of rifle ammunition, 800 rounds of link and two grenades: 66mm LAWs and ammunition for the M79 grenade-launchers were distributed around the sections.

Captain Ian Gardiner, a company commander in 45 Commando, carried over eighty-three pounds of equipment in the attack on Two Sisters. This included not only his rifle, bayonet, night sight, five full magazines, three grenades and a bandolier of fifty rounds, but also a twenty-four-hour ration pack, water and radio. 'I doubt if many men were carrying much less than me' he said. 'Most would have been about the same, and some – a good deal more.' He was adamant that none of this equipment was superfluous. 'We needed *all* that kit,' he declared,

> before our packs got sent up to us 36 hours later ... I would say that anyone sending his men into a battle of that nature with less than this is pushing his luck.
>
> We could not strip off for action and pick it up later. My objective was over 1,000 metres long and once we had taken it, we had to be prepared for counter attack. I certainly wasn't going to have men bimbling back and forward picking up kit (in the dark) while we were being shelled and were expecting a counter attack.

The modern soldier is fortunate in that, for at least part of the time, his pack or bergen will be flown out to him by helicopter, brought up before nightfall in his company's transport, or will simply stay in his Armoured Personnel Carrier. But if technology has helped him in one respect, it has made his life harder in another. Except under unusual circumstances night fighting was rare until the twentieth century. Siege operations were often carried on at night, and both besiegers and besieged attempted storms and sorties under the cover of darkness. Battles in the open field, however, usually stopped at last light, and were generally one-day affairs. Clausewitz advised against night operations, warning that: 'the attacker seldom if ever knows enough about the defence to make up for his lack of visual observation'. As late as August 1914, as evening fell on the battlefield of Mons, British soldiers were surprised to hear German bugles sounding the cease-fire.

The development of illuminants – parachute flares for guns and mortars of most calibres, Very pistols, hand-held Schermuly flares and trip flares – and night vision devices – image intensifiers and thermal imagers – has made it easier to fight at night. Moreover, despite Clausewitz's judgment, it is widely recognised that darkness may enable an attacker to minimise the effects of at least some of the defender's weapons. In short, night operations have become increasingly frequent since that strangely old-fashioned evening at Mons and, if the Falklands campaign is anything to go by, night attacks may become the rule rather than the exception. The US army's FM 30-102, *Handbook on Aggressor Forces*, states that Soviet troops on the offensive will attempt to sustain the same rate of advance by night as they will during the day. 'The short war of the future, as in the recent past, will be characterized by sustained combat operations,' wrote an American authority recently: 'Sustained combat operations are defined as those combat actions that are continuous for 24 or more hours without let up in the fighting.'[9] It may, of course, be that the short war assumption proves as flawed as the 'over by Christmas' belief of 1914. Nevertheless, the evidence of the Arab-Israeli conflicts of the past decade, the Iran–Iraq War, Vietnam and the Falklands indicates that, whatever the strategic picture might be, tactical pressures will compel the soldier to fight at night.

The net result of this increasing activity at night has been to deprive the soldier, already physically tired after a day's marching, fighting or digging, of sleep. During the First World War troops in the line would spend much of their night on guard, repairing wire or trenches, patrolling or carrying up the wire, duckboards and sandbags known by the collective euphemism of 'trench stores'. A senior NCO in a regular infantry battalion estimated that he had less than four hours sleep a night when his unit was in the line. A study of American soldiers in Italy in 1944 established that 31 per cent averaged less than four hours sleep a night, while another 54 per cent enjoyed less than six. Research on both sides of the Atlantic indicates that an adequate performance can be sustained for several weeks with as little as four hours sleep in a twenty-four-hour period, with six hours for more protracted operations. Even these small amounts of sleep are denied many soldiers.

Sustained operations do more than force men to stay awake. They also interfere with the body's diurnal cycle, the 'internal clock' which regulates many physiological functions. Most people are at the peak of their performance between 1200 and 2100 and are at their least effective between 0300 and 0600: Napoleon was right to value 'two in the morning courage' highly. A soldier engaged in operations during this period is likely to be considerably less efficient than he might be during the daytime, especially if he is woken harshly from an inadequate nap to face an unexpected crisis. Attacks delivered at, or shortly before, dawn, give the attacker an added advantage because his soldiers, although themselves at a metabolic low, have at least been awake long enough to make some of the necessary adjustments.

Even if sleep deprivation does not force the soldier to fight at his early-morning worst, it is likely to decrease his vigilance, interfere with his ability to think logically, concentrate and remember, and it can produce uncharacteristic behaviour patterns ranging from deep gloom to wild elation. Moreover, sleep loss is cumulative: a man deprived of sleep for forty-eight hours will recover after twelve hours of normal sleep, while a man who staggers on for ninety-six hours will need no less than 120 to recover. The US Army Research Institute for the Behavioral Sciences found that sleep deprivation affected some tasks more than others. Ironically, it is the leader, the very man likely to get least sleep, whose performance is most degraded by the lack of it.[10] A British study in 1980 found that after twenty-four hours without sleep military effectiveness 'had fallen off considerably'. After forty-eight sleepless hours, 'responses to simulated attacks ... were bad, with most soldiers over-reacting and misunderstanding orders, which were not always clearly given by the section commander'. The trial unit was 'unreliable as a fighting force' after sixty-eight hours without sleep.[11]

Lack of sleep and physical exhaustion affect most soldiers, often with serious consequences. Lieutenant Murdoch McDougall gives a graphic description of the effect of sustained operations on his comrades in 4 Commando in Normandy in 1944.

A man would lean back in his trench as I spoke to him and become unconscious before my eyes. Another, standing in his slit trench, fell asleep on his feet and slithered slowly to his knees, to finish huddled in the corner, still holding the mess-tin from which he had been eating as exhaustion overcame him.[12]

A Vietnam veteran put it more brusquely. 'I was constantly fatigued,' he said. 'The killing part is easy, but you're just so fucking tired all the fucking time.'

The effects of hunger are similar to many of those produced by tiredness. Hungry men are very susceptible to cold, get bored easily, take increasingly little interest in others, and can eventually assume a 'don't care' attitude which resembles the zombie-like trance of utter exhaustion. Even if there is sufficient food available to prevent the onset of these more extreme symptoms, the frequency with which food is eaten has a marked effect on a soldier's performance. As Peter Watson noted in *War on the Mind*, 'men who have had no breakfast or coffee only do significantly worse on target detection than men who did have breakfast, however light'.

Complaints about the qualitative or quantitative deficiencies of food are a constant feature of soldiers' letters, diaries and memoirs. 'I would say without hesitation', affirmed Brigadier Bernard Fergusson, 'that lack of food constitutes the single biggest single assault upon morale ... Apart from its purely chemical effects upon the body, it has woeful effects upon the mind. One is in the dismal condition of having nothing to look forward to.' Sometimes it is merely that the food available is not what the troops are used to. Colonel Auguste Ducrot, commanding the French 3rd of the Line on the Bomarsund expedition of 1854, told his wife of the difficulties caused by the unfamiliar British navy rations his men received during their voyage:

> soldiers have the habit of moaning in such a way that they complain constantly: the chocolate is not thick enough or is too thick, the soup too salty, the tea insipid; they've always got something to say. I've adopted the policy of putting all who complain on bread and biscuit; it is the only way of making them see reason.

On other occasions, it is the lack of variety that causes annoyance. The Russian soldier of the First World War enjoyed a diet distinguished only by its dreary predictability. There was bread for breakfast, cabbage soup with meat for lunch, and porridge for supper: the poor quality and uninteresting nature of this menu lowered morale and made its own contribution to the collapse of 1917. In the British army of the Second World War, daily rations often consisted of three meals of bully beef. This could be made palatable if cooked ingeniously: mixed with whatever else was available as an 'all-in-stew', livened up with curry powder, or given a pastry or biscuit-crumb topping to produce a savoury pie. All too often, alas, there was more bully than ingenuity, and it was simply wolfed down cold.

Monotonous food, even if uninspiring and lacking in vitamins, does at least keep body and soul together. But the logistic problems which beset armies have meant that, from time to time, food has run out altogether. Martin van Creveld warns in *Supplying War*: 'Before a commander can even start thinking of manœuvring or giving battle ... he has – or ought – to make sure of his ability to supply his soldiers with those 3,000 calories a day without which they will very soon cease to be any use as soldiers ...' Miscalculation, hostile action, or sudden changes in the weather all conspire to interfere with even the most robust logistic plans. Moreover, commanders may, in accordance with the current Soviet doctrine, decide to give priority to resupplying with the fuel and ammunition which enable soldiers to fight at the expense of the rations which enable them to live.

There was often a shortage of food in Napoleon's army. Soldiers were able to forage for themselves when operating in a central Europe well stocked after years of peace, and Napoleon's logistic system deserves, as van Crefeld points out, more credit than it generally receives. But things were naturally more difficult in the less populous areas of Eastern Europe and Spain, and by 1813 even the once-prosperous Germany had been stripped bare. Shortage of food lowered morale, eroded discipline and, on occasions in Russia and Spain, killed soldiers or left them vulnerable to disease or cold. As Jean Morvan put it in *Le Soldat impérial*, 'when food was lacking, veterans complained, conscripts groaned, guardsmen killed themselves, linesmen decamped'.

During the American Civil War the Confederacy, its own economy steadily crumbling, was increasingly unable to ensure that its armies were adequately fed. Even the Union army did not always make ends meet: Major-General William S. Rosecrans's men fought the Chattanooga campaign on half-rations. American soldiers fared even worse during the Meuse–Argonne battle in 1918, when some soldiers were reduced to scavenging for scraps of food amongst the dead. Just as the outcome of sieges in previous centuries had often depended upon the supply of rations, so too it was food rather than ammunition that determined the outcome of some Second World War battles. The American Army Historical Series volume on logistics affirms that 'lack of food probably more than any other single factor forced the end of resistance on Bataan', and the German defenders of Stalingrad were literally starving by the time of their capitulation. For the last fortnight of the battle German troops were rationed to a mere 50 grams of bread a day, eked out with horse-meat soup: many did not even receive this inadequate allowance. When Major Pohl, commanding 1st Battalion, 134th Infantry Regiment, won the Knight's Cross in mid-December 1941, General Paulus gave him a present whose value was commensurate with Pohl's courage: an army loaf and a tin of herrings.

The Falklands were no different. The Argentinians on Fanning Head, overlooking the British landing site at San Carlos, had received no rations for three days, and their morale was already eroded by the time that they were dislodged by a Special Boat Squadron patrol on the morning of 21 May. Many of the conscripts holding the positions round Stanley were hungry, and one of them told the journalist Daniel Kon of his indignation at discovering, after the Argentine surrender, that masses of food and equipment were piled up in the town, and had not been made available to the troops in their windswept positions. British troops were more fortunate, although the redoubtable 2 Para received only two days' rations in five days after its victory at Goose Green.

This shortage of food, which is so frequent a characteristic of military operations, does more than merely make men hungry, dispirited and increasingly ineffective. The preparation and consumption of food is as much a social ritual as it is a physical necessity. Cooking and eating take up slack time, break an otherwise interminable day into tolerable spans, and provide high spots whose anticipation lends point to an otherwise bleak existence. It brings men together and reinforces group identity. For centuries an army's basic unit, like the Roman legion's ten-man *conturbernium* or the Prussian army's seven-man *Kameradschaft*, was essentially a living and messing group rather than a tactical entity, and gained much of its cohesion from close contact in daily life. It is perhaps no coincidence that the Russians use the same word, *artel*, for messing unit and for trade union. The irregular arrival of rations threatens this little community: the rifle section that has not got the makings of a brew is poor and lonely indeed.

Captain Stuart Mawson, medical officer to a British parachute battalion at Arnhem, savoured a cup of tea in the aircraft on his way to the dropping zone. 'Something hot in the stomach', he wrote,

> was a stimulus to the vegetative nervous system. The fluid replaced that lost through the sweat of fear or exertion, the sugar replenished the level in the blood and supplied energy, while the mere fact of doing something familiar and pleasant in the company of others was as reassuring as the light of a fire in the jungle that keeps the wild animals away.

Mawson's remark perfectly sums up the physical and psychological value of food to the soldier. It is particularly important in times of stress, for amongst the physiological effects of the latter is a speeding-up of the metabolic rate, making men hungrier and thirstier than they normally are. Lance-Corporal A. Wallace of 2/5 Sherwood Foresters experienced a practical demonstration of this on 21 March 1918. His company sergeant-major walked along the forward trench during the German bombardment, distributing chunks of bread and bacon: 'Get this down you, lads – you'll be needing this.' 'We ate the food', recalled Wallace, 'and, with our water bottles, felt quite refreshed.' A correspondent in the Falklands wrote that fear was converted into hunger before an attack: 'All down the line of patiently waiting men you could hear the rustle of Garibaldi biscuits and Rolos being opened.'

Cigarettes are almost equally important. Fergusson thought that the inclusion of cigarettes in rations literally 'saved men's lives'. Cigarettes are appetite suppressants and, argued Fergusson, smokers worried less about food than non-smokers. It is hard to overstate the consumption of cigarettes in both World Wars. Denis Winter wrote that 'to light up was the first reaction to any dangerous situation'. 'Chain-smoking was widespread,' acknowledged W.H.A. Groom, 'and fifty cigarettes in twenty-four hours was not abnormal.' William

Manchester's sketch of his comrades on the Pacific would have been incomplete without the eternal cigarette.

> Mud-caked, unshaven, his uniform greasy and torn, he resembled a hobo, which in a way he was. Like tramps we smoked incessantly, carrying cigarettes in the cartridge pouches on our web belts (where they fitted perfectly), and slumped beneath the weight of our equipment, we looked both crippled and middle-aged.

A failure in cigarette supply could have a damaging effect on morale. 'Under the stresses of the battlefield,' wrote Norman Gladden, 'a smoker could become desperate enough to be willing to risk anything for his normal means of release from tension.'

The weather is a consideration of secondary interest to most Western men and women in the late twentieth century. Rain spoils a weekend or makes the walk to the station unusually unpleasant, and snow and ice bring traffic grinding to a halt. But what is merely an irritating backcloth to the average city-dweller is a matter of fundamental importance to the soldier, who lives out under the sky, often enjoying only such creature comforts as he has been able to carry on his back.

The miseries of campaigning in such areas as the Far East during the monsoon or Russia in winter are so striking as to need little emphasis, although Guy Sajer's account of the latter makes the point with sharp effectiveness.

> We urinated into our numbed hands to warm them, and, hopefully, to cauterise the gaping cuts in our fingers. Some men had patches of skin on the ends of their noses which had frozen and become infected. Similar infection was common in the folds of the eyelids, around the ears, and particularly in the hands. I myself was not seriously affected, but each movement of my fingers opened and closed deep crevices, which oozed blood.

It is the pressures of living in the field even in a temperate climate that deserve stressing. George Orwell's assessment of the priorities of life at the front are by no means untypical. 'In trench warfare five things are important: firewood, food, tobacco, candles and the enemy,' he wrote. 'In winter on the Zaragoza front they were important in that order, with the enemy a bad last.' Banal daily tasks such as eating, washing and weapon-cleaning take on a new character when they are carried out in the biting cold of winter. Two lines from David Jones's prose poem *In Parenthesis*, in which Jones describes frozen fingers fumbling to extract oil bottle and pull-through from the butt-trap of the Lee-Enfield rifle, somehow encapsulate the misery of cold: 'then were butt-heel-irons opened, and splintering of thumb nails with the jammed metal'.

Sergeant Wheeler of the British 51st Regiment was no stranger to that dampener of military ardour, rain. He spent a sleepless night on the eve of Waterloo:

> Being close to the enemy we could not use our blankets, the ground was too wet to lie down, we sat on our knapsacks until daylight without fires, there was no shelter against the weather: the water ran in streams from the cuffs of our jackets, in short we were as wet as if we had been plunged over head in a river.

Second-Lieutenant John Glubb was in similar straits a century later:

> Started at 2.30 p.m. in pouring rain, along a pavé road. Thousands of passing lorries covered us all with mud. On arrival in the dark, soaked with mud and water and shivering with cold, we found the billets allotted to us were occupied by gunners ... Perpetual rain, everything grey, everyone soaked.

Well might Henri Barbusse write: 'Dampness rusts men like rifles, more slowly but more deeply.'

In some respects today's soldier is better equipped to sustain this sort of discomfort than his forefathers were. Uniforms have become increasingly practical, and developments in textiles

have produced a variety of materials which cope much better
with the vagaries of climate than did the ubiquitous serge of
yesteryear. Even if waterproof jackets eventually let in water
around the seams, or make the wearer perspire so heavily that
he gets wet in any case, they are nevertheless a colossal improvement over the supposedly waterproof capes and ground-
sheets under whose flimsy protection previous generations of
soldiers hunched their soaking backs.

Yet, just as the acceleration of technology and industrialis-
ation provide the soldier with improved defences against the
weather, so urbanisation and the mechanisation of agriculture
ensure that the essentially rural environment in which the
soldier does so much of his living and fighting is increasingly
foreign to him. Even the Russian army, which for centuries
owed its formidable fighting qualities in great measure to the
hardy peasants who filled its ranks, no longer contains a
majority of soldiers of rural stock. In 1940 only 33 per cent of
Russians lived in towns, but by 1970 this had increased to 56
per cent. General von Bernhardi reviled townsmen as weak-
lings and drunkards, and the imperial German army believed
that they were socialist and subversive and tried, by laying
the burden of conscription most heavily upon the countryside,
to ensure that they were in a minority in its ranks. The demands of the First World War forced the Germans to conscript
townsmen in unprecedented numbers, leading some apologists
to blame the breakdown of German morale and discipline in
the latter stages of the war on the presence of these traditionally unreliable men. The tough countryman, for whom
the rigours of campaigning differed little from the grinding
hardship of everyday life, is a disappearing commodity in the
northern hemisphere. Marshal Canrobert, recalling his days as
a company commander in the 47th of the Line in Algeria in the
1830s, gives us a sketch of this vanishing breed.

As we returned, I turned round to watch my company
march past. These were not *grenadiers*, not *voltigeurs*, but
little soldiers from the *compagnies du centre*, linesmen, peasants

snatched from their homes to do their seven years. They did not even have the advantage of wearing a modest but distinctive sign, such as an epaulette – red or yellow. They marched round-shouldered under the weight of their loaded packs, tired by a day and a night of marching and fighting ... Despite their exhaustion ... without having taken a moment's rest, but with the satisfaction of having done their duty without flinching, they gave themselves to the hardest and most painful work.

Not only has the proportion of soldiers from the cities increased over the past century, but the nature of their home background has changed. John Baynes, in his study of Second Scottish Rifles at Neuve Chapelle, catalogues the wretched conditions of working-class life in Britain in the early years of this century. Food and living conditions were atrocious and violence was endemic. Football hooliganism is nothing new: in 1909 the annual Celtic versus Rangers match had to be stopped because the rioting got out of hand. Although the British army, recruiting as it did by voluntary enlistment rather than conscription, received more than its fair share of men from this sort of background, many of the soldiers who fought in the armies of the First World War had simply exchanged one harsh and violent environment for another. An infantry platoon analysed by Denis Winter contained a shepherd, a wheelwright, a labourer, a blacksmith, and several ironworkers and coalminers. They were working-class men in the old sense of the term, used to long days of unremittingly hard, dirty and physical labour.

The general increase in living standards in both Europe and North America has had its effect upon the urban soldier. He is now less likely than he was in the past to come from a home where physical discomfort and lack of food are the rule, although he is probably a good deal more used to violence than middle-class academics might like to think. Charles Anderson believed that the home life of what he calls 'the sons of working-class Americans [who] did the soldiering and dying in Vietnam' had a profound effect on the way they reacted to war.

In their zeal to relieve their offspring of the painful parts of life, the grunts' parents created a generation shielded from much of what has steeled every previous generation – the realization that a certain amount of adversity not necessarily deserved will be encountered in the course of one's life.

In sum, this tendency for soldiers to come increasingly from urban rather than rural backgrounds, and for these backgrounds to be relatively more comfortable than those of their fathers and grandfathers, makes the stresses imposed by separation from home and family, by terrain and climate, and by shortage of food all the more great. It would probably be wrong to claim that the change is so fundamental as to render modern soldiers immeasurably inferior to their ancestors in their ability to tolerate adversity. John Baynes is nevertheless right when he maintains:

> As men get more used to comfort, more sophisticated and more intelligent it becomes essential to take more trouble over their morale. The problem is not to discover what keeps the soldier in good heart, but how to apply lessons learnt throughout history to the pattern of modern life in its increasing complexity.

Paradoxically, the ability of military leaders to manage men under pressure may be declining at the very time when the maintenance of morale is more important than ever. The tendency for Western societies to be less deferential deprives officers of the unstated superiority which they often possessed in the past, and tactical imperatives demand dispersion and restrict movement, making physical contact between leaders and led more difficult and less frequent. Moreover, many of the stresses which we have examined in this chapter will bear as hard on officers as on their men, and may have the effect of weakening their authority. An early nineteenth-century French author warned that field service was bound to impose a strain on a soldier's respect for his superiors, since the officer would be seen 'too often in his dressing-gown'. A recent study made the same point in more measured terms, stating that 'formal leaders often suffer risk of displacement of status when environmental pressures on their group increase'.[13]

So much, then, for the effects of the wartime environment upon the soldier. Let us now accompany him as he moves up, bent under his pack, or crammed into the back of a truck, into what Ardant du Picq called 'the final objective of armies': battle.

4

Epitome of War

The battlefield is the epitome of war. All else in war, when war is perfectly conducted, exists but to serve the forces of the battlefield and to assure final success on the field.

S. L. A. Marshall, *Men Against Fire*

First Blood

Battle, whatever its frequency – or lack of it – is the end towards which most military training is directed, and is an event which comes to loom large in the soldier's mind. Before he comes within range of hostile fire the soldier will, as we have seen, have speculated about battle in general and his own role in it in particular. He may regard it as the supreme challenge to his manhood, like this Vietnam veteran:

> And I always wondered, like if I didn't go if it was just because I was afraid to go ... It may seem foolish ... after I got to Viet Nam and was in combat, I realised how foolish I was – I think, you know, that my reason was to find out, 'Am I gonna chicken out?'

Sometimes this speculation is enlivened by early enthusiasm, like that experienced by Ernst Jünger.

We had set out in a rain of flowers to seek the death of heroes. The war was our dream of greatness, power and glory. It was a man's work, a duel on the fields whose flowers would be stained with blood. There is no lovelier death in the world ... Anything rather than stay at home, anything to make one with the rest.

Roy Grinker and John Spiegel suggest that, before their departure for a combat zone, most men fantasise about their own performance.

Their minds are full of romanticized, Hollywood versions of their future activities in combat, coloured with vague ideas of being a hero and winning ribbons and decorations for startling exploits and with all sorts of exhibitionistic fantasies to which few would publicly admit.[1]

Philip Caputo spent the night before his first operation in Vietnam reflecting on the problems that might arise on the morrow. But, 'exhausted by the mental effort, I had entertained myself with fantasies of personal heroics. I had even imagined how the accounts of my bravery would sound in the local newspapers: "A Chicago-area marine has been awarded the Silver Star in Vietnam ... "'

Even if this feeling is as widespread as Grinker and Spiegel assert, it is certainly intermingled with a good deal of apprehension as contact with the enemy grows near. Sergeant Joseph Donaldson, who served with the 94th Regiment in the Peninsula, gave a good description of the mixture of emotions which assail men on the eve of their first battle. 'I felt a sensation something resembling delight,' he wrote, 'but it was of an awful kind – enthusiasm and sublimity, mixed with a sense of danger.'

Similar feelings have run through the minds of twentieth-century soldiers. Jack Chaffer, later to win a Military Medal with the Grenadier Guards in Italy, admitted that he was 'very apprehensive, but having been well trained at Caterham and Pirbright, I was raring to go'. Major Alan Briddon summed up his emotions prior to departure for the Western Desert as 'apprehensive but anticipatory', while an officer of the Suffolk Regiment looked forward to his arrival in Malaya during the Emergency with a 'very high pitch of nervous expectations'. Gordon Cormack, who served with anti-terrorist units in Rhodesia in the 1960s and 1970s, thought that battle seemed 'a normal progression of events' after training, but was: 'apprehensive also, like waiting for the start of the 440 yards. After all the bull you didn't want to let the side down.' The American psychiatrist Dr J. Dowling's expression 'apprehensive enthusiasm' is a good summary of most men's emotions during the period leading up to their first experience of combat.

As battle approaches, so enthusiasm wanes and apprehension increases. 'Our fevered thoughts cooled down as we marched through the heavy chalk loam of Champagne,' remembered Ernst Jünger. 'Pack and ammunition and rifle weighed on us like lead.' The physical symptoms of fear begin to make themselves felt. 'Most soldiers on approaching the firing line', notes a sober medical study of neurosis in war, 'displayed uneasiness and apprehension by restlessness, irritability, artificial jubilancy or silence and withdrawal, or by unusual perspiration, diarrhoea and frequency of micturition ... ' A First World War Australian NCO recalled: 'The tension affected the men different ways. I couldn't stop urinating, and we were all anxious for the barrage to begin.' Sergeant Timothy Gowing of the Royal Fusiliers, lying down before the Allied advance at the Alma in 1854, 'felt horribly sick, a cold shivering running through my veins'.

Lieutenant Frederick Hitchcock, adjutant of the 132nd Pennsylvania Volunteers, received his baptism of fire with Kimball's Brigade at Antietam on 17 September 1862. He described his sensations at some length.

These volleys of musketry we were approaching sounded in the distance like the rapid pouring of shot upon a tin pan, or the tearing of heavy canvas, with slight pauses interspersed by single shots, or desultory shooting. All this presaged fearful work for us, with what results to each personally the future, measured probably in moments, would reveal.

How does one feel under such conditions? To tell the truth, I realized the situation and felt most uncomfortable. Lest there might be some undue manifestation of this feeling in my conduct, I said to myself, this is the duty you have undertaken to perform for my country, and now I'll do it, and leave the results to God. My greater fear was not that I might be killed, but that I might be grievously wounded and left a victim of suffering on the field.

It is hard to exaggerate the degree of stress imposed by this feeling of pre-contact apprehension, which usually occurs, with varying intensity, before every battle in which a soldier participates. Charlton Ogburn wrote that 'the major enemy was not the Japanese themselves but your own apprehension'. Raleigh Trevelyan prayed, 'God give me strength for tomorrow, for I can think of nothing else.' An officer in 3 Para affirmed that he felt infinitely more scared on board *Canberra* approaching the Falklands than he did in action, and a platoon commander in the same battalion believed that the uncertainty and apprehension before battle were far more damaging than fear during it. R. N. Villar, a naval surgeon, concluded from his own experiences in the campaign that 'fear is an illogical sensation, but, however much you feel it, be sure that someone else feels it more. I found waiting the most worrying and doing the most relaxing ... '

Statistical evidence tends to support these views. John Dollard studied 300 American veterans of the Abraham Lincoln Brigade, which fought in the Spanish Civil War. Seventy-one per cent of them admitted to being afraid before action. 'Because of the terrific image of warfare drilled into me by years of training, I was much more afraid before I went into action,' recalled one veteran. By contrast, only 15 per cent remembered being frightened during the battle itself, and 14 per cent felt frightened afterwards. During the Second World

War the US Army approached the question of apprehension frankly. Its pamphlet *Army Life* told soldiers: 'YOU'LL BE SCARED. Sure you'll be scared. Before you go into battle, you'll be frightened at the uncertainty, at the thought of being killed.' Lance-Corporal Stuart Bain of Y Company, 45 Commando, echoed this when he remarked of his own experience of battle in the Falklands that 'people were frightened before it began rather than while it was going on'.

Apprehension before battle is by no means a unique phenomenon. Most of us experience at least some of the physical symptoms of apprehension before we embark upon any testing activity, and usually discover that they disappear once the trial is under way. A student quoted in D. Mechanic's *Students under Stress* said of an examination: 'Taking it is not as bad as anticipating it. It's not nearly so bad. You don't have time to worry while you are doing it.' The crucial point about apprehension is that it is not directed towards the solution of a real problem or to coping with a specific threat. Lazarus points out that the very concept of threat involves numerous cognitive processes – learning, perception, memory, judgment and thought. Sometimes this process of appraisal persuades us that the threat is more serious than is in fact the case. A study of air war and emotional stress suggested that air raids on Britain during the Second World War actually produced relief, because people 'had expected the attacks to be more devastating than they actually turned out to be'. Conversely, a very serious threat may not be perceived at all, because we do not know enough about it to carry out the process of appraisal.

A soldier who is unfamiliar with battle may invest combat with far more alarming characteristics than it turns out to possess, and may, as is so often the case, be surprised to discover how well he copes with it. But an experienced soldier, whose threat appraisal is based upon considerable objective evidence, may sustain as much stress in a relatively minor action late in his career as he did in his first battle. An experiment involving the administration of sham and real injections to patients lends support to the view that it is the individual's appraisal of the threat, rather than the real nature of the threat, which gives rise to anxiety. It concluded: 'the actual pain of the needle injection is not a primary factor ... Rather, the critical stimulation seemed to result from the frank realisation by the patient that he was to receive the injection and from the distress associated therewith.'

Freud distinguished between what he termed 'objective anxiety', or fear stemming from a genuine and identifiable threat, and 'neurotic anxiety', a free-floating, objectless anxiety, based upon a conflict between instinct and conscience. There is a learned dispute amongst psychologists as to whether or not anxiety serves to signal danger to an individual and, in so doing, to provoke a response: Freud argued that it did. What is clear, however, is that apprehension – while not necessarily synonymous with neurotic anxiety – does involve a struggle between the demands of the instinct and the dictates of conscience.

This is especially true before a soldier's first battle, when his apprehension focuses upon the conflict between an instinctive prompting to seek safety and a desire not to deviate from the standards expected of him by his leaders and comrades. John Dollard's research indicated that 'fear of being a coward' was the most strongly-felt sensation on the part of troops going into action for the first time. Other major fears – of being crippled, killed, captured and tortured, or painfully wounded – were markedly less common. Yet on the other hand only a very small proportion of veteran soldiers were concerned at the possibility of being a coward: for them, the fear of being crippled was infinitely more serious.

The letters and diaries of soldiers, and interviews with veterans, leave no doubt as to the pervasive nature of fear of failure. In January 1917, shortly before going into action for the first time, Captain J. E. H. Neville wrote to his father: 'The only thing I'm not certain about is whether I may get the wind up and show it. I'm afraid of being afraid.' 'My main hope', said Geoffrey Stavert, an artillery officer in Tunisia in 1942-3, 'was not to do anything which would let myself or my family down, and to put up a good appearance in front of the troops.' Charles MacDonald had the same problem. 'I must not appear afraid,' he wrote. 'I must give the men confidence in me despite the fact that they know I'm inexperienced.' Raleigh Trevelyan begged God not to let him disgrace himself, and, later, wrote:

> I remember father saying on embarkation leave that the worst part of battle was wondering how you were going to behave in front of other people ... I don't think even now I really fear death, or even the process of dying. It is only the thought of whether or not I shall acquit myself honourably that obsesses me.

This desire to appear a man amongst men, and the fear that one might fail the acid test of battle was widespread amongst members of the two Parachute battalions in the Falklands. A company commander in 2 Para believed that his soldiers were sustained by the desire not to let their comrades down, or to be seen to fail. 'Their own self-respect', he said, 'would not permit them to funk.' But this compelling need to live up to the regiment's proud traditions created powerful anxiety on the eve of the landings. Most of the soldiers I interviewed acknowledged that they were very frightened indeed before the battle started, and for many of them the greatest fear was not of being killed or wounded, but of 'bottling out', of showing cowardice. This supports John Ellis's comment on the Second World War that 'the fear of showing fear was often more powerful than the fear of death itself', and, in a deeper sense, echoes Montaigne's assertion that: 'The thing in the world I am most afraid of is fear.'

An individual's rank has an ambivalent effect upon his pre-battle apprehension. On the one hand, to all a leader's other concerns is added the worry that men's lives depend upon his action. Raleigh Trevelyan railed against the fact that twenty-seven lives were so dependent upon him, Philip Caputo was nervous that he might make 'some stupid mistake when the platoon hit the LZ', and Charles MacDonald found his role as a company commander made harder because of his 'love and admiration' for his soldiers. The commanding officer of a parachute battalion in the Falklands emphasised that his overriding emotion was the fear that his decisions might get soldiers killed needlessly. This strain built up to fever pitch after he had issued his orders and before the fighting started, at the very time when there was little that he could do to influence events.

On the other hand, an officer or NCO is often so busy with the chain of orders and preparation that leads up to battle that he will spend much of his time considering the practical problems of movement, supply, co-ordinating supporting fire, and so on, and will have little time available for general speculation. Moreover, a desire to preserve his status encourages him not to give way to anxiety. Sergeant-Major Michael Reed, who served with the Duke of Wellington's Regiment in France in 1940 felt afraid at the prospect of combat but, 'being a warrant officer I dared not show it'. Jack Chaffer was a lance-sergeant by the time he went into action, and this, he thought, 'helped me no end. One was expected to lead, and this I did to the best of my ability.' 'Everyone is horrified,' reflected Lieutenant-Colonel John Roberts, a company sergeant-major in the infantry for much of the Second World War, 'but so many including myself are driven on by pride, one cannot show oneself to be afraid in front of others. Subordinates look to their leaders for example.' Nevertheless, it was during the time between the issue of orders and the moment of crossing the start line that he was at his most anxious, to the extent of finding it 'difficult to take food, especially if I was not fully occupied'.

There are occasions when this desire to preserve status is quite literally stronger than the fear of death. For many centuries physical courage was a gentleman's essential attribute, and failure to display it would be certain to result in social ostracism. Lieutenant-Colonel Lord Portarlington was ruined by his absence from his regiment when it charged at Waterloo: he resigned, purchased a commission in another regiment, but was shunned by his brother officers and died broken and penniless. Captain Jahleel Brenton Carey was court-martialled for failing to prevent the death of Prince Napoleon in Zululand in 1879. The court's sentence of cashiering was quashed by the adjutant-general, but Carey was finished. 'He rejoined his regiment, which did not want him, and was put in Coventry for the rest of his life,' wrote Donald R. Morris. 'Officers turned their backs on him when he approached; conversations he tried to join ceased. He had neither the sense nor the courage to resign, and six years later he died in Bombay.'

Insistence on displaying the 'bottom' expected of a gentleman was sometimes taken to fatal extremes. At the Battle of Hopton Heath in 1643 the Earl of Northampton was unhorsed and surrounded by his enemies: his helmet was struck off, and he was bidden to surrender. 'I scorn to take quarter from such base rogues and rebels as you are,' rejoined the Earl, and was immediately cut down. Less dramatic but equally lethal was the behaviour of the officers of the 23rd Regiment at the Alma: after their regiment had taken the Great Redoubt, they stood about chatting under a brisk fire, and many of them paid the supreme penalty for carrying the manners of the drawing-room on to the battlefield.

Behaviour of this sort is not confined to individuals striving to conform to the standards of a social class. Soldiers often believe that their own status or their regiment's norms demand that they run added risks. A Marine sergeant in Vietnam declined to take cover, telling his platoon commander: 'I'm a Marine NCO, sir, and I ain't gonna go low crawling on my belly.' He was wounded moments later. But Sergeant Ingram was in good company: a Marine general went on record as saying that digging in was 'not the Marine way', an attitude which encouraged the journalist Michael Herr to suggest that the Marine Corps was the finest instrument ever devised for killing young Americans.

Typical of this attitude is the adherence to conspicuous dress in the field. A British officer who removed his epaulettes and took the plume and plate off his shako before an action in India was the victim of 'ridicule and criticism', and left his regiment soon afterwards. When Robert Graves joined the

2nd Royal Welch Fusiliers in France in 1915, he was accused of wearing 'a wind-up tunic', with his badges of rank inconspicuously on his shoulders rather than prominently on his cuffs, and was sent off to the master-tailor without delay. As the war progressed, British officers took to wearing privates' uniforms and equipment when in the line. Not all approved: Captain G. H. Greenwell lamented the arrival of a new brigadier who insisted on the practice. 'It is a sad departure', he complained, 'from the "Nelson touch" – all decorations won in battle and worn in battle.'

More recently, the parachutist's red beret has been an object of similar devotion. During the Indo-China War French paras considered that the practice of turning the beret inside out so as to look less conspicuous was 'cowardly', and on 6 May, a day before Dien Bien Phu fell, Colonel Langlais and Lieutenant-Colonel Bigeard defiantly wore their red berets when visiting their fellow paras on *Éliane*. British marines and parachutists wisely wore steel helmets in action in the Falklands, but replaced them with berets as soon as it was over. Surgeon Commander Rick Jolly, commanding the Falklands Field Hospital at Ajax Bay, commented sadly that several of the dead of 2 Para, killed at Goose Green, had spare victory berets tucked away in their clothing.

However much a soldier's self-respect helps him to resist the stresses of apprehension, the tension that builds up, especially before a set-piece action, can become almost unbearable. As he waited for battle to open at Waterloo, the Earl of Albemarle's sixteen-year-old son could not help remembering a conversation between his father and the prize-fighter Henry Pearce, the 'Game Chicken', on the eve of a contest. 'Well, Pearce, how do you feel?' asked the Earl. 'Why, my Lord, I wish it was *fit*,' replied Pearce. Norman Gladden, waiting to go into action with the Royal Northumberland Fusiliers at Ypres in 1917, found the tension so oppressive that 'I was literally consumed by a fatalistic desire to do something desperate to pierce the shroud by which we seemed to be divided from some awful truth.' 'It is a strange experience lying there waiting for zero,' recalled W. H. A. Groom, 'and one is very mentally alert – over-tensed, I suppose, beyond being frightened, just resigned to the inevitable.'

The start of an action may come as a surprise, or may be the culmination of much planning and preparation, but in either case the effects of hostile fire are varied. It is sometimes difficult for a man to accept that long-range small-arms fire is actually dangerous, and for many soldiers their first experience of coming under fire is one of surprise and disbelief. When Captain Walter Bloem's company withered under the scorching British musketry at Mons, his first thought was:

> Where was the enemy? Not the faintest sign of him anywhere, nothing except the cows that had become restless and were gadding about. One, as I watched, rose on its hind legs, and collapsed in a heap on the ground. And still the bullets kept coming over, over our heads and all about us.

Gordon Cormack thought that his own baptism of fire, a little more than half a century after Mons, was 'somewhat unreal. One moment everything was peaceful. Guns sounded a bit pathetic until it occurred to me that I could get killed.' 'It honestly wasn't until I saw some people fall overboard from the next craft that I realised we were actually being shot at,' remarked Major Dan Flunder, adjutant of 48 Commando on D-Day, and Sergeant John Shineton of the Fort Garry Horse, landing on the same beach, took some seconds to associate small holes in the canvas screen of his tank with the fact that he was being machine-gunned.

Added to this is a surprisingly powerful conviction that, in some profound way, the whole business is a ghastly mistake. Lieutenant David Tinker, a naval officer killed in the South Atlantic, was at least half-serious when he wrote of his first experience of shelling: 'They must be mad. Don't they know it's very unsafe shooting things at other people?' Fritz Nagel, a German gunner first under fire at Termonde in August 1914, was equally perplexed. 'Those people on the other side were trying to kill us,' he wrote. 'It seemed incredible to me.'

Sergeant Lee Childress of the 206th Assault Helicopter Company felt much the same in Vietnam. 'The first time you were under fire', he recalled,

> you thought, 'How the fuck can they do this to me? If only I could talk to the cocksuckers firing at me, we'd get along, everything would be all right.' I just had the overwhelming feeling that if I could talk to these people, that they really are the same as I am, that it's not us that are doing it ...

Similar thoughts ran through Philip Caputo's mind.

> My first reaction, rooted in the illusion that anyone trying to kill me must have a personal motive, was: 'Why does he want to kill *me?* What did I ever do to *him?*' A moment later, I realized there was nothing personal about it. All he saw was a man in the wrong uniform. He was trying to kill me and he would try again because that was his job.

Although the soldier in action is in immediate physical danger, the very fact that he is at last committed to battle often comes as a relief. Philip Caputo found that: 'The nervousness had left me the moment I got into the helicopter, and I felt happier than I ever had.' For Lance-Corporal George Mitchell, heading for the beach at Gallipoli in 1915, action banished anxiety. 'The key was being turned in the lock of the lid of hell,' he wrote. 'Some men crouched in the crowded boat, some sat up nonchalantly, some laughed and joked, while others cursed with ferocious delight ... Fear was not at home.' A fellow Australian described how, going into action on the Western Front in 1916, 'for the first few minutes I felt sick, then as steady as a rock', and another remembered that his 'knees knocked when the barrage opened, but after the start all trepidation vanished'.

For some, action comes as more than merely a relief from tension: it provides proof that their worst fears will not be realised, and that they will be able to stand the test of battle. Professor R. H. Tawney, serving as a sergeant in a New Army battalion of the Manchester Regiment on the Somme in 1916, found the first few moments of the advance – so fatal to so many – a time of almost sublime satisfaction.

> I hadn't gone ten yards before I felt a load fall from me ... I had been worried by the thought: suppose one should lose one's head and get other men cut up! Suppose one's legs should take fright and refuse to move! Now I knew it was all right. I shouldn't be frightened and I shouldn't lose my head. Just imagine the joy of that discovery!

Lieutenant J. H. Allen, later to be killed at Gallipoli, was positively exhilarated by his first action.

> I felt an overwhelming elation. It was not so much that one had left the firing line as that one had been in it. I often think of H. Benson's story of the man who was to be tortured and the agony of his dread. When he was put on the wheel they saw he smiled. His suffering was less than his suspense. Full of wretchedness and suspense as the last few days have been, I have enjoyed them. They have been intensely interesting. They have been wonderfully inspiring.

A soldier in 2 Para was understandably less literary in his description of Goose Green. 'Once it started,' he said, 'I stopped being really frightened: it was a right bastard, but I knew I could hack it.'

A View of the Field

His prose tracking almost like a film camera, Clausewitz describes the sensations a novice might experience as he moved across a battlefield, past the commander-in-chief – surrounded by bursting shells and trundling cannon balls – past the divisional commander, past the brigadier – where grape-shot rattles on the roofs of houses and cannon balls howl overhead – to the front line. There:

the infantry endures the hammering for hours with incredible steadfastness. The air is filled with hissing bullets that sound like a sharp crack if they pass close to one's head. For a final shock, the sight of men being killed and mutilated moves our pounding hearts to awe and pity.

The observer will undoubtedly sense, writes Clausewitz, that here ideas are governed by other factors, and 'the light of reason is refracted in a manner quite different from that which is normal in academic speculation'. In short, the battlefield is a unique and alien land, with logic, rules and values all of its own.

We have seen how pictorial representations of battle fail to do justice to a battlefield which, thanks to a variety of technological innovations like rifled weapons and smokeless powder, seems increasingly empty. S. L. A. Marshall believed: 'The battlefield is cold. It is the lonesomest place which men share together.' Once a man comes within range of the enemy's small-arms, he experiences a transition which is 'utterly abnormal. He had expected to see action. He sees nothing. There is nothing to be seen. The fire comes out of nowhere. He knows that it is fire because the sounds are unmistakable. But that is all he knows for certain.' A British field artillery officer looked with disbelief towards the German trenches on the first day of the Somme. 'Far as I could see not a single soldier could be seen,' he said, 'not a movement of any sort. Could it be that we held these trenches?' 'Battles of the First World War were rarely spectacular, since the shrapnel barrage obscured visibility,' asserted Charles Carrington, describing a bombardment during the same battle. 'A great noise and smoke-cloud filled the valley in which now and then one saw distant figures moving, aimlessly it seemed, like ants in a disturbed anthill.' Even a middle-ranking officer like Denys Reitz had very much a worm's eye view of the German offensive of March 1918. 'We were at any moment able to see how the tide ebbed and flowed beyond our immediate neighbourhood,' he wrote, 'and people in England knew more of its progress from day to day than we did.'

Two of the survivors of the German March offensive interviewed by Martin Middlebrook confirmed that the enemy was rarely seen and even less frequently engaged with small arms. 'I'd been in France ten months,' remarked Private F. Beardsell, 'and this was the first time I'd fired at the enemy.' During the battle Second-Lieutenant H. Jones shot some Germans with his revolver. 'That', he acknowledged, 'was the only occasion on which I shot any Germans in two and a half years of front-line soldiering.'

It is small wonder that rumour, which Shakespeare aptly called 'a pipe blown by surmises, jealousies, conjectures', flourishes in an environment where genuine information is notoriously hard to come by, and where there is a craving for news of any sort. David Jones's description of the bubbling pot of trench-rumour has an ageless ring. 'Up the line on Thursday afternoon – Monday – Thursday morning – Saturday night – back to the base – back to England – another part of the field – Corporal B. just said so – Signaller X. heard the Captain of "D" talking to ... ' As the long snake of 45 Commando stretched out across the Falklands peat on its way to Teal Inlet, a great whoop went up: 'Galtieri's dead – the Argies have surrendered.' It was eventually discovered, not without a little acrimony, that this rumour had originated in some wag corrupting 'Air-raid warning red' to 'Galtieri's dead'. Thereafter it was usually possible to raise a smile by the quip 'Galtieri's bought a shed', or, when contemplating a ration biscuit, 'I'll have a Garibaldi instead.' Rumour has an important psychological function in 'explaining and relieving emotional tensions felt by individuals'. But it often damages morale when the all too common rumours of peace, rest or leave are dispelled by a crueller reality.

The battlefield, given colour and texture by the rich palette of artists, writers and film-makers, is, as we have already observed, empty and drab to many of those who live upon it. It is sometimes so unspectacular that it may not even be identifiable as a battlefield. 'What impresses me most about the front line', wrote Woodrow Wyatt about Normandy, 'is not the violence but the absence of it.' Alan Moorehead came dangerously close to missing the front line altogether.

We rode through the whole American frontline position and got beyond the advanced scouts to within, I think, two turns of the road of the Germans, not only without being stopped but actually without seeing anybody. The week before, four German colonels had come down from Paris to look around and had similarly driven through both German and American positions. They pulled up in some bewilderment in our rear areas, thus making it from the fleshpots of Paris to the prisoner of war camps in Normandy in something under five hours without the least physical inconvenience.

There was one twenty-four-hour period in May 1953 when only thirty-seven enemy were seen on the whole of the US 8th Army front in Korea. During the Vietnam War, it was perfectly possible for a soldier – even in an infantry unit – to spend his year in-country without seeing a single enemy. One said, 'I ain't never seen a gook yet that was alive,' and Tim O'Brien, a rifleman in a front-line unit, saw the enemy only once, in a brief night action.

This is not to say that emptiness is a constant feature of even a modern battlefield. There were times in Korea when the empty hills around the 37th Parallel disgorged swarms of Chinese or North Korean infantry, and an American soldier in Vietnam, out of contact with the enemy for so much of his time, risked encountering them when he least expected it. Photographs of the anti-tank ditch in front of the Israeli position on the Golan Heights in 1973 show clusters of Syrian tanks, looking for all the world like models on a sand-table ravaged by a spiteful child, and Lieutenant-Colonel Avigdor Kahalani's account of the battle bears testimony to the frenetic intensity of the Golan fighting.

But for much of the time, even though the enemy's small-arms fire may be snapping past his head or hostile armour-piercing rounds clanging into the turret of his tank, the individual soldier sees comparatively little. In his novel *Red Eagle*, James Lucas, himself a Second World War infantryman, writes: 'The mental make up of any infantryman includes a peculiar detachment from events which are taking place around him. No infantryman sees at any one time during an attack any more than 200 metres ahead of him or much on either side of him.'

Tunnel vision is one of the consequences of stress. It is easy, even under the relatively banal stresses of everyday life, to experience this dangerous tendency to concentrate upon one particular item to the exclusion of all others. On the battlefield this blinkered view is also partly the result of men's desire not to look too closely at dangers they can do little about. A company commander in 2 Para watched his men as they lay down under fire at Goose Green, awaiting the order to move forward. 'Some soldiers stayed still and pressed their faces to the ground,' he said. 'Others were very animated, and pushed themselves up on their elbows to look around.' The smoke from explosions and from burning vehicles or houses, the improving techniques of camouflage and concealment, and the narrow field of view imposed by weapon sights all help to restrict the soldier's vision: despite the great number of Syrian tanks attacking Kahalani's battalion on the Golan, he often found it difficult to point out targets to his gunner.

Even when a man can see a good deal of what is going on around him, he is unlikely to be able to remember it accurately or to put his recollections into context. The reasons for this stem as much from the organisation of armies as they do from the workings of the human brain. It is only in the comparatively recent past that the average soldier was likely to see – or to understand – a map, or to be given a glimpse of the broad strategic picture by a verbal briefing or printed news sheet.

For the average British regular of 1914, for example, the period from August to November was a mosaic of exhausting marches, sharp and confusing battles, and rough and dangerous trench warfare. An NCO in the Royal Horse Guards believed that: 'We were told so little of the particular part we were to play in any action, that we just felt we were a number.' W. H. A. Groom never saw a map in twenty months in France, even as an NCO. It is almost twenty years since I paid my first visit to Ypres, impelled by a curiosity almost as morbid as it was academic. After the town fire brigade had sounded the Last Post under the Menin Gate, I caught sight of a tiny but upright figure, the pocket of whose blazer bore the sphinx badge of the South Wales Borderers, with the trio of First World War medals, 'Pip, Squeak and Wilfred', jingling above it. We fell into conversation and, slightly concerned that I might stir memories best left undisturbed, I inquired nervously about his time in the Salient. 'Lousy as rooks, we wass, lousy as rooks,' he said. 'Marching, shooting, bayonet fighting: lousy as rooks.' On discovering that he had been in the 1st Battalion of his regiment, which had played a distinguished part in the desperate defence of Gheluvelt Château on 31 October 1914, I asked him if he remembered it. 'Dunno, boy,' he replied. 'I never saw a map, so I dunno where we wass. The officers had maps, and we followed them everywhere. Lousy as rooks, though, I can tell you. Lousy as bloody rooks.'

Years later, visiting Ypres with an Old Contemptible whose battalion, 1 Queen's, had been reduced to two officers and twelve men in the same action, I asked him what it had been like.

> We went up a straight paved road [the Menin Road]. There were buggers with spiked hats, lying in the fields like sheep. We gave them stick when they came on: then some bastard shot me in the head, and I went back up the road with the walking wounded. I never saw any of my mates again.

That is an eyewitness account of a crucial moment in the First Battle of Ypres, when the fate of the war on the Western Front trembled in the balance, with only a few tired men – my informant amongst them – between the Germans and the Channel ports. He, too, had never seen a map.

The belief that an individual soldier can do little to influence the outcome of a battle springs from this inability to take a broader view of the field. There are occasions when the action of a particular individual, or of a small knot of determined men, has a profound effect upon the outcome of a battle. Wellington said that the most dangerous moment at Waterloo came when the giant *Sous-Lieutenant* Legros led a charge which burst through the main gate of Hougoumont. Lieutenant-Colonel James Macdonell and Sergeant James Graham closed the gate by main force, and Macdonell's guardsmen dealt with every Frenchman who had entered. Wellington declared: 'The success at the battle of Waterloo depended on the closing of the gates of Hougoumont.' But there is no suggestion that Macdonell or Graham believed that they had done more than do their best to win the gutter brawl inside the smoke-filled courtyard.

Even middle-piece officers, with access to maps and information, rarely believe that their actions are likely to prove of any broad relevance. Lieutenant-Colonel Brian Clark, who served with the Royal Irish Fusiliers during the Second World War, had a brisk answer to my question on the degree to which he felt that he could affect the outcome of any particular battle. 'Never felt it,' he wrote. 'Just did my bit for the Regiment.' A Second World War platoon commander affirmed that 'battle was too confused, too localised, too personal to give any thought to the outcome of anything but one's own "private" frontage'. Brigadier D. J. B. Houchin, a battalion commander in Italy, believed that he could affect the outcome of a battle 'Not at all. One was part of a larger fight.' Marshall quotes Major William R. Desobry, who commanded in the crucial action at Noville Wood which led to the saving of Bastogne: 'It was just another local affair. Not a man present had any idea of the importance of the engagement.'

So it is not merely that men forget. Very often they have no big picture to remember, and recall only disconnected snatches of unrelated events glimpsed over the parapet of a trench, through a rifle-sight or across the tail-board of a truck. Sometimes it is not until after the war that they discover where they were and what they achieved. The process of recall is also affected by postwar discussions and the very way in which military history – particularly official history – is written. There is a marked tendency to assume that because something happened, it happened for a reason and as the result of a plan: *post hoc ergo propter hoc*. Just as nature abhors a vacuum, so too military history tends to abhor chance and accident. During the process of interviewing veterans of the Falklands War, I was conscious of the way in which a carapace of accepted fact hardened almost before my eyes. One officer acknowledged a tendency to make behaviour seem more reasoned in retrospect than it had appeared at the time, and admitted that it was easy to suggest more planning and centralised control than he had recognised in the confusing reality of the moment. In a sense he was endorsing a comment by Charles Carrington, who remarked of the Battle of Broodseinde – part of the Third Battle of Ypres – that: 'What surprises me is that historians have elevated it into a tactical masterpiece like Messines. It was just all-in wrestling in the mud.'

The soldier's narrow view of the field, his tendency to add the experiences of his comrades to his own to form an image thick with accretions, and the overwhelming human desire to lend form and meaning to a bewildering series of random experiences, all help to colour the image of battle. Lieutenant Bill Little of the Fort Garry Horse summed up the process perfectly.

> Most people in battle have a narrow outlook. They're only concentrating on that which they are told to do or have to do. And as time goes, then as all battles do, they get embellished with the things that you hear from other people – your picture starts to build ... You actually develop from other people's ideas or thoughts, your own ideas. So you end up with a thought that may not be actual fact.

And the mind plays tricks of its own. Horrific events may be excised altogether by traumatic amnesia. William Manchester retained only snatches of the nightmare of Okinawa: 'Some flickers of unreal recollection remain: standing at the

foot of the hill, arms akimbo, quavering with senseless excitement and grinning maniacally.' Guy Sajer found it:

> difficult even to try to remember moments during which
> nothing is considered, foreseen or understood, when there
> is nothing under a steel helmet but an astonishingly empty
> head and a pair of eyes which translate nothing more than
> would the eyes of an animal facing mortal danger.

John Muir, a rifleman with 2nd Battalion, 1st Marines in
Vietnam in 1966, told Al Santoli how, during a pitched battle
with North Vietnamese regulars in the De-Militarised Zone:
'I lost my entire squad and I kind of went berserk. At least
I'm told I went berserk. I don't have the foggiest idea what
I was doing. I was told that I was throwing rocks at people.
I was really gung ho. I have no memory of it.'

Remembered events often have a dream- or film-like quality, like clips of film assembled haphazardly from the
cutting-room floor. Marc Bloch, an NCO in a French infantry
battalion in the summer of 1914, recalled his first battles as
'a discontinuous series of images, vivid in themselves but badly
arranged like a reel of movie film that showed here and there
large gaps and the unintended reversal of several scenes'. The
future Field-Marshal Alanbrooke, watching a British attack
on the Somme, wrote: 'One felt as if one was in a dream, or
that one was watching some extraordinary cinematograph
film, and that it could not all be true.' Norman Gladden,
advancing behind the barrage at the Battle of Menin Road
Ridge in 1917, experienced

> a peculiar, almost dreamlike illusion. Though my feet were
> moving with all the energy needed to carry me with my
> burden across the ground, I felt that they were, in fact,
> rooted to the earth, and that it was my surroundings that
> were moving all of their own accord.

Private Matthew's recollections of Iwo Jima were similarly
sporadic:

although I desperately wanted to form a picture of what it was like, what I had come through with was the recollection of my mental prodding and a few snapshots, disconnected in time and space, some of them faded as with age and out of focus and only one or two sharp and clear.

Spec 5 John A. David described an ambush in Vietnam as 'like a bad dream or a movie ... We couldn't be living it.' A Marine, wounded in the legs at Hue, told Michel Herr: 'I *hate* this movie.' Gad, an Israeli tank gunner, thought that the image in his gunsight resembled a television picture. 'You see it all as if it were happening on a TV screen,' he said. 'It occurred to me at the time; I see someone running and I shoot at him, and he falls, and it all looks like something on TV. I don't see people, that's one good thing about it.'

Often the mental camera zooms in on an apparently unimportant aspect of events. A Commando subaltern at Dieppe spent the landing wrestling with his trousers, which had fallen down: 'it is the trivial events which remain in mind, such as the descent of trousers'. As Captain Tony Farrar-Hockley of the Gloucesters sheltered from artillery fire which fell near his position on the Imjin River in Korea, he noticed a peculiar black and yellow beetle crawling up the wall of the trench. The creature stuck in his mind, although it was trivial in the context of the day's desperate battle. When Miles Tripp tracked down Ray Parke, a fellow member of his wartime Lancaster crew, they discussed their experiences: 'He had, he said, forgotten so much. He had a vivid memory of Les warming his hands on a mug of tea at breakfast each day but it was difficult to remember anything about the flying.' A soldier in 2 Para could recall few of the details of the fighting at Goose Green, but remembered that Gerry Rafferty's 'Baker Street' had spun round his brain throughout the battle. While Robert Graves waited on the firestep at Loos, his mind was a blank except for the popular song 'I Do Like a S'nice S'mince Pie'.

Frank Richardson asserts that the modern soldier's tunnel vision means that he will see fewer ghastly sights than his ancestors. 'The soldiers of the future,' he wrote, 'widely dispersed on their battlefields, are unlikely to see horrors like those seen by Marlborough's and Wellington's men.' This is not entirely true. In the first place, many of the horrors witnessed by soldiers on the battlefields of the eighteenth and nineteenth centuries were seen at close range. Once battle was joined, the infantryman of the Napoleonic period had little opportunity to look about him, even if the clouds of powder-smoke permitted observation. The crisis and the terror were alike very personal:

> a bayonet went through between my side and my clothes, to my knapsack, which stopped its progress. The Frenchman to whom the bayonet belonged fell, pierced by a musket ball from my rear-rank man. Whilst freeing myself from the bayonet, a ball took off part of my right shoulder wing and killed my rear-rank man, who fell upon me.

The modern soldier is likely to be spared the dreadful vision of a crowded battlefield the morning after. Sergeant Wheeler of the 51st wandered around Hougoumont the day after Waterloo. The orchard was 'full of dead and wounded Frenchmen. I went into the farmhouse, what a sight. Inside the yard the Guards lay in heaps, and many who had been wounded inside or near the buildings were roasted.' Yet a modern battlefield provides sights which are less hideous only in terms of scale. A Second World War medical officer blanched, nearly forty years after the event, as he spoke of extracting burned crewmen, their bodies still smoking, from their knocked-out Sherman on the Bourguébus Ridge in Normandy, and a parachute officer thought that the mutilation inflicted by a shell on the body of one of his soldiers was so dreadful that he did his best to bandage it so that others would not be dismayed by the sight.

Dispersion and a restricted field of view may not spare the soldier much in the way of horror. They will, however, increase his feeling of isolation, loneliness and uncertainty. Although the tactical disadvantages of dense formations are legion, there can be no doubting their value in psychological terms. 'It is perfectly clear', affirmed Wilfred Trotter, 'that a densely crowded formation has psychological advantages in the face of danger, which enable quite ordinary beings to perform what are in fact prodigies of valour.' Marshall made precisely the same point. 'Man is a gregarious animal,' he declared. 'He wants company. In his hour of greatest danger his herd instinct drives him towards his fellows. It is a source of comfort to him to be close to other men: it makes danger more endurable.'

The almost inevitable result of this need for company is that soldiers under fire tend to bunch. 'It is strange how men creep together for protection,' reported an Australian NCO, describing an attack on the Western Front. 'Soon, instead of four paces interval between the men, we came down to lying alongside each other, and no motioning could make them move apart.' Untried troops most need the sense of security provided by bunching. Experienced soldiers usually bunch less. This is partly because they realise, at a purely rational level, that a clump of soldiers offers a good target. It also reflects a deep-seated trust in their comrades: they have confidence in a support that may be invisible but is none the less perceptible. Training alone does not create this trust: a Canadian officer saw the dead of a well-trained British assault battalion on the beach in Normandy stacked like cordwood where their bunched formations had been raked by fire.

As men realise that they are under the enemy's fire, their natural impulse is to duck or to take cover. Colonel Ameller of the 66th of the Line, addressing his officers and sergeant-majors during the battle of Rezonville, took exception to the fact that they all ducked whenever a shell rustled overhead, and sharply ordered them to stop. He was, though, more polite than Colonel Lepic of the Horse Grenadiers, who, under fire at Eylau sixty-three years before, had shouted, 'Heads up! Those are bullets, not turds!' Learning to distinguish between effective fire and sporadic shelling or musketry is something which comes only with experience. Tom Rogers reckoned that it took him three months in Korea to become accustomed to such things. 'The sounds of war, incoming or outgoing mortars or shells, the fall of bullets around became so matter of fact,' he wrote. 'Even brewing up in the midst of it all.'

Overcoming the paralysis produced by hostile fire is not easy. Marshall investigated the tendency for American infantry in the central Pacific theatre to go to ground whenever they were engaged. He discovered that men became lost and uncertain, undergoing complete 'moral disintegration', when they took cover.

> Once halted, even if there has been no damage, the line never moves as strongly or as willingly again. After three or four such fruitless delays, men become morally spent rather than physically rested. All impetus is lost and the attack might better be called off for the day.

A number of factors prevail upon soldiers to advance under such circumstances, as we shall see in the following chapters: inspiring leadership, thorough training and tight group cohesion all play their part.

Above all, pressing on in the face of effective enemy fire requires considerable personal determination. Private C. A. McAnulty of the 2nd Australian Battalion kept a detailed diary in Gallipoli, and scribbled what were in fact his last thoughts during an attack.

> There was a clear space of 100 yards to cross without a patch of cover. I can't realise how I got across it, I seemed to be in a sort of trance. The rifle & machine gun fire was hellish. I remember dropping down and when we reached their trenches, looked around & saw Frank & 3 other men alongside me ... We were right out in the open ... I yelled out to the other 4 chaps, 'This is suicide boys. I'm going to make a jump for it.' I thought they said alright we'll follow. I sprang to my feet in one jump.

Private McAnulty was killed as he wrote.[2]

When soldiers do move forward, it is rarely with straight

back and measured tread. Michael Howard's description of
the Prussian Guard attacking across the bare uplands of Gravelotte on 18 August 1870 in the face of fierce rifle fire – 'as if
into a hailstorm, shoulders hunched, heads bowed' – is remarkably apt. The formidable Dr Bean, author of the Australian official history of the First World War, who spent his
time at the front, running the risks of the men whose achievements he was to immortalise, tells how the Australians advanced at Cape Helles: 'heads down, as if into fierce rain,
some men holding shovels before their faces like umbrellas in
a rain storm. The firing was by then intense, spurts of dust
rising from the plain like drops splashing in a thunder-shower.'
Alferez Peter Kemp of the Spanish Foreign Legion used precisely the same simile: the bullets 'seemed to come like rain,
with all the hiss and spatter of a heavy storm'. A soldier of
the 9th Massachusetts remembered how Union infantry, advancing up the slope at Fredericksburg in the face of a searing
fire, 'stood as though they were breasting a storm of rain and
sleet, their faces and bodies being only half turned to the
storm, with their shoulders shrugged'. Howard Pyle's painting
of the charge of the Minnesota regiments on Shy's Hill at
Nashville in December 1864 catches exactly this pose: the
soldiers look for all the world as if raindrops rather than bullets were the danger. John Fairley, writing of Arnhem, described 'that peculiar half-crouch that soldiers almost naturally slip into when they imagine themselves to be under
fire'.

These small knots of men, scuttling hunched against the
fire, or sheltering behind such cover as can be found, are
assailed by noise which is often, as Alanbrooke said of that at
the Battle of the Somme, 'unimaginable'. The sounds of battle
fill a broad spectrum from the soft moan of a wounded man
to the ear-splitting crash of a shell-burst. With practice, it is
possible to distinguish the noise made by various sorts of shell,
as Charles Carrington tells us.

Every gun and every kind of projectile had its own personality ... Sometimes a field-gun shell would leap jubilantly

with the pop of a Champagne cork from its muzzle, fly over with a steady buzzing crescendo, and burst with a fully expected bang; sometimes a shell would be released from a distant battery of heavies to roll across a huge arc of sky, gathering speed and noise like an approaching express train, ponderous and certain ... Some shells whistled, others shrieked, others wobbled through space gurgling like water poured from a decanter.

Charles Sorley thought that a quickfirer sounded like a cow coughing, and other guns resembled motor bikes, trains, or buffaloes with whooping cough.

George Orwell found that the shells fired by an old Nationalist heavy gun sounded 'like nothing so much as a man riding along on a bicycle and whistling', and Charlton Ogburn wrote of the 'toboggan slide rustle of air overhead' produced by his first hostile shell. 'Some shells scream, some whiz, some whistle, and others whir,' wrote the American cartoonist Bill Mauldin, who served as a sergeant in Italy and north-west Europe. 'Most flat-trajectory shells sound like rapidly ripped canvas. Howitzer shells seem to have a two-toned whisper.' The 'feathery shuffle' or 'delicate shush-shush' of the mortar bomb was especially sinister, giving little warning before the 'flat, grating, guttural crash' as the projectile arrived.

Small-arms fire similarly taxes men's descriptive powers. There is a clear distinction between the thump of the weapon being fired, and the crack of the bullet passing overhead. Major Martin Lindsay of the Gordon Highlanders, with a regular officer's understated matter-of-factness, compared being under close-range machine-gun fire with 'being in the butts during an LMG classification practice'. Patrick MacGill of the London Irish waxed more poetic: 'The air was vicious with bullets; a million invisible birds flapped their wings very close to my face.' David Jones, with his usual feel for *le mot juste*, described the vicious snap of a round passing 'like whip by angry ostler cracked'. Stan Goff wrote of the 'weird, shrill type of sound' produced by the AK–47, describing it as 'di-

dididididi shoom shoom'. On modern battlefields the din of shells and small-arms fire is punctuated by the distinctive sounds of mechanised warfare – the squeaky rattle of tank tracks above the rumble of engines, the metallic clang of APDS rounds hitting armour, the whup-whup-whup of helicopters and the reverberating boom of high-performance aircraft.

Some sounds have gone for ever. Lieutenant von Prittwitz recalled the rattling noise made by canister balls clattering against bayonets at Kolin in 1757, and Marshal Canrobert remembered the 'toc' of rifle-bullets hitting breastplates as the *Cuirassiers* of the Imperial Guard charged to destruction at Rezonville. Hand-to-hand fighting with edged weapons had a curiously tinny sound: the clang of British sabres striking French cuirasses at Waterloo reminded Sergeant Robertson of a thousand coppersmiths at work.

Music, too is a thing of the past. Its moral effect was once very considerable. In August 1431 the leaders of a German crusade against the Hussites rode to the top of a hill overlooking the enemy line of advance while the crusaders took up a defensive position. At first the assembled dignitaries were nonplussed to see columns of their own provision-wagons making off. Then, although the Hussites were still several miles away, the rattle of their war-carts, and the song 'All ye warriors of God', which the whole host was chanting, could be heard clearly. 'No resistance was even attempted,' records Count Lutzow, 'and before a single shot had been fired the whole German army, seized by a sudden panic, fled in the greatest disorder.' The effect of Prussian music at Zorndorf in 1758 may have been less dramatic, but it was none the less awe-inspiring, as a Protestant pastor in the Russian ranks remembered.

Then the menacing beat of the Prussian drums was carried to our ears. For a time their woodwind was inaudible, but as the Prussians approached, we could hear the oboes playing the well-known hymn 'Ich bin ja, Herr, in deiner Macht!' I cannot express what I felt at that instant, but I do not think that people will consider it odd when I say that never since in the course of my long life have I heard that tune without experiencing the utmost emotion.

The music played by a soldier's own side could raise his morale as much as it depressed that of his enemy. The Germans made widespread use of bugles to control their troops as they advanced in March 1918. *Fähnrich* Alfred Bruntsch of the 145th *Königs* Regiment was weeping quietly before the attack. 'I was emotionally finished,' he admitted, 'and glad in my heart when, after the four-hour barrage, the signal "spring up" sounded. This ancient call blown by our trumpeter helped me to get rid of my tears but the fear still remained.'

Men add to the cacophony of battle by their own shouts. War cries are a time-honoured means of boosting one's own fighting spirit and attempting to diminish the enemy's. The English shire levies barked their battle cry 'Out, out' as they withstood the wild rush of King David's Scots outside Northallerton in 1138. It is, perhaps, not too fanciful to think of the cries of 'Out, out, out,' shouted on picket lines or at demonstrations, as the folk-memory's imprint of the old war cry. The Zulu howl 'uSuthu' cracked the fragile morale of the Natal Native Contingent at Isandalwana in 1879, and the 'wild weird falsetto' of the rebel yell shook Union morale on many a battlefield, but rarely more so than on 2 May 1863, when Jackson's flank attack, a torrent of shrieking soldiers in butter-nut grey, swept away the flank of the unlucky XI Corps near Wilderness Tavern.

This particular war cry survived. William Manchester recalled how, during the Second World War, Southerners would charge with 'the shrill rebel yell of their grandfathers'. They were not alone. Charlton Ogburn described the cry of the 3rd Battalion of Merrill's Marauders: 'it was literally a two-syllabled obscenity, but as voiced it had the feral, doleful, spine tingling wail of a wolf's howl.' Russian infantry assaulted with hoarse shouts of 'Urra', and the Viet Minh hurled selves into the attack with cries of 'Tiên-Lên'. Second World War British parachutists used the strange war cry 'Woho Mahomet.' John Fairley cites Captain Eric Mackay's description of a night battle when his force ambushed some Germans.

> The night dissolved in sound, the din was hideous, the heavy crash of the Brens mixed with the high-pitched rattle of the Stens, the cries of wounded men punctuated by the sharp explosions of grenades and, swelling above it all, the triumphant war-cry, 'Woho Mahomet.'

In addition to these deliberate shouts, close-quarter battles are filled with the grunts and groans of men engaged in harsh exertion. When Pickett's charge reached its high-water mark at Gettysburg, the noise was 'strange and terrible, a sound that came from thousands of human throats, yet this was not a conmingling of shouts and yells, but rather a vast mournful roar'. Major Raymond Cooper heard a similar sound in Burma: 'Triumph or terror, British or Japanese, it was the primitive sound which comes when emotions are roused and unchecked.' Grunts and growls have both psychological and physiological motives, as professional tennis-players know. Not only do they help to unsettle an opponent, but they also accompany the expulsion of air by the diaphragm at a moment of intense muscular effort, thus fixing the chest wall and co-ordinating the movement.

Marshall regretted the fact that leaders were all too often silent in the moments after the enemy had opened fire, at the very time when any 'clear, commanding voice' would help soldiers overcome their initial shock. However, the other sounds of battle make verbal communication difficult, and sometimes shouting is counter-productive. During the bitter fighting in the Devil's Den at Gettysburg 'every soldier was his own general. Private soldiers gave commands as loud as officers; nobody paying any attention to either.' But there are times when a commanding voice does rise above the tumult. Corporal Morley of the 17th Lancers, capless, long hair streaming, rallied twenty of his comrades after the charge of the Light Brigade at Balaclava, booming in his Nottingham accent, 'Coom 'ere, coom 'ere, fall in, lads, fall in.' Not only did Morley get his troopers back up the valley safely, but he lived to fight the Union army during the Civil War. A thick accent was less of a disadvantage there than it had been in the British army, and Morley rose to the rank of captain. Lieutenant John Stevenson of the 1st Airborne Reconnaissance Squadron said of Arnhem:

> Of all my impressions of the battle, the one that has been most lasting has been the shouting of the German NCOs. Whenever you heard this loud parade-ground shouting and the answering 'Jawohls', you knew that there was an assault of some kind about to be mounted.

This shouting was in part a deliberate morale-boosting ploy, as 2nd Panzer Division reported from Normandy, where:

> The best results have been obtained by platoon and section commanders leaping forward and uttering a good old-fashioned yell. We have also revived the practice of bugle calls.

British troops in the Falklands shouted orders and warnings – 'grenade' and 'sixty-six' – much to the astonishment of Fabian E., who commented specifically on the practice in his interview with Daniel Kon. This tends to support Marshall's point on the value of verbal orders. It was precisely in low-level leadership and cohesion that the Argentinian army was weakest and the British strongest, and the lack of encouragement and orders amongst the former was at once a symptom and a cause of its collapse.

The noise of shellfire and small-arms, the cries of the wounded and the bellowing of officers and NCOs, subject soldiers to ferocious stress. This is accentuated when the cause of the noise cannot be seen. The garrisons of the French forts at Verdun in 1916 were safer from shellfire than their comrades who endured the bombardment lying out in the shellholes above ground, but the sheer din of shells smashing into the forts – it was, said one survivor, like being in an immense drum – and the agony of waiting for the arrival of the next shell drove men stark mad. Several Falklands veterans remarked on the fact that the worst place to be during an air attack on the fleet was below decks. Not only was the noise amplified, but there was no way of knowing what threat it portended. It was infinitely preferable – albeit actually more dangerous – to be up on deck, watching the Skyhawks as they ran the gauntlet of gun and missile fire.

With the eardrum-smashing, face-punching din of battle comes a hail of projectiles of all sorts. The damage they inflict is as much psychological as it is physical, for it is a striking fact that relatively few of the rounds fired by small-arms or artillery actually cause casualties. It is extremely difficult to be precise about the number of rounds required to produce a casualty in any given battle because, as one might expect, the available statistics are never adequate. Furthermore, small-arms are often used for 'reconnaissance by fire' rather than with the intention of causing casualties, just as artillery fire is sometimes employed primarily to destroy the enemy's field defences or communications rather than to kill or wound. But enough information is available to suggest certain conclusions.

Let us first consider the question of small-arms fire. The Comte de Guibert, in this respect the most optimistic of the theorists of the horse and musket age, thought that one million rounds of musketry produced 2,000 casualties: one hit, that is, for every 500 rounds. His colleagues Gassendi and Piobert were far less sanguine, believing that an expenditure of 3,000 rounds per casualty was the best that could be expected. Major-General B. P. Hughes, a modern authority, argues: 'It is impossible to accept that more than about 5% of the bullets that could have been fired were effective, and the rate often seems to have been appreciably lower.'

The Battle of Maida, fought on 4 July 1806 between a sea-landed British force under Major-General Sir John Stuart and a French army under General Reynier, consisted of three self-contained actions. In one of these Colonel James Kempt's Light Brigade, composed of the light companies of a number of infantry battalions, was attacked by two battalions of the French 1st Light Infantry. Kempt's force, 630-strong when officers and supernumeries are deducted, was formed two deep so that all muskets could bear. It fired three volleys, the first at 115 yards and the last at 30, and bayoneted the few brave Frenchmen who came to handstrokes. The French suffered 430 casualties, although a few lightly wounded men may have escaped the pursuit. In all, therefore, it took Kempt's 'light bobs' – picked men, with extra musketry training – 1,890 rounds to cause 430 casualties, or 4.4 rounds per hit. This is a remarkably good performance, which reflects the high standard of British marksmanship and fire discipline, the size of the target and the close range of the engagement. Few infantrymen of any era have done better.[3]

The muzzle-loading musket of the Napoleonic era was a notoriously inaccurate weapon. However, the rifled breechloaders of the latter part of the century performed no better. The French General Guillaume Bonnal analysed the Battle of Wissembourg, fought on 4 August 1870 between General Abel Douay's badly-outnumbered French division and elements of three German corps. He concluded that the Germans had expended 80,000 needle-gun rounds to kill or wound 400 of Douay's *turcos*, and that the *turcos* had fired 48,000 rounds to hit 404 Germans. The needle-gun, on the one hand, scored one hit per 200 rounds fired, and the *Chassepot*, on the other, one hit for a mere 119 rounds. Bonnal acknowledged that the figures were inconclusive, for, while the Germans were attacking across open country, the *turcos* were firing through loopholes or from behind cover. Moreover, some of the French casualties were caused by German shellfire rather than by musketry. This latter fact, though, makes the ineffectiveness of the German rifle fire even more striking.[4]

White soldiers did scarcely better against their tribal enemies. General Crook's men fired 25,000 rounds at Rosebud Creek on 16 June 1876, and caused 99 casualties amongst the Indians, or 252 rounds per hit.[5] The men of Lieutenant Gonville Bromhead's B Company, 2nd Battalion the 24th Regiment, defending the mission station at Rorke's Drift against the Zulus on 22 January 1897, fired over 20,000 rounds from their Martini-Henrys, many of them at very close range. About 370 bodies were picked up around the post, and the Zulus got at least another 100 away. But even if one triples this figure to allow for wounded, and assumes that all the Zulus fell to rifle fire, rather than to the Martini's wicked triangular socket-bayonet, Bromhead's men fired at the very least 13 rounds to hit a single Zulu.[6]

The British Expeditionary Force of 1914 is often regarded as the very apogee of skill at arms, and its performance at Mons certainly came as a stinging surprise to the Germans. Walter Bloem was the only company commander in his battalion to survive the action. 'In our company alone', he wrote, 'we lost five officers and half our men.' But this sort of damage was inflicted as much by the volume of British fire as by its accuracy. Individual soldiers often fired all the 120 rounds they carried with them, and frequently much more. On 23 October, for example, Private J. S. Barton of the Gloucesters fired 600 rounds, and his platoon shot its entire first-line supply of ammunition, much of it at ranges under 200 yards.

Some noisy and spectacular actions caused few casualties. On the night of 25–6 August three companies of 3rd Battalion, The Coldstream Guards and 2nd Battalion, The Grenadier Guards, supported by a single howitzer of 60th Battery Royal Field Artillery, were attacked in the little French town of Landrecies by a German battalion. The battle went on for perhaps two hours, and the British believed that they had killed or wounded 800–900 Germans. The Germans in fact reported their own loss at 127 men.[7]

In early November 1914 2nd Grenadiers held a sector in what was fast becoming the Ypres salient. The battalion was subjected to a series of fierce and determined attacks which, in a few cases, reached its lines. Repeated assaults during a long day's fighting left 300 German dead in front of a company position. In a similar action, fought a few days later, the same company fired 24,000 rounds. If one increases the German casualty figure by adding 300 seriously wounded and 300 lightly wounded, which were very roughly the rates prevailing at the time, and assumes that 24,000 rounds were consumed to inflict these casualties, then the Grenadiers were obtaining one hit for every 26·6 rounds fired.[8]

These calculations are all decidedly rough and ready: I use

them to illustrate, not to prove. They do, though, give an indication of the large numbers of rounds that even well-trained regular infantry might have to fire in order to hit – and not necessarily kill – an enemy.

The performance of their gunner colleagues was scarcely more impressive. J. T. MacCurdy maintains, in *The Structure of Morale*, that it took on average 1,400 shells to kill a man during the First World War. Although he marshals no evidence in support of this assertion, it may not be altogether wide of the mark. The majority of shells fired during the war were aimed at troops sheltering in trenches and dug-outs. During the Dhofar War of the 1970s, the very well dug-in position of Sarfait was hit by over 10,000 gun and mortar rounds in four years: six of its garrison were killed and twelve wounded.[9]

Attempts at relating the number of shells fired in a battle to the casualties produced are bedevilled by the same difficulties that confront us in our consideration of the hit-ratio of small-arms. There is also the added problem of interpreting German ten-day casualty returns, which did not include wounded men who remained with their units. But there is a clear picture of a vast amount of shells being fired to produce relatively few casualties. On 1 July 1916 alone, British guns fired 224,221 rounds, and the Germans suffered something under 6,000 killed and wounded. Many of these unfortunates fell victim to rifle and machine-gun fire, and to the grenade, bayonet, butt and shovel plied in the murderous trench mêlées. Conversely, a proportion of the shells fired were aimed not at German trenches or strongpoints, but at German wire. These two facts alone make accurate calculations impossible, but even the most sanguine British gunner would have been fortunate indeed to have hit, on average, one German for every thirty shells he fired into the rolling chalklands above the meandering Somme.[10]

The substantial total of rounds fired in the Somme bombardment was dwarfed by the 4,283,550 employed during the preliminary bombardment and opening engagement, between 15 July and 2 August, of the Third Battle of Ypres. Huge

amounts of shells were fired during deliberate attacks on prepared positions during the Second World War. 17 September
1944, when the artillery of a single corps fired 13,000 shells
into the Gothic Line, was 'quite a normal day'. It was certainly modest by the standards of the battle for Monte Camino
in December 1943, when the artillery of two corps fired
150,000 rounds in a twenty-four-hour period. Some targets
received eleven tons of shell per minute, and the gunners of
the British 10 Corps fired no less than 3,800 tons of ammunition. The sector under attack was held, if all reinforcements
received during the battle are included, by six German battalions which were badly clawed but certainly not annihilated.

Prodigious consumption of artillery ammunition has
characterised post-1945 limited wars. The Americans fired
77,349 rounds in two days in defence of the Arsenal, Dale and
Pork Chop Hill positions in Korea. The French defenders of
Dien Bien Phu, dependent upon resupply by air, none the less
managed to fire 15,055 rounds on 31 March 1954, 13,000 of
them from seventeen 105mm howitzers. During the first minute of the Egyptian assault in Sinai in 1973, 10,500 shells fell
on Israeli front-line positions, at the rate of 175 shells per
second. An Israeli eyewitness reported that 'the whole of Sinai
was on fire'. Finally, the British attack on the hills around
Port Stanley in June 1982 was delayed while 12,000 shells
were flown forward. During the final battle for Stanley five
batteries fired the equivalent of a regiment's training alloca-
tion for four years. 'All aspects of life on the gun positions',
wrote a battery commander, 'were dominated by the demands
of ammunition flow.'

Veterans frequently comment on the surprisingly ineffective
nature of so much fire. After scrambling back in from a patrol
amidst a hail of fire, Charles Carrington recorded: 'Home
with one man wounded, and for the twentieth time I mar-
velled how much ammunition can be spent without killing a
man.' Fred Majdalany said of Cassino that: 'The remarkable
thing about modern shelling is not how many it kills, but how
few,' and Martin Lindsay, inspecting heavily-shelled German
positions near Caen, complained: 'I walked round the battle-

field and found that only three Huns were killed by our barrage. They were all dug in and not a single dug-out had a
direct hit'. 'One of the things that amazed me is how many
bullets can be fired during a fire-fight without anyone getting
hurt,' remarked Douglas Graham, a medic with 3rd Battalion,
1st Marines, in Vietnam.

This vast, if surprisingly ineffective, volume of fire, and the
noise associated with it, is an essential ingredient in the stress
of battle. It helps turn real battle into something which has
little in common with the simulated battles of training. We
have already observed the tendency of historians to impart to
battle an order that rarely exists. The sheer disorganisation of
battle is at one and the same time the result of the pressures
produced by hostile fire, and a contributor, in its own right,
to battlefield stress.

The close-order formations of the horse and musket period
were a response to the inefficient short-range weapons of the
age and a device for promoting cohesion and assisting control.
Yet they seldom worked as their advocates hoped. Infantry
might get off a volley or two, but thereafter they tended to
load and fire as fast as they could. Lieutenant-Colonel Charles
Russell of the 1st Foot Guards wrote of the British foot at
Dettingen in 1743:

> They were under no command by way of Hyde Park firing,
> but the whole three ranks made a running fire of their own
> accord ... The French fired in the same manner, without
> waiting for words of command, and Lord Stair [the Allied
> commander] did often say he had seen many a battle, and
> never saw the infantry engage in any other manner.

Even in Frederick the Great's army, with its rigid discipline,
the reality of battle seldom corresponded to the theories of the
parade-ground. G. H. Berenhorst described how:

> You began by firing by platoons, and perhaps two or three
> would get off orderly volleys. But then would follow a
> general blazing away – the usual rolling fire when every-
> body blasted off as soon as he had loaded, when ranks and

files became intermingled, when the first rank was incapable of kneeling, even if it wanted to. The commanders, from subalterns to generals, would be incapable of getting the mass to perform anything else: they just had to wait until it finally set itself in motion forwards or backwards.

The officers who replied to Ardant du Picq's questionnaire in the 1860s painted a similar picture of disorganisation. Battalions disappeared as formed bodies once they had received the order to drop their packs. Du Picq noted sadly: 'Each man fires as much as possible, that is to say, as badly as possible ... The greater number fire from the hip.'

Excited soldiers were as much of a danger to their friends as to their enemies. Marshal Saint-Cyr estimated that one-quarter of French infantry casualties during the Napoleonic period were caused by men in the front rank being accidentally shot by those behind them. Lieutenant A. von Boguslawski, who fought with the 66th Lower Silesian Infantry Regiment at Rezonville, wrote that 'a good many soldiers fired into the air at long distances, a good many fired into their friends in front of them, notwithstanding all our careful musketry instruction.' His opposite number Lieutenant Devaureix of the French 66th Regiment was encountering the same problem at precisely the same time. He 'saw, with regret, a certain number of our soldiers fire almost in the air, without aiming, seeming to want to stun themselves, to become drunk on rifle fire during this gripping crisis'. A French regiment was briskly engaged when a strange brigadier appeared and gently reproved the men: '*Mes enfants*, you probably do not realise it, but you are firing on my brigade.'

The increasing tendency towards tactical dispersion has not made the task of preserving order any easier. Lieutenant George Roupell of the East Surreys, commanding a platoon at Mons, found that the only way of controlling his men's fire was to draw his sword and walk along the line 'beating the men on the backside and, as I got their attention, telling them to fire low'. Graham Greenwell's company began its attack on 6 April 1918 in text-book form.

I yelled myself hoarse doing the old dodge of short rushes forward and then lying flat, until my rear sergeant got annoyed with me, jumped up and against all regulations started a cheer. Everyone took it up and the whole Company became a great mob yelling and cheering like the devil.

Amongst all the confused and bitter actions in which he participated in 1944-5, Charles MacDonald recalled one set-piece attack that looked exactly like a training film. 'This was a mirage', he wrote, 'that was ridiculous because it was so wonderful and so true.' John Muir remarked upon the rarity of such manœuvres in Vietnam:

> You don't often get the chance to see a classic book-type assault: two platoons in front and one platoon in reserve, double-arm interval [two arms lengths between each man], rifle under your arm firing as you go ... It was just like the movies, for chrisakes.

These text-book, training-film battles are, and have always been, the exception rather than the rule. More common is the experience of 1st Battalion, 5th Marines in pouring rain twenty miles north-west of Chu Lai in August 1966.

> While Company A was attacking in the paddy, mortar shells had fallen along the road, just missing the battalion command group. The headquarters element, quite distinguishable with its fence of radio antennas, had hastily sought the concealment of the bushes and houses to the left of the road. The NCOs yelled at their sections to disperse yet stay close, and the radio operators tried to copy incoming messages and transmit at the same time. The officers were busy trying to pinpoint their position and decide on a course of action, when everyone was taken under small arms fire coming from all directions.[11]

This, then, is what the soldier encounters on the battlefield. His pre-battle tension disappears as the fighting starts, but it is replaced by the stresses produced by the noisy arrival of bullets and shells, an uneasy sensation of isolation, and the frustrating and confusing feeling of utter disorganisation. His brain records clips of experience, often in an erratic sequence. And, while he strives to do his job in an unfamiliar and perplexing environment, he becomes acutely aware that men – some of them his own comrades – are being killed and wounded.

5

Pale Battalions

When you see millions of the mouthless dead
Across your dreams in pale battalions go
                                    Charles Sorley

Death and wounds are an inseparable part of battle, and confront the soldier in a myriad guises. Charles Carrington saw death snatch Corporal Matthews before his very eyes on the Somme.

> I was looking straight at him as the bullet struck him and was profoundly affected by the remembrance of his face, though at the time I hardly thought of it. He was alive, and then he was dead, and there was nothing human left in him. He fell with a neat round hole in his forehead and the back of his head blown out.

William Manchester crouched below the sea-wall at Tarawa in November 1943 as an officer, deaf to his insistence that it was death to go forward, climbed it. He was riddled with bullets as he topped the wall. 'One moment he was looming above us in that heroic pose,' wrote Manchester, 'in the next moment red pits blossomed down him, four on his face alone, and a dozen others down his uniform.'

176

Sometimes the impact of bullet or shell fragment is clearly audible. Bullets make a solid thud or, more rarely, a metallic shriek as the spinning round is deflected by bone. Ken Harrison and his comrades were halted by a Japanese road block near Muar in Malaya, and, as he sprinted for the edge of the jungle, he heard 'the dull thwack of bullets' hitting the men immediately in front of him. The thing which most appalled me in the case of the one man I have seen killed was the sound of the projectile – the tail assembly of a 3·5-inch rocket – striking the upper part of his body: it was like a pick-helve hitting a bag of slightly gritty sand.

The first sight of a corpse, however much one has expected it, comes as a shock. 'We looked at all these dead with dislocated limbs, distorted faces, and the hideous colours of decay,' wrote Ernst Jünger of his first sight of a battlefield, 'as though we walked in a dream through a garden of strange plants, and we could not realise at first what we had all round us.' Richard Gale's first dead man made a lasting impression upon him.

> He was a German, and in his grey uniform I can see him now. His face was a ghastly grey colour, like marble in which there was a tinge of blue. His mouth was open and dried blood stuck to his chin where it had run down from his colourless lips ... the stench was sickening.

The smell of death is almost as disturbing as the sight of it. 'Those who die in great battles do not know the majesty of eternal rest,' declared Marc Bloch. 'The stench turns one's stomach.' William Frassinato suggested that the battlefield of Antietam could be smelt a mile away. The Western Front had its own characteristic odour. 'The smell of burnt and poisoned mud – acrid is, I think, the right epithet – was with us for months on end,' wrote Charles Carrington. 'And through it one could distinguish a more biotic flavour – the stink of corrupting human flesh.' It is not merely that long-dead corpses smell as they decay. Even the freshly-killed assail the nostrils with the blood-and-entrails reek of the slaughterhouse. The stench of death, cloying and pervasive, hung over Mount Longdon after its capture, and it was this, not the jumbled Argentinian corpses, that a sergeant in 3 Para retained as his abiding memory of the battle. This smell is woven into a tissue of other odours. First come those which characterise a whole era. For the horse and musket period the prevalent smell was the hydrogen sulphide bad-egg stink of black powder, while the smell of latrines – excrement and chloride of lime – predominated during the First World War. Mechanised war brings its own smell, the throat-catching stench of diesel and exhaust fumes. Particular battles have their distinctive smells, from the scent of half-ripe corn at Waterloo to the pervasive odour of cider apples in Normandy and the prickly tang of hexamine cooking fuel in the Falklands. 'The term "Russian Winter of 1941"', remembered a German veteran, 'brings to me very strongly a compound of smells: stale urine, excrement, suppurating wounds, and the not unpleasant smell of Kascha, a sort of buckwheat porridge.'

The effect of weapons upon the fragile and complex human body are bizarre and unpredictable. Men are blown to tatters by a direct hit. Gale was 'spattered all over with the blood and pieces' of a gunner subaltern. Private R. Le Brun of the 16th Canadian Machine-Gun Company saw his friend Private Tombs – the only other survivor of their section – hit in the head by a burst of machine-gun fire. 'His blood and brains, pieces of skull and lumps of hair, spattered all over the front of my greatcoat and gas mask,' said Le Brun. 'I stood there trying to get the bits off. It was a terrible feeling to be the only one left.' High-explosive projectiles scatter dreadful evidence of mortality. 'You tripped over strings of viscera fifteen feet long,' said William Manchester of Iwo Jima, 'over bodies which had been cut in half at the waist. Legs and arms, and heads bearing only necks, lay fifty feet from the closest torsos. As night fell the beachhead reeked with the stench of burning flesh.'

Flying fragments of the human body themselves cause wounds. Young Ensign Leeke was clutching his regiment's colour at Waterloo when a piece of skull from a soldier to his front slammed into his thumb. William Manchester had a piece of one of his men's tibia buried in his back, and a platoon commander in Italy was temporarily stunned by the impact of a soldier's forearm, easily recognisable from its tattoos. Sometimes a weapon's effects are more cruel and capricious, as Marc Bloch discovered. 'When a bullet strikes the skull at a certain angle, it explodes,' he wrote. 'That was the way L. died ... Half his face hung like a shutter whose hinges no longer held, and one could see inside the almost empty cranial box.'

On other occasions men are killed so cleanly – by blast which ruptures kidneys and spleen or by a minuscule fragment of shell or mortar bomb – that the victim looks as if he is only asleep. Martin Lindsay saw a Polish platoon headquarters killed like this in Normandy: 'They were still sitting upright, leaning back against the wall, the operator holding the microphone in front of his mouth.' John Glubb became fascinated by one corpse in the Bluff at Ypres.

He had been killed while climbing up the steep bank of the Bluff, and had one foot raised and a hand stretched out to pull himself up. By some miracle he remained in the same identical position. Except for the green colour of his face and hand, one would never have believed that he was dead.

The ebb and flow of battle often means that it is impossible to bury the dead, or that hastily-buried corpses are exhumed by shellfire or shovel. Men are therefore confronted not only by the newly-dead, but also by corpses in various states of decomposition. Glubb's sappers deepened a trench which had dead men trampled into its floor. 'They are pretty well decomposed,' he wrote, 'but a pickaxe brings up chips of bone and rags of clothing. The rest is putrid grey matter.' The horror is sharpened when one of the putrescent dead is a friend or relative. James Jack described the aftermath of an abortive attack in 1915: 'The Rifle Brigade dead lie all over No Man's Land, some hanging on the German wire which they were trying to cut or surmount when killed; amongst them one

whom I knew and is easily recognisable.' Billy Congreve –
killed on the Somme at the age of twenty-five, having won the
DSO and MC and earned a posthumous VC – spent several
nights in May 1915 searching for the body of his uncle, Major
Arthur King. He eventually found it 'simply riddled with
bullets and very far gone. He must have walked into a
machine-gun at least ... I have sent all he had on him, which
wasn't much, to Dorothy. The glasses were too smashed and
the torch too gruesome.'

For some the squalor of death in a ravaged landscape has
a peculiar poignancy. Sergeant Warner of the Somerset Light
Infantry saw, in February 1945, 'the bodies of three C Company fellows killed by a shell. They lie on the sodden field
under a dismal, damp sky; their equipment and rifles strewn
beside them.' Others are moved more profoundly by a set-
piece tableau of death. 'I came across a dead German officer,
already on a stretcher and half bandaged, with the two
stretcher bearers lying across him – testimony in death of their
devotion,' remembered John Horsfall, commanding a company of the Royal Irish Fusiliers in Tunisia in 1943. 'Few
things have affected me more.'

Most soldiers grow accustomed to the sight of so much
death. Jünger, shocked as he was by his first sight of a corpse,
admits that 'finally we were so accustomed to the horrible
that if we came on a dead body anywhere on a fire-step or in
a ditch we gave it no more than a passing thought and recognised it as we would a stone or a tree.' Some men become so
utterly blasé that they look upon the dead as a source of comfort in a harsh environment. Wheeler built himself a comforting wall of dead Frenchmen against the cutting wind on the
battlefield of Salamanca, and soon fell into a sound sleep.
Martin Lindsay found a sergeant who had strung a dead and
frozen German up to a tree and lit a wood fire beneath him:
'He was trying to thaw him out, in order to take off his boots.'
A sergeant in Peter Kemp's *bandera* of the Spanish Foreign
Legion cheerfully reported that he had used a mattress of
corpses to protect himself when sleeping on wet ground. One
of Kemp's brother officers saw a legionary hammering away

with his rifle-butt at the face of a dead militiaman. The officer told him that the man was already dead. 'I know sir,' he replied, 'but look! He has some fine gold teeth.' A First World War Irish soldier was less than pleased when a dead German's leg was cut out of the parapet of his trench, and grumbled that he would have to find something else to hang his equipment on. Binding testifies that this was not an isolated practice. 'The legs of an Englishman, still encased in puttees, stick out into a trench, the corpse being built into the parapet,' he wrote. 'A soldier hangs his rifle on them.'

It is more difficult to grow accustomed to the sight and sound of wounded men, although surgeons sometimes develop a gallows humour which, no doubt, helps them to cope: there is more than a little truth in the black comedy *M*A*S*H*. John Parrish recalled wry jokes being cracked round an operating table as surgeons worked on a desperately wounded man with both legs and one arm missing. 'The only part that really bothered me,' he reflected, 'was the brains under my fingernails.'

Most soldiers never construct this armour of professional detachment, and are more shaken by the sight of a badly wounded man than they are by that of a corpse. An Australian at Pozières in 1916 remembered looking towards a shell-burst:

> I turned and I saw through the smoke ... some black thing, a big black thing ... It was a shapeless black thing, flapping ... I ran over, ducking and weaving, till I got close. And it was a man, blackened, not a bit of flesh not burnt, rolling around, waving his arm stump with nothing on it.

Guy Sajer's friend Ernst Neubach was mortally wounded in Russia during the Second World War. Sajer looked at the ravaged face. 'He must have been hit in the lower jaw,' he wrote. 'His teeth were mixed with fragments of bone, and through the gore I could see the muscles of his face contracting, moving what was left of his features.' Raleigh Trevelyan witnessed something so frightful that he could not describe it

fully, even in the privacy of his diary: 'Yesterday evening there
was something on a stretcher that was the worst sight I have
even seen at this bridgehead ... *and it was still alive.*' Even the
armour of medical officers is not impenetrable. Charles Sarazin, working in a field hospital at Froeschwiller in August
1870, was horrified by the spectacle of one of his colleagues,
a regimental medical officer with the *turcos*, gut-shot, dying
lengthily, 'in all the agonies of peritonitis', almost equally
agonised by worrying about what would become of his wife
and family.

The sight of men being killed and wounded changes the
soldier's perception of fear. For soldiers in action for the first
time the greatest fear is, as we have seen, that of being a
coward. But for veterans the fear of being crippled and disfigured for life looms largest. John Dollard suggested: 'It may
be that the veteran acquires a more literal idea of the damage
caused by severe wounds.' Veterans also tend to be specific
about the sort of wounds they most fear. When Dollard's *Fear
in Battle* was first published, during the Second World War,
the most-feared wounds were those to the abdomen, eyes,
brain and genitals. Widely-publicised improvements in casualty evacuation and treatment, and the discovery of sulfa
drugs, went some way towards laying the spectre of the
stomach wound during and after the Second World War.

Damage to the genitals continue to rate highly amongst the
most-feared wounds. Michael Herr vividly described fear of
'the Wound' in Vietnam: 'Take my legs, take my hands, take
my eyes, take my fucking *life*, you Bastard, but please, please,
please don't take *those*.' Sergeant Bill Blyth of 48 Commando
was wounded in the legs on D-Day, and nervously asked Corporal Len Wakefield about 'the tackle'. 'Is it still there, Len?'
he inquired. 'I said if it's not, you can shoot me. But if it is,
let me live.' Wakefield took his hand to prove that all was well.
It requires no great feat of mental gymnastics to connect the
powerful pressures of *machismo* which spur on so many soldiers
early in their military careers to this fear of losing one's virility.
Ron Kovic, a crippled Vietnam veteran, made the connection
most aptly: 'I gave my dead dick for John Wayne.' Another

American speculated upon the long-term future of men wounded by the air-burst mine, nicknamed Bouncing Betty. 'They explode and get your thighs, take your penis, your rectum,' he said. 'So big deal, you get a guy to the hospital and you save his life, but if he's not a quadriplegic, he's got a colostomy, he can't have sex, he can't have kids.'[1]

Lesser wounds are sometimes welcomed. Lord Moran told of how 'a cushy wound, a blighty business, seems the most desirable thing in the world', and Groom wrote that 'lucky bastard' was the usual comment about a man even seriously but not dangerously wounded. Michael Herr observed the same phenomenon fifty years later. A young marine was wounded in the knee by shrapnel at Hue: when he heard he was to be evacuated, 'he couldn't stop smiling, and enormous tears ran down into his eyes'. 'To be hit and have his arm torn off, that was like somebody giving him two hundred thousand dollars,' said Stan Goff. 'That was how much his life was worth. His arm. To get out of the war, his contract was his arm.'

For others, even a blighty wound is an unwelcome visitor. Leaders resent being taken away from their men at the height of an action. Major-General Hans Kannengiesser, hit in the chest by a machine-gun bullet whilst getting his men into position to block the Suvla Bay landing in 1915, remarked: 'This was most annoying. Now I was forced to leave my brave Division just in this most critical moment.' A quiet infantry officer was visibly moved nearly forty years after the event as he described being wounded at the head of his company in Italy. 'I wasn't too badly hit and got them to prop me up so that I could still command the company,' he said, 'but the wretched medics insisted on taking me away.' It was only later that I heard – from another source – that he had received multiple wounds from close-range machine-gun fire and had spent months in hospital.

Sometimes it is a man's self-respect, his desire not to show weakness, that keeps him in battle despite his wound. John Glubb soldiered on with a foot wound, because he 'didn't want to be sent back and leave the men in the line'. A company commander in 2 Para, hit by the Argentinian anti-aircraft guns at Goose Green, resisted being evacuated until he came to the conclusion that he was causing his commanding officer extra problems by refusing to go. Lieutenant 'Birdie' Smith of the 7th Gurkhas, shot in the leg in the attack on Tavoleto in September 1944, declined to go to the Regimental Aid Post, paradoxically because he did not feel brave enough to do so. 'It would have taken more courage than I possessed,' he wrote, 'to have gone back to Battalion Headquarters with a flesh wound in my left leg to report that Charlie Company had disappeared into the night somewhere near Tavoleto.' He fought on, leading his company in an epic battle which was to earn him the DSO. One of the first casualties treated by Stuart Mawson at Arnhem was a company commander with his finger nearly severed. 'To try to persuade him to regard his wound from a medical point of view,' he reflected, 'was as hopeless as passing a bottle of milk around a sergeants' mess.'

Conduct of this sort is assisted by the way in which the body reacts to a wound. The sensation of being hit was summed up by Smith himself: 'a giant wearing heavy tipped boots hacked my feet from under me, down I crashed to the ground'. John Horsfall, wounded by a stick grenade in Tunisia, recalled how 'the sky in front of me turned into roaring flame with sledge-hammers mixed into it, and time for a while stood still'. Charles MacDonald was 'conscious of a sudden pain in the calf of my right leg, as if someone had hit me with a giant club swung by powerful arms ... a warm liquid flowed over my leg and into my boot'. 'I felt a numbing pain as if someone had whacked me on the funny bone with a sledge hammer,' wrote J.E.H. Neville, and for Raleigh Trevelyan there was 'a noise like a dinner gong going off inside my head'.

Very often the sensation is, quite literally, numbing. Martin Lindsay, an infantry officer with very considerable experience, saw only one recently-wounded man in pain from a wound, 'the shock being normally so great that nothing much is felt for hours'. Indeed, in the heat of the moment minor wounds may pass unnoticed, in much the same way that a football player may sustain a fracture during a game without being aware of it. Bob Sanders, wounded in Vietnam, recalled: 'At first, when I got hit, I didn't feel anything. I was too scared and I was concentrating on Charlie. I felt a little stinging, but I didn't think nothing of it.'

Private David Gray lost a leg at Goose Green.

> I just had a numb feeling from the waist downwards. I was laying on my stomach and I was just reaching up for my weapon and all I got was like a thud, all over a large thudding sound and I thought I was all right, I didn't feel any immediate pain and then when I looked down I saw the damage to my leg and screamed. I think it took a couple of seconds to register to my brain that I'd been hit, and then after that I got a drowsy sensation after a couple of hours. But I had no sort of pain, it was just numb from the waist downwards.

Even more serious wounds sometimes do not hurt immediately they have been inflicted. Commenting on farmworker Roy Tapping, whose arm was torn off in a baler in June 1983, Dr Clifford Woolf of University College London, said:

> It would be no good collapsing in agony ... it was inappropriate to his survival. The human nervous system contains various defence mechanisms. When his arm was torn off they went into action and switched off the pain. Mr Tapping had no choice in the matter. It was the only way he could survive. He may have felt no pain at all. Once help arrived, he probably felt the pain suddenly.[2]

Endorphins are released by the adrenal gland in moments of stress, and act as natural pain-killers, and the massive stimulus to the nerves produced by such a wound causes the brain to suppress pain.

This helps to explain the fact that soldiers often behave normally despite massive wounds. Charles Parquin was trotting forward with his regiment at Jena when he passed a sergeant of the 5th Hussars, a man of truly martial appearance, whose white pelisse was completely covered in blood. He had just had his left arm shattered by a cannon-ball and yet did not cease telling the chasseurs of our regiment whom he met as they advanced up the pass: 'Come on, my brave chasseurs! The Prussians are not all that bad.'

Devaureix saw a grenadier of the Guard walk calmly into a field ambulance at Rezonville, his right arm shot away, carrying his rifle in his left hand. Old General Strangways, commanding the Royal Artillery in the Crimea, was riding beside Lord Raglan at Inkerman in 1854 when his leg was mangled by a roundshot. He turned to one of his staff, and asked, 'in the tone of a man asking for a match', 'Would someone have the kindness to help me off my horse?' Told by a surgeon that his case was hopeless, the white-haired general asked simply: 'Then let me die among my gunners.' John Glubb believed that 'a direct hit on a limb so shatters the nerves that the victim feels no pain.' He noticed that one of his men who had lost an arm at the shoulder chatted cheerfully, and was not in pain. R. Melzack observed that there is no simple direct relationship between the wound itself and the pain experienced. 'The pain is in very large part determined by other factors,' he wrote, 'and of great importance here is the significance of the wound ... In the wounded soldier [the response to injury] was relief, thankfulness at his escape alive from the battlefield, even euphoria; to the civilian, his major surgery was a depressing, calamitous event.'

Most wounds become painful when the initial shock wears off, and some are agonising from the start. Men scream, either because of the pain itself, or in sheer panic and terror. Lieutenant Edwin Campion Vaughan of the Royal Warwicks, sheltering in a dugout in the dark nightmare of Passchendaele Ridge, tells how:

From the darkness on all sides came the groans and wails of wounded men; faint, long, sobbing moans of agony, and despairing shrieks. It was too horribly obvious to me that dozens of men with serious wounds must have crawled for safety into shell holes, and now the water was rising above them and, powerless to move, they were slowly drowning.

Michael Herr's description of a Viet Cong caught on the wire at Khe Sanh is equally moving. 'We heard then what sounded at first like a little girl crying,' he reported, 'a subdued, delicate wailing, and as we listened it became louder and more intense, taking on pain as it grew until it became a full, piercing shriek.'

These sounds testify to a pain which can be insupportable. Some wounded soldiers kill themselves. A Union artillery sergeant, hit in the abdomen at Antietam, was taken to an improvised aid station where he was told that his wound was mortal: 'In agony, his face lined with pain, the sergeant bit his lip, drew his Colt, and shot himself through the right temple.' Lieutenant Guérin, second-in-command of an Indo-Chinese company at Dien Bien Phu, committed altruistic suicide in the proper sense of the term. Wounded in both legs in the fighting for *Huguette*, he shot himself in the head rather than risk the lives of his men who had begun crawling back to rescue him.

Others are so badly wounded that they are quietly put down. The French surgeon Ambroise Paré, one of the fathers of military medicine, encountered three badly-burnt soldiers in Turin as the French army entered the city in 1536.

Beholding them with pity there came an old soldier who asked me if there was any means of curing them. I told him no. At once he approached them and cut their throats gently and, seeing this great cruelty, I shouted at him that he was a villain. He answered me that he prayed to God that should he be in such a state he might find someone who would do the same for him, to the end that he might not languish miserably.[3]

Guy Sajer admitted to doing much the same on the Eastern Front in the Second World War. 'We shot a great many men to put them out of their misery,' he wrote, 'although mercy killings were strictly forbidden.'

Some men beg for death. Private Roy Bealing of the 6th Wiltshires heard his chum Bill Parratt, desperately wounded on the first day of the Somme, calling out, 'Captain Lefroy, come and shoot me', and S.L.A. Marshall wrote of a sergeant wounded in Vietnam saying, 'If you would just give me a grenade, I'd blow my damned guts out.' It takes great moral courage to accede to such a request. Pioneer Georg Zobel passed through St Quentin just after the British had bombarded it with gas shells on the eve of the German March offensive.

> Here and there were men from other units who had been surprised by the gas. They sat or lay and vomited pieces of their corroded lungs. Horrible, this death! And, much as they implored us, nobody dared to give them the *coup de grâce*. We were badly shaken by it all.

A common solution is to do what Lefroy did, and to administer a heavy dose of morphia in the hope that it will ease the victim out of his agony. 'We always carried morphia for emergencies like that,' agreed Robert Graves. At Goose Green a sergeant in 2 Para shot a burning Argentinian who could not be rescued. Although his action caused some comment in the press, he was doing nothing more than render a fellow soldier a last service: there can be few of us who would not rather perish thus than, in Paré's words, languish miserably. Indeed, suicide pacts are not uncommon amongst soldiers. Bob Sanders's comrades often used to ask one another to finish them off if they were badly wounded: 'If I lose a leg or arm or something like that, blow me away, man, if you can do it without somebody seeing you.'

When men do get blown away by their friends, it is not always on purpose: accidental death is always a threat. The prospect of being killed or wounded is all the more alarming because of the capricious way in which death and injury strike in wartime. Until relatively recently more soldiers perished from disease than were killed in battle. Even today accidents of various sorts take their toll. John Parrish described how Americans in Vietnam fell victim not only to the Viet Cong but also to 'vehicles, snakes, plane crashes, overdoses of hard drugs, mud, water, bacteria, falls, bunker cave-ins, or even tigers'.

Accidents frequently happen when sentries fire on friendly strangers. The Prussian General von Verdy du Vernois admitted that 'many a one of our men had been hit in the dark by the bullets of his comrades', while the official records of his French opponents bear witness to the same difficulty. On the night of 25–6 July, for example, two sentries were shot dead and a captain wounded in a single corps. John Horsfall wrote sadly of a platoon commander killed by a picket in Tunisia: 'It was a hazard inseparable from war and only hard experience taught us how to avoid such things.'

The peril has grown with the advent of indirect fire weapons. General Percin, author of the aptly-named *La Massacre de Notre Infanterie*, estimated that 75,000 French soldiers were killed by their own artillery during the First World War. Worn barrels, faulty fuses, miscalculations on the gun position, inaccurate grid references, and, perhaps most seriously, the deliberate engagement of a friendly position which is not recognised as such, all play their part in making artillery something of a double-edged weapon. The record of air power is no better. Allied troops were severely bombed by their own aircraft in Italy and Normandy. On 24–5 July 1944, during the preparation for Operation Cobra, American bombers killed 111 American soldiers – including Lieutenant-General Lesley J. McNair, the highest-ranking American fatality of the war – and wounded another 490. These difficulties are, like accidental engagements between sentries or patrols, almost unavoidable. They do, however, cause feelings of resentment, irritation and guilt out of all proportion to the damage they inflict. The few accidental patrol clashes that occurred in the Falklands – 'friendly-friendlys' or 'blue on blue' – are recalled by some of those involved as more painful episodes than the battle for Mount Longdon.

The careless use of weapons has been a source of casualties, if the historian Herodotus is to be believed, ever since the Persian King Cambyses died in 522 BC after wounding himself with his own sword. A soldier of the 43rd Regiment was cleaning his musket after the capture of Badajoz when it went off, shooting a corporal through the head: the latter had survived the bloody storm, only to perish through a tired man's momentary inattention. Lieutenant-Colonel Thomas Gonne of the 17th Lancers shot himself while supervising NCOs' pistol practice on the day that his regiment received orders to leave for the Zulu War of 1879. *Sous-Lieutenant* Masson of the French 65th of the Line was more culpable. In September 1870, as the plight of the *Armée du Rhin* worsened, he sought solace in drink, and accidentally shot his company sergeant-major with his pistol.

Some mishaps are bitterly ironic. Amongst the first dead of the English Civil War were six Royalist gunners, killed when their piece burst, and the few casualties of a very early skirmish, in July 1642, included one man who had shot himself through the foot and another who had been shot in the back by his rear-rank man. Later, Lieutenant-Colonel Arthur Swayne was 'slain by his boy, teaching him to use his arms. He bid the boy aim at him (thinking the gun had not been charged) which he did only too well.' John Kincaid saw two of his riflemen blown up when their sword-bayonets struck sparks from an ammunition wagon they were cutting up for firewood after Waterloo. No sooner had the Duke of Wellington dismounted from his charger Copenhagen after the same battle than the beast lashed out and nearly brained him. One of the loyal sepoys who had helped defend the Baillie Guard Gate of the Lucknow Residency during the Indian Mutiny was shot by members of the relieving force, determined to take no chance in the half-light. He died, murmuring philosophically: 'It was fated. Victory to the Baillie Guard.' At the very end of the American Civil War, a Union officer who had lived through several hard-fought battles was killed when a horse trod on and discharged a loaded musket amongst a pile which had been used to corduroy a muddy road. Sergeant Nieweg, one of the very few Germans to escape from Stalingrad, was killed twenty-four hours later when a stray mortar bomb hit a dressing station. Raymond Cooper noted the death of 'two unfortunate Indians who, getting too near the supply dropping area, were hit on the head by bully beef tins'. Colonel C.A. McDowall recorded a similar incident, when an aircraft in difficulties jettisoned its cargo of bags of rice, one of which landed on a jeep and killed two of the four occupants.

Just as clashes between friendly patrols cause disproportionate distress, so too do these other accidents take their toll of men's spirit. For, dreadful though the sight of the dead and wounded men on a battlefield may be, it is none the less expected. Accidental death off a battlefield is often more damaging than deliberately-inflicted death on it. Marc Bloch was shocked by the death of some men who were killed when a hut collapsed. 'I would have felt less grief', he wrote, 'if they had succumbed to the enemy.' A soldier of the 71st recalled that the rows of dead and wounded at Waterloo were far less alarming than a single accidental death in barracks, and an NCO in 3 Para remarked that the sight of the dead on Mount Longdon did not disturb him, while a road accident 'really turned me up'.

Although casualty statistics veil the human cost of war by numbers which are so great as to be almost impossible to grasp, they do emphasise the frequency of accident. As late as the Second World War sickness caused more casualties than battle: there were rather more than two sick to every one wounded in both the British and American armies. But accidental injuries, too, accounted for more than their fair share of casualties. In Burma in 1942-3 there were roughly five times more non-battle than battle injuries, and it was only in 1944 that a British soldier in Italy was more likely to be hurt on the battlefield than off it. In Vietnam 41,853 Americans were killed in ground actions, but another 5,540 soldiers died from non-battle injuries. Just over a thousand of these perished in vehicle crashes, and almost as many were drowned or suffocated. Negligent discharges and accidental engagements contributed to 846 deaths from 'accidental self destruction' and another 939 'accidental homicides'.

The sad tally of accidental deaths in Vietnam underlines a common cause of death or injury in wartime: the fatal attraction of deadly games. Sergeant-Major Mike Kukler tells of the problems caused by Americans trying to outdraw one another, a sport that killed sixty men in the first four months of 1968.

Men would buy specially made low-slung holsters and the soldiers would face each other like cowboys and Indians looking for a fast draw. About half the deaths occurred in the 19, 20 and 21 year-old age groups. Thirty per cent of all deaths were caused when the fast drawer shot himself in the leg. One-fourth of these deaths were officer deaths.

Second World War Russian officers sometimes played a lethal game called 'cuckoo'. The players stood around the walls of a darkened room with loaded pistols. Each cried 'cuckoo' in turn and the others fired at where they thought the sound had come from.

Rick Jolly's first 'war' casualty in 1982 was a soldier who had been playing with a grenade. One of Peter Kemp's comrades was killed while competing with another officer to see who could pick up the most unexploded grenades, and *légionnaires* in beleaguered Dien Bien Phu crept out to the corpses of Viet Minh 'death volunteers' to recover the explosive they were carrying. It was no practical use to them: the ritual was, writes Bernard Fall: 'a gesture of pure bravado, of gratuitous defiance of fate and duly appreciated as such by all concerned'. By deliberately courting death on his own terms the soldier is not merely displaying bravery which he hopes will impress his fellows: he is also removing some of the randomness from the risks of war, and making its stresses more tolerable by facing them at a time and place of his own choosing.

Accidental death is utterly pointless, and its purposelessness is often highlighted by a commonplace environment to which death should be a stranger. Worse, the very fact that death – in the shape of a stray shell or badly-fused grenade – can reach out to grab men who feel themselves to be safe extends risk beyond the battlefield. This process has been going on for some time, although aircraft, long-range artillery and special forces have accelerated its development over the past fifty years. Colonel G.F.R. Henderson, writing almost a century ago, was more than usually prescient when he pointed out: 'The battlefield in the old days was a comparatively safe locality except at close quarters; but today death has a wider range and if the losses of a modern battle are relatively less the strain on the nerves is far more severe.' 'There was no such thing as one moment's complete security,' affirmed Moran. One of his fellow medical officers survived the fighting at Hooge in August 1915, only to have his head taken off by an isolated shell which fell in a wood in a quiet sector. Even if one is miles from the firing line, Mars still rolls his dice.

Survival on the battlefield itself often seems to depend upon what Frederick the Great called 'His Sacred Majesty Chance'. A trivial decision or unplanned movement can mean the difference between life and death. Stephen Westman left his company for a few moments to relieve himself. A shell burst squarely amongst his comrades, and the pack upon which his head had been resting an instant before was transfixed by a splinter. William Manchester was walking back to his squad when he tripped and fell: at that very instant they were obliterated by a shell. Hannah Arendt was right to maintain that 'nowhere else does Fortune, good or ill luck, play a more fateful role in human affairs than on the battlefield'.

Both dead and wounded have to be dealt with. An increasingly sophisticated chain of medical evacuation means that the wounded soldier has an excellent chance of being evacuated by vehicle or by helicopter, and receiving professional aid relatively quickly. Nevertheless, there are tactical circumstances in which immediate evacuation is impossible, and even in the best of cases a wounded man, urgently appealing to every human sympathy, will be the responsibility of his comrades for the first few crucial minutes.

There are two aspects to this particular problem. The most obvious is that of providing life-saving first aid under difficult conditions. Improvements in first-aid training and the advancement of medical science undoubtedly help, but the practical obstacles remain frighteningly unyielding. In April 1944 Birdie Smith was in a forward base planning a raid on a German mortar position when he heard mines explode in the darkness. The noise was followed by news that his friend Gunnar Keightly had been wounded in the leg. After much thought and a discussion with another officer Smith split his force and pressed on, while Keightly's escort carried him towards the British lines.

Smith's patrols were mortared and two riflemen were badly wounded: they too had to be evacuated, across rough country made dangerous by mines and the ever-present risk of mortar fire.

> One of the wounded was making loud wailing noises, groaning in terrible pain. There were no stretchers. Obviously Matt would have given both morphia injections but the men faced a harrowing ordeal, however careful the carriers were. 62 Balbahadur Rai did not survive the journey and the A Company sentry who challenged Matt's party saw the lifeless body of his friend carried in.

When Smith later asked the battalion's medical officer how Keightly was, the doctor replied sharply that his condition was serious, all the more so because the patrol's first aid had been so poor. 'Just think of all the hours I've spent trying to teach everyone in the Battalion the simple rudiments of first aid,' he complained. 'If he dies, well ...' Keightly did die, and Smith, writing in 1978, described how he continued to mourn him each Armistice Day, in part because 'I felt guilty at my failure to help and comfort a dear friend after he had been wounded by the mine.'

I examine this incident at length not only because it illustrates the practical difficulty of recovering the wounded from the battlefield, but also because it underlines the second problem created by a wounded man – that of continuing with the mission when all one's instincts are to help the victim. Successive generations of soldiers have been reminded that the job comes first. Sir Colin Campbell harrangued his Highland Brigade just before it crossed the Alma, warning the men to pay no attention to the wounded, who would be dealt with by the bandsmen and stretcher bearers. If any man stopped to help the wounded, his name would be put up in his village kirk. The same order was given before both the Somme and El Alamein, although on these occasions there was no recourse to the ultimate sanction of the kirk.

It is an order more easily given than obeyed. Paddy Griffith's comment on Vietnam, that care for the wounded often seemed to be given a higher priority than the continuation of battle, dovetails into John Parrish's description of how group aims were adjusted if a man was wounded: 'a marine becomes especially important if he is wounded ... The group is then sacrificed for the individual.' Few soldiers can remain deaf to the pleadings of a wounded man. 'We could hear someone over towards the German entanglements calling for a stretcher-bearer,' said an Australian soldier of the First World War. 'It was an appeal no man could stand against; so some of us rushed out & had a hunt; we found a fine haul of wounded & brought them in.'

There were occasions during the 1973 Arab-Israeli War when Israeli soldiers pulled working tanks out of the line to evacuate wounded. Some medical officers blamed this on inadequate training in first aid, and their hypothesis was tested in the Lebanon in 1982. During the preparation for the invasion selected units were given sixty hours of field first-aid training during their twelve weeks basic training. In the fighting itself, 'the units which had received this training had significantly less morbidity and mortality from combat trauma'.[4] British units on their way to the Falklands capitalised upon the time available to improve their standards of first aid. There was, at least in the case of 2 Para, a frank recognition that aggression could only be maintained if soldiers knew that they would be well looked after if they were wounded, and the battalion's second-in-command, Major Christopher Keeble, emphasised that efficient first aid and self-treatment made a vital contribution to success.

The recovery of wounded under fire is a constant feature of battle, with a curious poignancy all of its own. Often men are killed trying to rescue someone who is beyond help in any case. Robert Graves tells how a popular company commander was hit in No-Man's-Land at Loos. 'Samson lay groaning about twenty yards beyond the front trench,' wrote Graves. 'Several attempts were made to rescue him. He had been very badly hit. Three men got killed in these attempts; two officers and two men, wounded.' Graves found him that night, hit in seventeen places; he had forced his knuckles into his mouth to stop himself from crying out and attracting more men to their death. Max Hastings's account of A Company 2 Para at Goose Green has a strangely ageless ring:

Private Tuffen, just seventeen, was hit in the head and kept conscious by his mates for four and a half hours to save him from lapsing into a coma. Private Worrall was wounded. Corporals Abols and Prior ran out to drag him into cover, and were halfway back under fierce machine-gun fire when Prior was hit. Corporal Hardman now dashed to join Abols. Together they brought Prior to within a few feet of safety when a further bullet hit him in the head. They took his body to the safety of the gulley, and went out yet again, to bring in Worrall.

Stretcher-bearers and medical assistants come to occupy an important place in men's affections. Norman Gladden wrote warmly of the fat, lazy and easy-going Private Bell, 'who became a fearless, self-sacrificing hero when there was any succouring to be done'. Charles MacDonald paid tribute to his own company medic, killed as he jumped forward to assist a wounded rifleman. 'He was a "noncombatant", according to the rules of warfare,' wrote MacDonald, 'and was denied the privilege of wearing the combat infantryman badge and the ten dollars per month pittance for the dangers and hardships endured, but death had made no distinction.' Marshall, writing of Vietnam, declared: 'The unstinting faithfulness of the United States aid man to his duty is a phenomenon beyond explanation.' Stan Goff was more prosaic. 'The medics did their best,' he said. 'Those field medics, man, they busted their ass.' It was no accident that the most-decorated British soldier of the First World War – Private W.H. Coltman, VC, DCM and Bar, MM – was a stretcher-bearer.

Caring for the wounded is a task with immediate practical implications, and these can easily dwarf the importance of that other grim duty, dealing with the dead. But the disposal of the dead has a significance which goes far beyond the battlefield itself. Although most soldiers quickly adjust to the sight of the dead, or develop a rough humour which helps them to cope, a corpse provides convincing evidence of their own mortality. 'At the back of the mind', wrote Denis Winter, 'was the knowledge that the corpse was once a living man like oneself, in the same situation and therefore initially no more likely to meet death than oneself.' The sight of a corpse has a similar, if more profound, effect to that heart-stopping aphorism often used by medieval stonemasons:

> As you are now, so I once was
> As I am now, so will you be.

It is, by and large, young men who find themselves at the proverbial sharp end of war. An analysis of one million casualties of the First World War showed that 80 per cent were under thirty: Norman Gladden recalled that a man in his thirties 'seemed old to us'. George Orwell thought that the average age in the Republican militias was well under twenty. Bill Maudlin's inimitable cartoon characters Joe and Willie spanned the age spectrum of Second World War American infantry: 'Joe is in his early twenties and Willie is in his early thirties – pretty average age for the infantry.' The average age of Philippe de Pirey's comrades in a French parachute battalion in Indo-China in 1950 was twenty, and the members of B Company 2 Para in the Falklands were a year younger. Robert Santos, a rifle platoon leader in 101st Airborne Division in Vietnam in 1967–8, estimated that the average of his platoon was 'around nineteen. We had an old guy, Coogan. He was twenty-eight.'

Lord Moran connected the age of soldiers to their perception of death. 'War is the business of youth,' he wrote, 'and no young man thinks he can ever die.' Flight-Lieutenant Richard Hillary's views typify those of most young men. 'That I might be killed or in any way injured did not occur to me,' he reflected. 'Later, when we were losing pilots regularly, I did consider it in an abstract way when on the ground; but once in the air, never. I knew it could not happen to me.' 'It was easier to believe the sky would fall,' wrote Lord Lovat, 'than that any of us might one day be killed.' Glenn Gray argued that most soldiers 'are able to gain only a negative relation to death. For them, death is a state and a condition so foreign and unreal as to be incomprehensible.' In his 1981 Bronowski Memorial Lecture, Dr Nicholas Humphrey went even further, and declared:

> people do not really accept the fact of their own death. Like a suicide who leaves a note, 'I picture you reading this note when I am gone', people picture themselves standing above the chaos in which they themselves have died – and may experience a sickening excitement at the images of destruction and decay.

As the soldier's experience of war grows, however, he is forcibly reminded that death is no longer something which happens only to pets and grandparents. The death of his friends loosens his own hold on the illusion of immortality. Lord Moran tells of an admirable soldier who finally cracked when the last of his brothers was killed. 'I think, sir,' he said, 'when Tom went that did it.' One of Mark Baker's interviewees identified this change in his own feelings.

> The hardest thing to accept is that it's for real and forever. It was permanent. I'd been to funerals in my time. I'd been an altar boy and served at funerals. I had family friends and relatives that had died and I'd been to funeral parlors and seen dead people. But these guys were really young and peers of mine.

The manner in which death comes to the soldier, as well as the very fact of death itself, serves to alarm his friends. Many men are prepared to face a quick, clean death: indeed, they may even regard it as preferable to a crippling wound or to personal disgrace. But some of death's faces are particularly terrible. The prospect of being blown to pieces by a shell unmans many soldiers. It is, as Moran put it: 'something more than death, [and] all their plans for meeting it with decency and credit were suddenly battered down; it was not so much that their lives were in danger as that their self-respect had gone out of their hands'. Robert Jay Lifton observed that worries about dying without purpose or dignity were a recurrent dream amongst Vietnam veterans: 'I would end up shot, lying along the side of the road, dying in the mud.' Charlton Ogburn's first experience of shelling convinced him:

> They mean to blow your entrails out. And they may well succeed ... looking like something in a butcher's shop, you will be covered over with this musty-smelling, alien earth, the golden edifice of your future, sunlit tower upon sunlit tower reaching skyward, levelled to this indifferent leafmold acrawl with ants.

What happens to the body after death is a matter of greater concern than logic might suggest. In an article on the discovery of a massive ossuary at York in 1983, Bernard Levin wrote:

> it would be as surprising to find an era or a culture that did not surround death with elaborate and profound beliefs and rituals as it would be to find a race of men with three legs ... One of the greatest terrors that haunts any deathbed is that of the casual or contemptuous disposal of the dying one's body.

Many ancient judicial punishments were designed to make death painful, exemplary and destructive. Oliver Cromwell was exhumed and hanged after the Restoration, and his skull was left to whiten on a spike over Westminster Hall. In Britain commoners were hanged, drawn and quartered for high treason, and the grim terms of their sentence left them in no doubt that the process would not only be agonising, but that it would also desecrate their mortal remains.

> Let the prisoner be drawn to the gaol from whence he came; and from thence he must be drawn to the place of execution; and when he comes there he must be hanged by the neck, but not till he be dead, for he must be cut down alive; then his bowels must be taken out and burned before his face; then his head must be severed from his body, and his body divided into four quarters; and these must be at the King's disposal.

Barbarity of this sort was not confined to Britain. The stately elegance of eighteenth-century France in the age of the *philosophes* did not prevent Damiens, would-be assassin of Louis XV, from being publicly tortured with pincers and boiling liquids before being dismembered by four horses. Nor were the Germans much better: in 1710 a servant girl in Konigsberg who infected herself and her master with the plague was exhumed, hanged, and burnt at the foot of the gallows.

This grisly excursion into judicial savagery, if it reveals nothing else, illustrates the psychological importance of the disposal of the body after death, and re-emphasises the horror of the obliterating death by high explosive. Proper burial of the dead, accompanied by a degree of formalised mourning, is as necessary for those who die in battle as it is for those who perish in more peaceful circumstances. Having some sort of focus for mourning is useful for the dead soldier's comrades, but even more so for his family. The most powerful argument for repatriating the bodies of fallen soldiers is precisely that it gives comfort to their families by providing such a focus.

In contrast, it seems that most soldiers themselves would prefer to be buried where they fall. Lindsay had no doubts on the matter.

I wish they could all be left to lie where they have been so tenderly placed by those who loved them, near where they fell. I hate the idea of them being dug up and reinterred in some military cemetery, where the grave-stones will remain for posterity and their bodies will be dressed by the right, regimented in death.

William Manchester's section often discussed the subject, since it seemed that the question might soon cease to be hypothetical. 'The unanimous conviction', he wrote, 'was that our bodies ought to be spaded under out here on the islands.'

Burial near the battlefield allows a man's comrades to mourn, and to gain comfort thereby. Some sort of funeral, however informal it may be, also helps to camouflage the randomness and capriciousness of death, and even the most primitive of shrouds hides the ravages of bullets and shell fragments, restoring order and decency to a violated corpse. Soldiers take as much care as they can over digging their comrades' graves. Lance-Corporal Harold Chapin told his wife how two men had been buried in May 1915. 'Their chums were so particular', he wrote, 'to dig them a level grave and a *rectangular* grave and *parallel* graves, and to note who was in this grave and who in that.' Cyclist Jimmy Smith of the Northern Cyclist Battalion was less fortunate when burying his best friend, Ernie Gays. 'I took him by the ankles, the other two took him by the arms, and we laid him in and covered him up,' he wrote. 'I remember feeling a bit upset, for the grave was only about four feet deep. I knew he probably wouldn't be there for very long, because of the shell-fire.'

The distinguished South African Denys Reitz, then serving as a British infantry officer, saw a party of soldiers carrying their dead officer on the March retreat.

The moon shone full on the dead man's face, and I saw that it was Captain Newlands, whom I knew very well ... I asked the men where they were carrying the body to, and one of them said that they weren't going to allow no bl——dy Boche to bury the skipper, so the worthy fellows had taken upon themselves the self-imposed task of carrying their company commander back to the next line of defence, to ensure him against alien burial.

Moran observed that men worked hard to decorate the grave of a popular officer, and M. Warner, impressed as he was by the toughness of the East Yorkshires, assault troops on D-Day, noticed that some of them put roses on their comrades' graves.

Numerous soldiers – even those of no particular religious belief – find attending a comrade's burial a help in adjusting to the reality of his death. Billy Congreve was deeply moved by the funeral of his much-loved divisional commander, Major-General Hubert Hamilton.

> The scene was one of the strangest and most beautiful I have ever seen. The poor church battered by shells, the rough wooden coffin with a pewter plate on which we had stamped his name, a rough cross of flowers made by the men, the small guard with fixed bayonets and the group of twenty to thirty bareheaded officers and men. Above all, the incessant noise, so close, sometimes dying down only to redouble itself a few minutes later.

Brigadier Lord Lovat, another redoubtable fighting soldier, was similarly affected by a burial in a Normandy orchard.

> There was a tenderness under the apple trees as powder-grimed officers and men brought in the dead; a tenderness for lost comrades, who had fought together so often and so well, that went beyond reverence and compassion ... Funerals in the field, rough and ready though they be, seem less bleak than those performed with funeral rites, as though the soldier whose calling deals with sudden death can find a way to stand easy in its shadow.

Finally, Rick Jolly's account of the funeral of the dead of Goose Green has, for me, a quiet sadness all of its own, for I knew and respected one of them.

The funeral is a fierce event. Nearly 200 men stand in silence aroung the edge of the mass grave, heads uncovered, the majority with hands clasped loosely in prayer. Officers mix with soldiers, Paras mingle with Royal Marines. Above us is the dome of a perfectly blue sky, while, crystal-clear in the distance, snow gleams on the summit of Mount Kent.

In their repeated dealings with wounds and death, soldiers may eventually develop a shell of cynicism or indifference, or they may be so affected, particularly by the death of close friends, that they find it impossible to continue. But whatever the precise nature of men's response to it, there can be no doubting the fact that the fear of being killed or wounded, and the experience of watching others suffer and die, make a powerful contribution to the strain of battle.

6

The Real Enemy

The real enemy was Terror, and all this heel-click-
ing, saluting, bright brass and polish were our
charms and incantations for keeping him at bay.
        Alan Hanbury-Sparrow, *The Land-Locked Lake*

The Common Bond

Fear is the common bond between fighting men. The overwhelming majority of soldiers experience fear during or before
battle: what vary are its physical manifestations, its nature
and intensity, the threat which induces it, and the manner in
which it is managed. Only a tiny percentage of soldiers never
know fear at all. Field-Marshal Sir John French, writing pri-
vately and apparently honestly, denied that he had ever felt
frightened, and an American infantry officer of the Vietnam
era wrote that: 'Frankly, fear did not affect me, though I
thought at the time that I was appropriately prudent ... The
utter absence of fear in my recollections has been a puzzle to
me.' These are exceptional cases. In the former instance, a
deeply-held belief in the immortality of the soul probably
prevented French from being frightened of death, though it
can do little to explain his lack of fear of other threats. Given
that fear is, as MacCurdy puts it, 'the natural, and therefore

204

a reasonable, response to danger', this 'fearlessness' may well spring from the early and effective triumph of one of the coping systems which we shall examine shortly. It may also reflect the fact that a man's conception of battle often turns out to be more alarming than the real thing. As one of Mark Baker's interviewees put it, 'what was taking place was so much less terrifying than the pitched battles I had imagined in my head that the level of fear was just not that high'.

But for the great mass of the less fortunate, fear is present to a greater or lesser degree, and may be experienced as anything from mild apprehension to paralysing terror. Its physical symptoms are well documented, and one does not have to have survived battle to have experienced at least the most moderate of them. A violent pounding of the heart is the most common: at least 68 per cent of the soldiers questioned by Stouffer acknowledged this symptom, as did 69 per cent of John Dollard's veterans. A sinking feeling in the stomach, uncontrollable trembling, a cold sweat, a feeling of weakness or stiffness and vomiting were also reported, in more or less that order of frequency. Six per cent of Dollard's sample admitted to involuntary urination and 5 per cent to involuntary defecation. In one of the divisions examined by Stouffer, these symptoms were reported by 21 per cent and 10 per cent of those questioned.

Losing control of bladder and bowels are the symptoms of fear which tend to be most unwelcome, primarily because of the cultural taboos surrounding these bodily functions, and, of course, because they are difficult to conceal. Birdie Smith, dashing back to rejoin his company below the Castle at Cassino, was narrowly missed by a sniper. 'Once again the crack, crack, a blow on my haversack, and then the safety of another rock,' he wrote. 'Breathless, in tears and humbled to find that fear had caused my bowels to move, I lay as dead until a glance at my watch spurred me on.' Later, he briefed his NCOs, 'trying to ignore shaking hands and the tell-tale wet patch down my trouser legs'. Peter Halford-Thompson spoke of 'an embarrassing looseness in the bowels', and a Scottish infantry officer commented that 'of course one's bowels often turned to water'.

Before going into action for the first time, men are often more frightened of disgracing themselves than they are of being killed or wounded. This fear of disgrace spurs many soldiers, particularly officers and NCOs who feel that they have most to lose by showing weakness, into concealing the symptoms of fear as best they can. 'Most of all,' wrote a Second World War platoon commander in the Queen's Regiment, 'one was afraid of showing fear in front of one's men. This I feel is the main plank an officer or NCO has to keep him going.' Fear made Alan Briddon 'determined (if possible) not to show it', and Peter Halford-Thompson, too, was afraid of showing fear. 'Afraid of fear – death holds no fear', was the view of another experienced officer. Yet another wrote: 'There's only one way to fight it; strength; you must be strong with yourself, with your men, with everything; never weaken; never show you're afraid. Everybody cracks up in the end, of course, but you hope something will have happened by then.' Three-quarters of Dollard's veterans thought it important that they should suppress the signs of fear, and almost as many believed that their own behaviour in trying to set an example of courage to others made them 'a much better soldier'.

This approach to fear has several important ramifications. At the simplest level, suppression of the symptoms of fear by the leader may indeed make him remarkably effective in persuading others, by example, to overcome their own fear. This can promote that mutual stimulation of courage described in Tacitus's account of the German tribesman of the first century AD. 'On the field of battle', he wrote, 'it is a disgrace to a chief to be surpassed in courage by his followers, and to followers not to equal the courage of their chief.' Stuart Mawson was standing in a Dakota waiting to jump at Arnhem when the aircraft was hit by flak and several of the stick fell over. Lieutenant-Colonel George Lea, his commanding officer and first to jump, turned briefly from the open door and the hurtling world.

His face was grey and beads of perspiration stood on his forehead and trickled down the sides of his eyes.

'Stand steady there,' he commanded clearly. 'Stand steady.'

His voice contained:

> the conviction of the resolute that a surrender to fear is a surrender to the will of the enemy, and that battle is first and foremost a conflict of the spirit; and the men in the stick stood steady, while the plane that carried them plunged through the barrage.

Sometimes this iron repression of fear is achieved only at a great cost, and the inner conflict it engenders may lead to psychiatric illness. It may also make leaders reluctant to tolerate the symptoms of fear in others. In this case it does both leader and led a notable disservice. During the Second World War the American army adopted the explicit policy of building up a permissive attitude toward fear symptoms amongst the troops, and Stouffer's researches show that men who exhibited these symptoms were not necessarily poorly regarded by their comrades: 'The key factor which was stressed by the interviewees', he writes, 'was *effort to overcome the withdrawal tendencies engendered by intense fear.*'

Major-General Frank Richardson, a medical officer with extensive practical experience of both the consequences and the mitigation of stress in battle, argues that, as part of the measures employed to reduce psychiatric casualties, soldiers of all ranks should be told about such casualties and about fear and its symptoms. The physical symptoms of fear, writes Richardson, are 'simply due to rapid involuntary muscular action designed to warm up the body for the anticipated activity'. They do not mean that a man will crack, and imply no disgrace. Richardson drives home his point by citing the fact that 9th Armoured Division, to which he had given comprehensive pre-battle talks, experienced no psychiatric casualties at El Alamein. He used the same technique with a brigade of 51st (Highland) Division in Normandy in 1944, and the only battalion which he was not permitted to address later broke in panic. Thus, while there are undoubtedly benefits in leaders ruthlessly suppressing their own symptoms of fear, they should take care not to create a climate in which fear cannot be discussed.

We have already seen how, as a man's experience of battle grows, the object of his greatest fear is likely to change from the fear of proving a coward to that of suffering crippling wounds: the role played by the sight of the dead and wounded in shaping his perception of the threat is crucial. Dreadful sights may emphasise particular sorts of fear: during the First World War, for example, the spectre of being buried alive haunted many. Private T.C.H. Jacobs of the 15th London Regiment, crouching against the wall of his trench while the German barrage hammered British lines on the morning of 21 March 1918, remembered: 'Never at any time, then or later, did I think I might be killed, but I *was* afraid of being buried alive if the walls caved in.' In December 1914, Private P.H. Jones of the Queen's Westminsters noted that: 'Nightmares are very common and it is curious to note that everyone has the same dream of the dugout falling in and being buried alive. At times this dream is so vivid that a man wakes up yelling in a positive fever of anguish.'

Though fear of wounds and death looms large, there are other, apparently less logical fears. A British machine-gunner of the First World War had no hesitation in saying that rats, not shells, were his greatest fear.

> To enter a rat-infested dug-out or billet, tired and longing for sleep, haversack for a pillow containing the then iron rations of two or three biscuits, a tin with tea and sugar, Bovril cubes on the top. Then the rats trying to gnaw through the haversack – horrible.

John Harper was Staff Captain in an Indian Infantry Brigade during the retreat up Burma in 1942. The commanding officer of one of the brigade's battalions was shot dead beside him, and he had plenty of other evidence of the effects of Japanese artillery and small-arms fire. What worried him, however, was not the Japanese – 'I was too bloody busy for that' – but the prospect of catching a tropical disease.

An experienced soldier may even be more frightened of social embarrassment than of battle. In 1853, François du Barail, then *chef d'escadron* in the 5th Hussars, with a score of sharp actions behind him, attended an imperial *levée*, and admitted that: 'I was more worried in the *salon* at Saint-Cloud than I was before charging a great body of Arab cavalry.' Major F.S. Anderson, Royal Field Artillery, emerged from his sleeping bag on a French train to face a civic reception at a station. 'I have no recollection of ever having been so badly frightened before, during the whole war,' he wrote. Peter Bourne testified to similar fears in Vietnam, where one lieutenant 'was more apprehensive about his forthcoming wedding than about the bullets he faced every day'.

Fears of the effects of enemy weapons have a similar tendency towards illogicality: soldiers do not necessarily most fear those weapons which do the most damage. Dollard's subjects feared bombs most of all; then trench mortars, artillery shells, bayonet and knife, and expanding bullets; and finally grenades, strafing, machine-guns and tanks. Stouffer asked one group of veterans which weapon they rated as most frightening. The 88mm gun topped the list, distantly pursued by the dive bomber, mortar, horizontal bomber, light machine-gun, strafing, and land mines. When the same men were asked what enemy weapon they thought the most dangerous in terms of the numbers of men they believed it killed or wounded the batting order was similar – with two significant exceptions. The dive bomber was considered most frightening by 20 per cent of the men, but only 4 per cent felt it to be most dangerous, and the horizontal bomber, deemed most frightening by 12 per cent, was rated most dangerous by 5 per cent.

In strictly rational terms, mortar and artillery fire should be the most alarming, for it has been the greatest killer – although not necessarily a cost-effective killer – in the major wars of this century. Casualty statistics are a useful indication of what weapons do the most damage, although they need to be used with some care, because the method of calculation is rarely the same from war to war or even between theatres within the same conflict. During the First World War, shells and mortar bombs caused 58·51 per cent of British casualties, bullets 38·98 per cent, bombs and grenades 2·19 per cent and bayonets 0·32 per cent. In the Second World War mortars, grenades, aerial bombs and shells accounted for 75 per cent of British casualties, bullets and anti-tank shells for 10 per cent, with the remaining 15 per cent being produced by blast, crush, phosphorus and miscellaneous agents.

Small arms caused the American forces 3 per cent of their deaths and 27 per cent of their wounds in Korea, while shell and mortar fragments were responsible for 59 per cent and 61 per cent respectively. Despite the relative paucity of North Vietnamese and Viet Cong artillery in the Vietnam War, no less than 65 per cent of United States wounds and 36 per cent of deaths were caused by artillery and mortars, with small-arms producing 51 per cent of the fatal casualties and 16 per cent of the wounds. Finally, of British fatal casualties sustained in land operations in the Falklands, 47 were killed by gunshot wounds, 12 by fragments and 21 by blast. In this instance most of the blast casualties were caused by Argentinian artillery which was neither numerous nor, mercifully, notably effective.

A good deal of fear in battle is irrational, and is aroused because a particular weapon is felt to be especially frightening although, rationally, it may not be recognised as being particularly dangerous. Air attack causes a disproportionate amount of alarm. Tom Wintringham wrote: 'Aeroplanes are most effective against morale. They frighten; they exhaust; they break nerves. They do not, usually, in fact, kill many men.' The dive bomber is the classic example of this in the Second World War. The Junkers 87 Stuka suffered from numerous technical disadvantages: it was slow, and dangerously vulnerable in air-to-air combat. But its shrieking sound – a deliberate psychological warfare ploy – and its sinister gull-winged silhouette helped to make it far more frightening than the casualties it inflicted really warranted.

Central to the question of fear of a weapon is the soldier's perception of his ability to do something about it. Aimed rifle fire may be a direct personal threat, but it is a threat directed by another individual. Artillery or booby traps are different. 'I could deal with a man,' announced one of Mark Baker's interviewees. 'That meant my talent against his for survival, but how do you deal with him when he ain't even there?' An NCO in 3 Para used almost exactly the same form of words when describing why he found artillery fire more alarming than snipers: 'A sniper's just another man, and your training tells you what to do. But what do you do about some fucker four miles away?'

Mines have come to occupy an important place in the canon of fear-producing agents. They may not be notably effective, but they engender great fear. In part this is because they are an impersonal, inhuman threat, feared in the same way that Second World War pilots feared the impersonal flak more than the personal but more deadly fighters. Not only are mines and booby-traps impersonal, but both can strike at any time, without warning: they help to extend danger from the firing line through to the lines of communication. John Horsfall wrote:

> I never liked mining, either by our side or by the enemy, and our men detested this double-edged weapon which put defence in a straitjacket. All war is confusion and I should not be surprised if we lost more men by our mining than by that of the enemy.

Raleigh Trevelyan felt very much the same. 'I don't mind a fighting chance,' he wrote, 'but I have a dread of mines.' Tim O'Brien gives a penetrating account of the anxiety produced by mines in Vietnam.

> You hallucinate. You look ahead a few paces and wonder what your legs will resemble if there is more to the earth in

that spot than silicates and nitrogen. Will the pain be unbearable? Will you scream or fall silent? Will you be afraid
to look at your own body, afraid of the sight of your own
red flesh and white bone?

Some units found the threat of mines very serious in the Falklands: once one mine went off, it was all too easy for everybody to believe that they had found another.

Chemical weapons are also great fear-producers. Norman
Gladden recalled that First World War gas shells, widely used
after 1915 by both sides, 'inspired a fear that was out of all
proportion to the damage done', and Billy Congreve, un-
daunted by so much, complained that gas 'is a new horror in
this already horrible war, and there is something depressing
in gas'. 'It's damnable,' opined Robert Graves's comrade Captain Thomas gloomily – but depressingly accurately – about
gas on the eve of Loos. 'It's not soldiering to use stuff like
that, even though the Germans did start it. It's dirty, and it'll
bring us bad luck. We're sure to bungle it.' Alan Hanbury-
Sparrow called it 'the Devil's breath'.

It was Ahrimanic from the first velvety phut of the shell
burst to those corpse-like breaths that a man inhaled almost
unawares. It lingered about out of control. When he fired
it, man released an evil force that became free to bite friend
or foe till such time as it died into the earth. Above all, it
went against God-inspired conscience.

Gas attacks sometimes produced, in the form of 'gas hysteria', the ugly spectacle of collective panic. Lord Moran believed that gas was a major cause of psychiatric casualties: it
brought to a head a man's natural unfitness for war, although,
in his view, most of those so afflicted were more frightened
than hurt. Gas was regarded as a major threat by the American Expeditionary Force in France in 1918, although it
caused only a small proportion of American casualties: well
might the American historian William Langer call his memoirs *Gas and Flame in World War I*.

1 Battle piece: illusion. The bridge at Arcola, 1796

2 Battle piece: reality. Champagne, 1917

3 New baptism: US Marine recruits at Parris Island

4-5 The first ritual: British recruits, 1914 (*above*); German recruits, 1937 (*left*)

6-7 The empty battlefield: the Ypres salient, 1917 (*top*); Goose Green, 1982 (*above*)

8–9 Beasts of burden: East
Falkland, 1982 (*above*);
France, 1870–1 (*left*)

10–11 Straight back and
measured tread? North
Africa, 1942 (*opposite
above*); Vietnam, 1967
(*opposite below*)

12–15 Faces of war: British, 1916 (*top left*); German, 1945 (*top right*); French, 1954 (*above left*); Turkish, 1918 (*above right*)

16-17 Death in action: France, 1917 (*top*); Dien Bien Phu, 1954 (*above*)

18 Futility: a French medical officer recognises defeat, Indo-
    China, 1954
19 Comfort: a GI consoles a comrade whose buddy has been
    killed, Korea, August, 1950 (*opposite above*)
20 And bereavement: Vietnam, 1967 (*opposite below*)

21-2 Harvest of death: Antietam, 1862 (*top*); Korea, 1951 (*above*)

23-4 Rags of mortality: Cold Harbor, 1864 (*top*); the Somme, 1916 (*above*)

25-6 Props. Food: SS *panzergrenadiers* on the Russian Front, winter 1942–3 (*left*); and a cigarette: German troops in retreat, summer 1944 (*below*)

27-8 A common humanity? A wounded soldier chats with a prisoner, Pilkem Ridge, 1917 (*opposite above*); a French soldier and a wounded Viet Minh (*opposite below*)

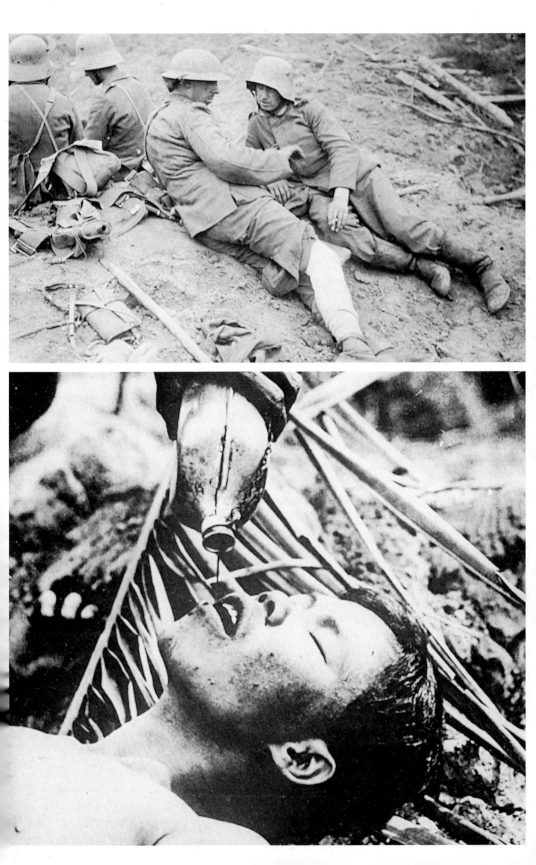

29-30 A bad thing to do. Spain: Goya's *This is Worse* (*above*);
My Lai, 1968 (*below*)

The paraphernalia of protective clothing and chemical detection kits required by soldiers operating in a nuclear, bacteriological or chemical environment saves lives but accentuates stress. Even the best-designed protective suits tend to be hot and uncomfortable. Respirators are curiously dehumanising: identifying familiar and trusted faces becomes difficult behind the rubber equivalent of the medieval pig-faced bascinet. Eating and drinking are tricky, urination is difficult and defecation a major operation.

Brigadier Simpkin has serious doubts as to how long battle can be sustained under such circumstances, particularly once chemical casualties arise. 'It strikes me as highly questionable whether morale can in fact be sustained in the face of even the minimum practical casualty level,' he declares. It may be that he is more pessimistic than the evidence warrants, for at times soldiers of the First World War operated for long periods in a gas-filled environment: if the gas used against them was less efficient than many of the chemical weapons now produced, their protection was also far more primitive than that available today. Lieutenant-Colonel Brian Chermol emphasises that thorough training can diminish the problem: 'There is less likelihood of BF [battle fatigue] casualties or mass "gas hysteria" ... if soldiers have confidence in their NBC equipment and can operate it correctly.' He is undoubtedly right. Nevertheless, in dealing with chemical weapons the soldier faces a threat with awesome practical and psychological aspects. I for one am haunted by Denis Winter's comment: 'In 1990 there will still be 400 men alive blinded by mustard [gas].'

Whatever the object of a soldier's fear, it is evident that both his fear and his ability to master it – his courage – evolve during his exposure to battle. Lord Moran, drawing on his own experience as a regimental medical officer in the trenches of the Western Front, compared a man's courage to his bank account. 'A man's courage is his capital,' he wrote, 'and he is always spending. The call on the bank may be only the daily drain of the front line or it may be a sudden draft which threatens to close the account.' He came to the same conclusions when studying air crews under stress in the Second World War.

> The first and last cause of a pilot's collapse is a persistent state of fear. Therefore more pilots break in Bomber Command than in any other section of the Air Force ... The pilot enters upon the summer of his career, a period of confidence ... of success and achievement ... But these summer months must pass, and when autumn comes the picture of the pilot's distress is no different from that of a soldier or a sailor, only the colouring varies.

Although some of Moran's arguments have been attacked by more recent theorists, there is a wide measure of agreement that the 'well of courage' theory is broadly correct. A study of Allied soldiers in Normandy in 1944 charted their learning curve to a period of maximum efficiency, followed by a decline as combat exhaustion set in.

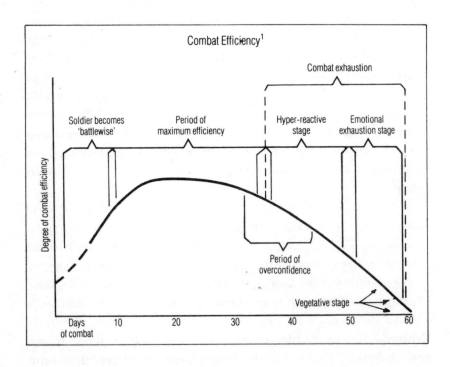

The amount of time required to produce combat exhaustion depends upon a number of factors, not least the intensity of combat. The figure of sixty days is relatively short, and reflects the intensity of the fighting amongst the *bocage* of Normandy. In a Second World War American study, Lieutenant-Colonel J.W. Appel and Captain G.W. Beebe denied that there was any such thing as 'getting used to combat'. 'Each moment of combat', they wrote,

> imposes a strain so great that men will break down in direct relation to the intensity and duration of their exposure ... Just as the average truck wears out after a certain number of miles, it appears that the doughboy wore out, either developing an acute incapacitating neurosis or else becoming hypersensitive to shell fire, so overtly cautious and jittery that he was ineffective and demoralising to the newer men. The average point at which this occurred appears to have been in the region of 200 to 240 aggregate combat days.

The British estimated that a rifleman would last for about 400 combat days. This longer period was because they tended to relieve troops in the line for a four-day rest after twelve days or so, whereas the Americans kept men in the line for 20–30 days, frequently for 30–40 days, and occasionally for 80 days.[2]

These figures are not dissimilar to First World War estimates. Robert Graves believed that it took an officer three weeks to find his way about the trenches. He was at his best between three and four weeks, after which his usefulness gradually declined.

> At six months he was still more or less all right, but by nine or ten months, unless he had been given a few weeks' rest on a technical course, or in hospital, he usually became a drag on the other company officers. After a year or fifteen months he was often worse than useless.

Breakdown in battle is not a twentieth-century phenomenon. A Prussian officer of the Seven Years War described how the Russian gunners at Zorndorf in 1758 'crouched under their pieces and let themselves be massacred'. Captain Cavalié Mercer, commanding a Royal Horse Artillery battery at Waterloo, saw men who 'fled not bodily to be sure, but spiritually, because their senses seemed to have left them'. The novelist Len Deighton, himself no mean historian, suggests that a man's inclination to show fear in this era was diminished by the fact that to do so would result in his being triced up to the halberds and flogged into insensibility, and, certainly, draconian discipline did play its part in suppressing the symptoms of fear.

But the crucial point here is that, while wars were often long, battles were short and relatively infrequent. If modern estimates of a man's tolerance of days of combat are applied to the soldiers of the Napoleonic period, then most of them could have fought for years without amassing as many combat days as, say, a British or American soldier in Italy in 1944–5. Nevertheless, sudden and traumatic shocks – like the concentrated gunfire at Zorndorf or Waterloo – might drain the well of courage dry at a single draught. Sieges, too, whose conditions often approximated to the dangerous stalemate on the Western Front in 1914–18, seemed to bruise men's tolerance more than battles in open field.

One of the major difficulties in the study of stress is that evidence is usually inadequate. It is either anecdotal, or is the product of experiments which tend to be unrealistic or unethical. Parachute jumping is a form of stressful, fear-inducing activity which enables researchers to measure heart rate, respiration rate, basal conductance and galvanic skin responses in order to determine when an individual is most stressed. W.D. Fenz, a leading authority in the field, has concluded that 'the performance of a jumper is related to the way in which he has learned to cope with his anxiety about a forthcoming jump'. Such research may have only limited relevance to fear in battle: there is, for example, no suggestion that parachutists necessarily experience a switchback curve like that of combat effectiveness. Nevertheless, many officers and men of 2 Para, the only unit to participate in two set-piece battles in the Falklands, at Goose Green and Wireless Ridge, commented on the way in which their view of battle had changed. They compared Goose Green to a first parachute jump, with a high degree of stress shortly before jumping, and Wireless Ridge to subsequent jumps, where the stress comes earlier. Thus the evidence derived from parachuting does seem to be useful, at least as far as the first few experiences of battle are concerned.

Personal accounts of battle help us to plot men's changing sensations. Martin Lindsay read a review of Lord Moran's book as he listened to British guns pound the right bank of the Rhine before the leading companies of his battalion crossed. It put his own experience into perspective.

> Nine months earlier, in the fields and orchards of Calvados, I had positively looked forward to the thrill of battle. Now, after some two dozen regimental actions, great and small, all my old zest seemed to have departed, and I was becoming increasingly imprudent in what I called acts of self-discipline.

D.J.B. Houchin felt very much the same, and his account is a classic description of the way in which the strain of combat affected a brave regular infantry officer.

> It became a greater and greater strain upon one's self-control and determination. I felt this depended upon one's sensitivity and mental capacity and of course character. I got a tired feeling of having to face it all again ... Each time in action a little bit of one's self-control was lost and one was inclined to look for excuses to avoid the unpleasant ... I did too much fighting and should have gone on the staff. I finished up a bit of a wreck.

Alan Hanbury-Sparrow, another regular from an earlier war, overdrew his account – already in peril, with repeated demands upon it since August 1914 – in a similar fashion. A gas-filled night at Passchendaele made out the final cheque.

By dawn we were all gassed. I had to send the rest of the HQ officers down, and face another night of it alone. As a result, I was rather bad. Passchendaele broke me. When I got out again in April, I lasted only three months, as I simply couldn't stand it any longer.

American psychiatrists listed the symptoms of men whose former efficiency had given way to combat exhaustion. There was:

a general slowing down of mental processes and apathy, as far as they were concerned the situation was one of absolute hopelessness ... The influence and reassurance of understanding officers and NCOs failed now to arouse these soldiers from their hopelessness ... The soldier was slow-witted ... Memory defects became so extreme that he could not be counted on to relay a verbal order ... He could then best be described as one leading a vegetative existence ... He remained almost constantly in or near his slit trench, and during acute actions took no part, trembling constantly.

Whereas their first few battles had helped such men grow in confidence and improve in tactical ability, subsequent actions tended to have the reverse effect. The loss of their friends affected them deeply, and they began to feel that their chances of survival diminished with each action. Donald Featherstone, an NCO in the Royal Tank Regiment, never plumbed the depths described above. Nevertheless, he recognised that his mood changed as time went on. 'I was always apprehensive,' he told me. 'Perhaps resignation and sense of fatalism became stronger. Handicapped by having vivid imagination that forced upon me a sense of self identification with comrades killed and wounded.' 'The instinct of self-preservation is always the same,' agreed Ernst Jünger.

It is a mistake to believe that soldiers toughen and become more brave in the course of a war. What they gain in technique, in knowing how to deal with the enemy, they lose in nervous exhaustion. There is only one support, and that is a sense of honour which it is given to few men to possess.

Some soldiers, notably officers and NCOs, struggle valiantly against this condition. Their plight is sharpened by the fact that they may have won decorations for bravery; leaders and subordinates alike may continue to expect great things of them, although they themselves recognise that they are well past their best. They may develop a psychiatric illness which forces them out of combat, or they may deliberately seek death in order to obtain an honourable release from an insupportable situation. Lord Moran discusses the case of Sergeant Taylor, who soldiered on resolutely until a near miss from a shell finally unhinged him.

This man came out with the battalion, was wounded and came back unchanged; he seemed proof against all the accidents of his life, he stood in the Company like a rock; men were swept up to him and eddied round him for a little time and ebbed away again, but he remained.

A Royal Armoured Corps officer, commissioned from the ranks and twice decorated for gallantry, felt relieved at losing a leg: it was, he thought, a better bargain than pressing on until he eventually made a mistake and got men killed.

Martin Lindsay, recognising the symptoms of over-exposure in himself, wrote angrily in his diary when an experienced corporal, with a Military Medal from the Western Desert, was sent out on patrol in north-west Europe in the winter of 1944–5.

If I were the CO I would break the company commander for choosing him. He cannot have thought at all: sending out an NCO who had done so much already when there are half a dozen others in the company who could well have profited by the experience.

He later told of the mortifying experience of seeing 'the lions of the desert, officers and NCOs with one or more gallantry decorations who had for so long been the linchpins of their platoons and companies, killed off one after the other and, it is important to note, all pretty well useless by that time'.

The sight of such men over-reacting in battle can have adverse effects upon those who look to them for example. Lieutenant Airey Neave, attached to the 60th Rifles at Calais in 1940, was surprised to see Major J.S. Poole, an officer with several First World War decorations for gallantry, show anxiety. 'I am afraid they may break through,' he warned. 'Get your people in the houses on either side of the bridge and fire from the windows. You must fight like bloody hell.' In Burma in 1942 John Harper was nonplussed at the prospect of a lieutenant-colonel, also with First World War decorations, muttering, 'God help us all, Gold help us all. Their aircraft'll be here in the morning.'

Just as a man's bravery may fluctuate from day to day, so too may a unit exhibit an inconsistency of courage. As Brigadier Smith tells us:

> courage is unpredictable. The riflemen who turned and ran on Monte Grillo, next day held fast and fought like lions: the same company of soldiers temporarily lost all fighting spirit below Tavoleto, only to be transformed into the band of fanatical furies who stormed and captured the village against all odds.

Some British regiments bolted before the charging clansmen at Falkirk in January 1746, but stood firm to face the Highland rush at Culloden three months later. Sir John Fortescue observed that 'the courage of some men is not the same on every day'. Glenn Gray went further, distinguishing the 'occasional coward', prone to temporary lapses, from the 'constitutional coward', totally unable to endure battle.

National or regional characteristics partly account for this inconsistency of valour. Nigel Balchin, in an unpublished paper on battle morale written in 1945, suggested that 'many aspects of morale are linked with national characteristics and ways of life. Results which are reliable for one nation may be quite unreliable for another'. The difference can be explained by reference to Jungian psychology or by a more practical emphasis on culture and upbringing. Whatever the reason, as Field-Marshal Montgomery asserted,

> It is essential to understand that all men are different ... Some men are good at night; others prefer to fight in daylight. Some are best at the fluid and mobile battle; others are more temperamentally adapted to the solid killing match in close country.

Nineteenth-century theorists confidently announced that the further north one went, the more stolid the inhabitants became. In 1866 a French officer proclaimed in the *Spectateur Militaire*:

> For all Frenchmen, battle is above all an individual action, the presence of dash, agility and the offensive spirit, that is to say, the attack with the bayonet; for the German, it is the fusillade ... individualism drowned in the mass, passive courage and the defensive.

There were believed to be differences in the way troops behaved even within the French army. Southerners were touchy and excitable, eager to charge but difficult to rally when broken. Northerners lacked *élan* but could stand hard pounding.

Colonel Albert Seaton linked racial and geographical factors to explain Second World War German fighting characteristics.

> An East Prussian and a Pomeranian, thanks to their admixture of Polish or Sorbish blood, were usually livelier than a Westphalian ... A Westphalian and an Oldenburger on the other hand were often more staid and steady than a Rhinelander or a Bavarian. All had different characteristics but all made good soldiers. Only the Saxons might perhaps be considered to be less martial.

John Baynes placed greater emphasis upon geographical than upon racial or cultural factors in assessing the soldiers of 2nd Scottish Rifles. Climate, type of soil and the general position of the countryside dictated the sort of life that was led there. From that sprang certain ways of doing things, which in time hardened into unmistakable characteristics.

George McWhiney and Perry Jamieson intriguingly link Confederate tactics in the American Civil War to the Celtic charge, pointing to cultural norms in the ante-bellum South which resembled those in seventeenth-century Scotland and Ireland, and tracing their transference to America by way of emigration from the Celtic fringes of Britain. It may be that they overstate their case, but the similarity between the heady rush of Southern infantry and the surge of charging clansmen is remarkable. Even the rebel yell – 'Woh-who-ey! Who-ey! Who-ey!' – bore a marked resemblance to the 'horrible and diverse yelling' that the Romans had heard from their Celtic enemies.

These characteristics are likely to affect not only the way in which a particular unit fights in a given battle, but also to influence its staying power and long-term battle-worthiness. In general, though, units and formations are apt to follow the same curve of apprehensive enthusiasm, efficiency, over-confidence and exhaustion as the soldiers who compose them, sometimes with the same tragic consequences that we have already observed in the case of over-stretched individuals.

There were two categories of British divisions in Normandy in 1944. The first were experienced formations, which had fought in North Africa, Sicily and Italy: 7th Armoured Division, 50th (Northumbrian) Division and 51st (Highland) Division. The second were new divisions without previous battle experience. Divisions in the second category performed far better than those in the first, whose conduct, in the early stages of the campaign, was frankly disappointing. Two of 7th Armoured's commanders were removed by a high command which did not really understand the problem. As Lindsay observes, 'all that was needed was the replacement of battle-worn tank crews, sending them home to train others'. The

51st Highland and 7th Armoured greatly distinguished themselves subsequently, but only after they had received so many
replacements that they were 'virtually new divisions'. Eversley
Belfield and Major-General Hubert Essame are right to add
the caveat:

> When judging any lack of enthusiasm displayed in action,
> especially by veterans of the 8th Army, it must be remem-
> bered that, for most front-line soldiers, the bleak rule was
> that you normally continued to fight on; either until you
> were killed, or so severely wounded as to be unfit for further
> active service in the line.

Taking the Strain

Every man has his breaking point, but most never reach it.
Although the cumulative strain of battle will ultimately over-
whelm even the most resolute, the majority of soldiers are
never stretched to the snapping point. They cope with battle
and its stresses in a variety of ways, some of them conscious
and some unconscious. Donald Featherstone's account of his
own wartime experience typifies that of many who struggle
honestly and manfully against fear.

> Consciously, I kept a low profile, did not project myself into
> any situations I considered dangerous or foolhardy – while
> admiring and envying those who were able to perform more
> creditably. At the same time I obeyed orders, did what I
> was told, and never ran – although often tempted! Con-
> scious of being a minute cog in a huge wheel, I tried in my
> own timid way to do my duty, support my comrades and,
> through them, the regiment and country.

The most obvious reactions to the stress of battle are those
involving direct action, in other words practical steps which
alter the individual's relationship with the source of stress. It
is significant that Featherstone mentions running, for coping
with stress by escaping from it is, after all, a not uncommon

reaction. The study of individual and collective panic is obstructed by the fact that most armies strive, for reasons as honourable as they are understandable, to preserve the fiction that *their* soldiers almost never run. In *The Afghan Wars* Tony Heathcote implied that part of the 66th Regiment had fled at Maiwand in 1880. The book was reviewed by a retired officer of the Royal Berkshire Regiment, descendant of the 66th, who fiercely denied that this could possibly have happened. But Heathcote's primary sources leave no room for doubt: an officer wrote that 'we retreated in panic', and amongst the casualties was a colour-sergeant, killed by falling on his company commander's sword in the rush. In fact, the soldiers of all armies panic from time to time, and if we are to understand the phenomenon we must be remorselessly objective in our approach to it.[3]

Let us begin by grasping the nettle, and examining an instructive instance of panic in the British army. On the afternoon of 6 November 1940 Brigadier – as he then was – Slim was driving up to the front line near Gallabat in Eritrea. He was with some Indian troops when part of a British unit roared past him in its first-line transport, its soldiers loudly intimating that all was lost. The unit concerned was 1st Battalion, the Essex Regiment. It had been ordered to hold the area around Gallabat Fort as a part of a general advance by 10th Indian Infantry Brigade. The advance proved abortive, with most of the handful of tanks engaged being knocked out, while the RAF lost five of its elderly Gloster Gladiators. One of 1 Essex's company positions was in an area about fifty yards square, and the ground was so hard that shell-scrapes six inches deep were the best that could be dug.

The battalion was accurately bombed, and the sight of the casualties, sent back on Bren carriers because the Regimental Aid Post had been accidentally lost, caused what the Official History gently calls 'some demoralization'. An ammunition vehicle was hit in the reserve company's area, and the sound of ammunition exploding suggested that the Italians had put in an attack on the battalion's rear. A platoon moved off in good order to deal with this supposed incursion, but some soldiers mistook this for a general retirement. Slim describes what happened then.

> This was too much for some men, already demoralized by the bombing, and they fled shouting to others to get out as the enemy were coming. The panic spread and was not checked until a number of men had broken away, seized first-line vehicles at the foot of the hill, and fled in them.

The Gallabat episode which, it must be said, briefly affected only a proportion of soldiers in a battalion which later fought well, is illustrative of the more general causes of panic. S.L.A. Marshall was convinced, after investigating seven panics among American infantry in Normandy, that there were usually two distinct processes to panic. Firstly, some perfectly legitimate act, like badly-explained orders for a minor withdrawal, was misunderstood. An initial over-reaction was followed by a blind, instinctive flight from something which made men 'suddenly and desperately fearful'. The move of the reserve platoon had a catalytic effect on the rest of 1 Essex at Gallabat, and a blind unreasoning panic took over thereafter.[4]

There was a similar misunderstanding at the Alma. The Scots Fusilier Guards were moving up the slope under heavy fire when the badly-mauled 23rd Regiment recoiled in disorder, colliding with the Guards and causing some confusion. At this juncture someone shouted, 'Fusiliers, retire!', and, although it was by no means certain that this order applied to the Scots Guards rather than to either of the other fusilier regiments in the area, most of the Scots Guards, in the words of one of their officers, 'went rapidly downhill'. This brisk retirement attracted the unfavourable notice of the Grenadier and Coldstream Guards, themselves coming into action, some of whom shouted: 'Shame! Shame! What about the Queen's favourites now?' Here we have some of the same ingredients as at Gallabat: a sudden shock – collision with the 23rd – and a misunderstood order.

What is doubly significant about Gallabat is the nature of

the initial shock to 1 Essex. It had never been under air attack before, and, although the attack caused relatively few casualties – there were forty-two killed and 125 wounded in the whole of the brigade that day – it had a disproportionate effect upon morale. It is often the real or imagined appearance of some new and terrible threat – sometimes one of the bogey-weapons we have already discussed – that initiates panic. Norman Gladden described how, in 1917, a German aircraft appeared at a delicate moment during a relief in the line, and panic set in.

> Never before, despite my capacity for fear, had I felt myself for so long in the grip of a terror so absolute. All around us was the continuing threat of instant death. Yet I saw no one fall ... The company that night was in the grip of a sort of communal terror, a hundred men running like rabbits.

Gas, liquid fire and tanks have all, from time to time, produced the same reaction. Tom Wintringham recounts how a shaky company commander in his International Brigade battalion was frightened by a flare in the Battle of the Jarama in February 1937: he shouted 'liquid fire', and ran, and about a third of the battalion followed him. In Marc Bloch's case it was bolting horses. 'Our men threw themselves off the road,' he wrote. 'The second lieutenant in command of our platoon was pushed into the ditch. I myself was half dragged, half carried into a field by a force that was all the more irresistible because it was so sudden.'

In much the same way that the appearance of one of the enemy's bogey-weapons can produce panic, the failure of a man's own weapons to live up to his expectations can have the same effect. British troops at Maiwand had been led to believe that their breech-loading Martini-Henry rifles gave them an immeasurable advantage over the Afghan army, and there had been talk of a battalion thus armed being able to march the length and breadth of Afghanistan as it pleased. The fact that breech-loaders did not stop a determined rush of *ghazis* caused dismay.

This factor played a part in most of the defeats of European armies by native opponents in the second half of the nineteenth century. There were also times during the Second World War when the failure of British anti-tank weapons to penetrate the armour of German tanks had very serious effects upon morale, even if it did not cause outright panic. The advent of weapons like the anti-tank missiles TOW and MILAN, with a high hit probability at medium or long range, may be fraught with peril if their ability to destroy armour does not live up to expectations. As Ardant du Picq warned:

> When confidence is placed in superiority of material means, valuable as they are against an enemy at a distance, it may be betrayed by the actions of the enemy. If he closes with you in spite of your superiority in means of destruction, the morale of the enemy mounts with your loss of confidence. His morale dominates yours. You flee.

Sometimes firm action nips panic in the bud, before it has the opportunity to reach full fruition. John Baynes tells how a soldier in a First World War field ambulance started a panic by shouting, 'Get out! Get out! We're all going to be killed,' just as a German attack was starting. A sergeant split his skull open with a shovel, quelling the panic before it had time to develop. Although James Jack had great confidence in his battalion, he posted the provost sergeant and regimental police to insure against just such an occurrence, recognising that 'one must guard against these inexplicable panics which seize brave men on rare occasions and which are so infectious. Moreover, false orders to retire, emanating possibly from a concealed enemy or shouted in error, have to be taken into account.' Sometimes even firm action fails to stem the flood, as Herbert Read discovered in March 1918. 'On the road, the straight white road leading to the Western safety, there was something like a stampede,' wrote Read. 'S. and the sergeant-major went and held it up with pointed revolvers. But it was all useless.'

Once a panic gets under way it develops a frenetic momentum of its own. Indeed, those involved seem to lose many of their human characteristics, and become animals, given over to the hysteria of the herd. Lord Moran described trench-mortar men running on the Somme as 'animals given up to their brute instincts', and General Louis Trochu, writing in 1867, discussed panics in the French army on the eve of Austerlitz and the night after Solferino, suggesting that such occurrences were common in crowds, whether of men or of animals. Gustave Le Bon used panic as an example of the 'collective mind' of the crowd. 'A panic that has seized on a few sheep soon extended to the whole flock,' he wrote. 'In the case of men collected in a crowd, all emotions are rapidly contagious, which explains the suddenness of panics.'

If Le Bon's explanation strikes a chord, so too does Freud's. He believed that 'panic arises either owing to an increase of the common danger or owing to the disappearance of the emotional ties which hold the group together'. The latter certainly occurs when the panic is in progress. A notable characteristic of panic is the way in which the old ties of comradeship and loyalty are severed, and it is, quite literally, every man for himself.

Another aspect of the Gallabat affair which merits further exploration is the question of command. There had been a change of command of 1 Essex a few days before the battle, and, shortly before that the battalion had been transferred to 5th Indian Division. The order for its move up to Gallabat had been issued, cancelled and reissued, in a sequence of order and counter-order almost deliberately calculated to increase stress and diminish confidence. In the Yom Kippur War of 1973, Major Dov, intelligence officer of the Barak Brigade, one of the formations holding the Golan Heights, encountered vehicles, guns and tanks withdrawing along the road from Nafekh to the Bnet Ya'akov Bridge: 'All signs pointed to a withdrawal motivated by panic.' He stopped them and sent them back, and discovered that: 'Many of the units were only too happy finally to receive orders, cut off as they had been as a result of the fighting from their chain of command.' The war correspondent Alan Moorehead, caught up in a panic in the Western Desert, felt that the absence of firm instructions played a large part in it. 'In ourselves we did not know what to do,' he wrote. 'Had there been someone in authority to say, "Stand here. Do this and that" – then half our fear would have vanished ... I badly wanted to receive orders. And so, I think, did the others.'

Collective panic is one of a number of ways of leaving the battlefield. Individuals may flee in isolation, although by doing so they risk being identified, pursued and prosecuted. Nevertheless, even the bravest may briefly give way to panic. Ernst Jünger's platoon was decimated by a shell which burst squarely amongst it. 'I will make no secret of it,' he admitted, 'that after a moment's blank horror, I took to my heels and ran aimlessly into the night. It was not till I had fallen head-over-heels into a small shell hole that I understood what had happened.' Well over half the Spanish Civil War veterans interviewed by John Dollard admitted losing their heads and being utterly useless as soldiers for a time.

Also not uncommon is a collective form of low-key combat exhaustion, in which a whole unit simply drifts, slowly and undramatically, away from the firing-line. Colonel W.N. Nicholson reported how British infantry on the retreat from Mons, having suffered heavily from shellfire, 'slowly trickled off', announcing that 'they had had enough'. General Sir Horace Smith-Dorrien watched the 5th Division coming out of action at Le Cateau on 26 August 1914, with 'the men ... walking steadily down the road – no formation of any sort. I likened it at the time to a crowd coming away from a race meeting.' Charles MacDonald saw his company look much the same as it crumpled under a German attack. His men began to fall back without orders. 'They walked slowly on toward the rear,' he wrote, 'half dazed expressions on their faces.'

If leaving the field of battle is one means of taking direct action against stress, aggression is another. Logically, it is what MacCurdy terms the attempt to remove danger by destruction of the noxious agent or agency. In his article 'Some Remarks on Slaughter', Dr W.B. Gault, a former US Army psychiatrist, declared:

A soldier is expected to be aggressive. General military principles emphasise the need to strike first, act swiftly and decisively, dominate the field of battle, control the lines of fire, keep the enemy on the run, search and destroy, etc. Moreover, in war, inaction is virtually unbearable.

The soldiers of a British infantry battalion under heavy fire in the Peninsula shouted, 'Are we to be massacred here? Let us go at them, let us give them Brummegum.' And give them Brummegum – their nickname for their Birmingham-made socket bayonets – is exactly what they did. French infantry strained at the leash as their ranks were winnowed by the iron gale at Rezonville. Old soldiers in the Grenadiers of the Imperial Guard begged their officers to order them forward: '*Mon commandant*, what are we waiting for? Let's do it like we did in Italy . . . Forward . . . Forward.' *Commandant* Philibert of the 25th of the Line wrote that 'my men cried forward', and a lieutenant of *zouaves* complained that 'nothing can be more discouraging and enervating for seasoned troops like ours than immobility'. Two days later Prince Kraft zu Hohenlohe-Ingelfingen, commanding the artillery of the Prussian Guard, watched the infantry covering his gun-line chafe at their inability to hit back at the French, whose *Chassepots* galled them so sorely. 'The brave soldiers of the Augusta regiment wished over and over to rush forward,' he wrote. Ardant du Picq argued that no body of troops could stand still under stress for any length of time: it would move rapidly in one direction or the other. Although his theories were taken to unreasonable lengths by his successors, there is more than an element of truth in his concept of 'the flight to the front'.

The pressure before a set-piece operation builds up to such a pitch that many of the participants are impelled by a desire to get it over. Lieutenant Rudolf Hartmann of the 483rd Regiment summed up the feeling in his unit before the German offensive of March 1918.

We didn't hate the English and French, especially the English for whom we had some understanding, being of the same stock ... This was the last desperate attempt to bring about a change in our fortunes. Maybe 20 to 30 per cent of our unit were keen because they hoped to find plenty of food and alcohol; they were mostly the young ones. But the rest of us weren't at all enthusiastic; we just wanted to get the war over and get home.

Musketier Wilhelm Boscheinen's comrades felt the same. 'The older men couldn't care less,' he recalled, 'only to be out of the shit.' On the other side of No Man's Land were men who, like Private T.C.H. Jacobs of the 15th London Regiment, were equally eager for the attack to end the stress and uncertainty of bombardment: 'fear was replaced by weary exasperation. I recall thinking "For Christ's sake pack it up, Jerry. Come over and fight, you bastards."'

Bombardment plays a key role in the creation of battlefield stress precisely because it renders either flight or aggression impossible and, by depriving men of the opportunity to cope with it by direct action, forces them to cope in other, potentially more damaging, ways. F.C. Bartlett believed that the hardest thing in war was 'to be afraid and sit still'. H.S. Clapham described the sensation of being under shellfire at Hooge in June 1915.

The worst of it was the inaction. Every minute several shells fell within a few yards and covered us with dust, and the smell of explosions poisoned my mouth ... And this went on for hours. I began to long for the shell that would put an end to everything, but in time my nerves became quite numbed, and I lay like a log until roused.

Charlton Ogburn recognised that the inactivity produced by being shelled did the real damage. 'Unless you've something to keep you occupied while it's going on,' he wrote, 'you're a gone goose.' One of Dollard's veterans said much the same: 'The most intense fear is during a hot action where the soldier is not occupied such as under bombardment or shelling.'

The bombardments of the Napoleonic period lacked the intensity or duration of those of the twentieth century, but the problem of inactivity under stress was well known even then. John Kincaid advised:

> If a body of troops is under fire, and so placed as to be unable to return it, the officer commanding should make it a rule to keep them constantly on the move, no matter if it is but two steps to the right and one to the front, it always makes them believe they are doing something, and prevents the mind from brooding over a situation which is the most trying of any.

Argentinian troops found this enforced immobility hard to tolerate. 'We were just targets for their artillery,' lamented one of them. 'Lots of times I felt like a duck on a lake, being shot at from all sides.'

The shell is impersonal, inhuman, and implacably hostile. William Langer thought that shellfire 'seemed a bit unfair ... Somehow it makes one feel so helpless, there is no chance of reprisal for the individual man. The advantage is all with the shell, and you have no comeback.' Paul Dubrulle, a Jesuit serving as a sergeant of French infantry at Verdun in 1916, gives an account of bombardment which captures its worst agonies.

> When one heard the whistle in the distance, one's whole body contracted to resist the too excessively potent vibrations of the explosion, and at each repetition it was a new attack, a new fatigue, a new suffering. Under this regime, the most solid nerves cannot resist for long; the moment arrives when the blood mounts to the head; when fever burns the body and where the nerves, exhausted, become incapable of reacting. Perhaps the best comparison is that of seasickness ... finally one abandons oneself to it, one has no longer even the strength to cover oneself with one's pack against splinters, and one scarcely still has left the strength to pray to God ... To die from a bullet seems to be nothing;

parts of our being remain intact; but to be dismembered, torn to pieces, reduced to pulp, this is a fear that flesh cannot support and which is fundamentally the great suffering of the bombardment.

The strain can prove so utterly intolerable that men commit suicide. Lieutenant von Rosen, acting commander of a company of 503 Heavy Tank Battalion in Normandy in 1944, lost fifty men to the heavy air bombardment which preceded Operation Goodwood: a further two men killed themselves, and a third had to be sent to a mental hospital.

Feelings of isolation and helplessness tend to aggravate most stressful situations, as, for example, in the case of serious illness. Lazarus believed that 'helplessness adds to the burden of the illness by increasing threat', and added that loneliness was particularly damaging: the mere physical presence of other patients with its accompanying sense of shared difficulties helps. Experimental studies in which subjects receive electric shocks indicate that delayed-action shocks are the most frightening, and 'knowledge about when to expect the punishment served to reduce the threat'. Bombardment isolates men from their comrades by its smoke, flame and debris; it leaves them in agonising uncertainty as to where the next shell will land; and it conjures up images of unspeakable, dehumanising mutilation.

It also highlights the second main category of devices for coping with stress. These do nothing practical about the stressor, but they make the individual under stress feel better. Chief amongst these palliative techniques is denial. The soldier becomes convinced that nothing will harm him. Sometimes this belief comes almost in a road-to-Damascus blinding flash. Hanbury-Sparrow wrote of 'the sudden, overwhelming knowledge that whatever happened in the trench you were not going to be killed'. One of my interviewees spoke of 'an amazing feeling of confidence and euphoria, the certain knowledge that whatever I did that day, they couldn't hit me'. More often, however, a man simply believes, quietly and undramatically, that the worst will never happen to him. Almost half the soldiers questioned by Dollard felt that they were lucky and would never be hit, and most of them recognised that this belief had been a help to them.

Denial is fragile armour. The death or injury of a friend, relative or member of the same infantry section or gun detachment easily cracks it. An NCO in 2 Para told me that it was not until he had been hit that he realised how dangerous it all was: till then it was 'only a game ... and you never think you'll be unlucky'. Grinker and Spiegel made the same point: 'Fear of enemy activity is seldom concrete until the flyer has seen a convincing demonstration of what damage can be inflicted, and how little can be done to avoid it.' The realisation that one is not invulnerable can be overcome by some in what Gray calls 'an indomitable will to power which refuses to recognise ordinary mortality'. In others, however, the shattering of denial is followed by unquestioning terror, and 'such soldiers feel that all bullets are intended for them and every shell is likely to land in the particular spot they have selected as temporary shelter'.

Hard work assists denial. Just as some terminally-ill patients press on with their careers as if the hovering death will never swoop, so busy soldiers concern themselves with practical tasks to the exclusion of rational reflection upon the dimensions of their real peril. Lord Moran, who wrote so perceptively about fear, had never experienced its physical symptoms, probably, he thought, because looking after the wounded gave him something to do. John Glubb wrote that 'one's mind is filled day and night with thoughts of the welfare of one's men and horses. There is very little time to think of oneself.' J.E.H. Neville told his father that he was surprised how cool he had been during his first bombardment. 'But then', he added, 'we had no time to think about anything.'

S.L.A. Marshall wrote of 'the mark of the warrior, this preoccupation with duty to the exclusion of worry. There is no other easement for combat stress.' Ernst Jünger shared this view. 'I have often observed in myself and in others', he remarked, 'that an officer's sense of responsibility drowns his personal fears. There is a sticking place, something to occupy the thoughts.' Shai, an Israeli infantry officer in the Six Day War, thought:

> One of the things that solves all an officer's problems is simply the fact of being in command. The need to set an example, the very fact that you're responsible for the men and their lives. It relieves you completely of the need to pretend.

Officers and NCOs in 2 and 3 Para frequently referred to the advantages they had enjoyed in battle. 'A commander commands,' said one, 'and he isn't under the same stress as a soldier.' A second believed that he had far too much to do during the battle for Goose Green to be worried, and a third commented that 'the pure mechanics of navigation' had filled his mind to the exclusion of much else. The work and worry produced by a leader's concern for his men is, however, a mixed blessing. While it may drive concern for personal safety from his thoughts, it engenders, as we have seen, stresses of its own. Lord Moran was spared fear on his own account, but wrote: 'I have another infirmity now. I am for ever worrying about the people I really like.' Ian Gardiner reflected on his own sensations before the attack on Two Sisters.

> Fear, certainly, plays a part, but it is not fear of death itself. It is more a sadness about the grief that will follow one's death among one's family. As a company commander responsible for the lives of some 150 men, I felt pretty lonely in that hour when our preparations were complete and before we moved off.

Sometimes the work which soldiers engage in to obliterate fear is of no military worth whatever. A German corporal forgot the horror of Stalingrad by assembling clocks in his dugout, and much of the trench art of the First World War – decorated shellcases, carved chalk or whittled wood – was inspired as much by the need to relieve stress as to defeat boredom.

Armies are ritualistic organisations. Military ritual is more than the delight of martinets, the bane of perennially scruffy soldiers and the abiding interest of a whole sub-species of military historians. It is a comprehensive framework of behaviour designed to serve, *inter alia*, as a precaution against disorder and a defence against the randomness of battle. Even military history is influenced by rituals of its own, and, in its 'battle pieces', can resemble what Lord Raglan calls 'dramatic ritual or ritual drama'. Parades stimulate individual and collective pride. Michael Grant believed that the Roman army's formal parades were an affirmative identification of the army with the gods. Christopher Duffy is sceptical about the purely military value of Frederick the Great's massive reviews. 'Where their true importance resided', he maintains, 'was in the ceremonial aspect, in the execution of the tribal ritual which bound the Prussian army to its king.'

There are powerful elements of ritual even in combat itself. Ethnologists have observed the tendency for potentially lethal combat within a species to be turned into a ritualised game: Eibl-Eibesfeldt writes that 'Intraspecific fighting amongst vertebrates is generally ritualized.' So is much fighting between humans, as we shall discover when we examine the soldier's bittersweet relationship with his enemy.

But we are concerned here with the function of ritual as a means of helping a soldier to cope with fear and stress. Collective ritual helps persuade its participants that all is well. Workers in factories due for closure tend to work on to the last day, with the cleaners and repair men maintaining the building as if it would be used for ever. Armies whose surrender is imminent often respond by increasing ritual. In September and October 1870, as the *Armée du Rhin* lingered in terminal misery around the fortress of Metz, it rediscovered its appetite – never far absent – for paperwork and bureaucracy. There were parades and inspections; ration returns were demanded by the *Intendance*; staff officers scanned the *Annuaire* to calculate promotions by seniority. With surrender days away, the Operations and Movements Section of General Headquarters demanded accurate strength returns by company rather than by battalion, complained that a local newspaper had published incorrect casualty figures, and submitted a list of decorations to be published as an Army General Order.

The wheels of military justice ground on. *Capitaine-adjutant-major* Planches of the 7th Hussars was awarded sixty days' imprisonment for striking a brother officer. The case exercised the Military Justice section of GQG, which eventually – protesting that the trial had been contrary to Article 229 of Chapter IV of the Military Code of Justice – quashed the sentence and released Planches. He went straight from French captivity into Prussian, for Metz surrendered while the lawyers were thumbing through their textbooks. Finally, with surrender decided upon, the army's account books were balanced and audited, almost as if the Prussians were more concerned with the intricacies of double-entry book-keeping than they were with taking over the greatest fortress on France's eastern frontier. But the ritual had its desired effect: despite some rumblings from the *troueurs*, who wanted to fight on regardless, the army's discipline held together until the last hours, when drink and despair produced some lapses.

On the battlefield ritual, often in the form of the drills rammed home in peacetime training, is a raft of familiarity in an uncertain environment. Sergeant Wheeler's commanding officer, Colonel Mainwaring, drilled his men under fire to steady them. 'I tell you again,' he shouted, 'they cannot hurt us if you are steady, if you get out of time you will be knocked down.' Major Charles Napier, commanding the 50th Foot at Corunna in 1809, had his men shoulder and order arms while roundshot bounded all around and his light company held off a cloud of *tirailleurs*. The 24th Michigan received its baptism of fire at Fredericksburg in December 1862 as it advanced to clear horse artillery and dismounted cavalry from some scrub. Jeb Stuart's horse gunners mauled the regiment as it advanced, but Colonel Henry Morrow halted it, and put it through the manual of arms. 'Then the 24th went ahead,' wrote Bruce Catton, 'taking great pains with its alignment and marching through that woodland like the West Point corps of cadets.'

Individuals fall back on ritual, to which they sometimes attribute magical properties, as a means of defending the *ego* against anxiety. In *No Man's Land: Combat and Identity in World War I*, Eric Leed wrote:

> The sheer scale of technologically administered violence seemed to force the regression of combatants to forms of thought and action that were magical, irrational and mystic ... Magic is an appropriate resort in situations where the basis of survival could not be guaranteed by any available technology.

In their efforts to load the dice of fortune, and to gain some comfort thereby, soldiers have for centuries cherished talismans or adopted talismanic behaviour. During the First World War, wrote Paul Fussell, 'no front-line officer or soldier was without his amulet, and every tunic pocket became a reliquary. Lucky coins, buttons, dried flowers, hair cuttings.' E.C. Vaughan fixed a holy medal given him by a nun to a ring on his braces, where there was soon 'an ever-increasing bunch presented from various people'. When Peter Kemp went off to fight in the Spanish Civil War, his father gave him a small black idol from the Congo, with the commendation: 'He's a lucky fellow.'

Second World War aircrews were particularly superstitious. 'All sorts of supposedly lucky objects are carried on missions,' observed Grinker and Spiegel: 'pictures, mementoes, a particularly insanitary and outworn article of clothing, a charm, a dog or some other animal. Sometimes a member of the crew or a certain airplane is believed to be lucky or unlucky.' Miles Tripp recalled the talismans of his Lancaster crew: Harry's red and blue scarf, Dig's hat, George and his girlfriend's brassière, Paul's yellow scarf patterned with red dragons. 'I flew with more charms than anyone else,' he wrote, 'a silk stocking, a land army brooch, a pink chiffon scarf and a tiny bone elephant.'

There was an undercurrent of superstition in the South Atlantic in 1982. Patrick Bishop and John Witherow described the 'strange outbreak of superstition' aboard *Canberra*. The vessel killed a whale, and this was regarded as a bad omen. Talismans abounded. A lance-corporal in 3 Para carried a St Christopher medal and touched it frequently. A private in the same battalion touched wood four times every morning, and another kept a pair of his wife's knickers in his pocket, and patted them in moments of tension. One soldier always put his left boot on first, and was sure that no harm would come to him providing that he did so. This parallels a Vietnam veteran's ritual of dressing: left sock, right sock, left boot, right boot. 'It was like an invisible protective shield,' he said.

Soldiers from both parachute battalions commented on the fact that, while few of them had taken talismans to the Falklands with them, many of them brought talismans back. Often an item – a shell fragment, empty case, or pierced relic of a near miss – would be endowed with special significance after a battle or patrol action, and would be religiously preserved thereafter. MacCurdy commented specifically on this practice.

In all but rare actions of the forlorn hope type the majority of combatants survive. If every one of these has had a talisman, the efficacy of the magic is proved to be 100 per cent, because no attention is paid to the corpse who fails to complain that the magic did not work.

There comes the moment when the treasured item is lost. Individuals often associate this with their imminent death. General Lasalle, darling of Napoleon's light cavalry, made a point of keeping a bottle of good brandy in one of his saddle holsters. At Wagram he reached down for a nip, but found only broken glass. 'What a wretched day,' he said. 'It is the sort of day on which I shall get killed.' His prediction came true two hours later. Some of these prophecies of death become self-fulfilling, as the individual concerned, convinced that he is doomed, takes unnecessary risks. His death may have the effect of reinforcing his comrades' belief in talismans. This is particularly true in the case of aerial combat, where a moment's inattention can prove fatal. 'The pilot who goes out on patrol and discovers only when he is in the air that he has left his lucky bit at home is unnerved,' writes MacCurdy. 'His confidence is lost and, with that, his skill in combat. So he is shot down. When his companions go over his effects they find the talisman – further proof to them of how essential magical protection is.'

Denial, hard work, and superstition are all devices for coping with stress. Fatalism, too, plays its part. Convinced that he can do little to protect himself in an environment thick with capricious death, the soldier may adopt a fatalistic resignation. This view is characteristic of soldiers of well-developed combat experience, men who have already seen just how nasty and random battle really is. A First World War Australian gunner officer summed up the soldier's fatalism:

if a shell or a bullet 'has my name on it' I will get it no matter how hard I try to dodge it. I have seen scores of our lads walking along while being shelled without quickening their pace or trying to get out of the line of fire & yet none of them got hit and again I have seen others run ... & run into a shell.

A British soldier in the Peninsula revealed how he had drained his emotions dry, and had become utterly fatalistic.

My mind had come to that pass: I took everything as it came without a thought. If I was at ease, with plenty, I was happy; if in the midst of the enemy's fire, or of the greatest privations, I was not concerned. I had been in so many changes of plenty and want, ease and danger, that they had ceased to be anticipated either with joy or fear.

This sort of fatalism is not necessarily useful for, although it makes an individual's existence bearable, it is likely to be accompanied by the symptoms of combat exhaustion. Stouffer described over-confident troops who had abandoned hope.

The Real Enemy

They don't give a damn whether they get killed or not.
They lose courage. They don't aim, can't hit the ground
fast. They're scared all right but they don't care. When
they're running they run about fifteen yards and then start
walking – don't give a damn.

Robert Graves's Welsh servant complained that units in this
state would 'waste men wicked'. A company commander in 3
Para detected signs of the same phenomenon as daylight
brought shells on Mount Longdon. 'Some soldiers walked
about casually under fire,' he remarked. 'They were utterly
fatalistic, and some of them got killed.'

It is a well-worn cliché that there are no atheists in foxholes.
The tendency for soldiers to pray under fire is demonstrated
by statistic and anecdote. Between 73 per cent and 84 per
cent of the infantrymen questioned by Stouffer in three American divisions answered that prayer 'helped a lot'. Over
three-quarters of his sample reported that their wartime experience had increased their faith in God. Interestingly, about
as many became more religious as became less so, which seems
to confirm the view expressed in a post-First World War
British report that war accentuates men's religion but not
necessarily their Christianity.

'I used to pray a lot,' admitted a Second World War American soldier. 'You automatically pray to yourself when you're
going in and you're in.' John Roberts wrote, 'in the heat of
battle one is ready, and indeed does say one's prayers to the
Almighty'. 'I also PRAYED quite a bit in sticky situations,'
recalled Alan Briddon. '*Genuinely* prayed, that is, although I
was not particularly religious.' John Shipp, writing over a
century before, was convinced that far more soldiers prayed
during battle than were prepared to admit it afterwards, 'for
in general soldiers deride religious comrades'. An Australian
soldier observed how respect for religion seemed to increase
with danger. 'Men, who months ago, would have been
ashamed to have it known that they had a bible are seen
reading it often,' he wrote. 'All [is] designed to draw men
nearer to God.' Church attendance in Britain rocketed in

1939, and declined thereafter. Chaplains on board troopships on their way to the Falklands enjoyed large congregations on the journey down and rather smaller ones on the way back.

For some soldiers a spiritual framework is an essential pre-requisite to acceptance of the probability of their own death. As Glenn Gray put it: 'Death is a fulfilment, not in the sense of a consummation, but as the final triumph of the spirit over the forces that would hinder it from the everlasting.' There are numerous soldiers in wartime who have no properly-defined or nicely-rounded concept of religion, but who have come to believe in an afterlife which makes their own sacrifice seem tolerable. 'Religion is supposed to be intensified in war,' thought Raymond Cooper. 'Religion in any theological sense I doubt, but easier appreciation of another world or at least of the existence of forces beyond man's control probably is.' Men who have no use for religion as such gain solace from putting themselves in a cosmic context. 'Andromeda and Pegasus are just over my head on this lovely night,' wrote a German soldier shortly to die at Stalingrad. 'I have been looking at them for a long time; soon I shall be near them. I can thank the stars for my contentment and serenity.'

But if war increases the spirituality of the majority, there is a minority of soldiers whose faith is shattered by their experiences, and who emerge from the crucible cynical and atheistic. A survivor of the Somme told how 'a chaplain tore his dog collar off in front of me and, with curses, said, "It is a mockery to wear it".' Private C. Bartram of the 94th Trench Mortar Battery lost his faith during the same battle. 'From that moment all my religion died,' he said. 'All my teaching and belief in God had left me, never to return.' W.H.A. Groom found that his 'belief in a church which condoned killing faded away'. For him, the war highlighted the dilemma of the padre. I shall consider the chaplain's role in fostering morale in Chapter 7.

Frank Richardson observed that there was often a touch of cynicism to religious faith in war, with jokes about 'fire insurance'. Soldiers have a remarkable ability to jest about even the most serious of subjects, and their humour is yet another aspect of the coping process. Even the dead can become the butt of jokes. As a New Jersey regiment marched across the old Bull Run battlefield, a private saw a hand protruding from a shallow grave. 'Look boys!' he cried. 'See the soldier putting out his hand for back pay!' In the ravaged village of Miraumont after the First World War, men of a Yorkshire battalion saw a pallid hand and a grey uniform cuff sticking up from the duckboards. A young soldier put the handle of a broken spade between the stiff fingers, saying, 'Now then, Jerry, get on wi'it; no bloody skrimshankin' 'ere.' As Irishmen of 1st Battalion the Royal Ulster Rifles passed through the Normandy village of Bréville in 1944, with the upper half of a German's body on the roadside, Lieutenant Alastair Morrison of the 4/7th Dragoon Guards was dismayed to see that 'they all shook him by the hand and passed some funny Irish remark'.

This bitter humour helps men to discharge dangerous tensions. In his study of students under the pressure of examinations, D. Mechanic recorded how his subjects sought to 'defend themselves against their feelings by behaving in a silly, manic way, and avoidance joking became very prevalent'. Lazarus suggests that this sort of avoidance joking keeps information that might prove disruptive out of one's frame of reference: by joking about a corpse, a soldier is avoiding contemplation of the sordid process of physical decay, or speculating upon how long it will be before he too is in the same state.

Bitter disappointment or personal tragedy can also be relieved by humour. As the authors of *The Winter War* observed, humour was, at one level, 'simply a case of laughing because otherwise you might cry; humour was the balm of tragedy'. In a ruined bunker under Chinese fire on Pork Chop Hill in Korea in April 1953 a soldier muttered: 'Jesus Christ, this is worse than Custer's last stand.' 'Were you there, too?' inquired an officer. 'No,' replied the private, 'but I've read about it.' When Raymond Cooper's company was strafed by Hurricanes, a soldier joked, 'I expect we've lent them the RAF to make it fairer.' John Parrish described the wry jokes of the wounded in Vietnam. 'Oh,' said one, 'I'm a commanding general disguised as a private. I'm here to inspect the hospital facilities, I figured the best way to slip in unnoticed was to blow off my foot.' 'If he puts another of these goddam tubes in my chest,' rejoined another, 'I'm taking my business elsewhere.' Rick Jolly has a similar story from the Falklands. A Royal Marine with his foot half blown off joked about the wound. 'Lucky really, sir, didn't get it quite right,' he said. 'If I'd stood on the bugger properly I'd have lost it all at the knee.'

Rum and Blood

One of the many valuable elements in John Keegan's contribution to our understanding of what happens on the battlefield is his treatment of battlefield narcosis. Some of the French knights at Agincourt had been drinking heavily on the eve of the battle, Corporal Shaw of the Life Guards was fighting drunk when he hewed nine Frenchmen through steel and bone at Waterloo, and some of the soldiers who advanced on the morning of 1 July 1916 were fortified by more than *esprit de corps*. During the Falklands War Lieutenant David Tinker testified, half-seriously, to the therapeutic effects of alcohol. 'The best thing to do is to have a few wets before an attack,' he advised. 'I'd had a drink before the Exocet attack and the pulse rate stayed very normal.' Drink and drugs are time-honoured ways of palliating stress, and their use is infinitely more widespread than bland official histories might suggest. The very expression 'Dutch courage' has military origins, dating from the predisposition of English soldiers in the Low Countries to fortify themselves with a nip or two of *genever*.

There are four main aspects to the question of alcohol and drug use in armies. Firstly, both drugs and drink have an entirely legitimate function in helping over-wrought men to sleep. Alcohol is more useful in this context than is often recognised: Rick Jolly made a plea for 'the traditional use of alcohol' to help stressed men sleep, and Frank Richardson found rum useful for the same purpose. Major J.R. Phillips, a regimental medical officer in 1940, was short of drugs: 'there was, however, an ample supply of alcohol, an excellent sedative, which proved most effective'. Alan Hanbury-Sparrow, on the receiving end, was utterly frank. 'Certainly strong drink saved you,' he acknowledged. 'For the whole of your moral forces were exhausted. Sleep alone could restore them, and sleep, thanks to this blessed alcohol, you got.'

Secondly, soldiers in garrison in both peace and war tend to overindulge in alcohol as a means of making an unbearable existence more tolerable. Brigadier Richard Simpkin declared: 'every army I know of – except the Swedish, Swiss and Israeli forces – conspires to make its conscripts' life so wretched that they are fully occupied in coming to terms with it or in using drink or drugs to distance themselves from it'. Jean Morvan recounted the spirited performance of a First Empire officer who habitually drank two bottles of wine with his lunch. He then had a well-deserved nap, enjoyed another bottle in bed, had dinner, and then took a short walk and another drink before turning in. On a more serious note, drink and drugs play an important part in crime in most armies: one-third of law violations by Soviet military personnel are carried out in a state of drunkenness.

Communal drinking also assists in the small-group bonding process. In the Anglo-Saxon hall thanes boasted over their drinking-horns about the deeds they would perform in battle. When Earl Byrhtnoth's men faced destruction at the Battle of Maldon in 991, they were reminded of the vows they had made in happier times, and encouraged to live up to them. 'Remember the times,' exhorted Aelfwine,

> when we spoke at the mead-drinking, when on the bench we uttered boasting, heroes in hall, about hard strife ... Thanes shall not reproach me among the people, that I wish to leave this army, to seek my home, now that my prince lies low, hewn down in battle.

Tired as they were by their march to Hastings in 1066, King Harold's men still spent much of the night before the battle drinking. A Norman chronicler gave a slightly bewildered version of the cries of 'drink-wassail' that rang out in the Saxon camp as Harold's host prepared for its last battle. Stuart Mawson noticed 'a subtle parade of manhood, an unconscious swagger in the manner of drinking' the night before the drop on Arnhem. Samuel Janney, who served with the 1st Infantry Division in Vietnam in 1968, was initiated into his platoon by a drinking party in the field. 'That was my platoon,' he said. 'And that was the first time I'd gotten loaded with them. I'd probably been in the unit for two weeks at that point. It makes a big difference being part of the group. They definitely initiated me.'

It is with the fourth aspect of alcohol and drug use – as a means of mitigating the stresses of battle – that we are most concerned. To a degree, at least, this use has been officially approved. The infantry divisions of Saint-Hilaire and Vandamme, given the crucial task of seizing the Pratzen at Austerlitz, were also given triple rations of brandy, nearly half a pint per man: small wonder that, as a French officer observed, 'the troops now burst with eagerness and enthusiasm'. Wheeler watched Sergeant Butley serving out the rum ration under fire at Badajoz in 1812, saving for himself the ration of those who were killed before they could drink it. Major O'Hare of the 95th chatted with Captain Jones of the 52nd as they waited in the dark to assault the fortress. O'Hare was depressed and fatalistic, and Jones tried to cheer him up. ' "Tut, tut, man! I have the same sort of feeling, but I keep it down with a drop of the *cratur*," answered the Captain, as he handed his calabash to the Major.' Wheeler and his comrades insulated themselves against the rain the night before Waterloo by stocking up with liquor: they were, he recalled, 'wet and comfortable'. For many years British soldiers enjoyed a rum ration, and care was often taken to issue it shortly before battle.

Officially-supplied drugs are not generally used for the same purpose: they are more often employed to help soldiers cope with lack of sleep. Benzedrine was widely used during and after the Second World War. At least 10 per cent of Second World War American troops took amphetamines at some time or other, and in 1947 one-quarter of the prisoners in US military jails were 'heavy and chronic users'. American medics often issued dexedrine to soldiers before they went out on night patrol in Vietnam. Michael Herr's description, 'Dexedrine breath like dead snakes kept too long in a jar', struck a chord with one of my subjects, who remembered poring over a map with another NCO in the musty darkness. The French army made widespread use of Maxiton: many of the garrison of Dien Bien Phu were able to stay on duty for days on end with its assistance.

Although modern Western armies tend to shun the use of hallucinogenic drugs as an aid to withstanding battle, such palliatives have a long history. The Vikings used small quantities of dried fly agaric – the red and white toadstool often associated with jolly gnomes in children's books – before battle. This mild hallucinogen often assisted in the process by which warriors went berserk in wild fighting frenzy. The word berserk literally means 'bear shirt', and berserkers regressed to the animal state, fighting without armour, snarling and biting at the linden wood of the enemy's shield-wall: a hallucinogen had a useful role in promoting this state. Similar preparations, chewed, smoked or drunk, helped many nineteenth- and twentieth-century tribesmen tolerate an unequal battle against a better-equipped European enemy. There is continuing interest in the question of chemical prophylaxis, although the risk of severe drop-off in performance when the drug wears off tends to make it a treatment useful only in clearly-specified circumstances.

If drugs helped tribesmen, their European opponents availed themselves of drink. In his study of European empires, V.G. Kiernan maintained that alcohol was vitally important to the soldiers of colonising powers. 'Alcohol was almost as indispensable as food,' he wrote. 'It supplied some nutrition, modified hardship, and sharpened appetite for battle ... Without this solace the Empire could not have been won.' Overindulgence in drink sometimes led soldiers to behave badly. During the Indian mutiny, Surgeon J.H. Sylvester, attached to the 14th Light Dragoons, witnessed Indians being roughly handled. 'Country spirit had been found in the village,' he wrote, 'and many of our European soldiery were drunk and committed atrocities among the villagers.' Drink did not always have this unpleasant effect. In 1879 there was enough champagne in officers' kits for a suitable celebration in Lord Chelmsford's square after his victory over the Zulus at Ulundi.

Nine years before, drink had helped French soldiers forget their disappointments as France's war plan went swiftly and irrevocably awry. General Desvaux noticed that things were going badly in this respect while the concentration of troops was still in progress. Travelling to the frontier by train, he wrote in his diary that: 'These big *carabiniers* are almost naked and drink flat out at each halt; they will soon be ill.' A month later Trochu saw drunken and dishevelled *zouaves* cavorting around a train at Châlons. He noted sadly that they had been excellent soldiers at Reichshoffen, when MacMahon's army had performed not discreditably against a superior German force. When Metz surrendered Desvaux was delighted to see that the Guard, of which he was the acting commander, had not a man drunk. Many linesmen, alas, could only face the dismal future well fortified with drink.

The function of alcohol as a morale booster in the British army of the First World War remains a matter of dispute. On the one hand there are those who argue that privately-purchased alcohol was in relatively short supply, and that its officially-issued cousin was not misused. Charles Carrington trenchantly observed that the cost of spirits put them out of the reach of many: 'Whisky – at seven and sixpence a bottle, a subaltern's daily pay – was a rarity which we husbanded.' And what of the issue rum, in its pottery jars marked SRD – Special Rations Department, but rumoured to mean Seldom Reaches Destination? General Jack pointed out that regulations clearly specified that it had to be drunk in the presence of an officer, and was 'in no sense a battle dope'.

On the other hand, there is abundant evidence that rum made an important contribution to battle morale, and both it, and privately-obtained liquor, were deliberately used to help men stand the strain of battle. One of the medical officers who testified before the War Office's 1922 Shell Shock Committee said, 'had it not been for the rum ration I do not think we should have won the war'. In his battalion of the Black Watch, they always tried to give the men a good meal and a double ration of rum in coffee before they went over the top. Colonel W.N. Nicholson recognised that rum had two specific functions. It helped make trench life bearable: 'The private soldier's ration of rum', he wrote, 'saved thousands of lives.' He also considered that it stiffened the spirit before or after battle: 'It is an urgent devil to the Highlander before action; a solace to the East Anglian countryman after the fight.' The practice of issuing rum after battle, to help men unwind, was followed by the Australians. 'For the boys who wanted rum there was plenty,' remembered one, '– in the AIF the rule was, no rum before a fight; the rum was given afterwards when the boys were dead beat.'

Rum looms large in the personal accounts of front-line soldiers. An infantryman recalled that the air smelt of 'rum and blood' during a British attack. Norman Gladden admitted that he and his comrades had drunk some smuggled rum in the trenches. 'Rarely had I seen a party in such a woeful situation so joyfully carefree,' he wrote. Lieutenant Vaughan, not long in the line, began to think how he would behave in an attack. The thought made him tremble all over, 'so that I was forced to go into the dugout and dispel the images with a whisky'. Thomas Penrose Marks thought the rum ration inadequate. 'The second ration [administered before battle] is supposed to give us Dutch courage,' he wrote. 'It might fulfil its purpose if it were handed out in more liberal doses ... It does not even make us merry. But every one of us welcomes it.' Robert Graves noticed his battalion's sick-list rose alarmingly when a zealous divisional commander stopped the rum issue. 'Our men looked forward to their tot of rum at dawn stand-to', he wrote, 'as the brightest moment of their twenty-four hours; when this was denied them, their resistance weakened.' In the maelstrom of a front-line trench at Loos, with the air heavy with gas, and many of his friends dead, Graves found a water-bottle full of rum and drank about half a pint. 'It quietened me,' he recalled, 'and my head remained clear.'

Rudolf Binding testifies that the need for alcohol was not confined to the British army. He observed that heavy bombardment produced a great desire for drink. 'They have a craving for brandy which can hardly be satisfied,' he wrote, 'and which shows how badly they yearn to lose the faculty for feeling.' A fierce desire to get hold of drink motivated many of the German soldiers involved in the March offensive. As Rudolf Hartmann revealed, about a quarter of his unit were keen because they hoped to loot food and drink. Many German soldiers succeeded in their self-imposed search-and-destroy missions. Binding lamented the fact that the cellars at Albert and Moreuil 'contained so much wine that the divisions, which ought properly to have marched through them, lay about unfit to fight in the rooms and cellars ... The disorder of the troops at these two places ... must have cost us a good fifty thousand men.' Stephen Westman bewailed the fact that the offensive was soon held up, 'not for lack of German fighting spirit, but on account of the abundance of Scottish drinking spirit'.

The British army persisted with its rum ration during the Second World War, with tots being issued when a medical officer was prepared to certify that the conditions warranted it. 'We simply kept going on rum,' admitted John Horsfall. 'Eventually it became unthinkable to go into action without it. Rum, and morphia to silence our wounded.' He described how one of his NCOs 'entered his penultimate battle reduced to the ranks, in close arrest and quite wonderfully drunk'. In his next battle this soldier was wounded and taken to the Regimental Aid Post, but, again fighting drunk, broke out and was later found dead in the German positions. 'He was a true Faugh with simple tastes,' reflected Horsfall, 'rum and the regiment.' As his battalion prepared to mount a diversionary attack, Martin Lindsay watched one officer walk round 'with a large earthenware jar, and everybody got well rummed-up, the first time I have seen this happen. They left in a state bordering on hilarity.' Raleigh Trevelyan asked a fellow platoon commander how he managed to tolerate the incessant rifle-grenading: 'Vat 69' was his answer. On the Eastern Front, both sides used whatever alcohol they could get their hands on to blur the horror. A wounded infantryman told Guy Sajer: "There's as much vodka, schnapps and Terek liquor on the front as there are Paks [anti-tank guns] … It's the easiest way to make heroes. Vodka purges the brain and expands the strength.'

American soldiers, in an army which was, in theory, 'dry', were less fortunate. In practice, as Charles MacDonald tells us, officers received a monthly allowance, which they had to pay for. In the winter of 1944–5 this amounted to one quart of Scotch, one pint of gin, one or two bottles of cognac, a bottle of champagne and a bottle of Cointreau. An officer would usually share this around his platoon, and there was little chance of wholesale drunkenness ensuing. In the Pacific, where drink was notoriously hard to obtain, men brewed up 'raisin jack' or 'swipe'. Aqua Velva aftershave, which could be mixed with grapefruit juice to make a passable Tom Collins, sold briskly. Bill Mauldin thought that his comrades drank 'because other recreational facilities are crowded or unavailable, and liquor can dull the sharp memories of war'. Two enterprising members of the Fort Garry Horse obliterated pre-battle tension on their voyage to Normandy by draining the alcohol from the compass in their tank, mixing it with powdered orange-juice, and drinking it. Plied with black coffee by their troop sergeant, they were sober by the time the regiment went ashore.

Although drink remained an important solace for American troops in Vietnam, it was overtaken by drugs. In 1971 50·9 per cent of US army personnel in Vietnam had smoked marijuana, 28·5 per cent had taken heroin or opium, and 30·8 per cent had experimented with other psychedelic drugs. Colonel George Walton quotes 1st Sergeant Ernest R. Davis in his book *The Tarnished Shield*. 'The Drug situation is horrible, really horrible,' said Davis. 'The further north you go in Vietnam, the more drugs there are. Some of the forward fire bases are among the worst. The men are using marijuana, heroin, and sometimes opium.' In 1970 over 11,000 US servicemen were charged with using hard drugs, but it was generally believed that the detection rate was only one in five.

Sometimes the effects of drugs were precisely what their users intended, and the strain of combat was reduced or even eliminated. 'In the field', said one soldier, 'I was not scared of booby traps or ambushes. I forgot I was a soldier.' Tim Page thought that the effects of drugs disappeared immediately battle started. 'OK,' he said, 'you can be stoned in combat for what it's worth. Though the first round will straighten you out ... There isn't a thing in the world that can bring you back that fast except a bullet.' At other times, however, drug-takers hallucinated with tragic consequences. One man shot and killed a lieutenant-colonel he had never previously met, explaining that inner voices had directed him to do so. A sentry smoking marijuana decided that everyone around him was hostile: he opened fire and killed several men. Gale Smith, a nurse in the 3rd Surgical Hospital, complained of drug abuse among medical orderlies. 'These guys would come into work stoned all the time. My medics would shoot up my patients.'

Drink and drugs, however undesirable some of their conse-quences may be, are well-established devices for assisting the soldier to escape from the wartime environment or to mask the ugly face of battle. On occasion, the escape is compounded by a physical transformation in which the drunken soldier – or even, on occasion, the sober one – dresses up in outrageous garb. On 28 March 1918 Rudolf Binding, sent forward to find out why the advance had slowed up, found 'men dressed up in comic disguise. Men with top hats on their heads. Men staggering. Men who could hardly walk.' Wheeler relates how, after the Battle of Vittoria: 'British soldiers were soon to be seen in French generals' and other officers' uniform covered with stars and military orders, others had attired themselves in female dresses, richly embroidered in gold and silver.' There was a bizarre carnival in the town of Fredericksburg after the battle. Not only was there a good deal of looting and vandal-ism, but Union soldiers leaped about in women's dresses and underwear. When men of the 18th Regiment fought their way into the outskirts of Sebastopol on 17 June 1855, a similar euphoria gripped them, and, in W. Baring Pemberton's words, they were soon 'dancing and pirouetting in bonnets and shawls on a plot of grass, regardless of the firing'.

Charles MacDonald's soldiers disguised themselves less strangely. He was surprised to see how, when his company was billeted in a former hat factory, 'three-fourths of the men had equipped themselves with fantastic civilian straws and felts'. In late January 1942, just before his Australian Mobile Workshop withdrew on to Singapore Island, Warrant Officer David Mason took a party into the Sultan of Johore's Palace. They entered in search of weapons, but emerged with other prizes.

As twenty-seven Mitsubishi bombers droned overhead on their way to Singapore, our brave boys capered and danced, clothed in red evening dresses, each one sporting

Prussian Hussars and the spoils of victory, 1757

wigs of varying hue. Round their necks like Hawaiian
wreaths were pearls and the missing ammunition belts, and
our biggest member, suitably nicknamed 'Brown Bomber'
hobbled uncomfortably in high heeled shoes.

An officer arrived to protest the following day, but desisted
after being threatened with an empty revolver 'by one of the
miscreants suffering from a Johnny Walker hangover'.

This fondness for dressing up is no doubt largely humorous,
but it is, in a curious way, the mirror-image of the way in
which women in wartime often tend to adopt military fashion
or even to don pseudo-uniforms *à l'Amazone*. It may, however,
have more serious overtones, and represent a soldier's desire
to dispense with his military identity altogether. Either way,
it is part, albeit a strange part, of the coping process.

Breaking Point

For a substantial minority of soldiers these processes either fail
to work adequately or are eroded by continual exposure to
battle, and breakdown results. These men are not merely extremely frightened, exhibiting all the usual physical symptoms
of fear but still amenable to discipline and support, and capable of being helped, urged or even threatened into continuing
to fight. They are ill: ill in the same sense that they would be
if they had influenza or malaria. Their symptoms vary greatly,
just as the symptoms of the physically ill do, and the severity
of their affliction may range from the temporary and minor
to the chronic and totally disabling. The very expression psychiatric casualty is a broad one – so broad, indeed, that Frank
Richardson terms it 'inelegant and etymologically incorrect'.
It includes men whose existing disorders are aggravated by
stress, men whose physical wounds – particularly disfigure-
ment or emasculation – are accompanied by psychiatric disorders, and those suffering from what is now generally termed
battle fatigue or battleshock.

It is not my purpose to discuss at length the diagnosis, and still less the treatment, of the psychiatric casualties of battle. Nevertheless, no consideration of the individual's performance in combat would be complete without reference to the question of these casualties, any more than it would without mention of the physically injured.

Writing in the US army's *Military Review*, Lieutenant-Colonel L.H. Ingraham and Major F.J. Manning suggest that 'psychiatric battle casualties are a phenomenon new with 20th-century warfare'. There is reason to doubt this. Not only are there descriptions, like those from Zorndorf and Waterloo, of soldiers suffering from what would today be recognised as battleshock, but medical evidence from nineteenth-century campaigns reveals that soldiers were treated for psychiatric illness induced by battle. During the American Civil War the Union Surgeon-General, William Hammond, recognised a condition he called 'nostalgia'. He encouraged the retention of its victims in the combat zone, in an attempt to keep them busy with steady but non-stressful work, a treatment not dissimilar to that advocated today. There were 5,213 cases in the first year of the war – 2·34 per 1,000 troops. This figure rose to 3·3 per 100 in the second year of the war, and there were substantial numbers of discharged for 'paralysis' and 'insanity'.

In 1922 the historian Sir John Fortescue, testifying before a War Office Committee, said that the evidence of history was not accurate enough for his contribution to be properly scientific. Nevertheless, he believed that 'even the bravest man cannot endure to be under fire for more than a consecutive number of days even if the fire be not very heavy'. He thought that noise had played a lesser part in former battles than it had in the First World War, but believed that standing still to face artillery fire was a dreadful ordeal even in the days of muzzle-loaders: 'the trial must have been too much for the nerves of many'. Lieutenant-General Sir Thomas Picton was reluctant to serve on the Waterloo campaign, and his letter to Wellington paints a sad picture of a man exhausted by the strain of command in an era when generals shared the risks of close-range battle with their troops. 'My Lord,' wrote Picton,

'I must give up. I am grown so nervous that when there is any service to be done it works upon my mind so that it is impossible for me to sleep at nights. I cannot possibly stand it, and I shall be forced to retire.' But Sir Thomas did not retire: he accompanied his old chief to Waterloo, where he was shot through the head while commanding the 5th Division.

Psychiatric casualties were undoubtedly relatively uncommon prior to the twentieth century. As we have already observed, soldiers were not generally subjected to sustained combat, and artillery bombardment lacked the qualities which have made it such an effective destroyer of mental stability this century. What is also crucial is that it was not until the First World War that military psychiatry came of age: the psychiatric casualties of previous wars often went undiagnosed and untreated.

The process of recognising that there was such a thing as psychiatric breakdown in battle was a painful one. Early in the First World War, as R.H. Ahrenfeldt writes in his history of British military psychiatry, it was almost a matter of chance whether a man suffering from a psychoneurotic breakdown was considered to be ill from 'shell shock', or to be a malingerer or even a deserter. It is beyond debate that some of the British soldiers shot for cowardice during the war were, by today's standards, sick men. By August 1916 the British Expeditionary Force had its own consulting psychiatrist and consulting neurologist, and by the end of the year special psychiatric centres had been set up in each army area, and specialists were appointed to the various bases provided with what were then termed 'mental wards'. Advanced psychiatric centres were in use by the middle of 1917, treating some patients and returning them to their units swiftly, and sending others back for treatment at base.

Soldiers suffering from psychiatric illness were initially diagnosed as having 'shell shock', in the belief that the patient's brain had been concussed by the proximity of an exploding shell. Those whose breakdown could not be associated with shelling were often, in the case of both the British and French

armies, accused of lacking moral fibre: they risked being subjected to therapies which might include the administration of
electric shocks. Nevertheless, by the end of the war there was
a widespread agreement amongst the Allied armies – including the Americans, who studied and copied British methods
– that casualties should be examined and sorted at field ambulances, with exhaustion, concussion and war neurosis as
recognised categories of illness. Light cases should be treated
in forward areas: often a rest in a safe but none the less military environment sufficed. More difficult cases could be sent
to the rear. Prisoners and men suspected of having self-inflicted wounds were also examined. As an index of the scale
of the problem, in 1917 psychiatric admissions ran at 1 per
1,000 for the civilian population of Britain, 2 per 1,000 for
troops on home service, and 4 per 1,000 for troops in the BEF.
As late as March 1939 120,000 men were still in receipt of
pensions or had received awards for primary psychiatric dis-
ability.

A 1922 War Office Committee considered the whole question of shell shock. It concluded that there were three sorts of
psychiatric casualty. Firstly, there was concussion, which was
relatively uncommon; secondly, exhaustion, which was far
more frequent; and thirdly, a number of real war neuroses.
Many of the witnesses testified that breakdown resulted from
continued exposure to stress, but there was widespread agreement that discipline, *esprit de corps* and leadership all helped to
reduce the incidence of breakdown.

During the Second World War the British army built upon
the foundations laid during and after the First. A Directorate
of Selection of Personnel was set up in June 1941, in an effort
to exclude from the services those likely to suffer early breakdown. In April the following year a Directorate of Army Psychiatry was established as part of the Army Medical Services.
Psychiatrists deployed well forward treated men who broke
down, and the activities of far-sighted general medical officers
like Frank Richardson ensured that fear and breakdown were
subjects which could be discussed to a greater degree than
ever before. There was, inevitably, some complaint that the

very fact of mentioning that there was such a thing as psychiatric breakdown encouraged some faint-hearted soldiers to feign its symptoms. Ahrenfeldt formally denied that this was a real risk. 'I have yet to meet a regimental medical officer', he wrote, 'who knows of a single instance of a good man being discouraged by the knowledge that if he became a casualty of any sort he would get looked after.' Richardson was less confident. 'Sometimes soldiers would wander back to the regimental aid post on their own,' he observed, 'announcing almost jauntily that they had "Exhaustion" and clearly feeling no stigma at having failed to stand up to conditions which they had left their comrades to face.'

Treatment followed a pattern similar to that during the latter stages of the First World War. Regimental medical officers sedated patients immediately after breakdown, and this was continued at the dressing station and the corps exhaustion centre. Here patients remained under military discipline, and were encouraged to think in terms of making an early return to duty. Rather less than 30 per cent of them were in fact returned to duty from the corps reception centre. The remainder went to an advanced psychiatric centre, where most of them were sufficiently rehabilitated to perform duty on the lines of communication within a month. The American army was initially far less successful, for, although there was a great amount of literature available on combat stress in the First World War, it was assumed that this would have little relevance in an age of mechanised warfare. As Peter Bourne acknowledges: 'There is little doubt that many of the casualties could have been averted had a more enlightened attitude prevailed at the time.' By 1944 the situation had improved enormously, with emphasis being given to treatment in the combat zone and the early return of many patients to duty.

The broad outline of the system of treatment used in the Second World War has changed little since, with the principles of treatment being recognised as immediacy, proximity and expectancy. In Vietnam, the Americans deployed a psychiatric consultant for their forces in the theatre, with two neuropsychiatric treatment-centre teams, and divisional

psychiatrists. Line officers received training on 'their responsibilities relative to the situational and social determinants of
combat adjustments', and general medical officers were well
aware of the psychiatric dimension of casualties.

In the fighting in the Lebanon in 1982 the Israeli army
made widespread use of front-line psychiatric stations, where
disturbed soldiers were visited by comrades from their unit,
who assured them that they were in no way disgraced and
would be welcomed back. Almost 60 per cent of patients were
returned to duty from these centres. The remainder went to
second-stage centres in Israel, where they remained about a
fortnight. The most seriously disturbed went to the army's
Combat Training Fitness Unit. Patients at all these centres
were treated as soldiers, and were required to wear uniform
and keep fit. Psychiatrists and therapists helped them overcome their problems, often feelings of guilt and shame at having left their comrades to carry on fighting, or aversion to
tanks or guns. Of the 600 Israeli soldiers evacuated with psychiatric problems, only sixty required further treatment, and
none of the latter needed long-term institutional care.

The incidence of psychiatric casualties is influenced by a
wide range of factors, such as the adequacy of selection processes before enlistment, the intensity of battle, the time spent
in combat by a unit or individual, the non-battle elements of
stress such as terrain and climate, the general attitude to fear
and breakdown, and the state of morale. During the Second
World War Allied troops sustained psychiatric casualties at a
rate which varied between about 8 per cent of all battle casualties – in the British 2nd Army in April–May 1945 – and
54 per cent – in the US 2nd Armored Division in forty-four
days of sustained operations in Italy in 1944. The latter instance is by no means isolated, however: in the ill-starred
Arakan offensive of 1942 the 14th Indian Division reached
such a low ebb that the command psychiatrist described the
entire division as 'a psychiatric casualty'.

In the case of the American army, evacuations for psychiatric reasons totalled 23 per cent of all evacuations, although
this figure reflects inadequate psychiatric care in the early

stages of the war. At one point in early 1943 psychiatric casualties were being discharged from the service faster than new
recruits were being drafted in. The highest overall rate of
psychiatric casualties was sustained by the US 1st Army in
Europe, averaging 101 per 1,000 troops per year. The British
2nd Army incurred psychiatric casualties at the rate of 10 per
cent of all its battle casualties on and immediately after D-
Day. This rose to 20 per cent in the period July–September
1944, and then declined steadily to 14 per cent in October–
December, 10 per cent in January–March 1945, and 8 per
cent in April–May.

In Korea, the Americans initially approached the Second
World War evacuation figure of 23 per cent, but this soon
dropped to 6 per cent as front-line treatment centres were
established. Almost three-quarters of patients were returned
to duty, with a relapse rate of 10 per cent. In Vietnam there
were relatively few cases of 'traditional' combat fatigue associated with sustained action, physical exhaustion and poor
diet. Psychiatric casualties totalled 5 per cent of evacuations
from Vietnam in 1965–6, and only 2–3 per cent in 1967–8.

Even the Israeli army, with its good morale, high level of
pre-war preparation, and wide popular support, is by no
means immune to psychiatric casualties. In the Six Day War
of 1967, with the tide flowing very much in Israel's favour,
they totalled less than 10 per cent of all Israeli casualties.
In 1973, however, when the Israelis were taken by surprise,
psychiatric casualties ran at 60 per cent for the first few
days of the war, reflecting a sharp dislocation of expectation as the Arabs launched a well-planned offensive which
the over-confident Israelis initially found it hard to contain.
This very high figure stimulated interest in the prevention
and treatment of psychiatric casualties, and, according to a
report in March 1983, Israeli forces in the Lebanon suffered
the much-reduced but still high rate of 23 per cent psychiatric
casualties.

Psychiatric disorders were uncommon in both the British
and Argentinian forces in the Falklands. In September 1983
the World Congress of Psychiatry was informed that only

twenty-one of the British wounded, 3·6 per cent, suffered from
mental illness, and 1·5 per cent from a combat reaction. Eight
received treatment for depression, and three for alcoholism,
stress-induced dizziness and extreme pain reaction. Dr Carlos
Collazo, psychiatric adviser to the Argentinian army, announced that only 3 per cent of his army's casualties had been
psychiatric.

These raw statistics help throw some light on to the reasons
for breakdown. The Second World War figures were very
much affected by the prevailing attitude to psychiatric illness.
There was no psychiatric specialist on the island of Malta
during the siege of 1941–2, largely because of what Ahrenfeldt
calls 'an intense hostility towards psychiatry, on the part of
the medical and non-medical administrative authorities in
Malta'. Soon after the bombing began, 50–60 per cent of
outpatients at the military hospital were psychiatric cases, and
about 25 per cent of the garrison showed 'a pathological
degree of response to aerial attack'. One officer reported that
they were 'very near to a crack in April, 1942'. There was
also little positive action that the garrison could take in the
face of air attack, and it suffered from the classic 'inactivity
under bombardment' syndrome.

The high level of psychiatric breakdown in American formations was due in great measure to the American system of
combat replacement. Divisions were kept in the line indefi-
nitely, and replacements were posted in as the need arose. A
replacement would therefore not only fight alongside men
he had had little opportunity to get to know, but he would
speedily realise that he was likely to fight until he dropped.
General Omar Bradley gave a moving account of the way the
infantryman felt under these circumstances.

The rifleman trudges into battle knowing that the odds are
stacked against his survival. He fights without promise of
either reward or relief. Behind every river, there's another
hill – and behind that hill, another river. After weeks or
months in the line only a wound can offer him the comfort
of safety, shelter and a bed. Those who are left to fight,

fight on, evading death, but knowing that with each day of evasion they have exhausted one more chance of survival. Sooner or later, unless victory comes, this chase must end on the litter or in the grave.

The shortcomings of this system persuaded the Americans to introduce a policy of rotation in Korea and Vietnam. In both conflicts units were topped up with replacements in the field, but an individual knew that he had only to serve in the theatre for a specified period of time. There were, of course, disadvantages inherent in this scheme. Individuals arrived in their new unit as strangers, often to be ostracised by those already there. In Vietnam the terms 'FNG' (fucking new guy' or 'cherry' (virgin) were common names for new arrivals. Bob Sanders's reception in the 173rd Brigade was not untypical: 'Yeah, you cherry, welcome to the Nam, you fucking bum ... I'm short, buddy, I'll be leaving outa here in a couple of days.' 'Look, FNG, I don't want to scare you,' remarked an old hand to Tim O'Brien after their camp had been mortared, 'but that stuff last night wasn't *shit!* Last night was a lark. Wait'll you see some really *bad* shit.'

Battle is confusing enough at the best of times, but for a replacement thrown in head first at the deep end it can be utterly perplexing. S.L.A. Marshall described the plight of Private Gerald Costello on a patrol action in Korea.

Costello was simply a lost soul wholly surrounded by meaningless wilderness. Given a number, a rifle and a responsible soldierly task to do by Uncle Sam, this hapless nephew was utterly incapable of understanding his relationship to anything about him.

Marshall argued that whatever rotation gave the soldier, it 'sacrificed most of the traditional values, such as earned promotion and citation, pride in unit and close comradeship, which are supposed to keep him steadfast'. General Donn A. Starry attacked the 'lousy system' of individual reinforcement, which created 'a lonesome soldier - 2,000 miles from home'.

Not only did the newly-arrived replacement in Korea or Vietnam find it difficult to adapt to his new environment, but his whole attitude to life changed significantly during the duration of his tour – a year, in the case of Vietnam. His apprehensive enthusiasm changed to resignation as he became integrated with his group and achieved a degree of mastery over his environment. This resignation was itself replaced by 'anxious apprehension' as DEROS – Date of Expected Return from Overseas – grew near. Men whose time was nearly up suffered from 'short-timer's fever'. They were markedly reluctant to run risks, and in some units it was accepted that they should not be sent on operations.

Yet, great though the disadvantages of the rotation system were, it was undoubtedly one of the main reasons for the low figure of American psychiatric casualties in Vietnam. There was always a horizon, never more than a year away, and getting closer day by day. In Peter Bourne's words: 'There is not the sense of hopelessness that prevailed in previous conflicts where death, injury or peace beame the only possible ways in which the soldier could find himself extricated from combat.' Bourne also made two other telling observations. The first was that there was a marked difference between the way in which the symptoms of stress-induced illness appeared in the American army and the army of the Republic of Vietnam. In the former, psychiatric symptoms were regarded as a legitimate manner of gaining acceptance as a casualty. In the latter, they were not, and physical equivalents were selected instead. This led Bourne to speculate that perhaps the various names for the psychiatric illnesses of war – shell shock, traumatic neurosis of war, combat neurosis and combat fatigue – 'were all coined consecutively in an attempt to pinpoint more accurately a clinical syndrome which may have been changing almost as rapidly as the names'. Secondly, Bourne considered the Australian army in Vietnam. Here, he concluded, the absence of a fixed tour caused some morale problems, but good leadership by company and platoon commanders helped prevent difficulties. The Australians constantly emphasised their own quality and criticised others. 'Closing their minds to all but the performance of their own unit against the Viet Cong,' wrote Bourne, 'they fought a private war in which their own military accomplishments take on meaning and significance.'

The conclusions drawn by the Israelis from their experience in 1982 are particularly interesting. The majority of their psychiatric casualties suffered from battleshock – from pure emotional reaction to the stress of battle. The psychiatric casualty tended to have a profile of his own. He was likely to be in his late twenties: soldiers between eighteen and twenty-one were the least and those between twenty-six and thirty the most vulnerable. Poor education, low motivation, low intelligence, being a reservist, being of low rank and being from a support unit were all likely attributes. As Lieutenant-Colonel Belenky observed, previous studies had indicated that low morale and poor unit cohesion made men more predisposed to breakdown in battle, and that the psychiatric casualties in elite units have generally been low. This was borne out in the Lebanon, where 'high unit morale correlated with a low incidence of psychiatric casualties'.

The low figure of psychiatric casualties in the Falklands may be something of a maverick. In the first place, the campaign was short. The Argentinian invasion occurred on 2 April, initial SAS and SBS landings took place on 1 May, the San Carlos landings began on 21 May and Port Stanley fell on 14 June. Even the luckless Argentine conscripts dug in on the hills around Stanley had to endure only three weeks of battle conditions and, demoralising though British land, sea and air bombardment was, it was light by the standards of the Second World War or, indeed, by projections of a future conflict on the Central Front. The combatants on both sides were anxious to get the war over. The soldiers of 2 Para found their wait on Sussex Mountain, before the march to Goose Green, most depressing precisely because it seemed to them that the war would drag on. Carlos, one of the Argentinians waiting for the attack, was also anxious to get it over with. 'We felt that the sooner they arrived, the sooner things would be settled,' he told Daniel Kon, 'and the sooner we could go home.' The battles themselves were also short. Goose Green, the longest, lasted some twenty-four hours: savage and confusing for many of those engaged, but without the mind-dulling drag of Second World War grinding-matches like El Alamein, Stalingrad, Kursk or Normandy.

Not only was the campaign short and of relatively low intensity but, at least as far as the British were concerned, it was fought by highly-motivated professional soldiers. The parachute battalions and marine commandos were fighting exactly the sort of war they had trained for: hence the common comparison with an exercise. Colonel P. Abraham, Professor of Psychiatry at the Royal Army Medical College argued that the Falklands should not be regarded as typical. Had the battles lasted longer,

> the number of those whose inability to fight was not attributable to sickness or injury would have escalated alarmingly. The chief reason for this assertion is that the number of such battleshock cases is inexorably linked to the number of wounded, and as the fabric of the unit is eroded by casualties, both physical and psychological, so does it become harder for the remainder to sustain themselves and each other in the face of bombardment and bereavement.

Estimates of the attrition rates in a future high-intensity conventional war suggest that, during the first thirty days of combat, psychiatric casualties will occur at the rate of at least one for every four battle casualties. Lieutenant-Colonel Chermol predicts that sustained nuclear, biological and chemical operations would increase this figure to one to three or even one to two. He goes on to say that after thirty days of continual combat, 'psychiatric casualties may well begin to exceed battle casualties, and most unit personnel may be psychologically ineffective after 60 days of continued, high-intensity combat'. Even this may be an optimistic projection.

Psychiatric breakdown can present itself in many forms. The classic symptoms of exhaustion are marked apprehension and nervousness, insomnia, headaches and nightmares. Denis

Sheil-Small was utterly exhausted when the battalion was taken out of the line and re-trained. 'Over and over again the faces of the wounded and dying appeared before me,' he recalled,

> until I was no longer living in the present but in the immediate past. The sudden transformation from battlefield to such training in such a short time was too quick. I could neither concentrate nor conform. My reserves of energy had vanished. Somewhere behind me, on the banks of the Irrawaddy ... I seemed to have left my true self; I had now become an empty shell.

Charlton Ogburn was in a similar state after his experiences with Merrill's Marauders. 'I had found myself with a strange debility that sometimes made me feel I could not stand up,' he wrote. 'I concluded that it must be mental, the result of the fear of Myitkyina, which brooded over that camp like the literal figure of death.'

Stephen Westman treated the commanding officer of his artillery regiment, an experienced major who had become convinced that nothing would happen to him so long as his dog was with him. But with the beast's disappearance:

> The major, a tall, good-looking man, became morose and desperate, although he was usually a resolute and tough person. He spoke about his impending death; he could not sleep, and I had to give him tranquillisers and sleeping-pills. He even started drinking, and I repeatedly found him dead drunk – a thing which he usually abhorred and which he would never have tolerated amongst his subordinates.

The major was eventually killed by a shell-splinter in the head, having failed to wear his steel helmet.

One of the most misunderstood reactions to battle is sleep. Grinding fatigue is in any case a natural result of being under fire. The men of Love Company, 27th Infantry, were in good condition when they crossed the start line in their assault on

Hill 440 in Korea, and had only 1,100 yards to cover from their assembly area till the time they came into action. The engagement started at 08.30, and from 11.30 onwards the main problem was keeping the soldiers awake. Under heavy bombardment, sleep is brought on not so much by fatigue but by a subconscious desire to withdraw from the battle. 'Artillery was the great leveller,' thought Private E. Atkinson of the East Yorkshires. 'Nobody could stand more than three hours of sustained shelling before they start falling sleepy and numb. You're hammered for three hours and you're there for the picking when he come over. It's a bit like being under an anaesthetic; you can't put a lot of resistance up.' Men often fall asleep under these circumstances. An Israeli thought his comrades in a bunker on the Suez Canal in 1973 were extremely cool to be able to drop off under the Egyptian bombardment: in fact, they were exhibiting a symptom of battleshock.

This mild symptom has more extreme forms. Some of the inmates of Nazi concentration camps withdrew from the intolerable present utterly, and became zombie-like creatures, nicknamed *Müselmanner* (Moslems) because their trance-like state was believed to resemble that of Moslem fanatics. Dr Bruno Bettelheim, himself a concentration camp survivor, wrote: 'come to feel that their environment was one over which they could exercise no influence whatsoever, these prisoners were, in a literal sense, walking corpses'. Writing of behaviour in an interrogation context, Joost van Meerloo discussed the tendency of victims to collapse. This, he suggested, 'serves as a protective device against danger. The victim seems to think, "If my torturer doesn't notice me, he will leave me alone."' Some soldiers do exactly the same thing. When Charles MacDonald's company arrived on a German position, they found one German lying covered with a blanket, shaking violently. 'Maybe he thinks he's an ostrich,' said one American. It is no bad analogy, and I term this phenomenon the ostrich syndrome. It is far more prevalent than one might suppose. John Keegan surmised that the piles of bodies depicted in medieval battle-paintings might in fact contain many men who had simply piled themselves up in the same way that small children huddle together for support.

Covering oneself with a blanket or sleeping bag on the battlefield has the same significance. Philippe de Pirey described a French corporal hiding under a mattress and sleeping bag as the Viet Minh overran an outpost of the Day River in May 1951. 'He reacted', wrote de Pirey, 'exactly as would a small child who wants to dodge his punishment.' After a bombardment in Burma, Lieutenant Logan E. Western found two Japanese in a foxhole, covered with a sack, 'paralysed and shaking with shock'. When the US Army's Dale outpost in Korea was stormed in April 1953, some of its occupants simply played possum. 'An infantryman', wrote Marshall of the incident, 'may play dead until by self-hypnosis he rejects thoughts of past and future, and minutes become contracted to seconds.' In the Hoa Hoi battles of October 1966 B Company, 1st Battalion, 12th Infantry killed forty Viet Cong in bunkers along a river: they would neither fight nor surrender, and were dispatched with grenades. The men of both 45 Commando, in the assault on Two Sisters, and 3 Para, in the attack on Mount Longdon, discovered Argentinians in sleeping bags. It was not that they hoped to escape detection, or that they had been surprised: they were simply dealing with a terrifying situation by escaping from it as best they could. Ian Gardiner wrote perceptively: 'The last citadel of a man's morale is his sleeping bag. The comfort and resource it offers is amazing. On subsequent occasions, when one was being shelled, or heard bombing close by, it was an instinctive automatic reaction to wriggle deeper into the "green slug".'

There is a variety of other symptoms. Some victims are silent and motionless. In the besieged Dien Bien Phu, Lieutenant-Colonel Keller, the French chief of staff had, as Bernard Fall tells us, 'suffered a nervous breakdown and could be seen in the deepest dugout of the headquarters complex, wearing a steel helmet'. Others sob like small children. Private Atkinson related how younger soldiers tended to give way first under the strain of bombardment. 'They would go up to one of the older ones – older in service that is – and maybe even cuddle up to him and start crying. An old soldier could be a great comfort to a young one.'

For some highly-motivated officers and men the conflict between the demands of duty and the knowledge that their chances of being killed or wounded are increasing daily produces serious physical symptoms. Thus, although First World War British officers, buoyed up by responsibility and activity, were half as likely to break down as their men, when they did snap it was often by displaying the symptoms of this hysterical conversion syndrome, in which a mental conflict is converted into, say, paralysis or blindness. This paralysis is no less real than it would be if it had a physical cause. It is amenable to treatment, and Richardson describes successfully dealing with an Indian Army officer who had a classic infantry officer's symptom, paralysis of the right arm. In the case of aircrew, for whom good eyesight is essential, blurring of vision is a common symptom. The hysterical conversion syndrome was relatively rare in the Second World War, and rarer still subsequently, largely because, in a climate where genuine psychiatric illness was recognised, an exhausted officer could admit to his condition without enduring the opprobrium that might have ensued in a less forgiving age.

For an unfortunate few, psychiatric breakdown ends not with effective treatment and a prompt return to duty, or even with a medical discharge and lasting but tolerable symptoms. Westman saw the worst sights of his war, not with the guns at the front, but in a hospital behind the lines.

The patients were kept in large wards, but the unruly cases were often put into padded cells, where they stood in an agitated state, talking constantly to themselves or to persons or things which existed only in their imagination. Others had hallucinations; they were still living through the horrors of an artillery bombardment or a gas attack. They covered their faces with their hands, so as to protect them from shell splinters. Others cried out for their gas masks, which they could not find, and still others heard voices under their pillows or under their bed covers, threatening them with death.

7

Competition, Diffidence and Glory

The first maketh men invade for Gain; the second, for Safety; and the third for Reputation. The first use Violence to make themselves Masters of other men's persons, wives, children and cattle; the second to defend them; the third, for trifles, as a word, a smile, a different opinion, and any other sign of undervalue, either direct in their Persons or by reflection in their Kindred, their friends, their Nation, their Profession or their Name.

Thomas Hobbes, *Leviathan*

The Reason Why

It is no secret that war is, as General Sherman told us, hell, and anyone who has read thus far will need no reminding of this. The fact remains, however, that successive generations, with abundant evidence before them, still persist in fighting. The question as to why men fight does not merely exercise professional soldiers and military theorists, who are concerned with the practicalities of persuading men to perform effectively on the battlefield: it is a moral issue of fundamental importance, all the more so in the era of *Kriegsstimmung*, war-mood, in which we now live.

Before moving on to examine more complex explanations, it is worth considering an unfashionable and surprising fact: some men actually enjoy war, and there are few soldiers for whom military service does not have, albeit in rosy retrospect, some attractions. Addressing the Royal United Service Institute in April 1969, Correlli Barnett described the cumulative effect of the military literature of the Great War as 'a generalised picture of idealism turning to sour disillusion, of the futility of the fighting on the Western Front, of the squalor of trench life, of the obscenity of death and mutilation on a modern battlefield'.

Yet it is perfectly clear that not everyone shared this view. 'I *adore* war,' announced Captain Julian Grenfell. 'It is like a big picnic without the objectlessness of a picnic. I have never been so well or happy.' This may very well reflect the fact that it was written early in the war: Grenfell was killed before disillusionment had the chance to set in. Not all early enthusiasms faded. The Harvard-educated Alan Seeger, serving in the ranks of the French Foreign Legion, told his mother in October 1914 that 'every minute here is worth weeks of ordinary *experience* ... This will spoil one for any other kind of life.' Days before he perished on the Somme, nearly two years later, he wrote to a friend: 'I am glad to be going in the first wave. If you are in this thing it is best to be in it to the limit. And this is the supreme experience.' Captain Graham Greenwell looked back upon the war years as:

> among the happiest I have ever spent. That they contained moments of boredom and depression, of sorrow for the loss of friends and of alarm for my personal safety is indeed true enough. But to be perfectly fit, to live among pleasant companions, to have responsibility and a clearly defined job – these are great compensations when one is very young.

In the spring of 1919, with the war safely over, Captain J.E.H. Neville was delighted to be detailed for services in Russia. 'Wartime soldiering was peculiarly fascinating,' he wrote at the time. 'Square-pushing bores me.'

One of the most savoury pleasures of war comes from the heightened sense of awareness sometimes brought on by the presence of danger. In J.T. MacCurdy's words, 'We are all of us not merely liable to fear, we are also prone to be afraid of being afraid, and the conquering of fear produces exhilaration – hence the joy of adventure.' Ernst Jünger probed deeply towards the truth when he quoted Stendhal: 'The perfection of civilisation would be to combine all the delicate pleasures of the nineteenth century with the most frequent presence of danger.' S.L.A. Marshall warmly agreed. He attacked 'the so-called realists of fiction' who:

> view through a glass clearly every last motion of the combat soldier. But what normal man would deny that some of the fullest and fairest days of his life have been spent at the front or that the sky ever seems more blue or the air more bracing than where there is just a hint of danger in the air.

Winston Churchill compared savouring danger to sipping champagne. 'A single glass of champagne imparts a feeling of exhilaration,' he declared. 'The nerves are braced; the imagination is agreeably stirred; the wits become more nimble. A bottle produces a contrary effect. So it is with war, and the quality of both is best discovered by sipping.'[1]

Even the majority, who find battle terrifying beyond even the merest hint of pleasure, none the less relish comradeship and a sense of importance as an individual within the group. 'Basically, I enjoyed Vietnam,' recalled one veteran. 'It was the most vivid part of my life. I enjoyed the anarchy of it. You know, self-law. No one ever bothered you ... You're living every minute. You're with guys who look after you. You can really trust them.' For another, 'Just hanging out was incredible, the feeling of life. You were so aware of time over there you could taste it.' Fred Majdalany esteemed the 'feeling of high comradeship' which binds men who have endured danger together. 'It is something that can only be known through the moral and emotional purge of battle,' he writes. 'It is the fighting man's reward.' They were echoing Joost van Meerlo:

> Many soldiers – tired by the rigidities of normal life – look back at violent moments of their war experiences despite the hunger and terror, as the monumental culminating experiences of their lives. There, in the *Bruderbund* of fighters, they felt happy for the first and only time in their lives.

A third source of enjoyment in war is the strangely wonderful sights which counterpoint the horror. Some of these are manmade, and others are the work of a nature which is often new to soldiers unfamiliar with the countryside. Michael Herr was struck by the majesty of tracer rounds: 'Even the incoming was beautiful at night, beautiful and deeply beautiful.' Some of Robert Jay Lifton's subjects felt that they looked at the world with an enhanced sense of appreciation: 'We would say, "Wow, look at this, look at the sweep of that gun barrel going out there ... against the sunset or against the stars" ... and look at it from just a new aspect.' The prospect of his first helicopter assault did not cloud Philip Caputo's vision of the strange beauty of Vietnam. 'The Cordillera looked especially beautiful at that hour,' he wrote, 'and, in the clear air, close enough to touch. It was golden-green high up where the new sun touched it, greenish-black lower down, and the line between light and shadow was as sharp as if it had been painted on.'

W.H.A. Groom found few compensations in army life, and his book deals extensively with the trials and tribulations endured by the front-line soldier. Nevertheless, he found that, when out of the line, 'amongst the trees, grass and wild life of the countryside there was a great affinity with nature, reminiscent of the times when during school holidays I would get up very early and walk up Nightingale valley'. There were flashes of wild beauty even in the line at Third Ypres. 'It was a marvellous sunrise,' wrote Groom, 'and I remember the huge red ball of the sun resting on the top of a distant pill box.' Guy Sajer's account of his experiences on the Eastern

Front during the Second World War is a farrago of horror and privation. But it, too, has its brief moments of beauty. In December 1942 he was on guard duty while his comrades celebrated Christmas, and he heard them singing 'O Stille Nacht'. 'This was, in its way,' said Sajer,

> the most beautiful Christmas I have ever seen, made entirely of disinterested emotion and stripped of all tawdry trimmings. I was all alone beneath an enormous starred sky, and I can remember a tear running down my frozen cheek – a tear neither of pain nor of joy but of emotion created by intense experience.

To the pleasures of comradeship and the glimpses of extraordinary beauty offered by war are added the not inconsiderable satisfactions of triumphing in a shared endeavour. As Robert E. Lee looked out across the Union dead who so thickly carpeted Marye's Heights at Fredericksburg, he reflected that it was as well that war was so terrible or we would become too fond of it. It was a sentiment Brigadier Julian Thompson repeated in the South Atlantic nearly a century and a quarter later.

These factors may motivate the few, and help moderate the strain of war for the many. But they do little to explain why the majority of men fight. What, then, about the simplest explanation: that soldiers fight for King and Country, and that they are impelled by patriotism? Patriotism undoubtedly does help persuade men to join up at the beginning of a war, and appeals to men's patriotism figure prominently in wartime recruiting posters. But the real motives behind enlistment are often anything but idealistic. Wellington had no doubts about the composition of his own 'infamous army'.

> Some people talk of their enlisting from their fine military feeling – all stuff – no such thing. Some of our men enlist from having got bastard children – some for minor offences – many more for drink; but you can hardly conceive such a set brought together, and it really is wonderful that we should have made them the fine fellows they are.

John Shipp, growing up in the 1790s, thought of little else but military service, and his ambition was, as he freely admitted, 'to make a name for myself in the field'.

In 1914 there was a surge of patriotic euphoria across the face of Europe. 'The spirit of patriotism of that age', wrote Richard Gale, 'had to be experienced to be believed. The whole nation rallied behind the colours.' But patriotism did not long endure the trenches. Robert Graves's comrades thought it 'too remote a sentiment, and at once rejected as fit only for civilians, or prisoners'. Moreover, not all those who marched away were imbued with it. For many younger men the war was a chance to travel, to break away from the shackles of a monotonous job, and to prove themselves in battle. 'It was not that I felt some definite urge to kill Germans,' wrote Groom, 'or that I had such a high sense of patriotism that I wanted to die for my country; it was simply that apart from curiosity – I wanted to see the front line – probably above all I wanted to say that I had been right in it.'

Once the war was well under way, the heady patriotism of its early days was replaced by a generalised sense of duty and responsibility. Denis Winter believes that 'men stood by their country as they might have stood by a pal whose luck was out'. Most would have gone home if there had been any way to do so with dignity, but the sticking point was 'Would you let Germany win?' For soldiers in the front line, the focus soon tightened on to their own immediate group. One company sergeant-major felt that he was fighting for 'the Regiment and its traditions, also my comrades'. His brother, an NCO in the Royal Horse Guards, said: 'I suppose we were fighting for our country but I'm doubtful if we gave it much thought. It was just a job to be done.' For Captain Neville, too, it was a job and little more. 'People at home', he wrote, 'seem obsessed with the idea that the army will fight to the death to avenge Belgium. Nothing is further from the truth. We shall go on fighting until we are told to stop.'

On the other side of the hill, Rudolf Binding briskly dismissed any abstract concept of the cause as a source of motivation in battle. 'I do not believe', he declared, that the individual fights for ideals – that is, really in the fight; he strikes out so that the other will not strike; he does not flee because he is fighting in an unrighteous cause, he does not attack because his cause is just; he flees because he is the weaker, he conquers because he is the stronger or because his leader has made him feel stronger. Ideals do not help him.

Lieutenant Fritz Nagel agreed. 'Lofty feelings of patriotism, love of country and so forth did not play a role,' he wrote. 'Nobody I knew thought in these terms.' Stephen Westman discerned not patriotism in conventional terms, but a general desire to protect a homeland under increasing threat. He said of his comrades that:

Whenever they spoke of their *Heimat*, the place where they came from, their eyes sparkled, although they often had to admit that they were born in ugly townships or villages. But 'Home' was something for which they all longed and which they were willing to defend to the last.

John Dollard asked his Abraham Lincoln Brigade veterans what they believed to be the most important thing in helping a man to overcome fear in battle. Over three-quarters of them included 'belief in war aims' in a list also containing such things as leadership, training and keeping busy. Dollard concluded that, although all stressed the value of believing that they fought for a better world, and recoiled in horror from the sort of world their enemy strove to create, 'the soldier in battle is not forever whispering, "My cause, my cause." He is too busy for that. Ideology functions *before* battle, to get the man in; and *after* battle by blocking thoughts of escape.'

Much the same was true in the Second World War. In response to the question 'What are we fighting for?', one of Stouffer's respondents replied: 'Ask any dogface on the line. You're fighting for your skin on the line. When I enlisted I was patriotic as all hell. There's no patriotism on the line. A boy up there 60 days in the line is in danger every minute. He ain't fighting for patriotism.' Only 5 per cent of the veterans of an infantry division with service in North Africa and Sicily cited idealistic reasons as a motive for encouraging them to do well. Indeed, the strongest group code identified by Stouffer and his researchers, apart from the condemnation of flagrant disloyalty, was the taboo against talk of a flag-waving variety. Combat soldiers particularly resented the mention of patriotic motives by men who did not themselves run the risk of battle. But once again there was a broad belief in the rightness of the cause, what Stouffer termed 'a tacit and fairly deep conviction that we were on the right side and that the war, once we were in it, was necessary'. A survey of troops in the Pacific indicated that the higher a man's conviction about America's war aims, the more likely he was to be willing to fight on. Anthony Kellett is undoubtedly right to point to 'a relationship between favourable attitudes to the war and behaviour in combat' as far as the American army was concerned.

In the case of Britain, the prevailing mood on the outbreak of war in 1939 was in sharp contrast to that in 1914. There was more resignation than jingoism, in part because of pervading memories of the Great War. Nevertheless, the fact that both the Germans and, later, the Japanese could, without too much difficulty, be portrayed as evil and threatening figures, helped to foster an underlying belief in the validity of the struggle. British commanders had contrasting views on the importance of patriotism. Montgomery, very much in concert with Stouffer's findings, maintained that the soldier of a democracy must be convinced of the rightness of his cause, even if only at a passive level. Such a belief would only give real moral support to comparatively few, but, conversely, no democratic society could hope to sustain a war if its citizens and soldiers were opposed to it. Slim, in contrast, held that the spiritual element, which he defined as faith in a cause, was the very foundation of morale. He preached not merely the defence of India or the reconquest of Burma, but the destruction of the Japanese army, an evil thing. Slim's views were undoubtedly coloured, and his inspiration of his soldiers assisted, by the fact that the Japanese army, with its aggressive strategy and harsh behaviour – not to mention the racial and cultural gulf between it and the British – *seemed* an evil thing to most of those who fought against it.

British soldiers of the Second World War are more likely, in retrospect, to list patriotism amongst their motives than are those of the First World War. My questionnaire asked them what they considered they were fighting for – 'your country, your regiment, your immediate comrades, or simply for survival?' H.L. Payne, a gunner officer in Malaya, believed that he fought for 'my country many miles away, which had a more important war on its doorstep'. Peter Halford-Thompson, who served in the same campaign, thought of 'King and Country – with a liberal dose of survival – which included my own men'. For Geoffrey Stavert even the question seemed puzzling. He fought for 'country, of course. What else?' Donald Featherstone recalls a mixture of motives. He fought:

> Certainly for my country – a deep sense of patriotism and chauvinism has always sustained me. I was immensely proud and sustained by being in the Royal Tank Regiment, and my own group were good. The lads around me – with whom I am still in regular contact – were first class ... The fight for survival was not the most conscious aspect, more an innate ever-present background.

For a Scottish wartime infantry officer, 'The rightness of the cause was beyond dispute. There were in addition tremendous bonds within platoons, companies, battalions of the Regiment based on comradeship and tradition.' Jack Chaffer 'always felt I was fighting for my Country, and always doing the best of my ability so as not to let down my Regiment and Comrades'.

The views of pre-war regulars tend to place less emphasis on patriotism and more on professional pride. Both Sergeant-Major Michael Reed and Lieutenant-Colonel Brian Clark put the regiment at the head of their priorities. John Roberts found country, regiment, comrades and survival all:

'compounded in the cause. There was great patriotism in the war, not so much in Korea: it was a long way away ... Regimental pride has been enhanced not lost in amalgamations. In the real heat of battle there is a sense of survival.' 'I fought because I was under orders to do so, and because I believed it right to do so; the Germans had to be defeated,' affirmed D.J.B. Houchin, already a regular for eleven years in 1939. 'Why did the Germans go on fighting when they knew the cause was lost and had lost faith in the Führer? They were professional soldiers as was I.'

The question of motivation in the German army towards the close of the war was examined in detail by Edward Shils and Morris Janowitz. They concluded:

> the unity of the German army was in fact sustained only to a very slight extent by the National Socialist convictions of its members, and that more important in the motivation of the determined resistance of the German soldier was the steady satisfaction of certain *primary* personality demands afforded by the social organization of the army.

A captured sergeant laughed when his interrogators inquired about the political opinions of his men. 'When you ask that question,' he replied, 'I realize well that you have no idea of what makes a soldier fight. The soldiers lie in their holes and are happy if they live through the next day. If we think at all, it's about the end of the war and then home.' *Heimat*: the very word used by Stephen Westman in his description of German soldiers of an earlier war.

Valid though this assessment may be for the great mass of German troops, there is no doubt that ideology played a greater role in forging and maintaining the morale of the *Waffen SS*. Charles Sydnor attributes the formidable fighting spirit of the *Totenkopfdivision*, in defeat as well as in victory, to two interrelated phenomena: the ideological legacy of the pre-war concentration camp system, and the energetic and fanatical style of leadership displayed by the division's senior officers. The SS recruit was drilled into unquestioning obedience, and encouraged to hate and despise the 'enemies behind the wire'. When war broke out, this hatred was readily transferred to the enemy beyond the frontier. 'The political antecedents of the *Totenkopfdivision*,' wrote Sydnor, 'the form and objectives of its ideological and military training programmes, and the character and quality of its leading personalities fashioned it into an extraordinary instrument of war.'

The Soviet Union responded to the German invasion of 1941, and the fluctuations in Russian fighting spirit that marked the first few months of the struggle, by changing the thrust of its propaganda. The Comintern was dissolved, and the previous emphasis upon the Soviet Union as standard-bearer of world communism was replaced by that of Russia fighting for its life against the invader. The concept of 'Mother Russia' came to the fore, and posters carried pictures of the warriors of tsarist days as well as more recent heroes, deliberately recalling former wars against earlier invaders. German behaviour in occupied areas made this line of argument all the more credible, and helped persuade Russians, many of whom had no affection for Stalin and his regime, to fight resolutely in defence of their homeland rather than of the regime which governed it. The British correspondent Alexander Werth said of the Russians that: 'The thought that this was *their* war was, in the main, as strong among the civilians as among the soldiers.' This fierce sense of defending a threatened homeland against a brutal enemy undoubtedly helped inspire Russian soldiers not only to expel the Germans from their soil, but to go on and take their revenge in Germany itself.

The great mass of memoirs of the Vietnam War tend to de-emphasise ideology as a motive for the American soldier. True though this may be for the latter part of the war, it does not accurately reflect feeling in its early stages. For Philip Caputo, 'counterinsurgency was still surrounded by the Kennedy mystique'. An infantry company commander stressed that he believed passionately in the American cause, and fought for: 'My country and its policies, and my unit. I was an apostle of our cause and worked to motivate my men not

only by self-concern but by the cause itself.' For younger conscripts, particularly those who arrived after 1968-9, ideology
played little part. David Parks wrote that: 'I never felt I was
fighting for any particular cause. I fought to stay alive, and I
killed to keep from being killed.' A Veterans' Administration
psychiatrist was sure that Vietnam combat veterans tended to
see their experience 'as an exercise in survival rather than a
defence of national values'. A soldier defined his own feelings
with a majestic double negative: 'I don't know who are the
good guys or the bad guys, us or the VC. But nobody that
fires at me ain't my friend.'

The role of ideology is well to the fore in the debate over
America's failure to win the war in Vietnam. In his important
book *Why the Vietcong Fought*, Lieutenant-Colonel W.D. Henderson blamed many of the American army's problems in
Vietnam on domestic politics, 'the greening of America', and
racial friction. But most of all, he maintained,

> The United States Army in Vietnam lost sight of the basic
> truth that combat is a group action, requiring the utmost
> in mutual cooperation; in 'good' units, cooperation is mo-
> tivated by an intense need on the part of the individual
> soldier to fulfil recognised obligations toward his fellow sol-
> diers.

R.A. Gabriel and P.L. Savage, in their controversial study of
the American Army in Vietnam, *Crisis in Command*, discerned
a progressive disintegration in the efficiency of small units, a
process which went on quite independently of sociopolitical
factors in American society as a whole. They went on to la-
ment the decline of officer professionalism within the army,
blaming an officer corps that was increasingly managerial for
its failure to give effective traditional leadership. American
failure, in short, was a predominantly military failure, and did
not stem from ideological weaknesses.

Charles Moskos observed what he termed a 'latent ideology'
amongst American troops in Vietnam. While they were not
necessarily patriotic in the conventional sense, they had a

deep-seated respect for the American way of life and the comforts it provided, and this conviction underlay their other, sometimes hostile, opinions about the war. There is more than a little similarity between the 'latent ideology' described by Moskos, and the generalised patriotism that we have already noticed on both sides in two World Wars. Finally, Kurt Lang expressed an opinion which has much in common with Field-Marshal Montgomery's comments on the importance of the cause. He argued that the US army in Vietnam inevitably reflected public doubts about the war. 'All this suggests', he wrote, 'that there are serious limits to the use of military force, except for small ventures, without significant popular support.'

With such eminent men in dispute, an overall judgment on the value of ideology in Vietnam is no easier. What is worth noting, however, is the manner in which the divergent opinions of Charles Moskos and Kurt Lang reflect views on patriotism and the cause held in two world wars. But what of America's enemy? As Henderson points out, the People's Liberation Army paid special attention to the organisation and control of primary groups, and, significantly, those Viet Cong who defected generally did so because of 'significant deterioration in unit cohesion' rather than because of any major shift in their personal ideological viewpoint. Unit political officers, who were deployed down to company level as is the case in most communist armies, represented the Party, and ensured both that the Party's view of the struggle was put before tne troops constantly, and that the aims of individual units did not diverge from those laid down by the Party. Henderson argues that the PLA failed in its attempt to politicise the mass of the soldiery by creating 'good communist soldiers'. Nevertheless, its ability to motivate and control its men allowed it 'to endure the disintegrative effects of sustained combat and hardship during the 1965-7 period, which resulted in the ultimate control of the battlefield'.

Samuel Rolbant discussed the combat motivation of Israeli soldiers in the light of an extensively distributed questionnaire. He established immediately that very few answers mentioned hatred of the Arabs as a motivating factor. There were, though, constant references to *ha-hevrah* (my buddies). 'Men said that what worried them most during combat', wrote Rolbant, 'was what others would think of them, or what their families or friends would feel about them when they came home.' In contrast, Major-General Y. Harkabi, a former chief of intelligence of the Israeli army, suggested that the Arab soldier was a lonely man in battle. 'Since social ties are weak,' he wrote, 'the formal framework holding the unit breaks down under the pressure of battle ... It is not that the Arab fighting man was not trained or indoctrinated sufficiently; but these precepts were cold and lifeless statues from which he drew no inspiration.'

The British soldiers and marines who recaptured the Falklands had few doubts about the righteousness of their particular cause. The Argentinians had seized something that was British and, if they did not leave voluntarily, they would have to be put off by force. Lieutenant David Tinker's view of an 'absolutely silly' situation, 'fighting a colonial war on the other side of the world; 28,000 men going to fight over a fairly dreadful piece of land inhabited by 1,800 people,' was not unique, but it was untypical. For most combatants, this broad canvas of patriotism was enlivened by splashes of bright colour. The parachute battalions, imbued with the mystique of 'the maroon machine', were anxious to demonstrate to the remainder of the British army as much as to the enemy that they were, in the words of a private soldier in 2 Para, 'better than any other fucker'. They were all regular soldiers, exercising the profession they had chosen. 'The boys went down to do a job we all wanted to do,' declared one commanding officer. Several soldiers, gratified though they were by the tremendous welcome they received on their return to England, were faintly surprised that they were deemed worthy of such euphoria for merely doing their job.

Their opponents were less fortunate. Not all the patriotic ardour on the mainland seeped through to the young conscripts who did the fighting. Guillermo, a soldier of the 7th Infantry Regiment, told Daniel Kon that: 'They didn't prepare us mentally ... Do you know how I felt? Like a piece of equipment. Where were we going? We didn't know. And, it has to be said, there were some people who didn't even know what they were fighting for.' His compatriot Carlos had no doubt that his cause was right. 'The church talks about "just wars",' he said, 'and the reconquest of the Malvinas for Argentina was just.' This belief was small compensation for the failure of the Argentinian army to produce well-motivated and cohesive small units. For most, the whole complex and intricate process of welding men together started only after they arrived on the Falklands. 'We formed groups,' explained Guillermo, 'small to start with, shut off from the others. And once these groups were consolidated, we made contact with others, we made friends with other groups ... we were like cavemen.' The quality of leadership was patchy. 'The major noticed stupid things such as whether your buttons were sewn on properly or if your trousers were dirty,' announced Jorge. A stretcher-bearer named Juan Carlos recalled:

> When some of the soldiers found themselves alone, in the middle of the night, in the total darkness, and they looked for the support of their superiors, they couldn't find them. So they too retreated. It was only logical. If the professionals had gone, what were mere conscripts expected to do?

Yet properly-trained and well-motivated Argentinians were capable of fighting stoutly. The 5th Marines gave a good account of themselves in their defence of Tumbledown Mountain against the Scots Guards. Pilots earned the respect of the very men they were trying to kill. 'If the guy who sunk *Ardent* walked in here now,' one naval officer told me, 'I would shake him by the hand and buy him a beer. He is an incredibly brave man.'

Events since the late 1930s do little to alter John Dollard's conclusions on the value of belief in the cause. Patriotism or ideology encourage men to go to war, and knowledge that the war enjoys popular support helps create a climate in which good battle morale can be maintained. But, as this brief survey has already shown, there are a variety of other factors at work.

Firstly, the fact that regular soldiers often feel very differently about a war than do their conscript or duration-only comrades is particularly important. Professional soldiers are encouraged to think of themselves as servants of the state, whose task is to defend their country against its internal and external enemies. They are unlikely to inquire too closely into the nature of those enemies: indeed, for them to do so might introduce a potentially dangerous element of uncertainty. When a *zouave* regiment marched to the Gare de Lyon to entrain for the 1859 campaign, its soldiers shouted, 'We're going to give those rascally Piedmontese a good thrashing,' a phrase which, no doubt, trips off the tongue more easily in its original French. They did nothing of the sort, for they were destined to fight on the same side as the Piedmontese, against the Austrians.

Regular soldiers can only have their aversion for politics reinforced by the ebb and flow of foreign policy. Britain and France had seemed perilously close to war over the Fashoda incident of 1898, and it was not until after the turn of the century that Britain saw Germany rather than France as her most likely potential enemy. The growth of anti-German, pro-French feeling in Britain was less marked within the army than outside it: the senior officers who landed in France in 1914 had spent most of their military careers planning to fight against the French rather than for them. The war cut across long-established personal and professional ties: the Royal Dragoons had the Kaiser as their Colonel, and the Commander-in-Chief of the BEF was proud of his Order of the Red Eagle and wrote warmly of 'the Emperor William' in his diary. There was widespread admiration amongst British regular officers for the soldierly qualities of the Germans, an approval which paralleled Edward Costello's judgment on his comrades-in-arms of the King's German Legion Peninsular War. 'I have always entertained a high respect for our Germans,' he wrote, 'which indeed they ever showed themselves deserving of ... not only on account of their humanity and general good feeling towards us, but from their determined bravery and discipline in the field.' In contrast, Robert Graves believed that 'troops serving in the Pas de Calais loathed the French'. Despite all this, however, the professionals in the British army got on with the job in hand. Major Tom Bridges went to war with the 4th Dragoon Guards in 1914, summing up the cavalry's motto as 'We'll do it; what is it?', and admitting that they would as soon have fought the French or Belgians as the Germans. 'Their job was to kill us,' said one British warrant officer, 'ours to kill them.'

When D.M. Mantell studied American Green Berets, he was surprised to discover that they were not 'ideologically engaged', and that when they volunteered for service in Vietnam they did so for 'private, professional or financial reasons'. He added:

> I was not talking to fervent and ideologically engaged persons but rather to socially and politically disinterested professional soldiers who were uninformed on the social and political issues of the day ... They made little attempt to disguise the fact that they saw themselves as hired guns, paid killers who were not particularly concerned with their employers or their victims.

Much as I might question the use of emotive terms like 'hired gun' and 'paid killer', I would not deny that this apolitical view of war is an essential component of the regular soldier's make-up. This is not to say that even the hardest professional should not have a moral or ideological sticking-point. John Akehurst felt that he had to consider the moral issue before accepting a loan service command in Oman. 'If one harboured any doubts,' he wrote, 'they were immediately dispelled by the nature of the opposition, who found it necessary to employ terrorism to pursue their aims and whose plans, no more democratic than the Sultan's, offered management of the country under close Russian control.'

Regular soldiers also share an intense professional curiosity as to how well their weapons, tactics and training will work in a real war. War is – and I mean this in no derogatory sense – the opportunity for them to apply what they have studied. Laying out a defensive position on a peacetime exercise inevitably conjures up the desire to see just how the plan would work in practice. Will the approaching armour be badly clawed by our tank and MILAN fire before it comes within range of our hand-held anti-armour weapons? How well will our bunkers, shored up with all the timber we have been able to lay our hands on, hold up against the savage bombardment which will inevitably precede the attack? Will the motor riflemen dismount there, where the arcs of my sustained fire machine-guns overlap, or there, in the dead ground where my mortar and artillery DFs will deal with them? Am I right to be dug in here, in a forward platoon position, where I can see what's happening, or should I command from further back? On coming under fire for the first time, D.J.B. Houchin was 'interested to see if my dispositions were correct'. A marine sergeant on his way to the Falklands believed that it was 'the best thing that's ever happened to me, I've been in twenty years and I'd given up hope that I'd ever see a shot fired in anger in a proper war'. 'I'm a professional soldier,' a sergeant in 3 Para told me, 'and of course I wanted a war. But one was enough.' Lieutenant-Colonel H. Jones was exasperated when the initial plan for a 'large-scale raid' against Goose Green was abandoned. 'I've waited twenty years for this,' he said, 'and now some fucking marine's cancelled it.'

For centuries men have been spurred on into battle and consoled in defeat by religion. We saw in Chapter 6 how religion, or at least an enhanced sense of spirituality, can help soldiers to cope with the trauma of battle. But religion has also been a major motivator across the centuries, easy though it is to forget it in an age when, in the West at least, its crusading fervour is muted. The linking of religion to the cause for which a war is fought arouses bitter controversy, and brings military chaplains into the moral firing-line. Norman Dixon highlighted what many have perceived as a role conflict between the chaplain as minister of God and as an officer in a belligerent army:

Their task is to *reassure* the military flock that since God is
on their side, the Sixth Commandment can be waived for
the duration. How they reconcile this with the knowledge
that enemy soldiers are in all probability receiving identical
advice from their chaplains remains one of the mysteries of
the ecclesiastical mind.

Robert Jay Lifton implied that religion was used to give moral
sanction to atrocities in Vietnam. At a funeral service on the
eve of the My Lai massacre both padre and commanding
officer spoke, 'the former lending spiritual legitimacy to the
latter's mixture of eulogy and exhortation to "kill everything
in the village".' 'Whatever we were doing – murder, atrocities
– God was always on our side,' said a Vietnam veteran.
Richard Falk described how: 'Even the regimental chaplain
endorsed the standing orders of the unit when he prayed for
"wisdom to find the bastards and the strength to pile it on".'
    I do not intend to become embroiled in this particularly
sensitive issue, and commend the works of Clarence Abercrombie and Gordon Zahn to those who wish to pursue it
further. I would emphasise, though, that for every soldier
aggrieved by the chaplain's stance, there are two who find the
chaplain a comfort. The German parachutists whose defence
of Monte Cassino was a truly epic display of determination in
the face of a prodigious land and air bombardment were a
branch of the *Luftwaffe* and, as such, had no chaplains. But
while the fighting was in progress a growing need for spiritual
comfort encouraged them unofficially to 'borrow' chaplains
from near-by army units. Bill Mauldin was not one to toe the
establishment line, but he had 'a lot of respect for those chaplains who keep up the spirits of the combat guys. They often
give the troops a pretty firm anchor to hang onto.' 'He didn't
push religion,' wrote John Parrish of his chaplain, 'but somehow made it known that support and comfort and talk and
God and all that stuff were available if we needed them.'
Many soldiers who fought in the Falklands found their chaplain a great help, and I suspect that had I spoken ill of their
padre to 2 Para I might have needed extensive dentistry.

The concept of holy war is acknowledged by Christianity and Islam, which have both shown themselves to be militant, fighting religions. Saint Augustine accepted that war could be waged by God's command, and in the ninth century Popes Leo IV and John VIII went further, declaring that those who fell in holy war died as martyrs and would have their sins remitted. Within two hundred years the Church was actively encouraging men to fight against the infidel, and the promise that they could take possession of any captured territory added material to spiritual reward. Crusaders were impelled by a variety of motives – including restlessness, boredom and sheer cupidity – and the conduct of luminaries like Reynald de Châtillon was no advertisement for Christianity. Nevertheless, the impact of religious enthusiasm should not be discounted. It had its dark side, producing over-confidence in battle and encouraging atrocities, but it generated formidable fighting morale, and was not least amongst the title-deeds of the Latin kingdom of Jerusalem.

Such religious fervour is now rare in the West, but its departure is relatively recent. Father Willie Doyle, killed at Third Ypres, firmly believed that the Irishmen of his battalion fought all the better for the comfort of their church. 'It is an admitted fact', he asserted, 'that the Irish Catholic soldier is the bravest and best in a fight, but few know that he draws his courage from the strong faith with which he is filled and the help which comes from the exercise of his religion.' He watched his countrymen scrambling forward into the mine debris at Messines in 1917, 'going to face death, as only Irish Catholic lads can do, confident of victory and cheered by the thought that the reward of heaven was theirs'. Peter Kemp saw martial religion in action in the Spanish Civil War, when his Carlist *Requeté* company was led into the attack 'by the captain and the chaplain, the one grasping his pistol and the other his missal'. Father Vincente rushed about the battlefield, kneeling over the dead and dying despite the heavy fire, and encouraging the men to shoot. Even during the Second World War, a commander's religious devotion could percolate down to his troops. 'We in the 8th Army', writes Frank Richardson, 'never doubted the sincerity of our general's faith, any more than Xenophon's Greeks doubted his.'

If the crusaders hoped for a somewhat austere heaven if they fell in battle, their opponents were sustained by the prospect of a more fleshly paradise filled with houris. Islam has been the fighting religion *par excellence*, with its own concept of holy war, the *jihad*. There can be no doubting the practical effect of their religion upon Islamic soldiers. Belief in the certainty of salvation, especially if one dies killing an unbeliever, draws death's sting. The Dervishes suffered 25,700 casualties, 9,700 of them dead, at Omdurman in 1898, about half their total force engaged. Lieutenant-Colonel B.A.C. Duncan calls this 'a poignant testimony to the supreme valour and devotion to duty which were the hallmarks of the Dervish soldier', and rightly lays great emphasis upon the importance of religion in inspiring it. In the Gulf War between Iran and Iraq, Iranian infantry, often ill-equipped and badly trained, have shown colossal determination, pressing home massed attacks with supreme disregard for casualties. The dogged defence of Khorramshahr by the Revolutionary Guards is a remarkable example of what infantry can achieve against mechanised forces. At the individual level, John Akehurst described flying by helicopter to Salalah with a wounded soldier who had lost a leg. 'He was very philosophical,' observed Akehurst, ' ... and if I had not realised it before I certainly realised then the power and comfort of total faith in Allah.' The driver of the explosives-packed truck that blew up the US Marine base in Beirut in 1983 was seen to smile seconds before he blew himself to pieces: we would do well not to dismiss lightly the religious fervour that can produce such effects.

The Valour of Simple Men

On 8 September 1916 Captain Thomas Kettle of the Royal Dublin Fusiliers committed his thoughts to paper in a moment of quiet before his battalion went forward. 'We are moving up tonight', he wrote, into the battle of the Somme. The bombardment, destruction and bloodshed are beyond all imagination, nor did I ever think the valour of simple men could be quite as beautiful as that of my Dublin Fusiliers. I have had two chances of leaving them – one on sick leave and the other on a staff job. I have chosen to stay with my comrades. I am calm and happy but desperately anxious to live.[2]

Captain Kettle was killed the next day, but his last letter lives on as a touching description of precisely that force that helps maintain the valour of simple men: the comradeship that binds soldiers together.

The white heat of ideology or the burning zeal of religion may sustain the few, or even, at particular moments in the world's history, inspire the many. But to the infantryman crouched behind a hummock of peat and heather while bullets snap over his head, or to the tank driver nudging through a hedge with the thrum of armour-piercing shot in his ears, neither ideology nor religion give much incentive for the one to get up and sprint to the next cover, or for the other to drive steadily across a field already scorched by his comrades' oily cremations. For the key to what makes men fight – not enlist, not cope, but fight – we must look hard at military groups and the bonds that link the men within them.

It is clear from the outset that membership of a military group can, in itself, foster a fighting spirit that has nothing to do with ideology or religion. Kettle's Dublin Fusiliers, for instance, were mostly Roman Catholics, fighting for a government to which they owed little allegiance, which had for centuries discriminated against Catholics, and against which many of their countrymen were already in rebellion. British troops patrolled Dublin, its centre heavily scarred by the fighting that accompanied the repression of the Easter Rising, and British firing-parties executed Irish nationalist leaders. Yet Irish soldiers fought fiercely against the Germans. Willie Doyle saw a British battalion break and bolt over his Irish Fusiliers. 'Brave Paddy from the Green Isle stood his ground and rose to the occasion,' he wrote, 'first shooting the men from Cornwall, and then hunting the Germans with cold steel.'

John Horsfall noticed the same phenomenon in Tunisia. His battalion was opposed by 962 *Schützen* Regiment, composed of 'political suspects, black marketeers and other pet aversions of Himmler, and they were here to be purified'. But instead of deserting in droves to escape from a regime which so many of them had actively opposed: 'These men fought us despite all logic, and they fought like furies ... ' They had, as Horsfall observed, very hard NCOs and picked officers, and enjoyed a robust battle morale which had nothing to do with politics.

The French Foreign Legion is an extreme example of the ability of *esprit de corps* to override all other considerations. In 1835 it was transferred *en masse* to the service of Queen Isabella of Spain for the First Carlist War. Its men were angered by the circumstances of the transfer and by the removal of their badges, and many of its officers resigned from the army in disgust. Once in Spain, the Legion was starved of supplies and mishandled by its allies. *Légionnaires* were flogged for minor disobedience, and tortured to death if they were captured. In April 1837 General Conrad summed up his command as 'exhausted and demoralized by no pay and continual privations'. On 2 June the Legion participated in a characteristically bungled Cristino attempt to seize the town of Barbastro from the Carlists. During the battle the Legion collided with the Carlist Foreign Legion in an olive-grove outside the town. Baron von Rahdon, serving with the Carlists, recorded the spectacle:

> the wood was held by our Foreign Legion, the throw-outs of various nations, it is true, French, Germans, Russians, but brave men with no fear of death ... They came to grips with the French Foreign Legion under General Conrad. Never before or since, in the course of my very tough military career, have I witnessed such a bloody struggle ... Men in the conflicting ranks recognised each other, called out to each other by their *bruder namen*, then proceeded to disembowel each other with the bayonet.

The French Foreign Legion emerged from the battle with only 160 of the 875 soldiers who had gone into it. The Carlist Legion had lost so heavily that it never took the field again.

The most decorated NCO in the Legion during the First World War was *Adjutant-Chef* Mader, who might have fought as gallantly for the country of his birth as he did for his adopted homeland had it not been for a bullying NCO whom Mader had throttled during his first period of military service – with the German army. In the short but tragic Syrian campaign of 1941 there were Legion units on both sides. The British-Free French force included the 13th Legion Demi-Brigade, while General Dentz's Vichy army contained the 6th Legion Infantry Regiment. The *légionnaires* on both sides fought with their accustomed determination. Many of the soldiers of the 6th sympathised with the very cause they fought so bravely against: once the armistice was signed, 1,400 of them joined the Free French forces.

Although the full flowering of group cohesion is to be seen in the regiment, whose corporate identity is often reinforced by distinctive uniforms and insignia, its roots lie deeply in the smallest of military groups. The importance of the primary group of up to ten, whose members were in regular face-to-face contact, was recognised long before psychologists or sociologists had turned their attention to the question of group behaviour. The Macedonian *syntagma* or battalion numbered 256 men, and drew up in sixteen files sixteen men deep, each headed by its file-leader with his second-in-command bringing up the rear. Files could manœuvre by halves or by quarters – in groups of eight or four. In every case, though, the pikeman fought between comrades he knew well, under the command of his file-leader and file-closer. The Roman legion of the imperial period contained ten cohorts, each subdivided into three maniples. There were two centuries in each maniple, and the century – in practice eighty strong – was formed from ten eight-man mess-units (*conturbernia*). The legionary identified with the larger body of his Legion – I *Germanica*, VII *Gemina*, IX *Hispana*, and so on – in the same way that an American might with his state or an Englishman with his county. But the century was his village and the mess-unit his home.

The overt purpose of these small units was either tactical, as in the case of a file of Macedonian pikemen or seventeenth-century musketeers, or administrative, as it was with the Roman mess-unit or the Prussian seven-man *Kameradschaft*. But it was recognised that the close relationship which sprang up between the members of the group had positive advantages in battle. Onasander advised that the commander should station 'brothers in ranks beside their brothers, friends beside friends; and lovers beside their favourites'. The Sacred Band of Thebes was organised to make the best use of the bonds of homosexual love which the Greeks regarded as perfectly normal. The Spartan Pausanias argued that 'the most valiant army would be recruited of lovers and their favourites', because all would be too ashamed to desert. Xenophon disagreed, believing that any soldier would feel ashamed at deserting his comrades.

The British *Regulations for the Rifle Corps* of 1800 emphasised comradeship, trust and respect as the basis for cohesion. Each company was to be divided into four equal parts, with a proportion of officers and NCOs. allocated to each portion on a permanent basis.

> The captain ... having formed his company thus equally, will arrange comrades. Every Corporal, Private and Bugler will elect a comrade of the rank differing from his own, i.e. front and rear rank, and is never to change him without the permission of his Captain. Comrades are always to have the same berth in quarters; and, that they may be as little separated as possible either in barracks or in the field, will form the same file on parade and go on the same duties with arms ...
>
> After this arrangement is made the Captain will then establish his messes, which are to be invariably by squads. Ten is the best number for a mess to consist of ...

In the wars of this century, the rifle squad or section, the fire team, or the weapon group built around a crew-served weapon, such as a mortar or artillery piece, have been the lowest common denominators of comradeship. In Charles Carrington's view:

> A corporal and six men in a trench were like shipwrecked sailors on a raft, completely committed to their social grouping, so that no one could have any doubts about the moral and physical failings of his pals since everyone's life depended on the reliability of each.

C.E. Montague used the same image. 'Our total host might be two millions strong, or ten millions,' he wrote, but,

> whatever its size a man's world was his section – at most, his platoon; all that mattered to him was the one little boatload of castaways with whom he was marooned on a desert island making shift to keep off the weather and any sudden attack of wild beasts.

When Norman Gladden was posted to a different battalion of his regiment, the Royal Northumberland Fusiliers, on his return to France from sick leave, he managed to join a Lewis-gun team, and his new comrades eased the shock of transition: they were 'a likeable group, who made us feel at home straight away'.

Lieutenant-Colonel Roger Little studied this comradeship at close range in Korea. For the American soldier in Korea, the buddy was all-important. 'The buddy role was an expectation of mutual loyalty and reciprocity attributed to another person at the same relative level in the organisation,' wrote Little. The soldiers whose opinions he recorded had a more down-to-earth view. 'When I joined the squad, Braun was *it*,' said one.

> Now he's the only one who was with us at Sandbag Castle. We depended on each other. I don't think that he would bug out, but if he did, it wouldn't make much difference. The only thing that would break us up would be if one of

us was killed or left the company. Bell has been buddying with us but he's still a new man and hasn't been through any of the things that Braun and I have been through.

One soldier summed up his relationship with his buddy with the comment that 'our minds seemed to run together', while another explained: 'A buddy shares everything; if you don't get mail, he lets you read his.'[3]

The buddy organisation within the American army in Korea was an informal grouping that sprang up spontaneously between soldiers in the same squad. The Chinese against whom the Americans were fighting employed a similar organisation quite deliberately, aiming not merely at producing cohesion, but at ensuring that the aims of the small group did not diverge from those of the larger organisation. The Chinese section was divided into three or four groups, each consisting of three or four men. General James Van Fleet believed that fear was the cement bonding men together in this system.

> The Red Chinese Army is divided at the very bottom into units of three men, with each assigned to watch the others and aware that they in turn are watching him ... The little teams of three, each man warily watching the others, begin the advance ... Yet – although terribly alone in the fight despite the two men at his side, made even more lonely by the doubt whether the two are there to help him or to spy on him – the Red soldier moves ever forward.

Van Fleet's judgment was unduly harsh, for there was a great deal more to morale in the Chinese army than the fear created by a system based upon political invigilation at all levels. Indeed, the effectiveness of the three-man pyramid had already been recognised in America. Major Evans Carlson of the US Marine Corps had been impressed by it in China in 1937, and in 1942 he organised his 2nd Raider Battalion on the basis of ten-man squads, with three fire teams of three and the tenth man as squad leader. 'Members of the Fire Team worked, slept and ate together,' wrote Alexander L. George;

'this structure developed an unusually strong cohesion. The men sensed this and saw how effectively the system worked in combat.'

The precise details of small unit organisation inevitably vary with the development of weapons and tactics, but it is striking how often groups of three or four and eight or ten have featured in units from the Macedonian file to the four-man 'brick' in Northern Ireland. The weapon group serving a machine-gun, mortar or artillery piece enjoys a particularly strong cohesion. This stems in part from their tendency to identify with their weapon and its powers, just as a pilot increases his own sense of power by identifying himself with his plane. Also, the demands of crew-served weapons mean that their detachments are kept busy tending them, both in the line and out of it. Weapons tend to be given collective nicknames, like Rosalie, for the long bayonet of the Lebel rifle, and Katyusha – 'Little Katie' – for the Soviet multi-barrelled rocket launcher. But the crew-served weapon usually gets a name of its own. The first three Shermans of Leclerc's *Deuxième Division Blindée* to squeak and clatter up to the Hôtel de Ville in Paris on 24 August 1944 were *Montmirail, Champaubert* and *Romilly*, named for battles of the 1814 campaign. The MOB-ATS of a British infantry battalion in the late 1970s bore the stencilled names Glamdring, Sting, Orcrist, Herugrim, Anglachel and Anduril – swords in Tolkien's *Lord of the Rings*. Round the central courtyard of Les Invalides in Paris stand cannon barrels, each proudly engraved with the weapon's name: *L'Hercule, Le Célèbre, Le Rigide, L'Éclatant* and *Le Pénétrant*.

In the case of artillery, the ties between the piece and its servants can easily assume mystical overtones. The process of casting guns in the Middle Ages was a branch of science bordering on the occult, and early gunnery had a quasi-religious mystique, strengthened by the practice of blessing guns, or that of bestowing upon them the honours given to regimental colours in the infantry. Artillery pieces became almost devotional objects to their detachments. A Russian gunner officer at Austerlitz encouraged his men to haul their guns across the frozen Satschan pond with the desperate entreaty: 'Don't leave your fine pieces to these enemies of Christ.'

Losing guns in battle has always been more bitterly regretted than the weapons' real military value might suggest, and artillerymen who might have run away to fight another day have often stood fast about their silent guns, selling their lives dearly with handspike and rammer. A British artilleryman watched Italian gunners dragging away their weapons after Caporetto.

> They were of an ancient type, which we had seen sometimes on the Carso, and not of very high military value. But the gunners took an affectionate and regimental pride in those old guns. They had neither tractors nor horses, but they dragged their beloved pieces for thirty miles from the rocky heights of the Carso, along good roads and bad, up and down hills, through impossible traffic blocks, and down on the plains as far as Palmonova, with nothing but long ropes and their own strong arms. They had forty men hauling on each gun.

Men become inordinately fond of such things. There were some 50-calibre machine-guns on motorised quadruple mounts at Dien Bien Phu. One of their crewmen discussed his weapon with Major Grauwin. 'He spoke of her lovingly,' remembered Grauwin, 'as a sportsman speaks of a racehorse. So I too developed an affection for her and I often used to listen to her when I had a chance to lie on my bed ... she fired up to the last minute.' The anniversary of the action at Bazeilles, a village outside Sedan where the *Infanterie de Marine* had fought to the last cartridge in 1870, was the regiment's traditional holiday. The wrecked tank *Bazeilles* thumped out the last rounds from the French strongpoint of *Éliane* on the morning of 7 May 1954. She was manned by Sergeants Balliat and Bruni of the 1st Colonial Parachute Battalion – which wore the old anchor insignia of the *Infanterie de Marine*.

There is more to the weapon group than the affection that its members share for their gun or vehicle. They are, of necessity, close together in battle, and do not suffer from that loneliness in battle which so easily overwhelms the individual rifleman. One of S.L.A. Marshall's more dramatic discoveries was that, on average, only 15 per cent of the men in American rifle companies in action in the central Pacific and European theatres of the Second World War actually fired their weapons in battle. A battalion of the 165th Infantry sustained a determined Japanese attack during a twelve-hour period on Makin Island in November 1944. 'Most of the killing', wrote Marshall, 'took place at less than a ten-yard interval. Half the American guns were knocked out and approximately half the occupants of the forward foxholes were either killed or wounded. Every position was ringed with enemy dead.' Only thirty-six members of the battalion had actually fired their weapons. 'The majority', said Marshall, 'were heavy weapons men. The really active firers were usually in small groups working together.'

Whatever the size of the small group, its effectiveness as a motivator is recognised by theorists and veterans alike. Lieutenant-Colonel L.H. Ingraham and Major F.J. Manning were convinced that: 'There is little doubt ... that morale and esprit, grounded in small group ties, is crucial in enabling soldiers to persist in combat under conditions of supreme privation, fear and uncertainty.'

In both World Wars men often deserted from hospitals or replacement depots to get back to their units. G.F. Maclean was commissioned from Sandhurst in 1915 at the age of eighteen, and joined 1st Battalion, the Argyll and Sutherland Highlanders, in France. 'The first man I saw wounded was an old soldier called Black Jock, he was carried off and I never expected to see him again,' he wrote.

> After a month he arrived back in the company. After a few days a note arrived saying Black Jock had been posted as a deserter. I spoke to him and after some thought he said, 'Oh! That. They put me in one of those convalescent camps. You never know where they will send you to from there, so I just came back up the line to the battalion.'

William Manchester was sent to hospital with a light wound on Okinawa. He escaped from the hospital and rejoined his friends in the line. 'It was an act of love,' he wrote.

> Those men on the line were my family, my home. They were closer to me than I can say, closer than any friends had been or ever would be. They had never let me down, and I couldn't do it to them ... Men, I now know, do not fight for flag or country, for the Marine Corps or glory or any other abstraction. They fight for one another. Any man in combat who lacks comrades who will die for him, or for whom he is willing to die, is not a man at all. He is truly damned.

Glenn Gray agreed that comradeship was stronger than the fear of death:

> Numberless soldiers have died, more or less willingly, not for country or honour or religious faith or for any other abstract good, but because they realised that by fleeing their posts and rescuing themselves, they would expose their companions to greater danger. Such loyalty to the group is the essence of fighting morale.

The readiness of soldiers to sacrifice their lives for their comrades can be demonstrated by a score of anecdotes. But examination of the winners of the Congressional Medal of Honor in the US Marine Corps makes the point concisely. Of the eight medals won by Marines on Peleliu in 1944, six were awarded to men who covered grenades with their bodies to save their comrades. In April 1952 Corporal Duane Dewey threw himself on a grenade, and Pfc Robert Simanek did likewise in August: both survived to win Medals of Honor. Finally, in the words of Robert Moskin's history of the US Marine Corps: 'Five black Marines earned the Medal of Honor in Vietnam. All five were killed shielding fellow Marines from exploding enemy grenades.'

Both Gray and Manchester deny that honour has any part in the formulation of group morale. They are right inasmuch as they mean honour in a wide and abstract sense. There is, though, more to the question of honour than Manchester's cold accusation that half the evil in the world is done in its name might suggest. Morris Janowitz maintained that honour was the basis of the military system, at least as far as professionals were concerned, and pointed to a single over-riding directive: 'The professional soldier always fights.' The Vichy French garrison of Syria had little hope of victory and some of its soldiers, as we have seen, actually sympathised with the men they were fighting against. But many regarded the struggle as a question of collective honour. 'You thought we were yellow, didn't you?' a Vichy sergeant asked Alan Moorehead. 'You thought we couldn't fight in France. You thought we were something like the Italians. Well, we've shown you.'

In part this honour is concerned with the obligations of the professional soldier, and in part it is a reflection of the 'manly honour' which encourages so many young men to enlist and buoys them up before their first battle. But, in a more specific sense, it is individual soldierly honour that impels a man to rejoin his unit when he has every reason not to, and prevails upon him to remain at his post even though flight would save him. Norman Dixon observed that military codes of honour have as their primary object not so much the control of fear, but rather the control of the sort of behaviour to which fear might give rise. They are designed to make the social consequences of flight more unpleasant than the physical consequences of battle. The one, argues Dixon, might lead to pain, mutilation and death, but the other produces, with much greater certainty, personal guilt and public shame. The effectiveness of such codes relies in no small measure upon the paradox that most men have more physical courage than they do moral courage, and regard the possibility of death or injury with less terror than they do the probability of disgrace. The agony of this disgrace is heightened when a man loses the respect of his comrades and his status within the unit. The ceremony of drumming a man out of the service with all its dishonourable symbolism of broken sword, and ripped-off

badges, buttons and braid – a common punishment for cowardice, which has survived into the twentieth century – is deliberately designed to underline the heinous nature of the
offence, and to serve as a warning to others. General George
Patton was certainly no psychologist, and his brusque
approach to psychiatric casualties caused a furore which
nearly cost him his job. Nevertheless, he was right in maintaining that the threat of ridicule is an effective weapon
against failure in battle.

S.L.A. Marshall was sure that: 'Personal honour is valued
more than life itself by the majority of men.' He told the story
of a young company runner who was hit by a shell at Car-
entan in 1944, collapsed into the arms of his company commander, 'and with his life swiftly ebbing, said "Captain, this
company has always called me a — — — —–— up. Tell me
that I wasn't one this time." The captain replied: "No, son,
you sure weren't," and the boy died with a smile on his face.'

At the very core of the matter of honour lies a man's sense
of obligation to his comrades and his desire to obtain and
retain their respect. Alfred de Vigny put what is perhaps its
best description into the mouth of Captain Renaud, recount-
ing their conversation while Renaud waited with his company
of grenadiers of the Royal Guard in the riot-torn Paris of July
1830. Renaud had sent in his papers a few weeks before, but
his resignation had not yet been officially accepted.

I went to the barracks to join those good fellows who are
going to be killed at every street corner, and who would
certainly have believed in their hearts that I was disgrace-
fully deserting them at a critical moment ... Look at our
old grenadier, Poirier, with his sullen, squinty eye, his bald
head and the sword-cuts across his cheek ... look at Bec-
caria with the profile of a Roman veteran; or Fréchou with
his white moustache; look at all that front rank with their
decorations and the three [service] stripes on their sleeves!
What would they have said, those veteran monks of the old
army, who have never wished to be other than grenadiers,
if I had failed them this morning?

Vigny concluded: 'Honour is manly decency. The shame of being found wanting in it means everything to us. Is this, then, the indefinable, the sacred thing?'

Shils and Janowitz believed that the concept of soldierly honour was one of the main reasons why the German army fought on in increasingly hopeless circumstances in 1944–5. 'Honour', they wrote, 'rooted in a rigid conscience (superego) served in the German army to keep men at their tasks better that individual reflection and evaluation could have done.' This sense of honour was particularly strong amongst professional soldiers. General Omar Bradley wrote of a captured German General who was asked why he had not surrendered sooner rather than struggle on in a hopeless cause. 'I am a professional,' he replied, 'and I obey my orders.'

A similar concept of caste honour, albeit in totally different circumstances, inspired French parachutists facing an equally hopeless situation at Dien Bien Phu in 1954. Seriously wounded men patched up in the field hospital left it to get back to their friends rather than leave them in the lurch. Major Paul Grauwin recalled their comments. 'Let me have that machine-gun.' said one. 'I've only got one leg ... Give me a chest to sit on and then you'll see what I can do with my hands.' Men parachuted into the shrinking perimeter when its collapse was only days away knew that the future was bleak. 'You know we've had it?' Grauwin asked one of them. 'Certainly, I know that,' he replied, 'but that's no reason for my staying in my bolt-hole at Nam-Dinh, while the blokes promoted with me, the ones in my old battalion and my old command post get smashed up. So I've come along to be smashed up with them, with you.' Within ten minutes of the news that 6th Colonial Parachute Battalion was in trouble, Grauwin's resuscitation ward was besieged by men of the 6th. 'There were men with only one leg, leaning on their comrades with two,' wrote Grauwin, 'others with only one arm, their thorax still encased in dressings; others with only one eye, asserting that they could see perfectly ...' A nineteen year-old parachutist from the *Nord* had a shell-splinter wound in his lung, which had to be drained every two hours. 'Major,' he told Grauwin, 'I want to return to my company. There are only seventeen of them left and if they are going to be killed off I want to be with them.'

What is soldierly honour to one man is the fear of scorn to another. A near miss by a roundshot made Wheeler's head ache. 'Had I been working in a place where there was no danger I should certainly have given up,' he wrote, 'but here I was ashamed to complain, lest any of my comrades should laugh at me.' Edward Costello told how a soldier in the Peninsular War who had helped the bandsmen carry away the wounded was shunned by his comrades: 'at length, during the latter part of the campaign, no good soldier would venture, under so frivolous a pretext, to expose himself to the indignation of his comrades'. Yigal, an officer in the Israeli armoured corps, made much the same point. 'It isn't patriotism or anything like that,' he said. 'When you fight, you're concerned with how you're going to win through, and how you'll look in other people's eyes.'

Yet it was not fear of ridicule that drove British soldiers of the Peninsula to volunteer for service in the 'forlorn hope', which spearheaded an attack on a fortress. Heavy casualties were almost a certainty in the face of close-range musketry and cannon-fire as the 'forlorn hope' wrestled with scaling-ladders in the fortress ditch or tried to burst through a defended breach. There were quarrels amongst the sergeants and men of George Hennell's regiment before the assault on San Sebastian, as all wished to take part. Eventually five sergeants went, three of them serving as temporary privates: both the 'official' sergeants were severely wounded. Major William Napier was denied permission to go. 'Being determined to go at all costs,' wrote Hennell, 'he took a musket and paraded in the ranks. He was spotted by General Alten and ordered back to his regiment.' Of the Light Division's seven officers in the forlorn hope, two were killed and four wounded. There were six volunteers for the two vacancies allocated to Costello's company of the Rifles: an offer of £20 – more than a year's pay for a private soldier – was made and refused for an exchange.

These brave men stood to gain little by their action. The 52nd Regiment gave the members of its forlorn hopes at Badajoz and Ciudad Rodrigo a badge bearing the letters VS, for Valiant Stormer, but the men of the 43rd and Rifles received no award. The display of spectacular courage might improve an officer's prospects, but it was certainly no guarantee of promotion. Many of those concerned were already men of proven valour. Lieutenant John O'Connell of the 52nd had commanded his regiment's forlorn hope at Ciudad Rodrigo and Badajoz before he did so at San Sebastian, and Major Napier had already been wounded twice, saved the Light Division by his handling of the rearguard on the River Coa in 1810, and led the 43rd Regiment in review order across three miles in the face of blistering fire at Salamanca. Even if the officers were encouraged by a desire to show gentlemanly 'bottom' at all times, what of the privates who had no class norms to maintain, and for whom a severe wound meant crippled destitution?

The desire to display bravery in the company of brave men is at least part of the reason for this sort of behaviour. This can be interpreted in terms of Adlerian psychology, with bravery as the soldier's Goal of Superiority, or it can be seen as the result of a cultural conditioning which emphasises courage as the ultimate manly quality. Showing resolution and stoicism was regarded as important by officers and men alike. Sergeant Michael Connelly of the 95th admonished a wounded man for groaning in the presence of French wounded. 'Hold your tongue, ye blathering devil,' he snapped, 'and don't be after disgracing your country in the teeth of these 'ere furriners, by dying hard ... For God's sake die like a man before these 'ere Frenchers.' At Waterloo, Ensign Leeke heard only one man cry out when wounded, 'but on one of the officers saying to him, "Oh man, don't make a noise," he instantly recollected himself and was quiet.' Flora Thompson observed the same values in Oxfordshire countrymen before the First World War. 'Their favourite virtue was endurance,' she wrote. 'Not to flinch from pain or hardship was their ideal.'

This emphasis on showing courage to the end is by no means confined to the British army in the Peninsula. The Australians of the First World War placed untold value on 'dying game'. A mortally-wounded man quipped to his friends: 'I feel pretty bad and expect I'm done for. But, strike me dead, that Turk could shoot all right.' Another muttered, 'Mafeesh [Australian Arabic for 'finished'] ... missus and kids – dirty swine', rose to his knees, fired a last shot, and died. Jack Seely saw the same attitude when his Canadian cavalry brigade attacked a Bavarian position near Moreuil in 1918.

> Hundreds of them were shot ... Hundreds more stood their ground and were shot at point-blank range or were killed with the bayonet. Not one single man surrendered. As I rode through the wood on Warrior with the dismounted squadron of Strathcona's, I saw a handsome young Bavarian twenty yards in front of me miss an approaching Strathcona, and, as a consequence, receive a bayonet thrust right through the neck. He sank down with his back against a tree, the blood pouring from his throat. As I came close up to him I shouted in German, 'Lie still, a stretcher-bearer will look after you.' His eyes in his ashen-grey face seemed to blaze fire as he snatched up his rifle and fired his last shot at me, saying loudly: '*Nein, nein. Ich will ungefangen sterben.*' [No, no. I will not die a prisoner.] Then he collapsed in a heap.[4]

Lieutenant Brounbrouck, commanding a battery of the 4th Colonial Artillery regiment at Dien Bien Phu, died in the wreckage of his command post, his back laid open by shell splinters. 'Keep firing,' he ordered, 'we've got to show them ...'

Field-Marshal Slim believed that courage was the supreme virtue. 'I don't believe there is any man', he wrote, 'who, in his heart of hearts, wouldn't rather be called brave than have any other virtue attributed to him.' Donald Featherstone, towards the other end of the military hierarchy, was equally certain in his judgment of courage. 'Even today,' he mused, 'I gloss over anything in a man decorated for gallantry – just as sins were forgiven in the Middle Ages by buying a pardon – to me Courage is a Man's Pardoner.'

Captain Johansen, Tim O'Brien's company commander in Vietnam, thought deeply about the question of bravery. 'I'd rather be brave,' he told O'Brien one day, 'I'd rather be brave than almost anything. How does that strike you?' O'Brien recalled that when he compared subsequent company commanders to Johansen, 'it was clear that he alone cared enough about being brave to think about it and try to do it'. For most men, wrote O'Brien, the pursuit of bravery was arduous. The easy aphorism that most men were neither cowards nor heroes was no help to:

> the middle man, the man who wants to try but has already died more than once, squirming under the bullets, going through the act of death and coming out embarrassingly alive. The bullets stop. As in slow motion, physical things gleam. Noise dissolves. You tentatively peek up, wondering if it is the end. Then you look at the other men, reading your own caved-in belly deep in their eyes. The fright dies in the same way novocaine wears off in the dentist's chair. You promise, almost moving your lips, to do better next time; that by itself is a kind of courage.

A soldier's immediate comrades, the men of his rifle section, tank crew or gun detachment, are those he identifies most closely with. But the widening ripple of secondary groups – platoon, company, battalion, regiment, and so on – are also important. It is inevitably the regiment that attracts most attention, although it is worth noting *en passant* that the company, which controls so much of the soldier's daily life in peace, and provides the horizon around him in war, is a greater focus of loyalty than we often recognise. Stouffer questioned the soldiers of an infantry division without combat experience: 56 per cent of them were proud or fairly proud of their company. In a veteran division no less than 78 per cent were proud of their company, a surprisingly high level of commitment in a survey which generally revealed a widespread dissatisfaction and low motivation.

There are two major difficulties in examining the regiment as an object of men's loyalty and a source of fighting spirit. The first is that no two armies have the same approach to regimental ideology, and that judgments which might be true for a 'regimental' army like the British have less validity for a more functional army like the West German. In this context my own partiality is bound to grin through the varnish, for I have spent my working life surrounded by badges, buttons, lanyards, tartan trews, coloured sidehats, spurs, sticks and shoulder-chains – all the paraphernalia of a regimental system for which Albuhera and Aliwal, Sobraon and the Somme are alive and well and living in the Regimental Museum. The second problem is that most comments on the regiment are made by regular officers or senior NCOs, the very men for whom regimental *esprit* is strongest, rather than by the temporary private soldiers whose appreciation of the finer points of regimental ideology may be lost in a fog of polishing and drilling.

John Masters believed that the regiment had been deliberately interposed between the individual and a greater cause which he might neither fully support nor understand.

> But in war it is necessary that all should pull together, and fight with a will, whatever their opinions of the rights and wrongs of the case. So, in the King's armies men were shielded from disturbing doubts by the interposition of a smaller cause, which no-one could cavil at, between themselves and the great national cause. The spirit was and is built on the regiment.

Masters is confusing cause and effect. The regiment came into being in sixteenth- and seventeenth-century Europe for administrative and tactical reasons, rather than for any thought of the psychology of motivation. Regiments were usually raised by proprietary colonels and officers nominated by them, and were named after their colonel – the excellent Prussian 18th Infantry Regiment bore, between 1740 and 1764, the designations Derschau, Prinz von Preussen and Prinz Friedrich

Wilhelm – or had a territorial title, like Picardie and Navarre of the French line under the *ancien régime* or the Sousdal, Uglitz, Kazan and Vladimir Regiments who held the Russian right at the Alma.

Many of the links between ancient regiments and their modern descendants are somewhat spurious, with amalgamations, and disbandments providing serious obstacles to honest genealogy, and a good deal of tradition being produced by sleight of hand. Even in the British army, which has the best record of historical continuity, it is as well not to inquire too closely into the origins of, say, the Royal Sussex Regiment's plume – supposedly won from the French Roussillon Regiment at Quebec in 1759, although the Roussillon Regiment wore no such embellishment – or the red hackle of the Black Watch. In the French army, tradition is bequeathed with the stroke of a pen. Thus the *94th Régiment d'Infanterie de Marine* is deemed to be the *Royal Hesse-Darmstadt*, a foreign regiment raised in 1709 and twice re-titled before it was disbanded in 1815. Re-raised for the Crimea in 1855, it perished in 1940, reappeared in 1944–5, was re-raised for Algeria in 1956–62, and re-raised yet again in 1967, when it obtained its *de Marine* suffix to commemorate the disappearing regiments of *Infanterie Coloniale*.

The *Kaiserheer* was equally robust in its approach to tradition. The Hanoverian army was disbanded in 1867, but its battle-honours – and those of the King's German Legion, the Hanoverian exiles who had fought for George III against Napoleon – were assumed, in 1899, by the German regiments raised in Hanover. So it was that British soldiers of the First World War found themselves fighting men who bore proudly the same battle-honours – Waterloo and Peninsula, El Bodon and Barossa – that were emblazoned on their own colours. Even the *Bundeswehr*, for all its emphasis on *Innere Führung*, manages to pluck at regimental identities from the mists of the past. So *Panzeraufklarungbataillon 11* has taken on the traditions of the inter-war *Reichswehr's* 17th Cavalry Regiment, itself the custodian of the traditions of the 2nd Prussian Dragoons from Schwedt-am-Oder: the *Schwedterdragoner* live on as an armoured reconnaissance battalion. A similar process of historical transfusion is going on in America even as I write, as the units of a newly-created regimental system acquire colours and traditions.[5]

Even the Russians are not to be left out. Although it is impossible to stretch regimental ideology beyond the Revolution, good use is made of units' distinguished records in the Second World War, and honorific 'Guards' titles are borne by regiments, divisions and armies. The flames of tradition are kept alive in the Regimental Culture Centre. Lieutenant-Colonel A. Cherkashin tells how unit club houses

> have Rooms of Combat Glory, where unit's relics illustrating their combat record are shown ... In the club's foyer the visitors could see attractively got-up stands familiarising them with Lenin's behests to the armed defenders of the country, telling about the regiment's heroes and those who had distinguished themselves in combat training and political education.

All this pursuit of regimental identity demonstrates that, whatever the origins of the regimental system may have been, it is now perceived as bestowing practical advantages in exactly the way which John Masters suggests. Armies have long sought to confer specific abilities on their soldiers by dressing them in a special way. Tony Heathcote describes the origin of the hussar uniform:

> Just as, at the present time, soldiers of elite corps in many parts of the world affect the red or green beret (itself originally a French peasant's headdress) adopted by the Allied special forces in World War II, so then it was deemed the smartest thing to wear a stylised and tailored version of the Hungarian herdsman's workaday clothing. The reasoning behind this was apparently that to make a man fight and operate like an Austro-Hungarian hussar, it was necessary to make him dress like one.

Regimental ideology has a similar function. It perpetuates military reputations, endowing the Glaswegian youth of 1983 with the attributes of the Scots Guardsmen who shut the gate at Hougoumont, and bestowing on a farmer's boy from the Home Counties the mantle of the men who withstood such a fearful hammering on the ridge at Albuhera.

In his study of the herd instinct, Wilfred Trotter maintained that 'The peace of mind, happiness and energy of the soldier come from his feeling himself to be a member of a body solidly united for a single purpose.' But, as other psychologists have shown, the regiment does more than merely provide this body. As J.T. MacCurdy observes, belonging to a long-standing organisation entails a feeling of membership, and this membership is not confined to those who are alive. Members of a particular nation may speak of 'us' when referring to their long-dead compatriots: members of a regiment with a long and distinguished history may similarly say, 'We had a bad day at Balaclava', or, 'We did rather well at First Ypres.'

The ideals of a long-established group belong to successive generations, and the group is immortal while the individuals who compose it are not. Thus a soldier may be able to accept his own death, the destruction of his section, even the annihilation of his battalion, knowing that his regiment will live on as a mystical entity. 'As long as the major portion of the man's interest and affection remains devoted to the welfare of the combat group,' declared Grinker and Spiegel, 'he will not develop strong anxiety over the possibility of his own injury or death.' While the primary group may easily be damaged, or even destroyed, by enemy action, the regiment, at once small enough to serve as a focus of identity and large enough to escape sudden catastrophe, marches on.

Group narcissism also plays its part. Many a soldier with serious doubts about his own ability will submerge them beneath his devotion to the unit and, particularly if he comes from a background of boredom and deprivation, he will gain inordinate satisfaction from the rewards offered within the regiment. The stormers' badge awarded to the soldiers of the 52nd Regiment may not seem like much of a recompense for running a great risk of death or injury, but it meant a very great deal to the men concerned.

The soldiers who join armies with a vigorous regimental system are left in no doubt as to their own good fortune. 'The 9th were ever the boldest Corps in the King's Army and the truest on parade,' an eighteenth-century sergeant told recruits. 'What is more, we fought at Fontenoy, Dettingen and Minden under the guiding eye of the Most High God.' The indoctrination of recruits in the Spanish Foreign Legion, as described here by Peter Kemp, is not untypical of the process employed in many armies of the nineteenth and early twentieth centuries, and, indeed, has more than an echo in present-day Aldershot, Pirbright or Quantico.

> From the moment he joined it was impressed on the recruit that he belonged to a corps apart – the finest fighting force, he was taught to believe, in the world; it was up to him to prove himself worthy of the privilege. Battle was to be the purpose of his life; death in action his greatest honour; cowardice the ultimate disgrace.

Even the cult of death is not confined to the Spanish Foreign Legion, with its nickname *Novios de Muerte*, bridegrooms of death. Death was seldom far away in the Middle Ages, and medieval art pays gruesome tribute to its prevalence. Dances of death show the grim reaper snatching the king from his court, the merchant from his counting-house, the mother from her children. Funeral statuary was often morbidly representative of the decay of the body after death. In the same way that the men and women of the Middle Ages faced death by robbing it of its mystery, so regimental ideography did the same. A foot regiment of the English Civil War marched into battle behind colours displaying the skull and crossbones. A skull and crossbones badge was worn by the British 17th and the German 16th Lancers, as well as by the German 1st and 2nd Hussars, and the 17th, the Black Hussars of Brunswick. During the Second World War *Panzertruppen* sported a metal death's head on their collar-patches, an affectation which led to many of them being shot out of hand after capture in mistake for members of the *Waffen SS*, who wore a similar badge.

To what extent does all this accretion of ideology and tradition really influence the soldier on the battlefield? Regular officers across the centuries have certainly believed that it was of real importance. When the 51st Regiment went into action in Holland on 1 August 1809, Colonel Mainwaring harangued his men, as was his wont. 'In the course of his address,' wrote Sergeant Wheeler, 'he recurred to his old favourite maxim of firing low, you will then hit them in the legs and there will be three gone, for two will pick him up and run away with him.' The good colonel went on to remind his listeners that it was the fiftieth anniversary of Minden, where the regiment had distinguished itself: he drew attention to the battle-honour on the colours and on the men's shoulder-belt plates. Six years later, as the square of the 28th Regiment staggered, under attack from three sides at Waterloo, it was rallied by Picton's great shout of 'Twenty-Eighth, remember Egypt!' Picton was referring to the 28th's performance at Alexandria in 1801 and, although few men had personal knowledge of the battle, this appeal to the regiment's pride stiffened its square in the hour of need.

Lord Moran was sure that 'Loyalty to a fine battalion may take hold of a man and stiffen his purpose.' The regiment, he believed, was 'the source of their strength, their abiding faith, it was the last of all the creeds that in historical times have steeled men against death'. Slim, too, spoke warmly of the regimental system. 'The moral strength of the British army', he wrote, 'is the sum of all these family or clan loyalties. They are the foundations of the British soldier's stubborn valour.' As far as Colonel Nicholson was concerned, the regiment was 'the only incentive to the regular soldier'.

A Second World War commanding officer told Frank Richardson that he had no doubts about how his soldiers would behave in their first battle.

As descendants of the men who gained such splendid victories in so many battles from 1702 onwards we are simply

unable to be cowardly. We've got to win our battle, whatever the cost, so that people will say 'They were worthy
descendants of the 32nd,' and that's saying a hell of a lot.

Sir Henry Lawrence, the distinguished soldier and statesman
of British India, thought that a unit's reputation had a tangible effect upon its members. 'Courage goes much by opinion,' he wrote, 'and many a man behaves as a hero or a
coward, according as he considers he is expected to behave.'
Martin Lindsay had felt the rough edge of war, but he too
was certain that

> by far and away the greatest single factor in a soldier's
> morale is regimental pride, based on centuries of tradition
> ... For my part I have no doubt how the battalion faced
> the enemy's fire sweeping across that wide, sullen river,
> the Rhine, on that dark night thirty years ago. We never
> wavered because, in the last resort, we were Gordon High-
> landers, we were the Highland Division.

Charlton Ogburn summed up the opinion of many of his
comrades when he complained that the designation of Merrill's Marauders, 5307th Composite Unit (Frovisional)
sounded like 'a street address in Los Angeles'. The US army
had, he thought, become too functional: 'you cannot expect
our army always to understand that an enduring continuity
suggested by a name like the Queen's Own Royal West Kent
Regiment ... can do something that a mobile snack bar cannot.' But the fact remains that units with short histories and
undramatic numerical designations performed well in the
American and German armies. Neither 503 Heavy Tank Battalion nor Assault Gun Battalion 200 had high-sounding titles,
but both were well to the fore in halting the British Goodwood
offensive in June 1944. Even the British army, with all its
respect for tradition, raised new armoured regiments from
scratch, and their conduct was in no way inferior to that of
those who had fought the *Maison du Roi* at Dettingen or
charged Sikh squares at Aliwal. Martin Lindsay, devotee of

the regimental system though he was, acknowledged that the British private soldier of the Second World War – and he might have added the last two years of the First – was a 'youth who typically was conscripted into the Army, posted overseas after a few months training, drafted to an unfamiliar regiment and only a few days later found himself in battle'.

Moreover, the soldiers of armies with no regimental system testify to the way in which a unit, however short its lineage, solidifies with battle experience and good leadership. Tom Wintringham's British Battalion of the International Brigades was short-lived. But he argued forcefully that its achievements sprang from its regimental cohesion: 'What we were able to do was done because individuals made themselves securely part of a fighting body, because group became part of a fellowship and our queerly-assorted ranks were, on the things that matter, of one mind.' Bob Sanders identified strongly with the 173rd Brigade (no soul-stirring title, that) in Vietnam.

> We felt tough and strong, because we had a unity and a harmony that I don't think was matched in Vietnam by any other unit. In fact, we not only felt that the Vietnamese couldn't beat us, we felt sure there was no other American unit that could beat us if it came to that.

Some of the regimental system's effects – for example in impeding inter-unit postings and thereby obstructing the promotion of the fittest – are undesirable. And it is certainly not essential: a spirit of martial teamwork can spring up in a numbered battalion or, for that matter, in a brigade, a division, or even an army. But a regimental system is undoubtedly useful in providing both a spiritual home for professional soldiers and a ready-made framework, shored up by attractive mystique, for temporary ones. Armies can survive well enough without it, particularly if they are accustomed to doing so. But, inefficient, illogical and, at times, irritating though it is, the regimental system makes it own unique contribution to the valour of simple men.

8

Precarious Valour

I have a very mean opinion of the infantry in general. I know their discipline to be bad, & their valour precarious. They are easily put into disorder, & hard to recover out of it; they frequently kill their Officers thro' fear, & murder one another in their confusion.

Lieutenant-Colonel James Wolfe to his father, 1755

Hell, No: We Won't Go

Marc Bloch recognised that, important though personal honour and group cohesion were, they did not necessarily produce fighting spirit. 'I believe', he wrote,

that few soldiers, except the most noble or the most intelligent, think of their country while conducting themselves bravely; they are much more often guided by a sense of personal honour, which is very strong when it is refined by the group. If a unit consisted of a majority of slackers, the point of honour would be to get out of any situation with the least harm possible.

In short, the creation of group spirit is no guarantee of military performance, for there is every chance that the group's

norms will conflict with the aims of the organisation of which
it forms a part. Recognition of this central truth is one of the
reasons for the system of political invigilation which exists in
most communist armies, where the *zampolit* ensures that the
aims of the group do not diverge from those of the organisation.

In its simplest form, this tendency is demonstrated by the
way in which individuals and units sometimes strive to avoid
combat, to the point of formally refusing to participate in it.
Groups that do this do not feel that they are behaving unreasonably. Their norms rate the survival of the group and its
members as all-important, and individuals who encourage the
group to fight will meet with suspicion, hostility and even
outright violence.

The phenomenon of collective combat refusal attained new
prominence during the Vietnam War. In August 1969 a company of the Americal Division refused to move out on an
offensive operation, and later two platoons of an armoured
cavalry troop declined to leave camp to rescue a disabled
vehicle between Lang Vei and the Laotian frontier. These
well-publicised incidents were merely the tip of the iceberg.
Richard Gabriel, using figures provided by official testimonies
to the US Senate, suggests that there were as many as 254
combat refusals in 1971 alone.

Small-scale avoidance of combat rarely reached the statistics. Patrols often went a short distance from camp, waited till
they were due back in, and returned to report that they had
had no contact with the enemy. Tim O'Brien testifies to the
fact that ambushes were frequently a charade: 'Often we faked
the whole thing, calling in the ambush co-ordinates to headquarters and then forgetting it.' Charles Anderson tells the
same story:

> Of the dozen ambushes run in the next two days, no more
> than three or four were strictly ready to react, according to
> doctrine. On the rest, the grunts simply walked out to the
> designated ambush site, hid under the grass or bush and
> wrote letters, slept, or just lay back on the ground with eyes
> closed.

'The object', said Sergeant Joe Curry, 'is to spend your year without getting shot at, or, if you do, to get fewest people hurt. We don't try to frustrate the Captain's attempt to kill gooks, but we don't put our heart in it.' Sometimes officers' legitimate concern for the safety of their men persuaded them that they were morally right in declining to go into action. In June 1966 a company commander in 2nd Battalion, 327th Infantry, firmly refused to risk his men without adequate supporting fire. 'Colonel,' he declared, 'I don't give a rat's ass what you say: I am not going.'[1]

These are simply recent examples of a practice which has gone on for centuries. Some of Wellington's Dutch-Belgian troops, imbued with an understandable reluctance to fight against an army in which many of them had recently served, left the field of Waterloo and withdrew into the Forest of Soignes to await the outcome of the battle. Lieutenant Basil Jackson of the Royal Staff Corps saw them: 'entire companies seemed there, with regularly piled arms, fire blazing under cooking kettles, while the men lay about smoking as coolly as if no enemy were within a day's march ...' These men were not panic-stricken cowards, ashamed of their conduct: they had simply decided that their interests were best served by the avoidance of battle.

In his book *Trench Warfare, 1914–18: the Live and Let Live System*, Tony Ashworth offers a generally convincing explanation for the phenomenon of the 'quiet sector' on the Western Front. He identifies sectors in which the soldiers of both sides took the view that aggressive action was not in their interest, and demonstrates that the Christmas truces of 1914 and 1915 were by no means isolated examples: breakfast truces, and truces to recover the wounded were both common. On the front occupied by the British 33rd Division, British and German patrols developed an elaborate system of signalling to one another, and would meet in No Man's Land before returning to their respective trenches to report that all was well. When that hardy warrior Brigadier-General Frank Crozier was commanding a battalion, he insisted that each of his patrols brought back a section of the German wire to prove that they had reached it. He was chagrined to learn that one company commander kept a roll of the wire in his dugout, and amused himself by forcing his subalterns to sit on it until the blood came: those who did so were rewarded by a short length which enabled them to avoid their next patrol. One British officer reckoned that the instinct for self-preservation reached very great proportions:

there developed a new spirit of taking care of one's self amongst the men, which ended, in late 1918, in few rifles being fired, and would, in a few weeks, have meant the cessation of the war, by the front line troops not refusing but quietly omitting to do duty. The Armistice came just in time.

The aggression of a group member endangered his comrades, for aggression produced retaliation. Graham Greenwell's company commander was by no means exceptional. 'Old Conny', he wrote, 'won't let us fire rifle grenades or trench mortars at them because they always send back at least four for every one of ours. He says he prefers a dignified silence unless they begin it.' Sergeant Warner felt very much the same on the borders of Germany in October 1944. His mortar fire brought a brisk reply from an 88mm, so, as he wrote in his diary: 'Decide not to fire unless absolutely necessary.' An officer in 3 Para discovered, during the battle for Mount Longdon, that 'the moment you opened fire you'd cop 200 per cent back, so we kept a low profile for a bit'. His regard for his men made him disinclined to risk their lives without what he regarded as sufficient cause. He found an Argentinian trench while out on patrol, but decided against attacking it. 'Why?' he asked. 'They'll lose some guys, but so will I. We can wait for a proper battle, instead of just eight men on a bare-arsed hillside ... The risks aren't worth it.'

On 27 August 1914, during the retreat from Mons, Lieutenant-Colonel John Elkington of 1st Battalion, the Royal Warwickshire Regiment, and Lieutenant-Colonel Arthur Mainwaring of 2nd Battalion, the Royal Dublin Fusiliers, decided to surrender rather than to fight and risk not only the destruction of their exhausted units but also the bombardment of St Quentin, where they had halted. Major Tom Bridges, commanding the two cavalry squadrons of the rearguard, found the soldiers of the two battalions 'in a queer, truculent mood'. Despite all the stigma attached to surrender, they were clearly prepared to stand by their commanding officers' decision. One man shouted out: 'Our old man [his colonel] has surrendered to the Germans, and we'll stick to him. *We don't want any bloody cavalry interfering!*' Bridges and his trumpeter improvised a band with a toy drum and a tin whistle, and persuaded most of the men to follow him. Both commanding officers were court-martialled and cashiered. Elkington joined the French Foreign Legion as a private soldier, was commissioned, decorated and severely wounded. He was awarded the Distinguished Service Order and restored to his rank in the British army by special command of the king. The incident did not stem from cowardice: rather, it reflected the tendency of officers whose decision-making was blurred by tiredness to over-identify with their equally exhausted soldiers.

Major-General Pilcher, commanding the 17th Division in the summer of 1916, was faced with a similar conflict between duty to his superiors and loyalty to his subordinates when ordered to carry out an attack on Mametz wood. He considered asking to be relieved of his command, but eventually decided to carry on, because a new commander might have got even more men killed. But he did not attack according to plan, and paid the price of disobedience. 'If I had obeyed the corps order more literally,' he wrote,

> I should have lost another two or three thousand men and achieved no more. I was, as you know, accused of want of push, and consequently sent home. It is very easy to sit a few miles in the rear, and get the credit for allowing men to be killed in an undertaking foredoomed to failure, but the part did not appeal to me and my protests against these useless attacks were not well received.[2]

The line between legitimate concern for the safety of one's group and the unreasonable flouting of superior orders is a thin one, and the whole issue is complicated by the soldier's concept of a contractual element in his role. The fighting record of the Australians was probably unparalleled during the First World War. None the less, on 8 July 1918 the 59th Battalion refused to advance. Its men felt, not without reason, that they were 'being put in to do other people's work', and, in their robust way, they applied the logic of the industrial dispute to the battlefield. Units who have been in action repeatedly easily come to believe that they have done their part to win the war, and are entitled to be relieved. As Lieutenant-General Sir Brian Horrocks, who took command of 30 Corps at a painful moment in its history, during the Normandy battle, put it: 'They begin to feel that it is time they had a rest and someone else did the fighting.' Kurt Lang linked lengthy battle experience to eventual combat refusal. 'What mainly differentiates the mutineer from other troops', he maintained, 'is exposure to unusually heavy combat stress.'

A sense of broken contract usually lies close to the heart of a mutiny. 'Constant pay' was one of the attractions of service in the New Model Army during the English Civil War. Its 1647 mutinies, often attributed to revolutionary stirrings amongst its rank and file, had more practical motives. 'Arrears and associated material grievances', writes one authority, 'were the engine behind the revolt of that year.'[3] Amongst the causes of the Indian Mutiny of 1857 was the sepoys' belief that they were being defiled by the introduction of a new rifle with a cartridge suspected – quite wrongly, in the event – of being greased with fat from pigs (unclean to Moslems) or cattle (sacred to Hindus). Their officers had, they thought, broken faith with them, and they believed themselves morally justified in rebelling. A massive sense of unfairness was a potent ingredient in the French army's mutiny in 1917: it was unfair that the soldier received a fraction of the daily wage of the munitions worker, unfair that officers enjoyed conspicuous privileges, unfair that the same units always seemed to be sent at the thickest part of the hedge. Privation and destruction of trained manpower did more damage to the tsarist army than did revolutionary propaganda during the first two years of the

First World War. Complaints about poor food were frequent, an inefficient bureaucracy proved utterly incapable of supplying adequate quantities of modern weapons and ammunition, and crippling casualties amongst regular officers weakened *esprit de corps*.

At times this sense of contract is very personal. Jack Bushby was 'surprised and, oddly enough, indignant under attack on the ground from the air. A feeling of "Hey! They can't mean me. I'm not a Regular. I only signed on for week-ends." Strange but abolutely true.' Just as William Langer regarded shelling as 'unfair', so a soldier in 2 Para thought that air attacks were somehow unreasonable. 'The second I saw the first Skyhawk,' he said, 'I thought, "Hello, someone's dropped a bollock; I'm an infantryman, and it's not my job to deal with those bastards."' British infantry at Waterloo were galled to see French *cuirassiers* walking their horses around the battalion squares. This, clearly, was not part of *their* contract. 'Where are our cavalry?' they shouted. 'Why don't they come and pitch into these French fellows.' Heavy bombardments and air attacks are convincing demonstrations of the enemy's power, and they sometimes persuade soldiers, not only that further resistance is hopeless, but also that their own superiors have behaved unreasonably in exposing them to such a threat and no longer deserve their loyalty.

Men often link their own performance to that of their officers. King James II, speaking of the Battle of Edgehill, remarked that English troops could be relied upon not to run away as long as their officers did not set them a bad example. Ensign John Colborne, later Field-Marshal Lord Seaton, overheard one Irish soldier standing behind him mutter to another: 'I'll stand as long as the officer stands.' Lieutenant Henry Harward of the 80th Regiment galloped away to fetch help when the Zulus overran a British detachment at Myer's Drift on the Intombi River in February 1879. When tried by general court martial, he pleaded that he had stayed with his command until it had disintegrated, and he was duly acquitted. Sir Garnet Wolseley, unable to quash the verdict, bitterly assailed what struck him as:

a monstrous theory, viz., that a regimental officer who is the only officer present with a party of soldiers actually and seriously engaged with the enemy can, under any pretext whatever, be justified in deserting them ... The more helpless the position in which an officer finds his men, the more it is his bounden duty to stay and share their fortune, whether for good or ill.[4]

Wolseley was being unduly rigid in Harward's case, but he was right in his recognition that, if leaders are not prepared to fight to the death, their followers may well decide not to. As the Argentinian stretcher-bearer Juan Carlos inquired, 'If the professionals had gone, what were mere conscripts expected to do?'

Nowhere is this sense of contract more important than when surrender is being contemplated. As Martin Middlebrook astutely observed in *The Kaiser's Battle:* 'The real limit of a Western soldier's resistance is the point at which he feels his individual honour has been satisfied.' He will fight on until he considers that the terms of his contract have been fulfilled and he has 'done his bit'. Lance-Bombardier Alan Toze of 122 Field Regiment Royal Artillery met a Scots deserter in Singapore shortly before the British surrender in February 1942. 'A man can stand so much,' he said. 'The Argylls have done their bit: we were too few against too many.'

The war in the Far East confirms the accuracy of Middlebrook's judgment on surrender. Unpleasant though it was for British or American soldiers to capitulate, the act was not surrounded by the deep-seated taboos which made surrender so disdained by the Japanese. In the Japanese army, heroism was commonplace and defence to the last man routine. When the Americans took Kwajalein Atoll in early 1944, only thirty-five members of its 5,000-man garrison surrendered, most of them already wounded. The rest fought to the death. A report by the commander of the Japanese 56th Regiment in Burma concluded, quite characteristically: 'The regiment will cover the withdrawal of the main body at the sacrifice of our lives. I believe this will be our final parting. Please give my best regards to the division commander.'

There have been times, particularly when they have been fighting a savage foe from whom no quarter could be expected, that Western soldiers have displayed the same determination to fight to the bitter end. But when men have reason to believe that captives will not be mistreated, then surrender is a far more easily-acceptable alternative than we might suppose. In March 1918 many of the British forward positions surrendered after only a token resistance. An officer wrote that the three battalions in the forward zone of his division 'fought it out on the spot and their heroism will live for ever in the annals of their regiments'. In fact, one of the battalions, 2/5th Worcesters, lost five officers and twenty-one men killed: 600 officers and men surrendered, and one witness saw them marching through St Quentin, in the German rear, with the battalion's transport, its aid post, and even its band. A large part of the unwillingness of many battalions to fight to the last man and the last round stemmed from a dislike and distrust of an improperly-understood defensive system. One experienced NCO prophesied: 'It don't suit us. The British army fights in line, and won't do any good in these bird cages.'

In some places British officers answered summonses to surrender with requests that the Germans bring up artillery, with undertakings to capitulate at a specified time, or with demands for a written document testifying to the determination of their defence. Lieutenant-Colonel Lord Farnham surrendered the Boadicea Redoubt, with eleven officers, 241 men and forty-one machine-guns and mortars, after requesting, and receiving, a paper stating that he had put up a good fight: honour was satisfied. On 27 June 1944 the boot was on the other foot. General Sattler, commander of the Arsenal at Cherbourg, told American emissaries that he would not surrender unless tanks were deployed against him. They duly appeared, and fired a few rounds: Sattler and his men marched out into captivity.

In these instances the decision to surrender, although taken by the commander, met with wide acceptance among his subordinates. There are, however, many occasions upon which a unit is prepared to go on fighting while numerous individuals within it are not. They may become psychiatric casualties or give way to panic. But they may also reduce their participation in battle to the absolute minimum or, if circumstances permit, withdraw it altogether. The nature of the twentieth-century battlefield has made this sort of combat avoidance increasingly easy. The wider the battlefield and the more isolated its soldiers, the easier it is for them to avoid participating in combat.

S.L.A. Marshall's work on the Second World War suggested that few American infantrymen actually fired their weapons in battle. His studies of small-unit action in Korea disclosed many soldiers who, without being psychiatric casualties in the proper sense of the term, hid in bunkers until the battle was over, and others who simply failed to fire their weapons despite a profusion of clear targets. Nevertheless, the fire ratio in Korea improved to about 50 per cent, and in Vietnam it was as high as 80 per cent. Tony Ashworth suspected that Marshall's logic was flawed, because he attributed non-firing to a psychological motive – reluctance to kill – and firing to a sociological cause – small-group cohesion. This inconsistency is not necessarily serious, and a mixture of motives probably applies in both cases.

My own deductions from the Falklands War are less valid than those of Marshall for the Second World War and Korea, Little for Korea, and Moskos for Vietnam, primarily because I interviewed my sample of soldiers several weeks after their experience of battle, when the skin of the accepted version of events was solidifying fast. Yet some useful conclusions did emerge. Firstly, the judgment of both parachute battalions on Marshall's statement that most infantrymen fail to fire in combat was epitomised by Chris Keeble's lapidary statement: 'Rubbish.' 'You had to fire,' explained a member of 2 Para, 'because you wanted to be part of that aggression, and firing was how you showed it.' The norms of the parachute battalions demanded aggression, and failing to fire came dangerously close to 'bottling out'. One soldier wished that men had not fired so much: his most dangerous moment in the campaign came when his company clerk engaged a passing Skyhawk and sprayed the surrounding area with bullets. Where the Marshall thesis did strike a chord was in British accounts of Argentinian fire. When I explained it to a group from 2 Para, there was immediate recognition that it applied to the Argentinians, whose snipers and machine-gunners had been very effective while their individual riflemen had not.

Isolation promotes combat refusal. The two-man trench has a bad track record in this respect. If one of its occupants is hit, his comrade is unlikely to go on firing. There are, moreover, numerous cases in the American, British and German armies of both occupants lying doggo, secure in the knowledge that their failure would be invisible, until the action was over. Charlton Ogburn wrote of 'youngsters who simply cowered in their foxholes, heads in arms, when the Japanese charged' and were bayoneted in the back. A Royal Marine officer described how his men initially reacted to an Indonesian attack in Borneo by crouching in their trenches: some had to be physically hauled to their feet.

The crews of armoured fighting vehicles are, of necessity, in a degree of isolation. I have encountered only one instance of outright combat refusal by an AFV crewman, a driver who declined to advance until pressed to do so by his commander's pistol. Nevertheless, as Richard Simpkin observed, 'armoured vehicle crewmen have considerable scope for less than ideal behaviour under fire, of kinds that may not be evident even to other members of their crew'. Sensitive equipment suddenly malfunctions so that the vehicle cannot proceed; drivers and commander manoeuvre into poor - but safe - fire positions; tanks mysteriously slew off minefield lanes and lose tracks. Tank commanders can be as anxious as infantrymen to avoid provoking an unpleasant response from the enemy. Brigadier James Hargest, a New Zealand observer whose account of the operations of 50th Division in Normandy is an invaluable record of the behaviour of men in battle, describes one such instance. On 17 June a tank of 8th Armoured Brigade waited at a British roadblock while several German vehicles moved along a straight road within easy range. 'The tank did not fire although the target was a perfect one,' noted Hargest. 'Neither did it call on the tanks in its troop nearby for support. The infantry Bde Comd sent down a message asking that the gun and cars be taken on. The reply was "If I do he will reply to my fire."'

Some failures to participate in battle are, then, explained by group norms which encourage such behaviour, or by the deliberate inaction of individuals or small groups, usually cloaked by isolation. But the devices used to bind men together with their comrades in the same unit can occasionally be so successful as to be counter-productive. In 1918 attempts to disband some Australian battalions in order to reinforce others provoked outright mutiny. The men of the 25th Battalion explained their refusal to disband in a dignified and articulate protest to their commanding officer, Lieutenant-Colonel Davis.

We have been taught that the regiment is everything. You have often told us that we must sacrifice everything for its honour. We have always obeyed you and we always will – in everything but what you now ask. We cannot obey you in this just for that reason – we would sacrifice everything for the battalion.

A far more serious example of the detrimental effects of group loyalty came at Salerno in September 1943. One hundred and ninety-two men from a reinforcement draft for the 46th Division refused to obey an order to pick up their kits and fall in to march to the Division's area. They were disarmed, shipped to Constantine in Algeria, and court-martialled. The privates were sentenced to seven years' penal servitude and the corporals to ten: the three sergeants involved were sentenced to death. All sentences were suspended on condition that the men would fight with new units, and this they did.

This was certainly not combat refusal in the conventional sense: most of those court-martialled had fought bravely in the past and were to do the same in the future. They were members of 50th (Northumbrian) Division and 51st (Highland) Division, both 8th Army formations with a high degree of divisional identity. They had believed that they were on their way back to their own divisions: they objected, not to fighting, but to fighting away from their comrades. The business was undoubtedly mishandled by the authorities at Salerno. The comedian Spike Milligan, who himself served there with an artillery regiment, blamed 'crass stupidity on both sides. If only an officer in charge had said to them, "Look, chaps, we are in a desperate situation. The bridgehead is barely holding. If we are pushed into the sea, it will put another two years on the war."'

The men's passionate identification with their parent divisions was certainly the mainspring of their mutiny. Major-General D.N. Wimberley, commander of the 51st, had always told his men that they were to ensure that they did not get drafted to other battalions, but were to return to the division. Alan Briddon understood how the mutineers felt.

I sympathise greatly with the deep desire of the NCOs and men to return to their own units. Such feeling was inculcated by Major-General Wimberley from the early days of the Highland Division and encouraged at every opportunity, thus welding fierce regimental spirit to the wider (but no less fiercely felt) division spirit. On discharge from a Cairo hospital, I myself deliberately 'missed out' the Base Depot Royal Artillery to which I had been ordered and hitch-hiked my way back to my own regiment in the line.

Members of the hard-pressed 46th Division may perhaps be forgiven for not seeing the matter in the same light, and one roundly declared that the mutineers 'deserved all that came to them'. None the less, it is hard not to sympathise with what one commentator called 'men caught in a Sophoclean web of inevitable tragedy'.[5]

The question of mutiny deserves more scholarly attention than it has so far received. Marxists tend to interpret it in purely class terms, the military establishment strives to shroud the whole ugly business in the dark folds of official secrecy, and popular historians eagerly address a subject which has an encouraging sales potential. Many of its manifestations lie outside the scope of this study. Nevertheless, some general points merit emphasis. The first is that, as General Serrigny observed, 'the crisis of confidence always starts among those who do not fight ... The crisis grows singularly with the greater distance from the battlefield.' That wise old campaigner Blaise de Montluc warned captains to keep a watchful eye on the rear, for it was there that disorder usually broke out.

Soldiers in fighting units are usually more resistant to mutiny than those in depots and training establishments. This was certainly true of the British and imperial Russian armies during the First World War, and General Donn A. Starry discerned a similar pattern in Vietnam. He maintained that most of the serious disciplinary problems occurred in base areas, where they gained a disproportionate degree of publicity because it was in precisely these areas that journalists were most active. Secondly, once the need to carry on fighting evaporates, then even units with excellent combat records can be affected by mutiny, as disturbances in the British army after the First World War and the American army after the Second amply demonstrate.

An aspect of mutiny which was well-documented in Vietnam is germane to this study. Officers, NCOs or even private soldiers who were identified as being too eager for action risked 'fragging'. The term was derived from the use of a fragmentation grenade, conveniently rolled into the victim's hooch at night, although assassination with small-arms fire in the confusion of a firefight was not unknown. The incidence of fragging peaked in 1971, with no less than 333 confirmed incidents and another 158 possible ones. Richard Gabriel suggested that at least 1,016 officers and NCOs were killed by fragging, and went on to speculate that as many as 20 per cent of the American officers killed in the war may have died at the hands of their own men. A less sanguinary alternative in the Navy or Air Force was 'fodding', the sabotage of aircraft by deliberate 'Foreign Object Damage', easily produced by a washer in an air intake. Charles Anderson argued:

> Every soldier, marine, sailor or airman who fragged a unit leader believed at the time of the incident that he acted with more than ample justification. Such a view may sound incredible now, but anyone who has seen combat and perceived what it does to one's thinking can appreciate the extreme difficulty, perhaps even the folly, or making value judgements on the thoughts and actions of men in a combat environment.

He cited interference with the date on which a man's tour ended and failure to rotate patrol responsibilities as common causes of fragging. More generally, what the troops called 'unnecessary harassment' made leaders vulnerable. Some of this was by no means as unnecessary as it seemed: a leader's insistence on improving defensive positions, wearing flak jackets and helmets, and taking malaria pills were all likely causes of resentment.

Fragging is not new: military leaders have always been at risk, living as they must among men used to violence in an atmosphere where life is cheap. The Pannonian mutiny of AD 14 was provoked partly by the fact that soldiers were being retained with the colours after their discharge date. It was marked by the murder of unpopular officers, including the centurion Lucilius, nicknamed 'another-please' from his habit of breaking his vine-staff on the backs of his men. The unpopular major commanding the 15th Foot at Blenheim turned to address his regiment before the battle, apologising for his bad behaviour in the past, and asking that, if he had to fall, it should be by the enemy's bullets. A grenadier shouted: 'March on, sir; the enemy is before you, and we have something else to do than to think of you now.' The action over, the major turned to the troops and raised his hat to call for a cheer: he was promptly shot through the head by an unknown marksman.

The French soldiers of the Napoleonic period were equally

direct in expressing their opinion. Jean Morvan tells how an unpopular general was fired on by his own troops, and some Paris students, detailed to form three batteries for the National Guard, actually killed the general sent to enlist them. Similar lapses were not unknown in Wellington's army. Tom Plunkett of the 95th was repeatedly promoted and just as repeatedly reduced to the ranks for drunkenness. On one occasion he determined to shoot his company commander and waited in ambush to do so, but was eventually coaxed into giving up his rifle. Colonel Cameron of Fassfern, commanding the 92nd Regiment, was shot dead at Quatre Bras, probably by a bad character whom he had had flogged a few days before.

The revival of the hand-grenade during the First World War saw the appearance of fragging in its literal sense. Brigadier-General Crozier knew of 'the bullying NCO who was blown to pieces by a bomb, with the pin extracted, being placed between his shirt and trousers'. Robert Graves's poem 'Sergeant-Major Money', in which two young Welsh soldiers bayonet a hard-driving sergeant-major, is founded on fact, and in *Goodbye to All That* Graves describes how two men in his battalion shot their company sergeant-major in mistake for their platoon sergeant. Two British soldiers were executed for murders committed in April 1918: one had shot his platoon sergeant, the other a lieutenant. The Australians were sharp with unpopular officers: some were 'sandbagged' or 'bottle-oed', and a few were shot. One Australian recalled throwing a lump of clay at an engineer officer who reprimanded him: 'He cleared off without a word, fearing worse treatment, for our rifles were handy, and a shot more or less is never noticed among the incessant firing during darkness.'

Stick and Carrot

The fact that soldiers sometimes refuse to fight, and may re-inforce this refusal by attacking those who wish to make them do so, is the single most important reason for the existence of military discipline. I am concerned here with battle discipline rather than with the discipline of polished buttons and crisp salutes, although we must remember that there is usually a direct link between the two. When Canrobert stopped at Malta on his way to the Crimea in 1854, he watched the British Guards at drill. 'Now do you understand Waterloo?' he asked a brother officer. There are numerous well-turned anecdotes about men who fight well but are not amenable to discipline, men who, as Marshall puts it, 'could fight like hell but couldn't soldier'. Drink often leads to their downfall. We have already met Tom Plunkett, lethal with his Baker rifle on the battlefield but almost equally deadly with the rum jar off it. John Glubb's Corporal Bush, marvellous leader that he was, was always demoted for drunkenness, and Robert Graves's Sergeant Dickens DCM and Bar, MM, *Médaille Militaire*, 'had been two or three times promoted to sergeant's rank and each time reduced for drunkenness'.

F.C. Bartlett describes discipline as 'enforced obedience to external authority'. This is too rigid a definition, for the most effective discipline is that which is self-imposed, which springs from the 'tribal' structure of small groups and from mutual confidence between leaders and led. Richard Simpkin is right to suggest that 'the nub of successful discipline is team spirit'. It is this sort of discipline which the members of good units recall with pride. 'We all knew one another very well,' wrote an officer in the Queen's Regiment of the platoon he commanded from January 1938 to January 1940, 'and there was a natural discipline which needed very little enforcement.' For another platoon commander, the end product of this sort of discipline was: 'A mutual confidence that what has to be done will be done whatever the circumstances. It enables rank barriers to be bridged without loss of respect.' Most of Bob Godfrey's Suffolks in Malaya in the early 1950s were conscripts. However, he found: 'Sharp conventional discipline not necessary. Persuasion and exhortation and, I suppose, example were all that were necessary ... National servicemen ... needed prodding a bit as the "days to do" charts appeared.' In Gordon

Cormack's anti-terrorist unit there was 'not parade-ground discipline, but a natural discipline founded on respect, affection and the knowledge that there was no room for shirkers'.

Nevertheless, there are times when this team spirit is inadequate as a basis for discipline. It takes time for a unit to acquire collective self-discipline and, as Moran observed, 'control from without ... can only be relaxed safely when it is replaced by something higher and better, control from within'. Moreover, heavy casualties, particularly amongst officers and NCOs, may so lacerate the fabric of a unit that its cohesion and self-discipline disappear. This process is likely to be accompanied by an increase in the number of psychiatric casualties and by large-scale failure in battle. The commanding officer of 6th Battalion, the Duke of Wellington's Regiment, painted a depressing picture of the way in which heavy fighting in Normandy, and the loss of twenty-three officers and 350 men, had ruined his unit.

75% of the men react adversely to enemy shelling and are 'jumpy'.

5 cases in 3 days of self-inflicted wounds – more possible cases.

Each time men are killed or wounded a number of men become casualties through shell shock or hysteria.

In addition to genuine hysteria a large number of men have left their positions after shelling on one pretext or another and gone to the rear ...

The new drafts have been affected, and 3 young soldiers became casualties with hysteria after hearing our own guns.

The situation has got worse each day as more key personnel have become casualties ...

State of discipline is bad, although the men are a cheerful pleasant type normally ...

NCO leadership is weak in most cases and the newly drafted officers are in consequence having to expose themselves unduly to try to get anything done ...

6 DWR is not fit to take its place in the line.[6]

There is a paradox inherent in military discipline. However draconian it might be, external discipline is imposed by the few upon the many, and relies upon what John Ellis accurately termed 'tacit consensus'. 'Orders are seldom obeyed to the letter and are often flagrantly disregarded,' wrote G.C. Homans of groups in general. 'Wise leaders know that nothing is so destructive of cooperation as the giving of orders that cannot or will not be obeyed.' Officers sometimes shrink from issuing contentious orders, suspecting that they will provoke direct disobedience which will crack the fragile shell of discipline altogether. In the winter of 1944 Charles MacDonald's company was attacked by five German tanks, against which it could offer little effective resistance. A troop of near-by American tanks refused to engage them without a direct order, which MacDonald's battalion commander, fearful of open disobedience, would not give. When the 78th Division went on the rampage in Cairo in Christmas 1943 the Military Police decided not to highlight the breakdown of discipline by making an issue of it: they either looked the other way or joined in. Colonial armies were often able to avoid the hard conclusion that their native troops refused to obey orders by the useful convention that an order which was disobeyed was one which had been misunderstood.

This care to preserve the fabric of discipline at all costs is an understandable one, since once the Emperor's-new-clothes nature of discipline is apparent to all, worse may follow. As Richard Watt remarked of the French mutinies of 1917, a dangerous moment was reached once 'the tissue of convention on which military discipline is ultimately based had become transparent to officers and enlisted men alike'. Once the psychological barriers against mutiny are broken down, indiscipline within an army, or conflict between an army and the government of its own state, can take on a curiously imitative character. Once the generals have initiated a *coup*, the barriers against the colonels staging their own are destroyed and, as numerous post-colonial states have discovered, the sergeants will probably not be far behind. Just as government rests ultimately upon the consent of the governed, so discipline relies upon the compliance of the mass with the wishes of the few. It is not surprising that the punishments for mutiny have, historically, often been the same as those for treason, for if treason strikes a fundamental blow at the nature of the state, mutiny threatens the whole structure of an army.

Ardant du Picq argued that discipline must be 'a state of mind, a social institution based on the salient virtues and defects of the nation', and Charles de Gaulle believed that an army's discipline must reflect the wider *mores* of civilian society. It is certainly true that military discipline reflects national culture. Colonel W.N. Nicholson was not alone in admiring the deep-seated discipline of German soldiers, which 'produced trenches and dug-outs that made our efforts look puny in comparison'. 'It is all rot the stuff one reads in the papers about the inferiority of the German soldiers to ours,' wrote Billy Congreve in October 1914. 'If anything, the German is the better, for though we are undoubtedly the more dogged and *impossible* to beat, they are the more highly disciplined.' An Australian sergeant attributed his countrymen's success to the absence of formal discipline. 'The Australian is not a soldier,' he remarked, 'but he is a fighter, a born fighter; each Australian has his separate individuality & his priceless initiative which made him ... infinitely better than the clockwork soldier.' Alan Briddon made the same observation of the Second World War Australian.

> My first action was with the Australian 9th Division before Alamein. I found it a total contrast to ours – first names etc, but *their* discipline was a very personal thing. Ours was corporate/regimental/Divisional and at times it irked but I was (& am) convinced that it was the right *métier* for the British.

There is also a tendency, as de Gaulle noted, for standards of military discipline to conform to the values of civilian society, a process which has become particularly pronounced in many Western armies over the last two decades. It is unrealistic – and, in political terms, probably dangerous – to

335

expect an army, especially one which contains conscript soldiers, not to mirror the society which produces it. None the less, however great our belief in rational discipline, *Innere Führung* or comradely spirit, we should not lose sight of an inescapable fact. For all that military sociologists have identified a 'narrowing skill differential' between the soldier and the civilian, the former still includes hazarding his life as an essential part of the job description. General Sir John Hackett called it 'the clause of unlimited liability'. There may come a moment in even the best-conducted, most democratic of armies, when a leader gives an order which will result in the certain death of his subordinates, and a framework of discipline which does not prepare for this eventuality does both army and society a disservice. As Major J.P. Isenhower put it: 'There is no doubt that current affection for the occupational model has contributed significantly to this problem [that of cohesion], for discipline is applied in the business world according to a different ideology from that in the military.'

The underlying principle behind the discipline of the horse and musket age was that, as Frederick the Great admitted quite candidly, 'the common soldier must fear his officer more than the enemy'. The Prussian soldier of the eighteenth century might be cuffed by his officer or NCO for the most trivial lapse, made to ride a sharp-backed wooden horse, branded, flogged, or invited to run the gauntlet – walking, stripped to the waist, between two ranks of soldiers armed with sticks. More serious offences merited hanging, shooting or being broken on the wheel. Draconian discipline like this was confined neither to the Prussian army nor to the eighteenth century. James Wolfe, the victor of Quebec, was a sensitive man with a taste for poetry. But there was nothing poetic about his regimental orders when commanding the 20th Foot at Canterbury in 1755: 'A soldier who quits his rank, or offers to flag, is instantly to be put to death by the officer who commands that platoon, or by the officer or sergeant in rear of that platoon; a soldier does not deserve to live who won't fight for his king and country.' British soldiers were flogged until

1881, although there was one case of unofficial flogging in Burma in 1944. Corporal punishment survived in the Russian army until 1904, was reintroduced shortly before the First World War, and was abolished after the Revolution. Officially-applied corporal punishment in France ended with the *ancien régime*, but vicious unofficial punishments like *crapaudine* lasted, notably in North Africa, till the 1930s. In the Spanish Foreign Legion of the Civil War period, defaulters were lambasted with *fustas*, pliant whips carried by officers and senior NCOs, and for serious disobedience the offender was shot on the spot. Argentinian conscripts in the Falklands suffered improvised physical punishments for misbehaving. Santiago described one man who was spreadeagled on the freezing ground for stealing food, and others were made to stand with their bare feet in icy water.

Draconian discipline was, even in the armies which applied it, only part of the picture. Some commanding officers set their faces firmly against corporal punishment, and used it rarely: others, like the sadistic Lieutenant-Colonel von Scheelen of the 1st Battalion of the *Garde*, laid it on vigorously. Sir John Moore's system of training had a lasting if limited impact on the British army. It was based, as Sir Arthur Bryant writes, 'on treating soldiers, not as the rigid drill automata of the 18th century army, but as human beings capable of individual initiative and self-improvement. His goal ... was "the thinking fighting man".'

In the end, though, it was the changing nature of Western society, rather than military recognition that harsh discipline was outmoded, that led to its disappearance. And the issue was, and remains, contentious. During the First World War 346 death sentences were carried out by the British army. The great majority (266, including two officers) were for desertion. Three were for mutiny, and the remainder were such diverse offences as murder, disobedience, striking or offering violence to a superior officer, sleeping on post, quitting post, and casting away arms. There is no doubt whatever that the justice was not done in at least some of these cases, as Anthony Babington's *For the Sake of Example* indicates. Public and parliamentary concern led to the abolition of the death penalty for desertion and cowardice in April 1930. The exact number of French soldiers executed during the First World War remains uncertain. Five hundred and fifty-four were sentenced to death for their part in the 1917 mutinies: forty-three are known to have been shot, and there are doubts in the cases of twenty-three more. In France, too, there was much post-war bitterness about courts martial, particularly when *cours de cassation* reviewed their proceedings.[7]

There were, none the less, those who argued, exactly as Frederick the Great had done, that if a soldier was not more frightened of his own officers than the enemy he might refuse to fight. Lieutenant-Colonel Lambert Ward described how a brigade of the 3rd Division 'had cracked to a man. You could not send them back to base, yet they were in such a state that they would willingly have taken ten years' penal servitude to stay out of the line. In these circumstances it was only fear of death that kept them at their posts.' It was a view shared by General von Ludendorff, who mourned the fact that the penalties at his disposal were less extreme than those available to his enemies. 'The Entente', he wrote, 'no doubt achieved more than we did with their considerably more severe punishments. This historic fact is well established.'

To the total of death penalties applied with the stark ritual of the dawn firing-party must be added the unknown sum of soldiers – British, French and German – who were shot out of hand by their own officers. One French divisional commander went so far as to order his artillery to fire on men who declined to leave their trenches, but his artillery commander refused to do so without a written order. Brigadier-General Crozier ended his life a pacifist. Even so, he firmly believed that he had done right to shoot soldiers to stop them running.

> Strictly from the military point of view I have no regrets for having killed a subaltern of British infantry on the same morning that I ordered our rifles and machine-guns to be turned on the fleeing Portuguese ... I, who am a soldier, know that it is difficult to leave the shelter of a shell-hole

for a final rush in the face of a deadly shower of bullets and the certain knowledge that cold steel awaits. It is less difficult, however, if there is the knowledge that a loaded revolver for use against the enemy is also loaded for use against you if you fail to jump forward when the barrage lifts.[8]

Lieutenant-Colonel Graham Seton Hutchison likewise had no doubts about ordering his machine-gunners to fire on a small body of British troops in April 1918 when they attempted to surrender. 'Such an action as this', he declared, 'will in a short time spread like dry rot through an army and is one of those dire military necessities which calls for immediate and prompt action.'

During the Second World War there were no formal executions for desertion or cowardice in the British army, and only one, that of Private Eddie Slovik, in the American. When British fortunes in the Western Desert were at a low ebb, Sir Claude Auchinleck, Commander-in-Chief Middle East, formally requested the reinstitution of the death penalty for desertion and cowardice, but his request was rejected. The Soviet army executed men for these offences both formally and informally: Order No. 356 of 1940 instructed commanders to use their weapons on their own men should compulsion be necessary.

The German army, despite the totalitarian character of the regime it served, was far more sparing in its use of execution until the very end of the war, when military police detachments roamed the rear areas, hanging stragglers who could not give a satisfactory reason for their presence there. Many of them were left hanging from lamp-posts, bearing placards announcing 'I am a cowardly swine: I betrayed my Führer.' There were also moments when a commander's pistol worked wonders. Colonel Hans von Luck, whose battle group of 21st Panzer Division did so much damage to British armour in Operation Goodwood, was faced with a *Luftwaffe* officer who maintained that his four 88s were for shooting at aircraft, not tanks. Luck drew his pistol, told the officer that he could 'either die now on my responsibility, or win a decoration on his own'. The guns came into action immediately, destroying sixteen tanks of the 2nd Fife and Forfar Yeomanry.

The discipline enforced by the officer's pistol or the firing-squad's volley is avowedly inferior to that produced by mutual respect and affection. And, if discipline is the stick which drives men on in battle, what are the carrots that lure them forward? We have already considered the crucial role of the group in contributing to fighting spirit. The relationship of the leader to the group is one which has attracted the attention of a large number of scholars, many of them concerned with establishing principles which will help with the training of leaders in industry as well as in the services. Definitions of leadership are legion but, at least in the military context, it is hard to better Correlli Barnett's assessment of it as:

> a psychological force that has nothing to do with morals or good character or even intelligence: nothing to do with ideals or idealism. It is a matter of relative will powers, a basic connection between one animal and the rest of the herd. Leadership is a process by which a single aim and unified action are imported to the herd. Not surprisingly it is most in evidence in times or circumstances of danger or challenge. Leadership is not imposed like authority. It is actually welcomed and wanted by the led.

John Adair discerned three different approaches to the question. First was 'the qualities approach', enshrined in the conviction that leaders are born not made. This produces many – sometimes very many – personal qualities which are put forward as essential attributes of leadership. Next came 'the situational approach', which suggested that the leadership characteristics required in a given case are the function of the specific situation. Finally, and most recently, came 'the functional approach', the result of objective research into human behaviour. Dr Adair's own theory of group needs is part of the functional approach. It makes use of A.H. Maslow's 'hierarchy of needs' to produce the 'three circles' concept of group needs, in which the circles of task, team maintenance and individual needs overlap. The leader has to perform various leadership functions to ensure that the group fulfils its task and is held together as a working team.

The Adair model is a useful aid to our reflections on military leadership, although, as has been the case throughout, I am concerned far less with the application of any particular model than I am with my own extrapolations from behaviour on the battlefields of history. Similarly, though there is much to be gained from recognition that there are a number of different types of leader – like Bartlett's institutional, dominant and persuasive – it proves little to scramble through history, eagerly dividing up leaders by type. My own field is in any case narrowed by the fact that it is with the battlefield in particular rather than war in general that I am concerned. There is certainly a connection between the individual soldier's motivation and his confidence in the upper echelons of his army's command structure. Yet this aspect of leadership seems to me to be far less important, as far as the soldier in the slit trench or tank turret is concerned, than what goes on at battalion, company and platoon level, where the links between leadership and life and death, success and failure, are both direct and visible.

The military leader's position is more difficult than that of most civilian leaders for, while he has discipline to help him, he is contending with situations in which the individual's basic physiological needs – food, drink and sleep – may be unsatisfied, and where there may be a direct clash between his safety needs and the fulfilment of the task. The leader of the late twentieth century must also relate to the soldiers produced by societies which are decreasingly deferential, and often has to do so as part of an army which has jettisoned the charismatic and heroic image of the leader in favour of the managerial model preferred by civilian society.

It is a fundamental truth that a military leader will not succeed in battle unless he is prepared to lead from the front and to risk the penalties of doing so. This need to lead from the front is as relevant to unpleasant tasks off the battlefield as to dangerous ones on it. Xenophon's account of Clearchus, commanding the rearguard with its cumbrous wagons on the retreat from Cunaxa in 401 BC, sets the tone perfectly:

> he had his spear in his left hand and a stick in his right, and whenever he thought that any one of the men ... was shirking, he would pick out the right man and deal him a blow, while at the same time he would get into the mud and lend a hand himself; the result was that everyone was ashamed not to match him in energy.

A resolute determination to share the discomforts of his soldiers is evident in Tu Mu's description of Wu Ch'i, a Chinese general of the Warring States period: 'He wore the same clothes and ate the same food as the meanest of his soldiers, refused to have either a horse to ride or a mat to sleep on, carried his own surplus rations wrapped in a panel, and shared every hardship with his men.'

But it is in battle that examples weighs most heavily. Field-Marshal Lord Carver wrote that the qualities required of a commanding officer have not altered much since the time of Julius Caesar, and supported his view with Caesar's description of his own behaviour in a battle against the Nervii in 57 BC.

> I recognised that this was a crisis; there were no reserves available. I had no shield with me but I snatched one from a soldier in the rear ranks and went forward with the front line. Once there, I called out to the Centurions by name and shouted encouragement to the rest of the men. I ordered them to advance and to open out their ranks so that they could use their swords more effectively. My arrival gave the troops fresh hope, their determination was restored because, with the Commander-in-Chief looking on, each man was eager to do his best whatever the risk to himself.[9]

In discussing the death of the much-loved Captain Uniacke, Edward Costello ventured some general comments on leadership.

During the Peninsular War our men had divided the officers into two classes; the 'come on' and the 'go on'; for as Tom Plunkett in action once observed to an officer, 'The words "go on" don't befit a leader, Sir.' ... But amongst the former, none were seen so often in the van as Uniacke; his affability and personal courage had rendered him the idol of the men of his company.

Rifleman Harris of the 95th watched a cavalry officer leading a charge at Vittoria:

He was a brave fellow, and bore himself like a hero; with his sword waving in the air, he cheered the men on, as he went dashing upon the enemy, and hewing and slashing them in tremendous style. I watched for him as the dragoons came off after that charge, *but saw him no more*; he had fallen. Fine fellow! his conduct indeed made an impression upon me that I shall never forget.

Personal leadership was also at a premium in the French army of the period. A British soldier wrote of French officers 'stimulating the men by their example, the men vociferating, each chaffing each until they appear in a fury, shouting, to the points of our bayonets'. We have already paid tribute to the bravery of Lieutenant-Colonel Macdonell and Sergeant Graham in closing the gates of Hougoumont: no less admirable was the valour of *Sous-Lieutenant* Legros of the 1st Light Infantry, who grabbed an axe from one of his pioneers and weakened the door before leading the charge which burst it in. The marshals of the First Empire had their failings as strategists, but their performance as junior leaders was superb. In April 1809 the Austrian garrison of Ratisbon repulsed two assaults by French infantry, and no more volunteers would step forward to pick up the scaling ladders. Marshal Lannes, in overall command of the operation, seized a ladder, saying, 'Oh, well! I am going to prove to you that before I was a marshal I was a grenadier – and so I am still.' His aides-de-camp struggled to take the ladder from him, and to carry it forward themselves. The sight inspired the waiting infantry, who rushed forward with other ladders: there was a sharp fight at the wall, but the French were not to be denied, and Ratisbon fell.

General von Waldersee argued that the national character of the French made it particularly important that they were led from the front, with the principle of '*Les épaulettes en avant*'. His countryman Prince Karl Kraft zu Hohenlohe-Ingelfingen suggested, however, that leadership was more important than discipline, even in the German army. Writing of the Franco-Prussian War, he said: 'The soldier endured all hardships, not from fear of punishment, but through confidence in his officers.' One private explained to a watching civilian, who could not understand why his unit had rushed forward into the teeth of heavy fire: 'When the lieutenant runs to the front, we must run with him.' Whatever may have separated French and German officers in 1870, it was not their admiration for courage, and their mutual recognition that the officer led personally in times of crisis. At a desperate moment at Rezonville Marshal Canrobert who, as a corps commander aged sixty-one, had ample excuse for being elsewhere, rode to the front of the 70th of the Line as Prussian shells furrowed its ranks. He found that the brigade commander had beaten him to it, and greeted him cheerily: 'Good day, Chanaleilles, I am pleased to see you. This is indeed the place for a gentleman and a soldier.'

This sort of leadership had a recognisable impact even in the grim conditions of the Western Front. And we should not take all the conventional strictures on woolly-minded generals and haughty staff officers at face value. Three British divisional commanders were killed at the Battle of Loos in 1915. One of them, Major-General Sir Thompson Capper, had very pronounced views on the importance of personal leadership, and had earlier described a day of fierce fighting as one on which no good officer should be alive. Accounts of his death vary, but it seems likely that he was killed, rifle and bayonet in hand, trying to persuade a shaky company to follow him. The commander-in-chief's military secretary told King George V: 'Capper had taken every chance of being killed ever since he came out, and it was only a matter of time.' At a rather lower level, John Glubb thought that the conspicuous bravery of Billy Congreve, then brigade major, had a noticeable impact upon the whole brigade.

Courage was the stock in trade of regimental officers. Even Brigadier-General Crozier, less than impresssed by the ability of the British officer to raise and train troops, agreed that he was 'still ready to die like a hero'. Sir John French was convinced that the performance of his troops depended upon good leadership. One of his staff told the King: 'of course we know that many officers are wanted to train the new troops, but if we are sent too many inexperienced youths from the OTC [Officers' Training Corps] ... we fear that the Regiments may become sticky'. A gunner's account of his battery's fight on 21 March 1918 leaves us in no doubt as to the effect of its commander's personal courage: 'Captain Heybittle, in full view of the Germans, stood on top on No 1 gun-pit ... our superb Captain Heybittle ... Our Captain Heybittle, whose leadership on that day had been beyond praise.' An Australian soldier wrote equally lovingly of Captain H.H. Moffat.

> He must have been as tired as any of us but he kept walking up and down the platoon with a cheering word here and there, and when he saw someone breaking under the strain he would help him along by relieving him of his rifle or other accoutrement. I saw him at one time carrying three rifles, and he finished the march with one on either shoulder ... When B Company heard that he had gone the way of all good men they wept, unashamedly too. I have seen hardened soldiers with tears in their eyes when they spoke of Captain Moffat, MC.

The German army's approach to officer leadership was rather different, with platoons being commanded by those senior non-commissioned personnel of which it had such a bewildering variety. Tasks which might have been entrusted to a subaltern in the British army were carried out by a *Feldwebel*, *Fähnrich* or *Offizierstellvertreter* in the German. But

345

German officers were not backward when it came to shedding blood. During the First World War the casualty rate for German infantry as a whole was 13·9 per cent: for infantry officers it was 75·5 per cent.

The same behaviour has produced the same effect during and after the Second World War. 'If you want your men to fight to the death,' said General George S. Patton, 'then lead them. Troops are like spaghetti; you can't push them around, you have to pull them.' John Horsfall lamented the fate of Lieutenant-Colonel 'Heaver' Allen of the Inniskillings. 'When one of his companies came under spandau fire as they were crossing those wadis,' he wrote, 'Heaver felt obliged to deal with the problem personally – and so paid a soldier's forfeit.' Major-General Kurt Meyer behaved in the Lannes tradition when panic-stricken soldiers of an infantry division bolted past him in August 1944.

> I realised that something had to be done to send these men back into the line to fight. I lit a cigar, stood in the middle of the road and asked them in a loud voice if they were going to leave me alone to cope with the enemy. Hearing a divisional commander address them in this way they stopped, hesitated and returned to their positions.

The affection of Guy Sajer's comrades for their commanding officer highlights the magnetism of a brave and fair leader. 'We all loved him,' wrote Sajer, 'and felt we had a true leader as well as a friend on whom we could count. Herr Hauptmann Wesreidau was a terror to the enemy, a father to his men.'

An American regimental commander in Korea attributed his men's fighting spirit to leadership. 'The boys up there aren't fighting for democracy now,' he said, 'they're fighting because the platoon leader is leading them.' Despite all friction between regular officers and conscript soldiers during the Vietnam War, the distrust of 'John Wayneism' and the contempt for 'heroes', charismatic leaders who coupled their drive with concern for their men could still achieve results. Tim O'Brien was, like so many of his countrymen, a reluctant soldier. But even he found something admirable in his platoon commander: 'he was insanely calm. He never showed fear. He was a professional soldier, an ideal leader of men in the field ... He did not yearn for battle. But neither was he concerned about the prospect.' There was also more than a trace of the old-style paternal relationship, even in Vietnam. 'I know all those kids and nobody else can take care of 'em like I can,' a Marine lieutenant told John Parrish. 'I love them kids. They're really great little soldiers. They fight their asses off when I tell them to. I really love the ignorant little bastards.' A young marine mourned the death of his gunnery sergeant. 'Hey, Doc, our gunny got it,' he told John Parrish. 'Right through the neck. The best fuckin' gunny in the Marine Corps. Toughest mother in the valley. He was like our dad.'

The death of Lieutenant-Colonel H. Jones of 2 Para, killed assaulting an Argentinian trench at Goose Green, not only provides the most recent example of robust personal leadership but highlights an inescapable question mark which hangs over such behaviour. On the one hand, thought Marshall, 'The need that a commander be seen by his men in all circumstances of war may ... be considered irreducible.' On the other, he was sure that the commander 'who practices self-exposure to danger in the hope of having a good moral effect on men, instead frays the nerves of troops and most frequently succeeds in getting himself killed under conditions which do no earthly good to the army'. Peter Kemp's commanding officer warned his officers that they should not expose themselves rashly. 'There will, no doubt, be plenty of suitable occasions for the display of courage,' he announced; 'otherwise, an officer must keep his vanity and exhibitionism under restraint.'

The trick is, of course, for a commander to get the balance right, and to intervene personally when his presence is genuinely required, but not to risk his neck when he does not need to do so. To describe this as a supremely difficult judgment, bearing in mind not only the confusion of the battlefield but also the bewildering mixture of motives in a man's mind as he debates whether or not to go forward, is probably an understatement. Major-General Pete Rees of 19th Indian Division illustrated his own awareness of the problem when one of his staff protested that he was taking risks. 'Obviously,' he said,

> it is no use to go and get killed unnecessarily, but on the other hand, what's the use of a general who is never seen by his troops. When things are a bit grim, it does cheer the *jawans* up, I think, to know their commander realises what they're doing, but still, I promise I'll be careful.

But there are inevitably times when a commander cannot afford to be careful, and, if he is to lead effectively, he must do so from the front. The cost is often heavy. Major-General Chaim Herzog, discussing the rescue of the Israeli garrison from a small post during the 1973 war, pointed out that the rescue group was led by the brigade commander, a battalion commander and the brigade artillery commander. 'It may be that this was a very expensive method,' he wrote, 'but it is an indication of the quality of leadership in the Israeli army and the self-sacrifice of officers who would not ask others to enter an area of danger which they were not prepared to enter themselves.' Almost half the Israeli casualties in 1956 and 1967 were officers, and in 1967 eight brigade commanders or above figured amongst the 781 all ranks killed.

These Israeli figures, extreme though they are, are not untypical: for much of history heavy officer casualties have been the corollary of personal leadership. Three examples from the horse and musket period show that death did not spare senior officers, and that officers, usually comprising about 5 per cent of the forces actually engaged, became casualties in far greater proportion. At Waterloo 32 out of 63 British commanding officers were killed or wounded: the Royal Scots lost 31 out of 36 officers and the 73rd Highlanders 22 out of 26. Nearly half the 840 infantry officers who fought at Waterloo or Quatre Bras were killed or wounded, and officers made up some 10 per cent of total British losses. The French lost 5 generals, 8 colonels and 823 other officers at the storming of the Malakoff on 8 September 1855: 12 per cent of all French casualties that day were officers. During the American Civil War, Confederate officers were profligate with their lives. No less than 55 per cent of Confederate generals were killed or wounded in battle: 6 of them fell in a single charge at Franklin in 1864. Colonel George Grenfell told a foreigner that 'the only way an officer could acquire influence over the Confederate soldier was by his personal conduct under fire ... every atom of authority has to be purchased by a drop of blood'.

Both Waterloo and the Malakoff were notably bloody actions, and the officers of this era attracted fire by their conspicuous dress. Nevertheless, in the First World War, when officers in the line dressed increasingly like the men they commanded, they continued to suffer disproportionately heavily: 27 per cent of the British officers who served on the Western Front were killed, compared with 12 per cent of the men. There were times when the demands of leadership increased this proportion still further. Although almost half the men in the 143 attacking battalions which attacked on the first day of the Somme were killed or wounded, only one in four of the officers remained unhurt at the end of the day. No less than fifty-three battalion commanders or above became casualties that day, and thirty-one of them were killed.

The plight of Second World War British infantry officers was no better. John Ellis's research shows that officers, 4–5 per cent of a battalion's strength, formed 10 per cent of the killed and 7·7 per cent of the wounded in Sicily, and 8·5 per cent of the killed and 7·7 per cent of the wounded in Tunisia. In north-west Europe in 1944–5, 50 per cent of the men in 50th Division were hit, as against 65·9 per cent of the officers. For the 15th Division comparable figures were 62·9 per cent men to 72·2 per cent officers. The difference is even more marked if fatal casualties are compared. The 50th division had 8·7 per cent of its men but 16·5 per cent of its officers killed, and the 15th 16·8 per cent and 28·7 per cent respectively. In 83 days of fighting in Normandy Lord Lovat's Commando Brigade lost 53 per cent of its officers and 36 per cent of its men, a melancholy total for such a short period. Brigadier Hargest wrote sadly that:

The high percentage of officer casualties is due to the necessity of them being *always* out in front to direct advances in difficult country. Since D-Day the Div has lost 2 Brigadiers and 12 Commanding Officers ... and a great number of Coy Cmdrs and Senior NCOs.

These statistics emphasise the crushing burden of casualties sustained by Second World War infantry, a burden which fell most heavily upon its officers.

The question of the proportion of officer casualties flared into prominence in the aftermath of the Vietnam War. Not only Gabriel and Savage, but also the author of the anonymous *Self Destruction: the Disintegration and Decay of the United States Army during the Vietnam Era*, pointed out that, although the proportion of officers to soldiers was, at 1:6+, higher than the 1:14 of the Second World War and the 1:11 of Korea, officer casualties were low. Four generals and eight colonels died in Vietnam, only one of the former because of hostile fire, and the overall fatality rate was 1·82 per 1,000 for officers and 1·87 for enlisted men. The author of *Self Destruction* affirmed that 'seeing few casualties among their own officers, grunts perceived that they were being led by men who lacked dedication'. Gabriel and Savage, for their part, compared the low proportion of American officer casualties in Vietnam with the high proportion of French officer casualties at Verdun in 1916.

Lieutenant-Colonel W. D. Henderson challenged the Gabriel and Savage thesis, suggesting that Verdun was widely regarded as 'a prime example of officer failure to recognise the changing nature of warfare, thus resulting in massive and unnecessary loss of life'. He maintained that the proportion of officers to enlisted men killed in Vietnam was higher, for most officer ranks, than in the Second World War and Korea, and that it was junior officers who suffered most because the nature of the war meant that generals and colonels were safer than they had been in other conflicts.

Henderson's arguments go a great way towards rebutting the case made by Gabriel and Savage. The dispute does, however, highlight the fact that in 1968 only 80,000 combat soldiers could be produced from a total American strength in Vietnam of 543,000 men, and that those who did the fighting felt discriminated against by comparison with those who inhabited what Charles Anderson called 'the world of the rear'. The large numbers of staff jobs open to an officer corps which had greatly increased in size, together with the fact that officers spent six months rather than a year in the field, suggested to the luckless few at the sharp end that officers were not, as a whole, accepting equality of sacrifice. This belief might, as Henderson suggests, have lacked a firm foundation, but that did not prevent it from being one of the most deeply-held and durable convictions of the war.

No similar complaints arose in the Falklands. There, traditional friction between teeth and tail found expression in some resentment of HQ 5th Infantry Brigade, but there was no suggestion that officers shirked their responsibilities in action. The Battle of Goose Green was won by section commanders and private soldiers, but 2 Para's officers demonstrated that blood is the price of epaulettes: of the eighteen dead, four were officers.

It would be wrong to imply that self-sacrifice is the only attribute of leadership, or that it is only officers that lead: in the latter context, the fact that the Cameron Highlanders lost over half their forty sergeants at Waterloo, and the price paid by NCOs in the Falklands shows that chevrons come no cheaper than epaulettes. I endorse all Marshall's warnings about the futility of pointless sacrifice. Nevertheless, in the last analysis it is determined and charismatic leadership, and the selflessness and dedication that it represents, that helps to pull men through the rigours of battle.

Other qualities are also important. Technical competence, the ability to do the right thing at the right time, must rate highly. Toughness and determination, too, are qualities without which the leader is unlikely to succeed. 'Not', as Lord Carver writes, 'the toughness of a loud-mouthed bruiser, but the tensile strength of mind, body and emotions that can stand up to the stresses, strains, the slings and arrows of outrageous fortune, and lead the way through them.' Edward Gibbon's description of Alaric the Goth – 'the invincible temper of mind which rises superior to every misfortune and derives resources from adversity' – captures this quality perfectly.

Some of the accidents of birth – like an imposing physique – give a leader a head start. One of W.H.A. Groom's company commanders got on well because of a proven track record, an impressive appearance and that other useful attribute, self-confidence. 'He was', wrote Groom, 'one of the original peacetime battalion privates who had won the DCM in 1915. He had an excellent parade voice, was good-looking and popular with the rankers because he always seemed to know what he was doing and exuded confidence.'

Those of us who are less favoured by nature should take comfort from the fact that there is not a direct correlation between a man's physical characteristics and his ability to lead in battle. As Frank Richardson pointed out, many of the great leaders of history would never have stumbled past a modern medical board. A British infantryman wrote of being led to safety on the Aisne in 1918 by 'a grand officer ... He is tall and rather ugly, and always quite undisturbed, yet thinking and "all there".' Even serious character defects are not, in themselves, fatal. Philippe de Pirey's company commander, Lieutenant Arbace, was unjust to his men, bullied them and stole from them. But, somehow: 'All the atrocities of which he was accused would be forgotten in the course of an engagement with the enemy, when his courage and calmness and battle-sense won him the praise of all his men.'

The currents of leadership do not flow only in one direction. Many leaders indulge, quite consciously, in role-playing, and strive to live up to the image expected of them by their group. Lieutenant Richards, a recently-commissioned Australian officer, fumed when a proposed attack was cancelled in 1918. 'I am sorry,' he wrote,

... as I want to show my frame up over that parapet with the rest of them and let them see that I got the courage.

352

It's remarkable how our Australians stick to their officers when they have proved their gameness. They hold off until they see a man properly tested and then they love him, but if he fails them he's right out wide in their estimation.

Tom Wintringham, commanding the British Battalion of the International Brigades, believed: 'The commander of the English battalion was partly, as any commander is, a creation of his battalion, a person trying continually (if seldom consciously) to be what his men needed and unconsciously desired.' E.C. Vaughan became a successful infantry officer and won a Military Cross at Passchendaele, but in his first battle his strength flowed from his men, not vice versa.

Dully I hauled myself out of the mud and gave the signal to advance, which was answered by every man rising and stepping unhesitatingly into the barrage. The effect was so striking that I felt no more that awful dread of the shellfire, but followed them calmly into the crashing, spitting hell.

Two other motives encourage men to fight, and both are contentious, albeit in very different ways. The first is the desire for plunder. It is only in relatively recent times that systematic attempts have been made to remove the plunder motive from war. Medieval warfare offered rich bounties to those who could capture an enemy worth ransoming. Froissart regretted that, at Aljubarotta in 1385, the English and Portuguese, fearing that the tide of battle would turn against them, had slain prisoners 'for whom they might otherwise have had ransoms of 400,000 francs'. By the thirteenth century not only ransom but also looting were systematised: after the sack of Constantinople in 1204 the loot was divided up according to rank, so that 'one mounted serjeant received as much as two serjeants on foot, one knight as much as two mounted serjeants'.

Personal gain remained a major motive for mercenaries from the Middle Ages to the present day. But until the nineteenth century even the soldiers of national armies could hope for prize money in some circumstances, and for free rein in a captured town in others. Captives and the fallen alike were pillaged as a matter of course. Sergeant Wheeler reaped a fine harvest at Waterloo: 'We had a rich booty, forty double Napoleons, and had just time to strip the lace off the clothing of the dead Huzzar when we were called to join the skirmishers.' Rifleman Harris was going through a dead Frenchman's pockets when an officer of the 60th Rifles suggested that he should rip open the lining of the man's coat, 'the place where the rascals carry their coin'. Returning to his regiment expecting a reprimand, Harris was congratulated by Major Travers, who regretted that the man's purse had not been better filled.

Looting was widespread in both World Wars, whatever military law-books may have said about it. Norman Gladden spoke of the 'natural utilitarian morality' of robbing the dead. Ernst Jünger hated the practice, but did not interfere with it, on the grounds that 'what they took was doomed to waste away' in any case. T.P. Marks believed that looting was universal.

> The plain fact of the matter is that every soldier on active service has, at some time or other, laid himself open to the charge of looting. Clearly it would not be possible to punish everybody, so the practice is to make an occasional descent upon someone, and make an example of him.

When Martin Lindsay's battalion reached Germany, he decided that looting was difficult to define, and allowed his men to take bedding and furniture, luxuries, forbidden articles such as shotguns, and wine. He had already encouraged them to loot prisoners: 'They soon had a fine collection of watches, fountain pens, pocket knives and not a few French francs.' He heard one corporal, before an attack, light-heartedly warning his section against indiscriminate shooting which might damage watches or fountain-pens.

With the exception of mercenaries who may be encouraged to participate in a hazardous operation by the prospect of personal gain, it seems unlikely that modern soldiers are much influenced by the profit motive on the battlefield, They are, of course, likely to seek 'souvenirs' – especially items of an easily-negotiable sort – as some recompense for their trouble. Argentinian binoculars and bayonets appeared with remarkable rapidity amongst the militaria dealers of the Aldershot area after the Falklands War.

If the prospect of financial gain is a time-honoured inducement for soldiers, the award of decorations also has ancient origins. Though it was generally not until the nineteenth century that systems of gallantry awards in the modern sense were established, collars, arm-bands and round discs worn in a harness over the corselet were awarded by the Romans, and a variety of other honorific titles or visible distinctions were used by most armies. Napoleon believed that it was by 'such baubles' that men were led, and in so saying he showed a good grasp of psychology. For, although F.C. Bartlett believed that medals were 'psychologically useless', many more modern theorists place greater emphasis on reward-motivated behaviour.

Two striking facts emerged during my own research. The first was that, whatever men might say in public about decorations, in private they were eager to discuss them at length, and my notes on decorations eventually came to fill more index-cards than those for any other single subject. Many of those who were most vocal had themselves been decorated, and were not concerned on their own behalf. Rather, they agreed with Martin Lindsay that 'the monstrously inadequate distribution of awards to other ranks' was a flaw in the British system, and they regretted that there had not been enough awards available for the brave men that they led.

Lieutenant-Colonel Dunnington-Jefferson was a regular officer in the Royal Fusiliers before the First World War. His battalion was in India when the war broke out, and he managed to obtain an attachment to GHQ in France, where he served on the intelligence staff throughout the war. He felt decidedly uneasy at the way in which a bountiful fortune had showered decorations upon him. 'I regret to record the following awards during the Great War,' he wrote,

all of which should have gone to somebody who had earned them by fighting Germans instead of to somebody who saw very little of the front line:-
Six Mentions in Dispatches
DSO and Brevet of Major
Foreign decorations – Italian Order of St Maurice and St Lazarus; Belgian Order of the Crown and Croix de Guerre; French Legion of Honour.

The second fact is that there is no general consensus on the subject of decorations, either amongst my own interviewees or in written accounts. Many agreed with Tom Rogers's opinion that any system of decorations is: 'A *farce*. 99 per cent of soldiers are not even thinking of brave or daring acts, they are doing the job they were trained to do. Only a rare few get seen doing so and get mentioned.' The proliferation of honours is also resented. 'To those who know, the only real war decoration will be the Iron Cross, First Class, and only if worn by a Captain, Subaltern, NCO or private,' thought Rudolf Binding. He went on to complain about the creation of new honours by the German states, waxing scornful about 'the order of Prince Tomnoddy with swords'. General Trochu had levelled similar criticism against the Legion of Honour sixty years before. Things had gone wrong since the First Empire, lamented Trochu: 'A General of Brigade, in those times of open war, was content with the rank of officer in the Legion, while in our times a colonel who has not got the cross of a commander holds himself to be incomplete and wronged.'

The debasement of medals was lambasted by critics of the US Army's performance in Vietnam. Enlisted men received the Army Commendation Medal for service in Vietnam. Junior officers received the Bronze Star, while Silver Stars descended upon colonels and Distinguished Flying Crosses upon generals in remarkable profusion. By early February 1971 1,273,987 medals for bravery had been awarded, a figure which compares with 50,258 in Korea and 1,766,546 in the whole of the Second World War. Fifty-six generals had returned from Vietnam by 1969, and twenty-six of them had gained awards for valour. As only four generals died in Vietnam, only one of them from enemy fire, this was quite possibly over-egging the pudding. The cheapening of honours led one major to admit that: 'The only decorations I admire are the Distinguished Service Cross and the Medal of Honor. All others are tainted by too often being awarded to people who do not deserve them.'

On the other hand, there are numerous men who wear their decorations with great pride. Marshal Maurice MacMahon was appointed a *chevalier* of the Legion of Honour for bravery in Algeria. He freely admitted: 'Neither the Grand Cross of the Legion of Honour, nor the baton of a Marshal of France gave me as much pleasure. It's pointless to speak of the Presidency of the Republic, which was in no way agreeable to me.' Ernst Jünger won the Knight's Cross of the House of Hohenzollern, with swords. 'The war ended by giving me peculiar views as to orders and decorations,' he wrote, 'and yet I confess that I was proud to pin the enamel cross with the gold rim to my breast.' Martin Lindsay was surprised and delighted by the signal which announced the award of his DSO.

> Of course, I was astonished. It is about two years since anything really nice has happened to me. In the next hour I turned on my torch several times just to make sure I'd made no mistake. Then I gave up trying to sleep and got up and wrote and told Joyce all about it.

'I am more proud of winning a Military Cross at Passchendaele', Charles Carrington told me modestly, 'than of any other achievement in my largely un-successful career.' George Patton was warned (wrongly, as it happened) that he might not get a DSC for which he had been recommended in 1918. 'Sir,' he replied, 'I'd rather be a second lieutenant with a DSC than a general without it.'

For all the controversy surrounding them, decorations are welcomed by very many soldiers as a recompense for acts of bravery. 'Civilians may think it's a little juvenile to worry about ribbons,' wrote Bill Mauldin, 'but a civilian has a house and a bankroll to show what he's done for the past four years.' Their inequitable distribution, with officers being disproportionately favoured in either quantity or quality of award, causes bitterness, but in general they help to increase the self-esteem of individuals and the *esprit de corps* of units. Status markers, like the US army's Combat Infantryman badge are also useful, although the conditions governing their award often suffer from problems of definition which enable them to be obtained by men who have not really earned them.

What remains open to question is the extent to which the desire to obtain a medal actually influences a man's behaviour in battle. All armies have their fair share of 'pot-hunters', afflicted by what the Germans delightfully call *Brustschmerzen* – chest trouble. But few of them seem to be spurred on in battle by their desire for well-covered chests. Lieutenant-Colonel Peter Halford-Thompson was sure that he knew of one such instance.

> Hunting of decorations is a menace. A fellow officer was determined to get a bar to his MC. He became a very dangerous bore and caused many unnecessary casualties before he himself was killed. The very brave ... are often quiet people doing their job superlatively well under fire.

Siegfried Sassoon was sure that:

> Books about war psychology ought to contain a chapter on 'medal reflexes' and 'decoration complexes'. Much might be written ... about medals and their stimulating effect on those who really risked their lives for them. But the safest thing to be said is that nobody knew how much a decoration was worth except the man who received it.

James Hebron, a fire-team leader with 1/26 Marines at Khe Sanh in 1967-8, knew of a corporal in his unit who was encouraged to behave bravely by his desire for a decoration.

> This guy had firmly stated that he wanted to become a Medal of Honor winner. That was his whole raison d'etre

for being involved in the Vietnam War. He was a crazy fucker, ballsiest son of a bitch I ever met. [When he was killed] There was nobody there to write up his Medal of Honor papers.

Such instances are probably rare. More common is the paradox that men who win awards may be encouraged to behave bravely in the future, in an effort to live up to their new-found status. Such conduct can, alas, lead to eventual disaster, for the decorated man may easily feel compelled to push himself to the point where only death or a wound brings release from the breakdown he dreads.

Major Peter Cochrane won two gallantry awards, a DSO and an MC, as a subaltern in the Cameron Highlanders during the Second World War. In his book *Charlie Company* he makes a judgment which provides a fitting conclusion to this chapter. In the last analysis, he writes,

> trust depends on a man's knowing that his commander thinks of him as a person and therefore treats him fairly, and looks after him – food, weapons, clothing – as well as conditions permit.
>
> Cohesion follows as a matter of course, and this is the root of it. Men are inclined to do what their comrades expect them to do or, more accurately, because nobody actually wants to fight, they do what they imagine their comrades expect them to do ... In the good unit – and trust and cohesion both grow from and create a good unit – the assumption is, of course, that actions will be governed by those never-mentioned concepts, duty and honour.

9

I Am the Enemy

I am the enemy you killed, my friend.
I knew you in this dark; for so you frowned
Yesterday through me as you jabbed and killed.
I parried; but my hands were loath and cold.
Let us sleep now . . .

Wilfred Owen, 'Strange Meeting'

Fighting Talk

'The basic aim of a nation at war in establishing an image of
the enemy', wrote Glenn Gray, 'is to distinguish as sharply as
possible the act of killing from the act of murder by making
the former into one deserving of all honour and praise.' The
soldier goes to war with an abstract image of the enemy in his
mind's eye, an image sometimes sullied by officially-inspired
propaganda and almost always spattered by the mud thrown
by the popular press. His training will have featured 'aggressor
forces' or 'terrorists', and the very language he is encouraged
to use will suggest that he is dealing, not with another human
being thrust by the turn of the dice into a different uniform,
but with a mere object of hostility belonging to some different
tribe - almost to a another species. E.P. Thompson and Dan
Smith saw this process as a 'deformation of culture', which

makes possible a disjunction between the rationality and moral sensibility of individual men and women and the effective political and military process. A certain kind of 'realist' and 'technical' vocabulary effects a closure which seals out the imagination and prevents the reason from following the most manifest sequence of cause and consequence.

This should be no cause for astonishment. A soldier who constantly reflected upon the knee-smashing, widow-making characteristics of his weapon, or who always thought of the enemy as a man exactly like himself, doing much the same task and subjected to exactly the same stresses and strains, would find it difficult to operate effectively in battle. Any army at war is pursuing, as Clausewitz put it, state policy by other means. Its soldiers are fighting not so much individual Russians or Germans, Americans or British, but are struggling against the servants of a hostile state. Without the creation of abstract images of the enemy, and without the depersonalisation of the enemy during training, battle would become impossible to sustain. But if the abstract image is overdrawn or depersonalisation is stretched into hatred, the restraints on human behaviour in war are easily swept aside. If, on the other hand, men reflect too deeply upon their enemy's common humanity, then they risk being unable to proceed with a task whose aims may be eminently just and legitimate. This conundrum lies, like a Gordian knot linking the diverse strands of hostility and affection, at the very heart of the soldier's relationship with his enemy.

J.A. Blake maintained: 'The paramount function of language in the world of combat is its instrumentality – instigating and furthering action ... The language of combat reality is an exhortatory, private language.'[1] Even out of combat language is a tangible barrier between soldiers and outsiders. Henri Barbusse spoke of how a language 'made up of a mixture of workshop and barrack slang, and *patois*, seasoned with a few newly-coined words, binds us, like a sauce, to the compact mass of men who ... have emptied France to concentrate in the North-East'. Max Hastings described how journalists on the *Canberra* became:

> institutionalised in the midst of a large military force. We have slipped into their speech, demanding a 'wet' whenever there is tea to be had, scouring the ship for 'gash' camouflage material or arctic clothing. We agree thoughtfully that we think we could 'hack' that, a phrase I had never heard before boarding the ship except to describe journalists ...

Equipment was 'proffed' or 'rassed', a close friend was an 'oppo', worthless kit was 'binned' (by soldiers) or 'ditched' (by sailors and marines). Learning the new language takes time, and the process marks an individual's acceptance into the group. When William Manchester joined the US Marines:

> A bar was a *slopchute*, a latrine a *head*; swamps were *boon-docks*, and field boots *boondockers*. A rumour was *scuttle-butt* ... a deception was a *snow job*, gossiping was *shooting the breeze*, information was *dope*, news was *the scoop*, confirmed information was *the word*.

The language used by soldiers is liberally spiced with swear words and blasphemies, sometimes to such a degree that any honest attempt to capture it would risk being accused of gratuitous coarseness. Yet without the right language, portrayals of soldiers, whether in print or on film, lack authenticity and reality. It is only relatively recently that authors have felt able to avoid circumlocution or the discreet use of dashes. David Jones was unusually robust for his times, but he relied on cockney slang like 'you prize Maria Hunt' or near misses like 'effing'. The British soldier's language has long been colourful and descriptive, ever since the seventeeth century when, in the probably apocryphal expression, 'the army passed over into Flanders and swore horribly'. George Hennell, in common with young officers of later generations, found it all rather hard to cope with. 'The want of reflection in numbers of the men surprised me,' he wrote after the storm of Badajoz. 'They were singing and swearing and talking of having had a damned narrow escape while their comrades lay round them in heaps dead.'

In May 1916 the commander of the Australian 5th Division told his men that he was anxious 'that members of the division should drop the use of two words in particular which unfortunately are too commonly heard at the present time. Probably everyone knows that these words are F ... and B ..... They are both beastly, especially the first.' This well-intentioned attempt to clean up language was foredoomed to failure. Glenn Gray wrote:

> The most common word in the mouths of American soldiers has been a vulgar expression for sexual intercourse. This word does duty as adjective, adverb, verb, noun and in any other form it can possibly be used, however inappropriate or ridiculous in application.

He might equally well have said English-speaking soldiers in general. Birdie Smith was hitch-hiking back to his battalion in Italy when the vehicle, driven by Tiny, a New Zealander, broke down. 'The f.....g f.....'s f....d,' cursed Tiny, his remark neatly bowdlerised by Smith. It was all too much for the curé of Dickebush during the First World War.

> I have looked it up phonetically in my little English dictionary (fah-ke) and I find, to my surprise, that the word 'fake' means 'false, unreal or not true to life'. Why the soldiers should refer to us in this way is difficult to understand, and yet everywhere one hears them talk of 'fake Belgium' and 'fake Belgians'.[2]

Spicy epithets are not confined to the rank and file. Numerous officers, including a number of very distinguished ones, have sworn like the proverbial trooper: Napoleon was noted for the foulness of his language. Sergeant Wheeler was surprised to find that, at times, General Sir Frederick Adam was 'very passionate, when he will vie with any soldier under his command in swearing'. Major-General J.L. Pennefather encouraged his men at Inkerman with shouts of 'blood and 'ounds, boys'. His chief, Lord Raglan, came close to uttering the forbidden word during a conversation with Marshal Bosquet, his French counterpart, during the same battle. 'Nous sommes ... Nous sommes ... Vous avez un mot d'argot qui exprime bien ce que je veux dire,' mumbled Raglan. 'Nous sommes foutus, milord?' replied the unblushing Bosquet. 'J'espère que non.' Just as children tend to have two sets of language, one used at home and the other at school, so generations of officers have used what Robert Graves called 'unrestrainedly foul language' when speaking to their men, and a different set of language in more genteel company.

But it is in its application to weapons and their effects, and to the enemy upon whom they are used, that military language plays its most important role. The soldiers of the First World War did not die: they 'fell', were 'knocked out' or 'went under'. Germans were 'knocked over', and, in language borrowed from the shoot, some units made 'a bigger bag' than others or 'picked up' more Germans. In the Falklands, Argentinians were never killed: they were 'taken out' or 'wasted'. British troops were not shelled: they were 'brassed up', 'banjoed' or 'malleted'. The Argentinians were either the frankly derisive 'spicks' or the more neutral 'Argies'. Sometimes men use the language of sport: one brave Australian, dying game, told his mates that he was still playing and still had a jersey. At other times there are domestic or medical euphemisms, like 'disinfection', 'cleansing' and 'mopping up', which struck Norman Dixon as being of some psychological significance.

The Vietnam War highlights the way in which language both depersonalises the enemy and cloaks the act of killing in euphemisms. Tim Page told how: 'all the stoned freaks in combat were hanging out, talking about putting their weapon on rock'n roll, which means fully automatic ... Hose it down. Putting out some heavy pee, man. Zapped the Cong today. Just zonked. Copping some zees now.' For Michael Herr, fire was a 'discreet burst', a 'probe', a 'prime selection' or a 'constructive load'. Richard Falk described how replacements had to crash their way through an undergrowth of language:

They learned that grunts never die, they get 'greased'. They never said yes, they said 'That's a Roge', or 'Roger that'. ... grunts would not put on their equipment, they would 'saddle up'. They didn't stage ambushes, they 'blew bushes'. They 'humped the boonies' or 'busted bush'. Some of them never looked for the enemy, they went 'Chuck-hunting'.[3]

As for the Vietnamese, they were ginks, dinks, slants or slopes, and the Viet Cong was Charlie: sometimes, in admiration, Mr Charlie or even Sir Charlie. Weapons had names which belied their destructive nature: Puff the Magic Dragon, Gravel, Grasshopper, Walleye and Maverick.

A Noble Enemy?

'For at least a thousand years', wrote Michael Glover, 'mankind has struggled to mitigate the hardships and savagery of war.' These attempts, codified in scores of documents from the Dutch jurist Grotius's *The Laws of War and Peace* of 1625 to the recently-ratified Geneva protocols dealing with the treatment of guerrillas, have paralleled, and done little to contain, rapid increases in the destructive effects of weapons. They are also based upon a dialogue between potential and actual adversaries, a dialogue which has become increasingly difficult as political ideology has strengthened its hold upon men's minds. Thus, warned Alfred Vagts,

enemies are to be deemed criminals in advance, guilty of starting the war; the business of locating the aggressor is to begin before or shortly after the outbreak of war; the methods of the enemy in conducting the war are to be branded as criminal; and victory is not to be a triumph of honour and bravery over honour and bravery but the climax of a police hunt for bloodthirsty wretches who have violated law, order, and everything else esteemed good and holy.

These developments have meant that the soldier has for centuries been the target of advice and instruction which, however good their intentions, are both confusing and impracticable. The legitimate need to de-fuse deep-seated cultural and psychological taboos against killing is an inseparable part of military training, and we have already seen some of its consequences. This almost obligatory dehumanisation of the enemy is particularly pronounced when there are radical ideological differences between the opponents, differences which, as Vagts has suggested, may portray the enemy as the foe of civilisation and the enemy of progress, as a 'Godless Communist' or a 'Capitalist-Imperialist bloodsucker'. Racial and cultural differences accelerate this process. Eibl-Eibesfeldt warned against exactly this phenomenon of cultural pseudo-speciation: 'The fact that the other party is denied a share in our common humanity shifts the conflict to the interspecific level, and interspecific aggression is generally destructive in the animal kingdom too.' Stouffer's researches showed that, in an average American combat performance group, 44 per cent of those questioned would 'really like to kill a Japanese soldier', while another 32 per cent would 'feel that it was just part of the job, without liking it or disliking it'. In the case of a German enemy, however, while 52 per cent were prepared to kill as part of the job, only 6 per cent expressed enthusiasm at the prospect.

But at the same time that the soldier is being trained to kill, he is also instructed that there are circumstances when he must exercise restraint. Even on the medieval battlefield, where what went on was 'bloody murder' at its most horrific, there were still recognisable standards of behaviour, whose contravention would earn the offender the disapproval of chroniclers. The Swiss were notorious for refusal to give quarter, and at Courtai in 1302 the Flemings, wielding the terrible spiked maces called *godendags* – literally 'good mornings', an unsubtle Low Country jest – were more interested in braining Robert of Artois's horsemen than in collecting ransom. During the sixteenth and seventeenth centuries the introduction of a religious element into European war had much the same effect that ideology has had on more recent conflicts. Combatants might not acknowledge one another's right to be in the field at all, and would regard rough treatment of an enemy as, in Cromwell's words, 'a righteous judgement of God upon these barbarous wretches'. For all the courtesies exchanged between rival commanders during the English Civil War, Irish Catholics captured under arms in England, and Montrose's men who formally surrendered on terms at Philiphaugh in 1645, were 'knocked on the head' – another euphemism – along with their womenfolk.

It is more difficult to train soldiers in the exercise of deliberate restraint than it is to imbue them with combative zeal. In the first place, the laws of war are complex enough to generate learned debates in military journals, and as long as well-educated officers are unable to agree upon whether or not the defence of superior orders is valid in British military law, the plight of the individual rifleman must remain puzzling.[4] Secondly, the logic which underlies a nation's interpretation of the Geneva Convention may serve only to confuse the issue still further. The principle of proportionality, for example, suggests that an artillery officer who bombards a large, inhabited town because he thinks it might contain a very small party of the enemy is guilty of a war crime, because the means he uses are out of proportion to the aim he hopes to achieve. But the same nation that instructs its gunners or airmen in the principle of proportionality may also maintain weapons whose prime targets are centres of civilian population. At a lower level, a rifleman who, in frustration and despair, shoots a civilian who he believes to be a terrorist sympathiser risks a punishment which a pilot who jettisons his bombs short of the target, killing many more civilians, will be likely to escape.

Finally, although a few soldiers of victorious armies may indeed be tried for war crimes – the cases of Lieutenant Harry Morant in the Boer War and the Americans Captain Compton and Sergeant West in the Second World War attracted some publicity – in general it is the vanquished who face the tribunals. These factors combine to ensure that many soldiers, most particularly the conscript soldiers of nations which are already engaged in major war, leave for the front cherishing the image of an enemy who is 'not an individual man or woman, but a hostile power intent upon destroying our people and our lives', an enemy who is likely to fight without restraint, and against whom the most extreme measures may have to be employed. A racial, religious or ideological element will make this abstract image of the enemy seem even more inhuman: Menachem Begin's description of the Palestinians as 'beasts walking on two legs' is only one in a long line of dehumanising epithets.

This concept of a hateful and inhuman enemy rarely survives contact with him as an individual. This meeting may take some time to come, even at the front. For weeks Charles Carrington heard wagon wheels, wiring parties, coughs and sneezes, and even the sound of a sergeant-major castigating an offending soldier, until he eventually saw his first German. The first sight of a real enemy came as a strange surprise to Raleigh Trevelyan.

> He was tall and bare-headed, a well-built man with straight, fair hair. He walked towards us, apparently quite composed, without even lifting his hands. The situation was ridiculous. We stood there as he approached, feeling like children in our nervous excited state, guilty children who have been caught with cigarettes in their mouths.

At last the enemy has a human face. 'The essence of the concrete image', argued Gray, 'is the realisation that the enemy is neither entirely evil nor entirely different from oneself – as portrayed in simple abstract images – but a complex being of both good and bad impulses.' King George's men soon established a good working relationship with the Corsican ogre's troops in Spain. Wheeler found himself on a boat with some wounded and prisoners, and soon struck up a friendship with a Frenchman. 'The French corporal', he wrote, 'could speak English well, was about three years older than myself, as light hearted and merry companion as I could wish.' Edward Costello and his comrades established 'a very amicable feeling' for the French, 'apart from duty in the field'. Pickets and outposts regularly fraternised, and it was the height of boorishness to fire upon sentries: when a major move was imminent, the opposing outposts would usually be given a chance to decamp.

During the First World War the way in which trench warfare forced the adversaries to live within literally a stone's throw of each other helped break down the barriers created by rumour and propaganda. How could one hate a man who shouted: 'Good morning, Tommy, have you any biscuits?' Or another who shared a common passion: 'It is I, Fritz the Bunmaker of London. What is the Football news?' Small wonder that Bill, the most aggressive man in his section – and a Chelsea supporter, though doubtless those two facts are not related – was nonplussed to discover that his opposite number also supported Chelsea. 'A blurry supporter of blurry Chelsea,' he muttered. ''E must be a damned good sort of sausage eater.'[5] Lieutenant-Colonel Arthur Osburn thought that some German troopers captured in one of the first battles of the war were 'Bavarian ploughboys in German uniforms', ordinary fellows caught up by something beyond their control.

Colonel W.N. Nicholson observed that this sort of attitude actually made things more difficult for senior commanders. 'It is a commentary on modern war that commanders should fear lest the soldiers on each side become friendly,' he wrote. 'Our soldiers had no quarrel with "Fritz" save during the heat of battle or in retaliation for some blow below the belt.' Brigadier-General Count Gleichen, going round the trenches one day, asked a man if he had shot any Germans. The man replied that there was a bald, bearded gentleman opposite, who often showed himself over the parapet. 'Well, why don't you shoot him?' asked Gleichen. 'Shoot him,' said the man, 'why, Lor' bless you sir, 'e's never done me no harm.' Lord Moran had seen 'more cold cruelty in a month of the competitive life of London in peace than came my way in more than two years with a battalion in war'. He believed that hatred, whipped up by atrocity stories, was 'the big blunderbuss in the armoury of those in authority, to be fired off whenever they wished to stiffen the people against the enemy'.

There were, as Tony Ashworth has described, other ways of ensuring that the men at the front did not become so friendly that they forgot to fight: the generally unpopular policy of raiding, and the use of trench-mortars and artillery to goad the enemy into a response which broke local truces, were just two of the methods employed. It was easier for regulars, who felt that their professional standards demanded that they remain aggressive. But, as one of them explained, the fact that he was a regular did not endow him with any feelings of hostility. He had: 'None whatever, sometimes a chummy feeling ... At night I would fire short bursts (Pom-tiddly-pom-pom, pom-pom). Back would come the answer, and I often thought how I would like to have met my opposite gunner – probably a lousy young corporal like me.' Ernst Jünger, too, strove to maintain professional standards. 'It has always been my ideal in war', he wrote, 'to eliminate all feelings of hatred and to treat my enemy as an enemy only in battle and to honour him as a man according to his courage.' A Commando officer who organised an ambush on D-Day said that in doing so he had: 'Nothing personal against the Germans, but we thought that if we set up a decent ambush we might be able to shoot a few.'

During the Second World War, although the real issues dividing the British and the Germans were more marked than in the First, hostility often evaporated with personal contact. M. Warner saw his first Germans on D-Day. They were prisoners, the first of them 'a burly, ruddy-faced corporal in torn and dusty uniform ... These men appear to be all ages, some look decent chaps, all are very straight-faced.' Later, the searching of prisoners served to emphasise their common humanity.

> Old chap of fifty empties his pockets, including his photos of wife and kiddy and his old pipe. Realise more than ever this business is crazy ... The prisoners all have a wallet of photos, just as we carry, and we let them keep them, also

their little boxes of tobacco. The thought often comes into my mind: 'Are these chaps so different to us?' It is their leaders like ours who can kid us up. They have the same love of home and family as us.

There were quiet periods even on the Eastern Front, where the combination of ideology, racialism and revenge usually made the fighting far more bitter than it was in the west. Guy Sajer recalled that Russians were not shot at during one quiet period. 'We just couldn't shoot them,' said a German. 'For once, let's all stick our noses out without getting a bullet between the eyes.' Once, in dreadful conditions, Sajer and his comrades shared their rations with some Russian prisoners.

We all grinned at each other without distinction, like players from two teams in the showers after a match. There was no longer any feeling of hatred or vengeance, only a sense of life preserved and overwhelming exhaustion ... We were able to forget the hate which divided us, as our stupefied senses reawakened to an awareness of life.

The British forces in the Falklands were regulars, were subjected to no official hate-propaganda, and little of the Argie-bashing of the popular press rubbed off on them. As far as most of them were concerned, the Argentinians were cyphers. 'I felt neither hatred nor friendliness towards the Argentinians,' said Corporal Harry Siddall of 45 Commando. 'I simply thought about the job in hand, and they happened to be in the way of getting the job done.' A soldier in 2 Para admitted that he had 'always hated them', until 'you saw what sad creatures they were when you went through a position'. Another thought they were nothing more nor less than Figure 11 [man-shaped] targets: they were on the position being attacked, so would have to be disposed of. A platoon commander in 3 Para was more philosophical. 'The poor buggers were there because they'd been sent there,' he said. 'Those guys had been rubber dicked.'

Often it is adversity that strikes the chord of humanity. John Shipp, waiting while a fort was bombarded in India, was painfully reminded of what was happening inside it. 'Even at that distance,' he wrote, 'we could distinctly hear the cries of the wounded, and knew from our own experience what they must be suffering.' As Norman Gladden watched the British barrage he thought of 'the unfortunate enemy caught in such a storm of death', and E.C. Vaughan, seeing a German counter-attack flayed by fire, 'felt terribly sorry for them, for they looked very new and untried, and I was so tired and weary myself'. Marc Bloch threw a grenade at a group of Germans, and terrible cries followed its explosion: 'Although we had become terribly hardened, my blood froze.' An American infantryman experienced the same sensation in Vietnam:

> One day during a fire fight, for the first time in my life, I heard the cries of the Vietnamese wounded, and I understood them. When somebody gets wounded, they call out for their mothers, their wives, their girl friends. There I was listening to the VC cry for the same things. That's when the futility of the war really dawned on me.

Soon, far from hating his enemy, the soldier may come to respect him for his fighting qualities. 'Ours was indeed a noble enemy,' declared Edward Costello. Horace Churchill could not help admiring the big *cuirassiers* who came on, time and time again, into the musketry at Waterloo. 'Never was such devotion witnessed as the French *cuirassiers*,' he wrote. 'I could not help exclaiming when the mêlée was going on, "By God, those fellows deserve Bonaparte, they fight so nobly for him."' A British officer spoke admiringly of the German machine-gunners who remained faithful unto death. 'Topping fellows. Fight until they are killed. They gave us hell.' James Jack could not disguise his professional respect for the conduct of the German rearguards in the withdrawal to the Aisne in 1914. 'On the whole, though,' he wrote, 'their rear-guards have put up a fine defence – in many cases a superb defence.' T.E. Lawrence gave unstinted praise to the German detachments who alone held together amidst the rout of the Turkish Fourth Army in October 1918.

I grew proud of the enemy who had killed my brothers. They were two thousand miles from home, without hope and without guides, in conditions bad enough to break the bravest nerves. Yet their sections held together, sheering through the wrack of Turk and Arab like armoured ships, high-faced and silent. When attacked they halted, took position, fired to order. There was no haste, no crying, no hesitation. They were glorious.

C.E. Montague heard a Highlander in the postwar army of occupation tell a stout burgher: 'Och, dinna tak' it to hairt, mon. I tell ye that your lads were grond.' Nor was this admiration one-sided. A German soldier paid tribute to the men of 2nd Battalion, the Rifle Brigade, at Aubers Ridge in 1915. 'Almost every single man of them', he wrote, 'had to be put out of action with hand grenades. They were heroes all, brave and true to the end, until death.'

David Jones included 'the enemy front fighters who shared our pains against whom we found ourselves by misadventure' in his dedication to *In Parenthesis*. John Horsfall's *The Wild Geese are Flighting* was dedicated to 'our friends, and adversaries, who fought in the line in Tunisia, and whom we left behind us,' reflecting Horsfall's own high regard for his enemy. The men of Lieutenant-Colonel Walter Koch's 5th Parachute Regiment were, Horsfall acknowledged, dangerous as enemies, but 'they fought a clean war, and pleasantries were passed whenever the circumstances permitted'. Brigadier Derek Mills-Roberts respected the bravery of the crew of a German self-propelled gun which had got right into his lines in Normandy: 'It takes courage to drive a self-propelled gun into an enemy area without infantry protection. We buried them in the field where we had made a place for our own dead.' For John Roberts, the war held:

No personal hostility whatever. Indeed, when an enemy position had been taken, one tended to take the same attitude of care and welfare to the dead and wounded as if they belonged to our own side. There was an abhorrence of

373

any maltreatment of prisoners ... especially when they had put up a good fight.

I have encountered few British veterans of the Second World War who have much affection for the Japanese. 'If one of them passed by this minute,' snapped one, 'I would cheerfully saw his head off and roll it in the gutter.' The differences in race and culture, and the expression that these found in Japanese treatment of Allied prisoners of war, remain an obstacle to understanding or forgiveness as far as many survivors are concerned. Although Japanese harshness had a long-established cultural basis, aggression was encouraged by hate propaganda. Colonel Masonobu Tsuji, who masterminded Japanese planning for the invasion of Malaya, wrote a tract designed, amongst other things, to screw his soldiers to a pitch of fighting fury.

When you encounter the enemy after landing, think of yourself as an avenger come at last face to face with your father's murderer. Here is the man whose death will lighten your heart of its burden of brooding anger. If you fail to destroy him utterly you can never rest in peace.

But if affection for the Japanese is rare, there is more than a trace of admiration in the accounts of some Allied survivors. Kenneth Harrison fought in Malaya as a sergeant in an Australian anti-tank battery, and afterwards endured the rigours of captivity. For him, the Japanese

came in all sizes and shapes and most were barbaric and sadistic ...

But good or bad, kind or sadistic, they had one supreme virtue – in the final analysis their Sun God imbued each and every one of them with a courage that I believe to be unequalled in our time.

Whatever their other qualities might be, to me they are – with envy – the brave Japanese.

Denis Sheil-Small felt sorry for dead Japanese until he remembered what the Japanese had done to their prisoners. Even so, he was impressed by the courage they showed in recovering their dead: 'One must grudgingly admit that they showed great bravery on these occasions and also in their efforts to succour their wounded.' Lieutenant Meredith Caldwell of Merrill's Marauders witnessed the death of two Japanese observers who had remained hidden in an American position. 'If they'd been in our army,' he affirmed, 'they'd have got the Congressional Medal of Honor.'

There are flickers of admiration for the enemy in a variety of post-1945 conflicts. Bob Sanders thought that the Viet Cong fighting 'was good. "Sir Charlie," that was what we called him. We respected Charlie.' John Akehurst quotes Captain Ian Gardiner's opinion of his adversaries in Dhofar, revealing a relationship based on hostility mixed with affection, similar to that between nineteenth-century British officers and their tribal opponents on the North-West Frontier of India.

> Their personal mobility was superb and their eye for ground was faultless. Whenever we moved they seemed to be watching us and waiting for a tactical mistake to exploit. If the opportunity came they pounced ... As men the *adoo* were truly remarkable. It would be an honour to command such a group.

Rick Jolly and his comrades had mixed feeling as HMS *Exeter*'s Sea Dart claimed a high-flying Argentinian aircraft:

> the crew must have seen their deaths coming for ten or fifteen seconds. What a way to die! ... Once again we are up against the paradox of war. We can admire our enemies, even respect their courage and skill, but also cheer when they are removed violently from the battlefield.

A Bad Thing to Do

This vision of the noble adversary is, alas, no more durable than that of the inhuman enemy. Some soldiers do feel hatred for their enemies, if only briefly and for a specific reason; others never rid themselves of the abstract image of hostility; most apply the hard logic of the battlefield, which makes surrendering in combat a hazardous business; and still others display what R.H. Tawney called 'joyful cunning in destruction'.

Fred Majdalany stressed that 'most of the killing you do in modern war is impersonal ... Very few men – even in the Infantry – actually have the experience of aiming a weapon at a German and seeing the man fall.' Most of the veterans I interviewed were infantrymen with front-line service, yet fewer than half of them believed that they had actually killed an enemy, and often this belief was based on the thinnest of evidence. 'I like to think I killed a few,' said one parachutist. 'Certainly I fired a hell of a lot of rounds and I must have got lucky with some of them.'

The act of killing is often so blurred by the distance separating killer and victim that it seems like a game, or is swamped by a feeling of technical satisfaction in marksmanship. The future Field-Marshal Slim shot a Turk in Mesopotamia in 1917. 'I suppose it is brutal,' he wrote, 'but I had a feeling of the most intense satisfaction as the wretched Turk went spinning down.' An Australian soldier described shooting Turks as being 'just like potting kangaroos in the bush'. 'It's great fun shooting human rabbits,' said J.E.H. Neville. Lieutenant Bill Little of the Fort Garry Horse reached the back of the village of St Aubin in his Sherman tank on D-Day just as the German garrision was evacuating it. At first he thought that the cluster of men were friends, but then:

> lo and behold I could see the coalscuttle helmets ... They were Germans ... The excitement was just fantastic, and I talked to my other tank and said ... 'Let 'em have it.' Well then, it was just a real bird shoot ... This was the first time

we'd actually hit German soldiers and the exhilaration, after all the years of training, the tremendous feeling of lift, of excitement, of exhilaration, it was like the first time you go deer hunting.

Two of the Green Berets interviewed by D.M. Mantell used the same analogy. 'It's an accomplishment, more or less stalking a person, stalking something live, just like going hunting for deer.' 'Did you ever go deer hunting?' asked another. 'You lead. It's just a lucky shot. Felt like having a party. Just a freak, lucky shot.' The much-decorated Staff-Sergeant Patrick Tadina said that he did not particularly like killing people, 'just outsmarting them'. At the time he was credited with killing 109 Viet Cong.

Even the antisepsis of distance is no guarantee that a sense of clinical detachment will prevail, and the sensations which accompany the first kill can be traumatic. The first time that Edward Costello shot a Frenchman he was overcome with horror. 'I reproached myself as his destroyer,' he wrote. 'An indescribable uneasiness came over me, I felt almost like a criminal.' A First World War Australian sniper recalled how, after shooting a German observer: 'a queer thrill shot through me, it was a different feeling to that which I had when I shot my first kangaroo when I was a boy. For an instant I felt sick and faint; but the feeling soon passed; and I was my normal self again, and looking for more shots.' G.T. Rudge was a seventeen-year-old private in the Essex Regiment when he killed a German on the Somme. 'This was the first time I had killed anybody and when things quietened down I went and looked at a German I knew I had shot,' he said. 'I remember thinking that he looked old enough to have a family and I felt very sorry.' 'I'll tell you a man sure feels funny inside', remarked an American infantryman, 'the first time he squeezes down on a Kraut.'

Hand-to-hand fighting is rarer than Hollywood might lead us to suppose. Indeed, it has probably been the exception rather than the rule from the eighteenth century onwards, for, as Ardant du Picq pointed out, one side or the other usually recalls an urgent appointment elsewhere before bayonets cross. 'Each nation in Europe', he wrote, 'says:. "No one stands his ground before a bayonet charge made by us." And all are right.' General Trochu saw only one bayonet fight in his whole career, when the 3rd *Chasseurs-à-Pied* and 6th of the Line accidentally collided with a Russian regiment in the fog at Inkerman. 'This was not, strictly speaking, a "charge bayonets",' said a Confederate colonel of an attack at Fort Donelson, 'but it would have been one if the enemy had not fled.'

Edward Costello argued that bayonets were vital for their moral effect. They were rarely pushed home, but 'the bayonets had better remain in present use until such time as we can bargain with the French or other enemies to disuse them'. Hohenlohe-Ingelfingen agreed: 'he who has not made up his mind to come at last to the bayonet can never win, for he can have no serious intention to assault'. Fred Majdalany knew that there was:

> A lot of loose talk about the use of the bayonet. But relatively few soldiers could truthfully say that they had stuck a bayonet into a German. It is the threat of the bayonet and the sight of the point that usually does the work. The man almost invariably surrenders *before* the point is stuck into him.

R.G. Lee's recent *Introduction to Battlefield Weapons Systems and Technology* takes much the same tone. 'The fixing of bayonets is more than a fixing of steel to the rifle since it puts iron into the soul of the soldier doing the fixing,' wrote Lee. The bayonet was 'an emotive rather than a seriously practical weapon'.

But for all this, there are times, even in very recent wars, when men have fought hand to hand: men were killed with the bayonet in both Vietnam and the Falklands. The feeling of killing a man in close combat is a very personal one indeed. Stephen Westman was a lance-corporal in the German infantry in 1915. 'We got the order to storm a French position, strongly held by the enemy,' he wrote, and during the ensuing mêlée a French corporal suddenly stood before me, both our bayonets at the ready, he to kill me, I to kill him. Sabre duels in Freiburg had taught me to be quicker than he and pushing his weapon aside I stabbed him through the chest. He dropped his rifle and fell, and the blood shot out of his mouth. I stood over him for a few seconds and then I gave him the *coup de grâce.* After we had taken the enemy position, I felt giddy, my knees shook, and I was actually sick.

The dead Frenchman haunted Westman's dreams for many nights thereafter. I.L. Idriess of the 5th Australian Light Horse described bayonet fighting during the first battle of Gaza in March 1917 as:

just berserk slaughter. A man sprang at the closest Turk and thrust and sprang aside and thrust again and again ... the grunting breaths, the gritting teeth and the staring eyes of the lunging Turk, the sobbing scream as the bayonet ripped home ... Bayonet-fighting is indescribable – a man's emotions race at feverish speed and afterwards words are incapable of describing feelings.

Despite all the bayonet training that soldiers received, in close combat they very often reversed their weapons and used them as clubs. Prince Frederick Charles asked a German infantryman why he did this. 'I don't know,' replied the soldier. 'When you get your dander up the thing turns round in your hand of itself.' The Germans seem to have had a positive preference for using the butt rather than the bayonet. Indeed, the difference in French and German styles of hand-to-hand fighting is epitomised in the different design of their First World War infantry weapons. The French Lebel mounted a long needle-bayonet, while the most common of the many variants of bayonet for the German Mauser 98 was the massive 'butcher's knife'. In close-in trench fighting, the Germans preferred clubs, coshes and sharpened spades, the French knives and daggers.

For some, killing has a satisfaction that goes far beyond the pleasure of the rifle range or the duck shoot. Erich Fromm saw it as 'one way of experiencing that one *is* and that one can produce an effect on another human being'. A GI spoke of killing at My Lai as being like 'scratching an itch ... it's going to drive you mad unless you do it', and another compared it to the closely-linked guilt and satisfaction which accompany masturbation. 'I could kill a VC right now,' a Green Beret told D.M. Mantell. 'Being a combat soldier was one of the most rewarding experiences of my life.'

Killing is easier if the opponent looks like a soldier. Combatants on both sides in the First World War recognised that the introduction of the steel helmet marked a deepening of hostility. Edmund Blunden was sorry to see helmets replace 'friendly soft caps', and thought that the change marked a transition from a 'personal crusade into a vast machine of violence'. For Ernst Jünger, the appearance of the helmet marked the new era of bureaucratically-organised violence: the Somme was the turning point. 'After this battle,' he wrote, 'the German soldier wore the steel helmet.' Brigadier Peter Young, in the Second World War, had no more regret about shooting a helmeted German than he would about 'banging a nail on the head'. But somehow he could never bring himself to shoot a bareheaded man. Corporal Charles McCartin, an American who survived the 'Death March' on Bataan in 1942, watched Japanese soldiers in trucks hitting men over the head as they passed. 'They seemed especially to pick on Americans wearing steel helmets,' he said. 'Since I too was wearing a helmet, I stayed away from the trucks after I saw the first incident.'[6]

It is not surprising that the helmet helps promote hostility, for part of the purpose of military uniform is to define the wearer's warrior status and to impress opponents, and the steel helmet, with its medieval overtones, does so particularly well. Military equipment also signals that its wearer is a soldier: German packs, made of hide with the hair still attached, radiated a feral aura which British soldiers found peculiarly hostile. Small wonder that soldiers who surrender – and survive the experience – not only throw away their weapons, but also discard their packs and helmets. They may also, if they are wise, strive to appease their captors. Eighteenth-century officers used to hold out their purses and watches. Twentieth-century soldiers, like those described by Jünger, used a similar tactic: 'Most of them showed by their confident smiles that they trusted in us as human beings. Others held out cigarettes and chocolates in order to conciliate us.' When male Barbary apes wish to approach a senior male, they borrow a young animal which they carry, in order to inhibit the senior's aggression. Some soldiers do likewise. A British infantryman watched Germans emerging from a dugout to surrender on the Somme: 'They were holding up photographs of their families and offering watches and other valuables in an attempt to gain mercy but as the Germans came up the steps, a soldier, not from our battalion, shot each one in the stomach with a burst from his Lewis gun.'

This incident illustrates all too clearly that surrendering during battle is a difficult business. Charles Carrington suggested, 'No soldier can claim a right to "quarter" if he fights to the extremity.' T.P. Marks saw seven German machine-gunners shot. 'They were defenceless,' he wrote, 'but they have chosen to make themselves so. We did not ask them to abandon their guns. They only did so when they saw that those of us who were not mown down were getting closer to them and that the boot was now on the other foot.' Ernst Jünger agreed that the defender had no moral right to surrender in these circumstances:

the defending force, after driving their bullets into the attacking one at five paces' distance, must take the consequences. A man cannot change his feelings again during the last rush with a veil of blood before his eyes. He does not want to take prisoners but to kill.

During the cavalry action at Moncel on 7 September 1914 Sergeant James Taylor of the 9th Lancers saw how difficult it was to restrain excited men. 'Then there was a bit of a mêlée,'

he said, 'horses neighing and a lot of yelling and shouting ...
I remembered seeing Corporal Bolte run his lance right
through a dismounted German who had his hands up and
thinking that this was rather a bad thing to do.' Harold Dearden, a medical officer on the Western Front, read a letter
written by a young soldier to his mother. 'When we jumped
into their trench, mother, they all held up their hands and
shouted "Camerad, Camerad," and that means "I give in" in
their language,' it ran. 'But they had to have it, mother. I
think that is all from your loving Albert.'

In the First World War, both sides habitually bombed
dugouts containing men who might have surrendered had
they been given a chance to do so. A British soldier, newly
captured in March 1918, told his captor that there were some
wounded in one of the dugouts: 'He took a stick grenade out,
pulled the pin out and threw it down the dug-out. We heard
the shrieks and were nauseated, but we were completely powerless. But it was all in a *mêlée* and we might have done the
same in the circumstances.' The remarkable thing about the
German March offensive was not how many British soldiers
were killed while trying to surrender, but how few. Survivors'
testimony indicates that the Germans were remarkably scru-
pulous about accepting surrender in circumstances when, in
hot blood, they might easily have killed out of hand. Private
J. Parkinson was changing belts on his machine-gun when a
German officer put a pistol in his back and said: 'Come along,
Tommy. You've done enough.' Parkinson rightly commented
that the officer 'must have been a real gentleman'.

No soldier who fights until his enemy is at close small-arms
range, in any war, has more than perhaps a fifty-fifty chance
of being granted quarter. If he stands up to surrender he risks
being shot with the time-honoured comment, 'Too late,
chum'. If he lies low, he will fall victim to the grenades of the
mopping-up party, in no mood to take chances. Ironically,
once he has had his surrender accepted, the prisoner of war is
likely to be well treated by his former adversaries, and to
experience increasingly worse treatment as he goes back along
the enemy's lines of communication. E.C. Vaughan's men

shared shell holes with their prisoners, and 'made a great fuss of them, sharing their scanty rations with them'. Major Vandeleur of the Cameronians was well treated by his captors in August 1914, only to have his greatcoat stolen off him when he was half-way back to Germany.

This inclination to take no risks is often stropped to a sharp edge by the stories about misuse of the white flag which are such a frequent accompaniment of war. The British cavalry who charged the Boers at Elandslaagte in October 1899 were reluctant to take prisoners, for word had just gone out that the Boers had fired on a party of British who went forward to accept their surrender. White-flag stories were common during the First World War, and appeared again in the Second. During the Falklands War, Lieutenant Jim Barry of 2 Para was shot dead moving up to accept the surrender of a group of Argentinians at Goose Green, and the popular press complained bitterly that the white flag had been abused.

There may perhaps have been some instances when feigned surrender has been employed as a stratagem, but these are few and far between. Genuine misunderstandings – like the Goose Green affair – are far more common, as James Jack noted in his diary in 1914.

> We have had several unfortunate – and I think very stupid – incidents due to our troops leaving their trenches to 'accept the surrender' of Germans approaching under a white flag. Others of the enemy, having no intention of giving in, thereupon opened fire upon friend and foe with dire results to both.

It was not only Germans that believed it their duty to stop impromptu surrenders by firing on the participants. Captain W. Tickler of the 5th Lancashire Fusiliers saw a German officer taking the surrender of a British sergeant and some of his men at Passchendaele in 1917. 'So I screamed across at this bloke, "What the hell are you doing giving yourselves up?" I didn't wait for him to answer me, I just let fly with my revolver. I was aiming at the German officers, but they were all mixed up together.' One of Charles MacDonald's platoon commanders encountered the same problem in reverse in 1945. 'Some of them wanted to surrender,' he said, 'but every time a kraut would jump out of his hole to surrender, some other kraut s.o.b. would shoot him right in the back.'

Armies are naturally eager to avoid any ambiguity about the question of surrender, and, understandably enough, encourage their soldiers to regard an enemy as hostile unless it is quite obvious that he has stopped fighting. A GHQ order of August 1916 was blunt. It was the duty of troops to use their weapons against the enemy:

> until it is beyond all doubt that these have not only ceased all resistance, but ... that they have definitely and finally abandoned all hope or intention of resisting further. In the case of apparent surrender, it lies with the enemy to prove his intention beyond the possibility of misunderstanding, before the surrender can be accepted as genuine.

The same logic applied amongst the rocks of Tumbledown and Mount Longdon. 'What was I meant to do,' one soldier asked me rhetorically, 'creep around their bunkers and ask if they'd decided to jack in, and would they mind coming out? Of course not. You've got to go in hard, and you can't afford to fuck about.'

Sometimes prisoners are simply a nuisance. In one attack, Jünger's men would take none, 'for how could we get them through the barrage? It was bad enough on our own without prisoners to see to.' During the Second World War, Brigadier Fitzroy Maclean, head of the British military mission to Yugoslavia, asked a Russian officer how they dealt with prisoners. 'If they surrender in large groups,' replied the Russian, 'we send them back to base; but if ... there are only a few of them, we don't bother.' Later Maclean saw a row of corpses, 'like ninepins knocked over by the same ball. They had clearly not died in battle.' This led him to speculate as to how many actually comprised a large group.

On some occasions the killing of prisoners is an open secret:

on others, officers see exactly what is going on. C.A. McDow-all, newly commissioned into the Burma Frontier Force in 1940, dealt effectively with attacks on the Indian community by rioters. 'I did what I could to help,' he wrote, 'and we caught one or two of the thugs and gave them a thorough thrashing, tied to a tree, while some others happened to get shot under circumstances into which I did not enquire too closely.' During an attack on a cold, snowy night, Charles MacDonald sent two men off with a wounded prisoner. They were soon back. 'To tell you the truth, Cap'n, we didn't get to A Company,' said one. 'The sonofabitch tried to make a run for it. Know what I mean.' Some months later, one of his sergeants told MacDonald over the radio that he had cap-tured three prisoners but could not withdraw with them. 'Roger,' answered MacDonald, 'do what you can.' The pla-toon returned without its prisoners. 'Today Company G com-mitted a war crime,' wrote MacDonald. 'They are going to win the war, however, so I don't suppose it matters.' During the British Commando raid on Vaagso in December 1941 a German sailor threw a hand-grenade at Lieutenant-Colonel J.F. Durnford-Slater, missed, and raised his hands. A sergeant advanced upon the sailor, rifle at the hip. 'Nein, nein,' cried the sailor. 'Ja, ja!' replied Sergeant Mills, and shot him. 'Yeah, well, Mills, you shouldn't have done that,' said Durnford-Slater.

Reluctance to accept surrender, or bitterness against men who have clearly ceased fighting, is fuelled on the one hand by the racial and ideological factors which we have already noted, and on the other by a sense of personal animus which stems from a particular incident. In the American Civil War, Major-General Ben Butler earned notoriety in the Confeder-acy for ordering that any woman of New Orleans who insulted a Union soldier was to be regarded as 'a woman of the town plying her avocation'. His decision cost lives, for, as a Louis-iana *zouave* recounted, when a Union soldier threw down his arms in a battle soon afterwards and called for quarter, 'I say no quatta for de Bootla. I stick wid de bayonet.'

The death of a friend or relative is a more common reason

for this sort of behaviour. Edward Costello saw a Portuguese soldier who had returned home to find his parents murdered and his sister dying fling himself on a line of passing French prisoners, killing one and wounding another before the escort could stop him. W.H.A. Groom witnessed a party of Germans run up to surrender, throwing off their packs and helmets. Then: 'One of our men, not in my platoon, quite near me shot and killed at close range one of the Germans running with his hands in the air and I heard him say, "That's for my brother."' In the autumn of 1942, Guy Sajer saw a wounded man knife a Russian prisoner in a fury, despite the efforts of other Germans to stop him. William Manchester recorded how, on Okinawa in 1945, 'Bob Fowler, F Company's popular, towheaded commander, had bled to death after being hit in the spleen. His orderly, who adored him, snatched up a submachine gun and unforgivably massacred a line of unarmed Japanese soldiers who had just surrendered.' 'I was so pissed off when my buddy got it', remarked an American soldier in Vietnam, 'that I blew up two kids riding a water buffalo.'

Soldiers who man bogey weapons may find it hard to have their surrender accepted. Blaise de Montluc warned his readers against despising their enemies. Arquebusiers, however, were different: Montluc made a point of hanging them whenever he caught them, because they used a weapon that he regarded as inhuman. 'Would to heaven that this accursed engine had never been invented,' he complained. 'I had not then received those wounds which I now languish under, neither had so many valiant men been slain for the most part by the pitiful fellows and the greatest cowards.' During the First World War, enemy machine-gunners were often regarded as an admirable foe. 'Real professionals,' said one veteran, 'they were a pleasure to fight.' Trench-mortar men were far less respected. Disliked by their own side because of the shelling that their activities often provoked, they were hated as well as feared by their opponents. Edmund Blunden was annoyed when a flimsy trench was shelled by *minenwerfers*: 'for once a little hate was possible', he wrote. 'To throw minnies into that ghost of a front line!' The Germans used a buried wooden mortar to bombard British lines at Fricourt on the Somme with large explosive canisters. When the Royal Welch Fusiliers attacked on 1 July they overran the weapon. 'The crew offered to surrender,' wrote Robert Graves, 'but our men had sworn for months to get them.'

A variety of other weapons have brought misfortune to their users. Some British tank-crews at Cambrai in 1917 were killed or beaten up by the Germans who had been so terrified of these 'fire-vomiting iron dragons'. Germans carrying the saw-backed pioneer bayonet for the Mauser KAR 98 were often brutally treated by captors who thought that the weapon was deliberately designed to cause added suffering, and flame-thrower operators were detested – and very occasionally burned alive after capture – in both World Wars.

It is their organisation and tactics, rather than their weapons, which make irregulars – partisans, guerrillas, call them what you will – susceptible to harsh treatment. The French did not regard Spanish guerrillas as legitimate combatants during the Peninsular War, and were similarly brusque in their treatment of German irregulars in 1813–14. Conversely, when the Germans were attacked by French *francs-tireurs* in 1870–1, they responded violently. 'We are hunting them down pitilessly,' said Bismarck. 'They are not soldiers; we are treating them as murderers.' It only needs a few partisan attacks for soldiers to be ready to over-react at the slightest provocation unless they are very carefully controlled. Fritz Nagel and his comrades found rumours of Belgian partisans particularly unsettling in 1914: these stories produced 'savage and merciless slaughter at the slightest provocation'. Stephen Westman agreed that civilians were sometimes shot: 'But I know how it felt to be fired on from behind by snipers and the rage into which the soldiers were driven when they saw their comrades killed right and left by men who claimed for themselves to be treated as "non combatants".'

Historically, officially-applied atrocity has occasionally been defended on the same grounds used to justify harsh and exemplary punishment: that it has a deterrent effect and therefore saves lives in the long run. A fifteenth-century French commander massacred civilians in the Pyrenees, and urged that his action should not be misjudged. 'Do not think', he said, '... that I caused this slaughter to be made so much out of revenge for the wound I had received as to strike terror into the country, that they might not dare to make head against our army.' For centuries it was customary to summon a fortress or town to surrender once a practicable breach had been made in its walls and assault was imminent. Lawyers quibbled as to the precise meaning of 'practicable breach'. Some said that it was a breach up which a horseman could ride, while others maintained that men should be able to walk through it without using their hands. Should the governor refuse to surrender, he and his garrison could be killed out of hand when the place was stormed. Cromwell summoned Drogheda on 10 September 1649. His initial assault was repulsed, but the town was stormed two days later and the garrison was put to the sword: perhaps 4,000 soldiers and civilians perished.

This dreadful policy was designed to save life rather than to take it. The logic of it was that a garrison, by refusing to surrender once a breach had been made, was behaving unreasonably. The attackers would ultimately win, and a last-ditch defence would simply cause needless casualties. Wellington believed that had he slaughtered the garrison of Ciudad Rodrigo he would have saved 5,000 Allied lives at Badajoz, which would have capitulated when summoned. As late as 1820 he maintained that 'the practice which refuses quarter to a garrison that stands an assault is not a *useless* effusion of blood'.

But this sort of behaviour, whether it results from rational calculation, personal or collective fury, or even criminal malice, invites reprisal and risks initiating the ghastly round of atrocity and counter-atrocity, with rumour playing its own deadly part. In his book *Humanity in Warfare*, Geoffrey Best quotes a line from John Roebuck's review of Napier's *Peninsular War*: 'Cruelty begets cruelty – one atrocity creates another, by way of reprisal – and national animosity is kept alive and heightened by a desire to gratify personal hatred and revenge.' Fighting between the Australians and Turks during the First World War, bitter though it was, had little of the 'needle match' about it. The Germans, however, were regarded in a different light, not only because they were blamed for starting the war but also because they were credited with having committed atrocities. Many Australians felt genuine hatred for them, and acted accordingly. 'I accounted for 5 or 6 Germans with bombs,' said one, 'and we had orders to bayonet all wounded Germans and they received it hot and strong.' Another described, with undeniable satisfaction, the fate of Germans who tried to surrender.

> Strike me pink the square heads are dead mongrels. They will keep firing until you are two yds. off them & then drop their rifles & ask for mercy. They get it too right where the chicken gets the axe ... I ... will fix a few more before I have finished. Its good sport father when the bayonet goes in there eyes bulge out like a prawns.

The Second World War on the Eastern Front was made especially savage by German ideology, which portrayed Russians, in a classic example of dehumanisation, as *untermenschen*. German soldiers were encouraged to think of their opponents as sub-human, and a good measure of the misery experienced by Russian prisoners stemmed from the simple neglect and casual brutality which this policy helped bring about. Erich Fromm suggests that making the enemy a 'non-person' removes the human sense of empathy. 'There is good clinical evidence', he writes, 'for the assumption that destructive aggression occurs, at least to a large degree, in conjunction with a momentary or chronic emotional withdrawal.' The Russians used atrocity stories as morale-boosters, and German behaviour in occupied areas soon gave substance to these tales. In the words of Albert Seaton:

> As the Red Army approached the borders of Germany the propaganda was intensified and as an act of policy the troops were told that personal property and German

women were theirs by right and that they were not account-
able by law for civil crime committed in Germany.

They were spurred on by Ilya Ehrenburg's exhortation to:

Kill! There is nothing that is innocent in the German.
Neither in the living nor in the unborn. Follow the directive
of Comrade Stalin and trample into the ground forever the
Fascist beast in his cave. Break by force the racial haughti-
ness of German women! Take them as your lawful prey!
Kill, you brave advancing Red soldiers!

Guy Sajer saw the process of atrocity and counter-atrocity at
first hand, and acknowledged that, 'Russian excesses did not
in any way excuse us for excesses by our own side. War always
reaches the depths of horror because of idiots who perpetuate
terror from generation to generation under the pretext of
vengeance.'

Even if the soldier is spared broad-brush propaganda designed to discredit the enemy collectively, aspects of his training
will have encouraged the depersonalisation of the individual.
Training for hand-to-hand combat is perhaps the best example of this process. In the First World War, Colonel Campbell's bayonet-training in the Bull Ring at Étaples was intended
'to arouse the pugnacity of the men'. Hanbury-Sparrow complained: 'It was all the rage, this brainless bayonet-fighting.'
But he was a regular, and did not need his resolve stiffening
by such training. However, Lieutenant R.F. Calloway, a
priest who served as a chaplain before taking a combatant
commission, thought it more useful. He found Campbell's lecture 'extraordinarily good, but to me the interest of the lecture
lay not so much in the lecture itself as in what the lecture
stood for – the entire conversion of our whole attitude of mind
as a nation ... if the war is to be won we must fight to kill'.
He was killed, at the age of forty-four, on the Somme in
September 1916.

Vigorous training for hand-to-hand combat, very much in
the style of the Bull Ring, was given to the American soldiers

who fought in Vietnam. David Parks found it rather funny: 'You run around this horse-shoe-shaped course lined with dummies you're supposed to stick with your bayonet, yelling "Kill!" Funny. I always yell "Ha-ha" instead.' 'Dinks are little shits,' bellowed Tim O'Brien's drill sergeant. 'If you want their guts, you gotta go low. Crouch and dig.' O'Brien attributed much of what went wrong in Vietnam to the effects of this sort of training. 'To understand what happens to the GI among the mine fields of My Lai,' he wrote, 'you must know something about what happens in America. You must understand Fort Lewis, Washington. You must understand a thing called basic training.'

The massacre at My Lai draws together many of the strands woven in this chapter. The road to My Lai was paved, first and foremost, by the dehumanisation of the Vietnamese and the 'mere gook rule' which declared that killing a Vietnamese civilian did not really count. Lieutenant Calley's unit had been bled steadily, often in actions against half-seen enemies who seemed to melt back amongst the population. The day before the massacre, the popular Sergeant Cox was killed by a booby-trapped shell. Captain Medina's briefing to his company was at best easily misunderstood. One of those present recalled his words as follows:

'Our job is to go in rapidly, and to neutralise everything. To kill everything.'

'Captain Medina? Do you mean women and children, too?'

'I mean everything.'

There were suggestions from the Military Police that prisoners would be unwelcome. 'I'd love to be in the field with you,' one MP told Calley. 'I'd take every prisoner and I'd kill every damn one. Do it, Lieutenant, or you're going to see these people back.' After the massacre, the military hierarchy did its best to cover up the event: officers were reluctant to take proceedings against those who had fought an ugly war in harsh conditions.

An officer quoted by John Parrish summed up the pressures on the ordinary, basically decent American conscripts.

> You put those same kids in the jungle for a while, get them real scared, deprive them of sleep, and let a few incidents change some of their fears to hate. Give them a sergeant who has seen too many of his men killed by booby traps and by lack of distrust, and who feels that Vietnamese are dumb, dirty and weak, because they are not like him. Add a little mob pressure, and those nice kids who accompanies us today would rape like champions. Kill, rape and steal is the name of the game.

The My Lai affair spread its ripples wide, and it, and other incidents like it, have attracted serious scholarly attention which, for reasons of space, if for no others, I cannot hope to equal. But the issue of atrocities in Vietnam did open a debate which cannot be ignored in any work which seeks to examine the soldier's behaviour on the battlefield. On the one hand there are those like Ashley King, who wrote to the editor of the *New York Times* on 22 March 1970, who argue: 'The criminals are all of us. The war itself is the great atrocity that spawns the lesser atrocities.' On the other, some would agree with Captain William H. Miller's letter in the Bridgeport *Post* on 17 February 1970. 'Let the military fight the wars,' he urged, 'and let the politicians run the government, and ask not the butcher how he kills the pig, for he too has an unpleasant task.'

For Peter Bourne, there was a certain inevitability to the affair. 'There can be little doubt', he wrote, 'that in the combat situation it becomes often meaningless to ask the soldier to make fine discriminations that distinguish a "legitimate" act of war from a war crime.' This is a view with which I would warmly concur. But it has two essential corollaries. The first is that we should spare no effort to give the soldier every chance of making this judgment. The second is that societies which ask men to fight on their behalf should be aware of what the consequences of their action may so easily be.[7]

For all that his attitude may oscillate between aggression and affection, between atrocity and admiration, there is a final paradox in a man's relationship with his enemy. The enemy soldier, too, has to undergo the readjustments that come with enlistment and basic training, the gnawing anticipation on the eve of battle, and the experience of battle itself. The enemy may wear a different disguise or march to a different rhetoric. Yet he is an image, albeit seen in a grubby and distorting mirror, of the soldier himself. When Captain Sam's company killed nineteen and wounded four North Vietnamese on Hill 130, the marines relished the taste of revenge, rifled the enemy's discarded packs, and told war stories. Some, thought Charles Anderson, reached the bottom level of reflection and 'came to see the young Vietnamese they had killed as allies in a bigger war of individual existence, as young men with whom they were united throughout their lives against the big impersonal "thems" of the world ... In killing the grunts of North Vietnam, the grunts of America had killed a part of themselves.'

IO

A Peaceful World

There is in many today as great a fear of a sterile and unexciting peace as of a great war. We are often puzzled by our continual failure to enlist in the pursuit of a peaceful world the united effort, cheerfulness in sacrifice, determination and persistence that arise almost spontaneously in the pursuit of war.

Glenn Gray, *The Warriors*

The Old Life

Battle is a watershed even in the lives of those who survive it without visible scars. Military training, the forging of the bonds of comradeship, and the traumatic events of the battle-field itself are never entirely forgotten. By some they are frequently and freshly remembered, and by others they are locked away like an album of horrible photographs, and are viewed only with pain and reluctance: indeed, a few of the images may be so hideous that they are excised altogether.

Most ex-soldiers remember war with mixed feelings, aware that it has altered the way they look at the world, conscious that they have faced perhaps the greatest challenge of their

394

lives, grateful for some elements of the experience and profoundly moved by others. Few regard war as anything other than an evil, unavoidable in some circumstances, but an evil none the less: yet at the same time they do not regret their own participation in it. The majority feel that their experience of war links them to others who share it, as firmly as it separates them from those who do not. 'The war, *mon vieux*,' wrote Jacques Meyer, 'was our buried, secret, youth.' 'In the 1920s', admitted Charles Carrington, 'I used to catch myself despising men of my own age who had not been in the trenches.' The flood of military memoirs and myriad of wartime anecdotes are only one side of the equation: on the other is reticence. Sometimes a reluctance to talk about 'their' war reflects not only veterans' desire to avoid rummaging amongst unpleasant memories, or their feeling that an outsider cannot possibly understand what they have to say: they are also reluctant to let someone else into a world which belongs to a group from their own generation. It was their war and remains their memory, and is a currency not to be cheapened by inflation.

Donald Featherstone thought that his own experience of war was

the greatest moulding of my life. To my wife's disgust, I am today – 40 years later – the product of the British Army. All the good and bad qualities I possess emanate from the six and a half years I spent in the Army. I shudder to think what I would have been like without it – yet shudder at the realisation of what it has made me! In retrospect – and I say that with slight doubts – I think if I had my life again I would do it all again as it happened.

A First World War company sergeant-major told me: 'When I left France wounded after two years there I felt and still feel that war is a vile, soul-destroying and uncivilising evil. But if I were a younger man I would fight again.' Peter Halford-Thompson struck the same note. 'I would not have missed it for worlds,' he wrote, 'which is not to say that I would encourage war which is unutterably ghastly and, ultimately, futile.' Although the journalist Robert Fox was not a combatant in the Falklands, he shared many of the fighting man's risks. 'One feels mildly affronted for it to be suggested that such an extraordinary experience, which so nearly cost me my life, was worthless,' he affirmed. 'The days in that wild landscape, the companionship of many of the men in the field were enjoyable more often than not; fear and danger were exhilarating too ... For me it was an existential dream.'

Sometimes it is a specific battle, usually the individual's first, that epitomises the experience. 'I wouldn't say that I enjoyed it,' said Jack Ward, who landed with 48 Commando on D-Day. 'But I'm very pleased that I saw it, and I'm very pleased that I was there ... I wouldn't have missed it for anything.' Bill Little of the Fort Garry Horse described D-Day as:

> the most exciting and frightening day I've ever gone through in my life. I've gone through other battles after that but I think this was the initial indoctrination into war ... it was perhaps the most important day in the sense of accomplishment, in the sense of change from a boy to a man, literally.

This feeling of having grown up as a result of war is almost universal. An Israeli paratrooper frankly acknowledged the horror of war. 'I'll tell you in two words what the battle was,' he said. 'Murder and fear, murder and fear.' But the experience had changed him, and not necessarily for the worse. 'I know I'll never be the same person again,' he admitted. 'All the things that used to bother me are so small and silly. I know what life is worth, now I've seen so much death.' Several British parachutists commented, on their return from the Falklands, on the way in which their experiences had matured them. 'It helps you put your life in perspective,' remarked one. 'If you've survived all that, somehow the mortgage and the car don't seem to be too much of a problem.' A young officer believed that his men were more mature and self-assured on their return. They were less concerned with looking 'alley' on exercises, girt about with non-regulation kit, fighting knives, and so on. There was less off-duty brawling. 'If I saw a bloke eyeing me up in a pub,' said one private, 'I might have to give him one, know what I mean? Now I don't need to. I've done it all.' Their opponents, too, felt that they had grown up. 'Before the war I was still a bit of a baby,' said Jorge. 'Now I realize I've begun to be a bit of a man ... I think this has been one of the fundamental things in my life, something that's going to leave its trace for ever.'

Even the men of 2 and 3 Para, tough professionals though they were, were anxious to get the war over and to come home. It was relatively easy for them to re-adjust to peace, for the war had been short, and there was still the supportive framework of the unit and the usual round of exercises, cadres and inspections. But for the conscript soldiers of large armies, facing the end of the war and demobilisation is an ambivalent process. The euphoria of getting back into civilian clothes is mixed with the sadness of leaving trusted friends. An Australian soldier summed it up well:

One is jolly glad to be out of it, yet ... men you have been friendly with and stood side by side for months or perhaps into years ... have been killed – one's heart fills with sadness – and one has a hankering to be back over there with 'the boys' once more. Whatever one may be in private life when you are in the line facing the same enemies fear, death & other horrors you are absolutely one, and one gets momentary glimpses of that truer and greater democracy which is gradually opening out to solve all human problems.

Another described the agony of feeling his battalion 'drifting to pieces. The links that connected us with the unforgotten dead seemed to be snapping one by one.'

Guy Chapman contemplated imminent demobilisation with regret. 'Looking back at those firm ranks as they marched into billets,' he wrote, 'I found that a body of men had become so much a part of me that its disintegration would tear away something I cared for more dearly than I could have believed.

I was it, and it was I.' The mock-tragic song 'When This Lousy War is Over' had its peacetime version.

> Now the bleedin war is over
> Oh, how happy I was there;
> Now old Fritz and I have parted,
> Life's one everlasting care.
> No more *estaminets* to sing in,
> No mamoiselles to make me gay;
> Civvie life's a bleedin failure,
> I was happy yesterday.

It is the comradeship that men remember most warmly. George Chissel's service on the Western Front convinced him that 'war is a curse that has to be endured'. But he remembered with affection: 'The fellowship generated in my platoon ... All good chaps.' 'The comradeship and *esprit de corps*' were the most memorable aspects of Jack Chaffer's war. Alan Briddon, too, liked to remember 'comradeship in action/hardship, and travel overseas (at a young, impressionable age)'. A platoon commander looked back upon 'all the selfless acts of comradeship and sharing. How wonderful the human spirit can be and how privations, fear, hunger, cold, wet and all the horrors of war serve to bring out the very best in people'. For Donald Featherstone, the most pleasant memories were of

> the comradeship and togetherness; the careless, live-for-today attitude. The awareness of being in it together. The pride of wearing uniform, and the insignia of a first class regiment, that put one in an ordered class beyond the haphazard scope of civilians. Seeing places and doing things in strange parts.

It is largely this sense of comradeship which men seek to re-create in ex-servicemen's organisations. Even Vietnam Veterans Against the War, opposed though it was to the very war in which its members had fought, helped some veterans recapture their security and confidence through contact with their own kind, and the post-Vietnam 'rap groups' mirrored, in a strange way, the small-unit loyalties of combat. Just as some soldiers feel unable to exist outside a war, so some of these veterans depended on the continuation of the war for their own survival. 'Our life is being against the war,' one of them told Robert Jay Lifton. 'When the war ends, then we end as people.'

There are also darker memories, buried but all too easily exhumed. Often they concern the dead: either the dead of one's own side, whose memory drifts back to 'ghost' survivors as if to reproach them for still being alive, or the enemy dead, laying death-guilt at the doors of their slayers. Most often, though, it is a short clip of memory of a single incident which sums up all that is worst in war. A brave and distinguished old gentleman wept softly, nearly seventy years after the event, as he described a popular officer walking out of the barrage clutching his stomach. He went to help him, and discovered that he had been literally disembowelled by a shell fragment. Brian Clark regretted a runner's mistake. When adjutant of an Irish battalion in North Africa, he sent for two company commanders: 'A runner brought the *companies* up a wadi; 45 casualties from 2 SP gun shells.'

Seeing friends killed, or, almost worse, being unable to help them when wounded, leaves enduring scars. One of the veterans quoted in Patsy Adam-Smith's *The Anzacs* recalled: 'the useless slaughter of young men. The older I get the sadder I feel about the uselessness of it all, but in particular the deaths of my comrades.' Another reflected: 'We thought we had managed all right, kept the awful things out of our minds, but now I'm an old man and they come out from where I hid them. Every night.' Younger men, too, have haunted sleep: a soldier in 3 Para described how machine-gun fire scythed down fleeing Argentinians, night after night, in his dreams.

Other memories are less overtly unpleasant but are recalled with reluctance. Most preconceptions of battle presume that the civilian population has been removed from the battlefield as if by magic. In fact, civilians cling to the fringes of battlefields, and sometimes find themselves on them, trying to carry on with their lives as if the war were some monstrous aberration which will soon disappear. Both Jack Chaffer, in Italy, and Tom Rogers, in Korea, were upset at the plight of refugees. Wheeler wrote of the bombardment of Flushing in 1809 that 'the heart-rending cries of the poor women and children, beggar description'. Lieutenant de Forsanz survived the Battle of St Privat, when his corps was battered for hours by the fire of 180 German guns before being prised out of the village by infantry assault. But what stuck in his mind was the vision of an old woman trotting around the wreckage of her garden, wailing, 'My cauliflowers, my cauliflowers.' A German officer found the expulsion of civilians from the area of the Hindenburg Line 'a heart-rending business, more ghastly than murder'. The destruction of property in the area given up when the Germans withdrew to the Hindenburg Line alarmed even those who inflicted the damage. 'Do not be angry: only be surprised' begged a placard left in the square at Péronne.

Donald Featherstone's objection to 'the petty injustices of the Army, the unfeeling unintelligent attitudes and actions of many in positions of command; the gulf between the average officer and other ranks' was endorsed by several other British veterans of the two World Wars. An American infantry officer remembered his wound, and, more specifically, 'the frustration of being out of the fight after being evacuated for wounds. I remember seeing President Nixon pointing out enemy targets in Cambodia while in hospital and reflecting angrily that I should have been there instead of in bed.'

Readjustment to civilian life is at best uncomfortable and at worst impossible. A few men grow so used to the rough fabric of war that nothing else sits comfortably upon them. 'I cannot go home and start the old life,' lamented a German soldier of the First World War. 'My Germany is where the Very lights illuminate the sky, where the time of day is estimated according to the strength of the artillery barrage.' Others miss the sheer excitement, the feeling of being wanted, being relevant, being alive. 'You know that I do not love war or want it to return,' a Frenchman assured Glenn Gray in 1955. 'But at least it made me feel alive as I have not felt alive before or since.' A Vietnam veteran took to armed robbery. 'It wasn't the money with me,' he told Mark Baker. 'I was doing things for a handshake. I wanted the adrenalin pump.'

Then there are the professional crises that must be faced by soldiers, both regular and temporary, when peace breaks out. Regulars rue the loss of their acting rank: the 1919 and 1946 Army Lists are filled with temporary brigadiers who went crashing back to major. Wartime officers and NCOs have to compress themselves back into old niches in civilian life, or struggle to carve new ones. H. Gordon Bennett left his job as an actuarial clerk in 1914. He returned five years later a brigadier, having seen most of his brother officers killed or wounded and having earned the CB, CMG and DSO. He was offered his clerk's job back on the old terms, and his employers thought that they were doing him a favour.

There is also the practical problem of losing the habits which have become almost conditioned reflexes. Numerous middle-class Englishmen came back from the First World War with a penchant for swearing and the easy habit of unbuttoning by the roadside. Glenn Gray, returning to America in 1946, 'felt curiously undressed without a pistol on my hip, and I trod softly for a while on loose soil, unconsciously fearing booby traps'. Philip Caputo diagnosed combat veteranitis from his own symptoms, to whit:

> an inability to concentrate, a childlike fear of darkness, a tendency to tire easily, chronic nightmares, an intolerance of loud noises – especially doors slamming and cars backfiring – and alternating moods of depression and rage that came over me for no apparent reason.

Postwar enthusiasm for soldiers does not long survive the victory parades. The way in which societies have treated the men who have fought for them has often been little short of shameful. Frederick the Great housed a few of his veterans in the Invalid House in Berlin: most others were given a licence to beg, and a few would waylay the king's coach. When he was in a good mood he would throw them a thaler, but when he was not he would simply order his pages to 'Drive the scum away.' So much for the men who rolled up the Austrian line at Leuthen and stood firm in the savage close-range infantry firefight at Zorndorf. Many of Wellington's Peninsula veterans ended their days begging on the streets of London. The condition of Rifleman Harris, travelling home ill, was a source of constant anxiety to his coach driver. 'Here's a nice go,' he grumbled. 'Catch me ever taking up a sick soldier again if I can help it. This here poor devil's going to make a die of it in my coach.' Ron Kovic, paralysed by a bullet wound in Vietnam, found little compassion or gratitude in hospital in the United States. 'Urine bags are constantly overflowing on to the floor while the aides play poker on the toilet bowls in the enema room,' he wrote. 'The sheets are never changed and many of the men stink from not being properly bathed.'

The survivors of world wars can at least console themselves with the knowledge that the war they fought was the focus of major national effort, and that the demands it made on manpower mean that most men of their age will enjoy the community of shared experiences. They might have fewer practical advantages, for these wars ravaged even most of the victors' economies, and many veterans discovered that, whatever else they had been doing, they had not built a land fit for heroes to live in. Stouffer's researches revealed that, although there was generally little bitterness and resentment in postwar America, most veterans felt that their military service had hurt them more than it had helped them. A few were openly resentful at their welcome. 'When you come back they treat you just like scum,' one complained. 'If you ever get the boys all together they will probably kill all the civilians. They [the civilians] aren't worth anything anyway.'

Those who fight in smaller wars, and especially ones which arouse opposition at home, are far less fortunate. Philippe de Pirey thought that 'the wall of utter indifference' that greeted soldiers returning from Indo-China was almost worthy of a book in itself. The veterans of another unpopular Asian war found readjustment to 'The World' almost as difficult. 'Back in the States,' wrote Charles Anderson, he felt alone, naked, exposed to the dumb peering and probing of those afraid to get involved with things outside their own life-cocoons. He wanted to be left alone to heal his wound, to 'get his thing together', so he could somehow face tomorrows that looked too bright, too hard.

The mismatch between aspiration and fact is often hardest to bear. Thinking, talking and writing letters about what he will do when he gets back home helps many a soldier through the long periods of boredom which he endures. Wives grow more desirable, civilian jobs – no matter how humdrum – look positively attractive, and even a scruffy tenement is more comfortable than a trench. But, as Grinker and Spiegel pointed out, 'all anticipation of the return home is extremely unrealistic since the returnee expects the perfection of paradise in the "new life" '. He soon discovers that he is a centre of interest only briefly, and that mothers and brothers soon have other things to do. He may find the process of sexual readjustment difficult, particularly if, as is so often the case, he married shortly before going overseas, or during leave. Suddenly the other world, the one he has left, begins to seem far more attractive than it ever did while he was in it. In 1919 an American marine wistfully looked back a year. 'These our United States are truly artificial and bare,' he wrote. 'There is no romance or colour here, nothing to suffer for and laugh at.' A Vietnam veteran reflected upon an experience that had been horrific but which somehow, in retrospect, had a glimmer of attraction. 'Thinking about Vietnam,' he said, 'once in a while, in a crazy kind of way, I wish that just for an hour I could be there. And then be transported back. Maybe just to be there so I'd wish I was back here again.'

The Will to Warfare

The political mainsprings for war still exist. Indeed, as we near the end of the millennium, it seems to me that these springs are more tightly stretched than ever over the struggle for resources in a world divided as much between north and south as between east and west. In *The Coming End of War*, Werner Levi reached decidedly optimistic conclusions. He argued that 'popular antiwar attitudes make the use or threat of war as a political instrument difficult' in open societies and, to a lesser extent, even under totalitarian regimes. This view neglects the fact that the current wave of antiwar protest is by no means unique: the widespread and deeply-felt pacifism of the 1930s failed to prevent the Second World War. Moreover, it is easy to confuse protest against nuclear war with opposition to war in general. While nuclear war is widely recognised as being a strategy of no returns, the events of 1982-3 in the Middle East, the Caribbean and the South Atlantic all suggest that conventional war retains utility as a political instrument.

Glenn Gray detected some hope in the fact that there was a change which he saw as 'novel and important – our growing unwillingness to glorify war and the military virtues'. Here he has a point. Nevertheless, if the great wave of popular anti-war literature of the 1920s and 1930s – unrepresentative though it may have been of the views of all those who fought in the First World War – failed to achieve a radical change in attitudes, I see no reason why more recent literary endeavours should do so. The portrayal of war in films, and its reporting on television, is also no guarantee that it will become obsolete. Indeed, it may have precisely the reverse effect. One can see shells smashing houses in Beirut, or the huddled corpses of the victims of left-wing guerrillas or right-wing death squads in central America, in the privacy of one's sitting-room on almost any night of the week. There is certainly nothing romantic about it. But neither is it really shocking. War has become moving wallpaper, and its familiar pattern no longer horrifies us.

If political, ideological and economic pressures cause wars, will men continue to fight them? John Keegan speculated, in *The Face of Battle*, that battle may have abolished itself by simply becoming intolerable for its participants. The evidence of the last decade does not support such a sanguine view, and it would undoubtedly have made John Keegan less optimistic had he written in 1984 rather than a decade earlier. It may be the case that sleep deprivation and physical weariness will force the battles of the future to assume a more sporadic character than many current theorists suggest, that the tempo of operations will inevitably slow down as soldiers grow more tired, and that the widespread destruction of high-cost, high-value weapon systems will lead to a 'broken-backed war' or even the stalemate of mutual exhaustion.

It is clear that all the ingredients of battle still exist. Military organisations continue to bond their soldiers together in the small groups which form the basis of battle morale: ideologies and religions form abstract images of a hateful enemy. The development of new weapon systems enables the soldier, even on the battlefield, to fire more lethal weapons more accurately to longer ranges: his enemy is, increasingly, an anonymous figure encircled by a gunsight, glowing on a thermal imager, or shrouded in armour plate. We should not, then, assume that battle will abolish itself because those who actually fight it are unable or unwilling to continue. At one level, we are the inhabitants of the taught world of the 1980s, increasingly able to control our environment, harnessing galloping technology, and probing far beyond the confines of our own planet. At another, we are prisoners of our development and culture, and, with all the mixed feelings of our fathers or grandfathers, we stand on the start line, waiting only for the whistle.

Notes

1 Start Line

1   John Connell, 'Writing about Soldiers', *Journal of the Royal United Services Institute*, August 1965, p. 221.
2   Ibid., p. 222.
3   Ibid., p. 224.
4   Quoted in E.B. Greenwood, *Tolstoy: the Comprehensive Vision* (London, 1975), p. 29.
5   G.R. Elton, *Political History: Principles and Practice* (London, 1970), p. 53.
6   Basil Liddell Hart, *Strategy: the Indirect Approach* (London, 1964), pp. 23-4.
7   W.H.A. Groom, *Poor Bloody Infantry* (London, 1976), p. 22.
8   Robert Fox, 'The Violent Imagination', in Peter Marsh and Anne Campbell (eds), *Aggression and Violence* (Oxford, 1982), p. 7.
9   Lieutenant-Colonel Roger Little, 'Buddy Relations and Combat Performance', in Morris Janowitz (ed.), *The New Military* (New York, 1969).

2 Mysterious Fraternity

1   Quoted in Christopher Duffy, *The Army of Frederick the Great* (Newton Abbot, 1974), p. 57.
2   J.H. Faris, 'The Impact of Basic Training: the Role of the Drill Sergeant', in Nancy L. Goldman and David R. Segal (eds), *The Social Psychology of Military Service* (London, 1976).
3   Asa Baber, 'Role Models', *Playboy*, April 1982.

4   Peter Bourne, 'From Boot Camp to My Lai', in Richard A. Falk (ed.), *Crimes of War* (New York, 1971).

5   B. Simon and I. Bradley (eds), *The Victorian Public School* (London, 1975).

6   E. Dinter, *Held Oder Feigling* (Herford, 1982). An English edition is imminent, but had not appeared when this book went to press.

7   Peter Bourne (ed.), *The Psychology and Physiology of Stress* (New York, 1969).

8   'General Sir John Hackett on World War II Films', *Sunday Times Supplement*, 20 March 1983.

9   L.H. Suid, *Guts and Glory: Great American War Movies* (New York, 1978).

3   The Painful Field

1   General Charles Thoumas, *Les Transformations de l'armée française*, 2 vols (Paris, 1887), i, p. 18.

2   Nancy L. Goldman and David R. Segal (eds), *The Social Psychology of Military Service* (London, 1976), p. 275.

3   Guether Lewy, *America in Vietnam* (New York, 1978), p. 157.

4   R. S. Lazarus, *Psychological Stress and the Coping Process* (New York, 1966), p. 20.

5   David M. Kennedy, *Over Here: the First World War and American Society* (Oxford, 1980), p. 187.

6   Major R.L. Nabors, 'Women in the Army: Do They Measure Up?', *Military Review*, October 1982.

7   Bruce Catton, *Glory Road* (New York, 1964), p. 210.

8   Lieutenant-Colonel's H.W.R. Pike's letter, *Journal of the Royal United Services Institute for Defence Studies*, March 1983, p. 79.

9   Lieutenant-Colonel H.L. Thompson, 'Sleep Loss and its Effect in Combat', *Military Review*, September 1983, p. 15.

10 Ibid., pp. 18-19.

11 D.R. Haslam, 'The Effects of Sleep Loss upon the Motivation, Morale and Mood of the Soldier', paper presented to the NATO symposium on motivation and morale in the NATO Forces, Brussels, 1980.

12 Quoted in Lord Lovat, *March Past* (London, 1978), p. 338.

13 R.W. Seaton, 'Deterioration of Military Work Groups under Deprivation Stress', in Morris Janowitz (ed.), *The New Military* (New York, 1969), p. 239.

4 Epitome of War

1 Roy R. Grinker and John P. Spiegel, *Men under Stress* (New York, 1963), p. 44.
2 Diary of Private C.A. McAnulty, quoted in Bill Gammage, *The Broken Years: Australian Soldiers in the Great War* (Canberra, 1974), pp. 70–1.
3 The Hon. J.W. Fortescue, *The History of the British Army*, vol. v (London, 1910), pp. 343–50.
4 General G.A. Bonnal, *Froeschwiller: récit commenté des événements ...* (Paris, 1899), pp. 138–40.
5 Stephen E. Ambrose, *Crazy Horse and Custer* (New York, 1975), p. 423.
6 Donald R. Morris, *The Washing of the Spears* (London, 1978), p. 423.
7 Brigadier-General Sir J.E. Edmonds, *Military Operations: France and Belgium, 1914*, vol. I (London, 1933) pp. 134–5.
8 J.M. Craster (ed.), *Fifteen Rounds a Minute: the Grenadiers at War, August to December 1914* (London, 1976), pp. 143, 147.
9 John Akehurst, *We Won a War* (Salisbury, 1982), p. 69.
10 Martin Middlebrook, *The First Day on the Somme* (London, 1971), p. 264.
11 F.J. West, *Small Unit Action in Vietnam, Summer 1966* (Washington, 1967), p. 93.

5 Pale Battalions

1 Ron Kovic, *Born on the Fourth of July* (New York, 1976), p. 98; Mark Baker, *Nam* (New York, 1981), p. 276.
2 *Daily Express*, 29 June 1983.
3 John Laffin, *Surgeons in the Field* (London, 1970), p. 29.
4 Lieutenant-Colonel G.L. Belenkey, *Psychiatric Casualties in Israeli Forces during the War in Lebanon* (Washington, 1983).

6 The Real Enemy

1 From R. Swank and W. Marchand, 'Combat Neuroses: the Development of Combat Exhaustion', *Archives of Neurology and Psychiatry*, vol. 55, 1946.
2 See John Ellis, *The Sharp End of War* (Newton Abbot, 1980), pp. 250–5.

3 T.A. Heathcote, *The Afghan Wars, 1839* (London, 1980). The book was reviewed in the *Journal of the Royal United Services Institute* in March 1981, and generated an instructive correspondence in that journal's September and December 1981 issues.

4 For the Gallabat episode see Field-Marshal Sir William Slim, *Unofficial History* (London, 1960), p. 142; T.A. Martin, *The Essex Regiment, 1929–1950* (Brentwood, 1952), pp. 34-8; I.S.O. Playfair, *The Mediterranean and the Middle East*, vol. 1 (London, 1954), pp. 398-9; and Anthony Brett-James, *Ball of Fire* (Aldershot, 1951), pp. 27-8.

7 Competition, Diffidence and Glory

1 W.S. Churchill, *The Malakand Field Force* (London, 1901), p. 13.

2 Quoted in John Laffin (ed.), *Letters from the Front* (London, 1973), p. 70.

3 R. Little in Morris Janowitz (ed.), *The New Military* (New York, 1969).

4 Major-General J.E.B. Seely, *Adventure* (London, 1930), pp. 304-5.

5 John Keegan, 'Inventing Military Traditions', unpublished paper presented at the Past and Present Society Annual Conference, London, 1977.

8 Precarious Valour

1 See R.A. Gabriel and P.L. Savage, *Crisis in Command: Mismanagement in the Army* (New York, 1979), pp. 42-5; S.L.A Marshall, *Vietnam: Three Battles* (New York, 1971), p. 65.

2 Quoted in Colin Hughes, *Mametz* (London, 1982), p. 127.

3 I. Gentles, 'Arrears of Pay and Ideology in the Army Revolt of 1647', in B. Bond and I. Roy (eds), *War and Society: a Yearbook of Military History* (London, 1975), pp. 44-66.

4 Quoted in Donald R. Morris, *The Washing of the Spears* (London, 1968), pp. 474-5.

5 Alan Patient, 'Mutiny at Salerno', *Listener*, 25 February 1982; letters in *Listener*, 11 March 1982.

6 Report in Public Record Office WO 205/5G. I must acknowledge my debt to Lieutenant-Colonel Carlo d'Este, without whose *Decision in Normandy* (London, 1983) I would not have known of the existence of this document.

7   See William Moore, *The Thin Yellow Line* (London, 1974), for an informed discussion of the British and French figures.
8   Brigadier-General F.P. Crozier, *The Men I Killed* (London, 1937), p. 68.
9   Field-Marshal Lord Carver *et al.*, 'Thoughts on Command in Battle', *British Army Review*, no. 69, December 1981.

9   I Am the Enemy

1   J.A. Blake, 'The Organization as an Instrument of Violence', *Sociological Quarterly*, vol. II, Part 3, 1970, p. 334.
2   Quoted in Lyn Macdonald, *They Called It Passchendaele* (London, 1978), p. 74.
3   Richard A. Falk (ed.), *Crimes of War* (New York, 1971), p. 449.
4   Lieutenant C.J.L.F. Anderson, 'The Defence of Superior Orders', *Journal of the Royal United Services Institute for Defence Studies*, vol. CXXVI, no. 2, June 1981.
5   Tony Ashworth, *Trench Warfare 1914–18: the Live and Let Live System* (London, 1980), p. 139.
6   Donald Knox, *Death March: the Survivors of Bataan* (New York, 1981), p. 129.
7   For the issue in general see Falk (ed.), *Crimes of War*; John Sack, *Body Count: Lieutenant Calley's Story* (London, 1971); Peter Karsten, *Law, Soldiers and Combat* (Westport, Conn., 1978); and Richard A. Gabriel, *To Serve with Honor* (Westport, Conn., 1982).

Select Bibliography

Books

ABERCROMBIE, CLARENCE L., *The Military Chaplain* (London, 1977).

ADAIR, JOHN, *Training for Leadership* (London, 1968).

ADAM-SMITH, PATSY, *The Anzacs* (London, 1978).

AHRENFELDT, R.H., *Psychiatry in the British Army in the Second World War* (London, 1958).

AKEHURST, JOHN, *We Won a War* (Salisbury, 1982).

AMBROSE, STEPHEN E., *Crazy Horse and Custer* (New York, 1975).

ANDERSON, CHARLES R., *The Grunts* (Novato, Cal., 1983).

——, *Vietnam: the Other War* (Novato, Cal., 1982).

ANNAND, A. McKENZIE (ed.), *Cavalry Surgeon* (London, 1971).

ARENDT, HANNAH, *On Violence* (London, 1970).

ASCOLI, DAVID, *The Mons Star* (London, 1981).

ASHWORTH, TONY, *Trench Warfare, 1914–18: the Live and Let Live System* (London, 1980).

BABINGTON, ANTHONY, *For the Sake of Example* (London, 1983).

BAKER, MARK, *Nam* (New York, 1981).

BAPST, GERMAIN, *Le Maréchal Canrobert: souvenirs d'un siècle*, 6 vols (Paris, 1899).

BARAIL, F.C. DU, *Mes souvenirs*, 3 vols (Paris, 1894).

BARBUSSE, HENRI, *Le Feu* (Paris, 1917).

BARTLETT, F.C., *Psychology and the Soldier* (Cambridge, 1927).

BAYNES, JOHN, *Morale: a study of Men and Courage* (London, 1967).

BELFIELD, E., and ESSAME, H., *The Battle for Normandy* (London, 1965).

BERGMAN, A.E., *Women of Vietnam* (San Francisco, 1975).

BEST, GEOFFREY, *Humanity in Warfare* (London, 1980).

BETTELHEIM, BRUNO, *The Informed Heart* (New York, 1960).

BIDWELL, SHELFORD, *Modern Warfare* (London, 1973).

BINDING, RUDOLF, *A Fatalist at War* (London, 1929).

BISHOP, PATRICK, and WITHEROW, JOHN, *The Winter War: the Falklands* (London, 1972).

BLOCH, MARC, *Memoirs of War, 1914–15* (London, 1980).

BLUNDEN, EDMUND, *Undertones of War* (London, 1966).

BOGUSLAWSKI, A. VON, *Tactical Deductions from the War of 1870–71* (London, 1874).

BOURNE, PETER G., *Men, Stress and Vietnam* (Boston, 1970).

—— (ed.), *The Psychology and Physiology of Stress* (New York, 1969).

BRETT-JAMES, ANTHONY, *Ball of Fire* (Aldershot, 1951).

—— (ed.), *Edward Costello* (London, 1967).

BURNS, J. M., *Leadership* (New York, 1978).

CARRINGTON, CHARLES, *Rudyard Kipling: His Life and Work* (London, 1955).

——, *Soldier from the Wars Returning* (London, 1965). See also Edmonds, Charles.

CATTON, BRUCE, *Glory Road* (New York, 1964).

CHAPMAN, GUY, *Vain Glory* (London, 1968).

CINCINNATUS (*pseud.* Cecil B. Currey), *Self Destruction: the Disintegration and Decay of the United States Army during the Vietnam Era* (New York, 1981).

CLAUSEWITZ, C. M. VON, *On War*, ed. and trans. Michael Howard and Peter Paret (Princeton, 1976).

CLAVELL, JAMES (ed.), *The Art of War by Sun Tsu* (London, 1982).

COCHRANE, PETER, *Charlie Company* (London, 1977).

CONGREVE, WILLIAM LA T., *Armageddon Road*, ed. Terry Norman (London, 1983).

COOPER, RAYMOND, *B Company* (London, 1978).

CRASTER, J. M. (ed.), *Fifteen Rounds a Minute: the Grenadiers at War, August to December 1914* (London, 1976).

CROW, F. A. E., *The Army Medical Services*, 5 vols (London, 1956–66).

CROZIER, F. P., *The Men I Killed* (London, 1937).

DEARDEN, HAROLD, *Medicine and Duty* (London, 1928).

DEVAUREIX, A. A., *Souvenirs et observations sur la campagne de 1870 (Armée du Rhin)* (Paris, 1909).

DINTER, ELMAR, *Held oder Feigling: die körperlichen und seelischen Belastungen des Soldaten im Krieg* (Herford, 1982).

DIXON, NORMAN F., *On the Psychology of Military Incompetence* (London, 1976).

DOLLARD, JOHN, *Fear in Battle* (Westport, Conn., 1977).

DUFFY, CHRISTOPHER, *The Army of Frederick the Great* (Newton Abbot, 1974).

DUPUY, T. N., *Numbers, Predictions and War* (London, 1979).

DURKHEIM, EMILE, *Suicide: a Study in Sociology* (London, 1963).

EDMONDS, CHARLES (*pseud.* Carrington, Charles), *A Subaltern's War* (London, 1929).

EIBL-EIBESFELDT, IRENAUS, *The Biology of Peace and War* (London, 1979).

ELLIS, JOHN, *The Sharp End of War* (Newton Abbot, 1980).

ELTON, G.R., *Political History: Principles and Practice* (London, 1970).

ENLOE, CYNTHIA, *Does Khaki Become You: the Militarisation of Women's Lives* (London, 1983).

ERIKSON, ERIK, *Childhood and Society* (London, 1977).

FAIRLEY, JOHN, *Remember Arnhem* (Aldershot, 1978).

FALK, RICHARD A. (ed.), *Crimes of War* (New York, 1971).

FALL, BERNARD B., *Hell in a Very Small Place* (London, 1967).

——, *Street without Joy* (London, 1963).

FALLS, C., *War Books* (London, 1930).

FARAGO, LADISLAS, *Patton: Ordeal and Triumph* (London, 1963).

FARRAR-HOCKLEY, ANTHONY, *The Edge of the Sword* (London, 1954).

FERGUSSON, BERNARD, *The Wild Green Earth* (London, 1946).

FRANKEL, N., and SMITH, L., *Patton's Best* (New York, 1978).

FRASER, DAVID, *Alanbrooke* (London, 1982).

FRASER, JOHN, *Violence in the Arts* (Cambridge, 1956).

FRASSANITO, WILLIAM A., *America's Bloodiest Day: the Battle of Antietam 1862* (New York, 1979).

FREUD, SIGMUND, *Group Psychology and the Analysis of the Ego* (London, 1959).

——, *Totem and Taboo* (London, 1972).

FROMM, ERICH, *The Anatomy of Human Destructiveness* (London, 1977).

FULLER, J.F.C., *The Conduct of War* (London, 1961).

FUSSELL, PAUL, *The Great War and Modern Memory* (London, 1975).

GALE, SIR RICHARD, *Call to Arms: an Autobiography* (London, 1968).

GAMMAGE, BILL, *The Broken Years: Australian Soldiers in the Great War* (Canberra, 1974).

GENNEP, ARNOLD VAN, *The Rites of Passage* (London, 1977).

GEORGE, ALEXANDER L., *The Chinese Communist Army in Action* (London, 1967).

GITTINGS, JOHN, *The Role of the Chinese Army* (London, 1967).

GLADDEN, NORMAN, *Ypres, 1917* (London, 1967).

GLOVER, MICHAEL, *A Gentleman Volunteer: the Letters of George Hennell from the Peninsular War, 1812–13* (London, 1979).

——, *The Velvet Glove: the Decline and Fall of Moderation in War* (London, 1982).

GLUBB, SIR JOHN, *Into Battle: a Soldier's Diary of the Great War* (London, 1978).

GOFF, STANLEY, and SANDERS, ROBERT, with SMITH, CLARK, *Brothers: Black Soldiers in the Nam* (Novato, Cal., 1982).

GOLDHAMMER, HERBERT, *The Soviet Soldier* (London, 1975).

GOLDMAN, NANCY L., and SEGAL, DAVID R., *The Social Psychology of Military Service* (London, 1976).

GORDON, R.K. (ed.), *Anglo-Saxon Poetry* (London, 1954).

GRANT, MICHAEL, *The Army of the Caesars* (London, 1974).

GRAUWIN, P., *Doctor at Dien Bien Phu* (London, 1955).

GRAVES, ROBERT, *Goodbye to All That* (London, 1969).

GRAY, J. GLENN, *The Warriors: Reflections on Men in Battle* (London, 1970).

GREENWELL, GRAHAM H., *An Infant in Arms* (London, 1972).

GREENWOOD, E.B., *Tolstoy: the Comprehensive Vision* (London, 1975).

GRIFFITH, PADDY, *Forward into Battle* (Chichester, 1981).

GRINKER, R.R., and SPIEGEL, J.P., *Men under Stress* (New York, 1963).

GROOM, W.H.A., *Poor Bloody Infantry* (London, 1976).

HANBURY-SPARROW, A.A., *The Land-Locked Lake* (London, 1932).

HARRIS, ROBERT, *Gotcha! The Media, the Government and the Falklands Crisis* (London, 1983).

HARRISON, KENNETH, *The Brave Japanese* (London, 1968).

HASTINGS, MAX, and JENKINS, SIMON, *The Battle for the Falklands* (London, 1983).

HAYES, DENNIS, *The Challenge of Conscience* (London, 1949).

HENDERSON, W.D., *Why the Vietcong Fought* (Westport, Conn., 1979).

HERR, MICHAEL, *Dispatches* (London, 1978).

HERZOG, CHAIM, *The War of Atonement* (London, 1975).

HIBBERT, CHRISTOPHER (ed.), *A Soldier of the Seventy-First* (London, 1976).

HILLARY, RICHARD, *The Last Enemy* (London, 1949).

HOHENLOHE INGELFINGEN, PRINCE KRAFT ZU, *Letters on Infantry* (London, 1892).

HOMANS, G.C., *The Human Group* (London, 1957).

HORSFALL, JOHN, *The Wild Geese are Flighting* (Kineton, 1976).

HOWARD, MICHAEL, *War and the Liberal Conscience* (London, 1978).

HUGHES, COLIN, *Mametz* (London, 1982).

HUXLEY, JULIAN, *Essays of a Humanist* (London, 1964).

ISHERWOOD, CHRISTOPHER, *Lions and Shadows* (London, 1953).

JANIS, I., *Air War and Emotional Stress* (New York, 1951).

JANOWITZ, MORRIS, *The Professional Soldier* (Toronto, 1964).

—— (ed.), *The New Military* (New York, 1969).

JOHNSON, GARRY, and DUNPHIE, CHRISTOPHER, *Brightly Shone the Dawn* (London, 1980).

JOLLY, RICK, *The Red and Green Life Machine* (London, 1983).

JONES, DAVID, *In Parenthesis* (London, 1938).

JUNGER, ERNST, *The Storm of Steel* (London, 1929).

KARSTEN, PETER, *Law, Soldiers and Combat* (Westport, Conn., 1978).

KEEGAN, JOHN, *The Face of Battle* (London, 1976).

KELLETT, ANTHONY, *Combat Motivation* (New York, 1982).

KEMP, PETER, *Mine Were of Trouble* (London, 1957).

KENNEDY, DAVID M., *Over Here: the First World War and American Society* (Oxford, 1980).

KIERNAN, V.G., *European Empires from Conquest to Collapse, 1815–1960* (London, 1982).

KINCAID, SIR JOHN, *Adventures of the Rifle Brigade and Random Shots from a Rifleman* (London, ND).

KNOEBL, KUNO, *Victor Charlie: the Face of War in Vietnam* (London, 1967).

KNOX, DONALD, *Death March: the Survivors of Bataan* (New York, 1981).

KON, DANIEL, *Los Chicos de la Guerra* (London, 1983).

KOVIC, RON, *Born on the Fourth of July* (New York, 1976).

KUKLER, MIKE, *Operation Barooom* (Gastonia, North Carolina, 1980).

LAFFIN, JOHN (ed.), *Letters from the Front*, (London, 1973).

——, *Women in Battle* (London, 1967).

LAMB, DAVE, *Mutinies: 1917–1920* (Oxford, 1978).

LANGER, WILLIAM, *Gas and Flame in World War I* (New York, 1965).

LAWFORD, JAMES (ed.), *The Cavalry* (New York, 1976).

LAZARUS, R.S., *Psychological Stress and the Coping Process* (New York, 1966).

LE BON, GUSTAVE, *The Crowd: a Study of the Popular Mind* (London, 1920).

LEE, R.G., *Introduction to Battlefield Weapons Systems and Technology* (London, 1981).

LEED, E.J., *No Man's Land: Combat and Identity in World War I* (Cambridge, 1981).

LEVI, WERNER, *The Coming End of War* (London, 1981).

LEWY, GUENTHER, *America in Vietnam* (New York, 1978).

LIDDELL HART, B.H., *Strategy: the Indirect Approach* (London, 1964).

—— (ed.), *The Letters of Private Wheeler, 1809–1828* (London, 1952).

LIFTON, ROBERT JAY, *Home from the War* (New York, 1973).

LINDSAY, MARTIN, *So Few Got Through* (London, 1946).

LORENZ, KONRAD, *On Aggression* (London, 1966).

LOVAT, LORD, *March Past* (London, 1978).

LUCAS, JAMES, *War on the Eastern Front* (London, 1979).

LUDENDORFF, E., *Memoirs, 1914–18* (London, ND).

LÜTZOW, COUNT, *The Hussite Wars* (London, 1914).

MacCURDY, J.T., *The Structure of Morale* (Cambridge, 1943).

MacDONALD, CHARLES B., *Company Commander* (Washington, 1947).

MACDONALD, LYN, *Somme* (London, 1983).

——, *They Called It Passchendaele* (London, 1978).

McDOWALL, C.A., *Some Were Lucky* (unpublished typescript).

MACK, JOHN E., *A Prince of Our Disorder: the Life of T.E. Lawrence* (London, 1976).

MACLEAN, FITZROY, *Eastern Approaches* (London, 1951).

MACMAHON, M. DE, *Mémoires du Maréchal de MacMahon* (Paris, 1932).

McWHINEY, GRADY, and JAMIESON, PERRY D., *Attack and Die: Civil War Military Tactics and the Southern Heritage* (University, Alabama, 1982).

MAJDALANY, FRED, *The Monastery* (London, 1950).

MANCHESTER, WILLIAM, *Goodbye, Darkness* (London, 1981).

MANTELL, D.M., *True Americanism: Green Berets and War Resisters* (New York, 1974).

MARKS, THOMAS PENROSE, *The Laughter Goes from Life* (London, 1971).

MARSH, PETER, and CAMPBELL, ANNE (eds), *Aggression and Violence* (Oxford, 1982).

MARSHALL, S.L.A., *Ambush* (New York, 1969).

——, *Battles in the Monsoon* (New York, 1967).

——, *Men Against Fire* (New York, 1947).

——, *Pork Chop Hill* (New York, 1956).

——, *Vietnam: Three Battles* (New York, 1971).

MARTIN, T.A., *The Essex Regiment, 1929-1950* (Brentwood, 1952).

MASTERS, JOHN, *Bugles and a Tiger* (London, 1956).

——, *The Road Past Mandalay* (London, 1961).

MAULDIN, BILL, *Up Front* (New York, 1945).

MAWSON, STUART, *Arnhem Doctor* (London, 1981).

MAZRUI, ALI A. (ed.), *The Warrior Tradition in Modern Africa* (Leiden, 1977).

MECHANIC, D., *Students under Stress* (Glencoe, Ill., 1962).

MEERLOO, J.A.M., *Mental Seduction and Menticide* (London, 1957).

MEYERS, S.M., and BIDERMAN, A., *Mass Behaviour in Battle and Captivity* (London, 1968).

MIDDLEBROOK, MARTIN, *The First Day on the Somme* (London, 1971).

——, *The Kaiser's Battle* (London, 1978).

MILES, BRUCE, *Night Witches* (Edinburgh, 1981).

MITCHELL, T.J., and SMITH, G.M., *History of the Great War Based on Official Documents. Medical Services: Casualties and Medical Statistics of the Great War* (London, 1931).

MOCKLER, ANTHONY, *Mercenaries* (London, 1970).

MONTAGUE, C.E., *Disenchantment* (London, 1922).

MONTGOMERY, VISCOUNT, *The Memoirs of Field-Marshal the Viscount Montgomery of Alamein* (London, 1958).

MOORE, WILLIAM, *The Thin Yellow Line* (London, 1974).

MOOREHEAD, ALAN, *African Trilogy* (London, 1959).

MORAN, LORD, *The Anatomy of Courage* (London, 1966).

MORRIS, DONALD R., *The Washing of the Spears* (London, 1978).

MORRIS, MICHAEL, *Terrorism* (Cape Town, 1971).

MORVAN, JEAN, *Le Soldat imperial*, 2 vols (Paris, 1904).

MOSKIN, J. ROBERT., *The Story of the US Marine Corps* (New York, 1979).

MOSKOS, CHARLES C., *The American Enlisted Man* (New York, 1970).

—— (ed.), *Public Opinion and the Military Establishment* (Beverly Hills, 1971).

MOUSSAC, GEORGES DE, *Dans la mêlée: journal d'un cuirassier de 1870-71* (Paris, 1911).

MOYNIHAN, MICHAEL, *God on our Side* (London, 1983).

NAGEL, FRITZ, *Fritz: the World War I Memoirs of a German Lieutenant* (Huntington, West Virginia, 1981).

NEAVE, AIREY, *The Flames of Calais* (London, 1972).

NEVILLE, J.E.H., *The War Letters of a Light Infantryman* (London, 1930).

NICHOLSON, W.N., *Behind the Lines* (London, 1939).

NOYCE, W., *They Survived: a Study of the Will to Live* (London, 1962).

O'BRIEN, TIM, *If I Die in a Combat Zone* (London, 1973).

OGBURN, CHARLTON, *The Marauders* (New York, 1959).

PARISH, PETER J., *The American Civil War* (London, 1975).

PARKS, DAVID, *GI Diary* (New York, 1968).

PARRISH, JOHN, *Journal of a Plague Year* (London, 1979).

PASKINS, BARRY, and DOCKRILL, MICHAEL, *The Ethics of War* (London, 1979).

PATRICK, JAMES, *A Glasgow Gang Observed* (London, 1973).

PICQ, CHARLES ARDENT DU, *Battle Studies: Ancient and Modern Battle* (Harrisburg, Penn., 1956).

PIREY, PHILIPPE DE, *Operation Waste* (London, 1954).

PLAYFAIR, I.S.O., *The Mediterranean and the Middle East*, vol. 1 (London, 1954).

PRICE-WILLIAMS, D.R., *Introductory Psychology* (London, 1958).

QUIRK, RANDOLPH, *Style and Communication in the English Language* (London, 1982).

RAE, JOHN, *Conscience and Politics* (London, 1970).

RAGLAN, LORD, *The Hero: a Study in Tradition, Myth and Drama* (London, 1949).

REITLINGER, GERALD, *The SS: Alibi of a Nation* (New York, 1968).

RICHARDSON, F.M., *Fighting Spirit: a Study of Psychological Factors in War* (London, 1978).

ROLBANT, SAMUEL, *The Israeli Soldier* (London, 1970).

ROMMEL, ERWIN, *Attacks* (Vienna, Virginia, 1979).

ROTHENBERG, GUNTHER E., *The Army of Francis Joseph* (West Lafayette, Ind., 1976).

ROY, IAN (ed.), *Blaise de Montluc* (London, 1971).

SACK, JOHN, *Body Count: Lieutenant Calley's Story* (London, 1971).

SAJER, GUY, *The Forgotten Soldier* (London, 1971).

SARAZIN, C., *Récits sur la dernière guerre franco-allemande* (Paris, 1887).

SASSOON, SIEGFRIED, *Memoirs of a Foxhunting Man* (London, 1971).

——, *Memoirs of an Infantry Officer* (London, 1971).

SEATON, ALBERT, *The German Army, 1933–45* (London, 1982).

——, *The Russo-German War, 1941–45* (London, 1971).

The Seventh Day: Soldiers' Talk about the Six Day War (London, 1970).

SHEIL-SMALL, DENIS, *Green Shadows: a Gurkha Story* (London, 1982).

SHIPP, JOHN, *The Path of Glory* (London, 1969).

SIMON, B., and BRADLEY, I. (eds), *The Victorian Public School* (London, 1975).

SIMPKIN, RICHARD E., *Human Factors in Mechanised Warfare* (London, 1983).

SLIM, VISCOUNT, *Courage and Other Broadcasts* (London, 1957).

——, *Unofficial History* (London, 1960).

SMITH, E. D., *Even the Brave Falter* (London, 1978).

SMITH, MYRON J., *War Story Guide: an Annotated Bibliography of Military Fiction* (London, 1980).

STOUFFER, S. A., *et al.*, *The American Soldier*, vol. I, *Adjustment during Army Life*, vol. II, *Combat and its Aftermath* (Princeton, 1965).

SUID, LAWRENCE H., *Guts and Glory: Great American War Movies* (New York, 1978).

SULZBACH, HERBERT, *With the German Guns* (London, 1981).

SYDNOR, CHARLES W., *Soldiers of Destruction* (Princeton, 1977).

TERRAINE, JOHN (ed.), *General Jack's Diary* (London, 1964).

THOMPSON, E. P., and SMITH, DAN (eds.), *Protest and Survive* (London, 1980).

THOMPSON, FLORA, *Lark Rise* (London, 1979).

TINKER, HUGH (ed.), *A Message from the Falklands* (London, 1982).

TOLSTOY, LEO, *Sebastopol* (London, ND).

——, *War and Peace* (London, 1972).

TREVELYAN, RALEIGH, *The Fortress* (London, 1956).

TRIPP, MILES, *The Eighth Passenger* (London, 1979).

TROCHU, L. J., *Œuvres Posthumes*, 2 vols (Paris, 1896).

TROTTER, WILFRED, *Instincts of the Herd in Peace and War* (London, 1947).

VAGTS, ALFRED, *A History of Militarism* (New York, 1959).

VAUGHAN, EDWARD CAMPION, *Some Desperate Glory* (London, 1981).

VIGNY, ALFRED DE, *The Military Necessity* (London, 1953).

WALTON, GEORGE, *The Tarnished Shield: a Report on Today's Army* (New York, 1973).

WATSON, PETER, *War on the Mind: the Military Uses and Abuses of Psychology* (London, 1978).

WATT, RICHARD M., *Dare Call it Treason* (London, 1964).

WEBER, MAX, *Theory of Social and Economic Organisation* (London, 1947).

WEST, F.J., *Small Unit Action in Vietnam, Summer 1966* (Washington, 1967).

WESTMAN, STEPHEN, *Surgeon with the Kaiser's Army* (London, 1968).

WILDMAN, A.K., *The End of the Russian Imperial Army* (Princeton, 1980).

WINTER, DENIS, *Death's Men* (London, 1978).

WINTRINGHAM, TOM, *English Captain* (London, 1939).

WRIGHT, SAM, *Crowds and Riots: a Study in Social Organization* (London, 1978).

XENOPHON, *Anabasis*, 2 vols (London, 1950).

YOUNG, PETER (ed.), *Richard Atkyns*, and NORMAN TUCKER (ed.), *John Gwyn* (London, 1967).

ZAHN, GORDON, *The Military Chaplaincy: a Study of Role Tension in the RAF* (Manchester, 1969).

Articles

ABRAHAM, P., 'Training for Battleshock', *Journal of the Royal Army Medical Corps*, no. 128, 1982.

ANDERSON, C.J.L.F., 'The Defence of Superior Orders', *Journal of the Royal United Services Institute for Defence Studies*, vol. CXXVI, no. 2, June 1981.

BELENKY, G.L., 'Psychiatric Casualties in Israeli Forces during the War in Lebanon', *Walter Reed Army Institute of Research*, 1983.

BLAKE, J.A., 'The Organization as an Instrument of Violence', *Sociological Quarterly*, vol. II, no. 3, 1970.

CHERKASHIN, A., 'Regimental Culture Centre', *Soviet Military Review*, no. 12, 1981.

CHERMOL, B.H., 'Psychiatric Casualties in Combat', *Military Review*, July 1983.

CHODOFF, ELLIOT P., 'Ideology and Primary Groups', *Armed Forces and Society*, vol. IX, no. 4, Summer 1983.

CLAYTON, A.H. LE Q., 'Sport and African Soldiers: the Military Diffusion of Western Sports throughout Sub-Saharan Africa', University of London, Institute of Commonwealth Studies, Postgraduate Seminar, 10 February 1983.

CONNELL, JOHN, 'Writing about Soldiers', *Journal of the Royal United Services Institute*, August 1965.

FENZ, W., 'Coping Mechanisms and Performance Stress', *Medicina dello Sport*, vol. XXIX, no. 3, March 1976.

FOLKMAN, SUSAN, 'An Approach to the Measurement of Coping', *Journal of Occupational Behaviour*, vol. III, 1982.

GAULT, W.B., 'Some Remarks on Slaughter', *American Journal of Psychiatry*, 128:4, October 1971.

GERHARDT, I.D., 'Offensive Spirit: the Vital Ingredient', *Military Review*, October 1981.

GLOVER, MICHAEL, 'A Profusion of Honours', *Military History*, January 1983.

——, 'Uniform: Regulation and Reality', *Military History*, February 1983.

HART, T.S., 'Determination in Battle', paper presented to the Royal Armoured Corps Conference, November 1978.

HASLAM, DIANA R., 'The Effect of Sleep Loss upon the Motivation, Morale and Mood of the Soldier', paper presented at the NATO symposium on motivation and morale in the NATO Forces, Brussels 1980.

HEGGE, FREDERICK W., and MARLOWE, DAVID, 'Some Human Dimensions of Continuous Land Combat: 2000 AD', Walter Reed Army Institute of Research, 1983.

HUMPHREY, NICHOLAS, 'Four Minutes to Midnight', Bronowski Memorial Lecture 1981, *Listener*, 29 October 1981.

INGRAHAM, L.H., and MANNING, F.J., 'Cohesion: Who Needs It, What Is It?', *Military Review*, June 1981.

ISENHOWER, J.P., 'Cohesion: Finding the Key', *Military Review*, October 1981.

JEAPES, TONY, 'Stress in Battle', *British Army Review*, no. 60, December 1980.

KEEGAN, JOHN, 'Inventing Military Traditions', unpublished paper presented at the Past and Present Society Annual Conference, London, 1977.

LABUC, S., and ELLIS, K., 'Battle Stress and Morale as International Variables', paper presented at NATO Seminar on the Human as a Limiting Element in Military Systems, Toronto, May 1983.

LANG, KURT, 'American Military Performance in Vietnam: Background and Analysis', *Journal of Political and Military Sociology*, vol. VIII, Autumn 1980.

L'ETANG, HUGH, 'Demoralisation in War and Peace', *Brassey's Annual*, 1967.

——, 'Fighting Spirit', *Brassey's Annual*, 1969.

——, 'Some Actualities of War', *Journal of the Royal United Services Institute for Defence Studies*, March 1972.

——, 'Some Thoughts on Panic in War', *Brassey's Annual*, 1966.

LINDSAY OF DOWHILL, SIR MARTIN, 'Courage and Fear', *British Army Review*, no. 57, 1977.

——, 'Gallantry Awards', *British Army Review*, no. 67, 1981.

—— *et al.*, 'Thoughts on Command in Battle', *British Army Review*, no. 69, 1981.

MELZACK, R., 'The Perception of Pain', *Scientific American*, no. 204, 1961.

NABORS, R.L., 'Women in the Army: Do They Measure Up?', *Military Review*, October 1982.

PATIENT, ALAN, 'Mutiny at Salerno', *Listener*, 25 February 1982.

REILLY, J.C., 'An Attitude to Drill', *British Army Review*, no. 37, April 1971.

SHILS, EDWARD A., and JANOWITZ, MORRIS, 'Cohesion and Disintegration in the Wehrmacht in World War II', *Public Opinion Quarterly*, vol. XII, no. 2, Summer 1948.

SOHLBERG, SHAUL C., 'Stress Experiences and Combat Fatigue during the Yom Kippur War', *Psychological Reports 1976*, no. 38.

VILLAR, R.N., 'A Personal View', *British Medical Journal*, vol. CCLXXXVII, 20 August 1983.

Index

Majdalany, Major Fred, 96, 110,
117, 171, 272, 376, 378
Manchester, William, 51, 60, 70, 76,
97, 120, 129-30, 155, 164, 176,
178, 193, 201, 300-1, 362, 386
Mann, Delbert, 68
Manning, Major F.J., 11, 255, 299
Mantell, D.M., 93, 286, 377, 380
maps, 152-4
marching, 115-25
Marks, Thomas Penrose, 249, 354,
381
Marshall, S.L.A., 11, 13, 53, 58, 66,
73, 136, 149, 159, 160, 165, 166,
188, 196-7, 225, 234, 262, 272,
299, 301, 325, 332, 347, 351
Maslow, A.H., 27, 340-1
Mason, Warrant Officer David, 253
Masson, Sous-Lieutenant, 190
Masters, Lieutenant-Colonel John,
38, 308, 310
Matthews, Corporal, 176
Matthews, Private, 156
Mauldin, Bill, 28, 76, 77, 78, 88,
162, 197, 251, 357-8
Mawson, Captain Stuart, 129, 184,
206, 246
Mazuri, Ali, 57
Mechanic, D., 140, 243
medals, 355-9
Medina, Captain, 391
Meerloo, Joost van, 267
Meinhof, Ulrike, 102
Melzack, R., 186
memories, 394-403
memory, 154-7
mercenaries, 353-5
Mercer, Captain Cavalié, 63, 216
mercy killings, 187-8
Meyer, Jacques, 395
Meyer, Major-General Kurt, 346
Middlebrook, Martin, 11, 66, 150,
323
military history: and military values,
8; and the actualities of war, 7-18;
function, 5; operational research,
12-13; oral, 10-11; personal
experience and, 8-10; popularity,
4-5; psychology and, 15-16;
sociology and, 12

military justice, 237
Miller, Captain William H., 392
Milligan, Spike, 328
Mills, Sergeant, 385
Mills-Roberts, Brigadier Derek, 373
mines, 211-12
Mitchell, George, 147
modesty, 111
Moffat, Captain H.H., 345
Montague, C.E., 115, 295, 373
Montaigne, 142
Montgomery, Field-Marshal, 51-2,
96, 99, 221, 277, 282
Montluc, Blaise de, 94, 329, 386
Moore, Sir John, 337
Moorehead, Alan, 150-1, 228, 301
morale, 25, 26, 29, 42, 109, 130, 164,
166, 220-1, 227, 248, 264. See also
fear; stress
Moran, Lord, 14, 57, 109, 113, 183,
193, 198, 199, 202, 212, 213-14,
217, 219, 228, 234, 235, 313, 333,
369
Morant, Lieutenant Harry, 367
Morley, Corporal, 165-6
Morris, Desmond, 20
Morris, Donald R., 144
Morris, Michael, 88
Morrison, Lieutenant Alastair, 243
Morrow, Colonel Henry, 237
mortar fire, 209-10
Morvan, Jean, 127, 245, 331
Moskin, Robert, 300
Moskos, Charles, 76, 281-2, 325
mosquitoes, 114
motivation, 270-90
Moussac, Georges de, 63
moving forward, 160-2
Muir, John, 156, 174
Murphy, Audie, 69
music, 163-4
muskets, 168
mutiny, 328-30
My Lai, 391-2

Nabors, Major R.L., 101-2
Nagel, Lieutenant Fritz, 146, 276,
387
Napier, Major Charles, 237
Napier, Major William, 304, 305, 388